The Definitive
Handbook of
Business Continuity
Management

# The Definitive Handbook of Business Continuity Management

Edited by

**Andrew Hiles**
*Chairman, Survive!*

**Peter Barnes**
*General Manager, Survive!*

JOHN WILEY & SONS, LTD
Chichester • New York • Weinheim • Brisbane • Singapore • Toronto

Copyright © 1999 by John Wiley & Sons Ltd.
Baffins Lane, Chichester,
West Sussex PO19 1UD, England

National        01243 779777
International   (+44) 1243 779777
e-mail (for orders and customer service enquiries): cs-books@wiley.co.uk
Visit our Home Page on http://www.wiley.co.uk
                  or http://www.wiley.com

Copyright to Chapter 1 has been retained by *Arthur Andersen* as detailed on the Chapter title page.
Copyright to Chapter 7 has been retained by the author as detailed on the Chapter title page.
Copyright to Chapter 9 has been retained by the author as detailed on the Chapter title page.
Copyright to Chapter 17 has been retained by the authors as detailed on the Chapter title page.

*Other Wiley Editorial Offices*

John Wiley & Sons, Inc., 605 Third Avenue,
New York, NY 10158-0012, USA

WILEY-VCH Verlag GmbH, Pappelallee 3,
D-69469 Weinheim, Germany

Jacaranda Wiley Ltd, 33 Park Road, Milton,
Queensland 4064, Australia

John Wiley & Sons (Asia) Pte Ltd, 2 Clementi Loop #02-01,
Jin Xing Distripark, Singapore 129809

John Wiley & Sons (Canada) Ltd, 22 Worcester Road,
Rexdale, Ontario M9W 1L1, Canada

*British Library Cataloguing in Publication Data*

A catalogue record for this book is available from the British Library

ISBN 0-471-98622-4

Typeset in 10/12pt Garamond by Dorwyn Ltd, Rowlands Castle, Hants
Printed and bound in Great Britain by Bookcraft (Bath) Ltd, Midsomer Norton, Somerset
This book is printed on acid-free paper responsibly manufactured from sustainable forestry, in which
at least two trees are planted for each one used.

# Contents

# Contents

# Contributors

TIM ARMIT
*Senior Consultant, Insight Consulting, Churchfield House, 5 The Quintet, Churchfield Road, Walton-on-Thames, Surrey KT12 2TZ, UK*

GREGG BEATTY
*Vice President, The Darien Group, 11 Regency Plaza, Glen Mills, PA 19342, USA*

LYNDON BIRD FCBI
*Director, CPA Ltd., The Elms, 20 Broad Street, Wokingham, Berks RG40 1AB, UK*

IAN CHARTERS MBCI
*Consultant, Continuity Systems Ltd., 37 Hookstone Drive, Harrogate HG2 8PR, UK*

MALCOLM CORNISH FCBI
*Head of CSG Europe, Comdisco Continuity Services, 1000 Great West Road, Brentford, Middlesex TW8 9HJ, UK*

NEAL COURTNEY
*Sales and Managing Director, Imbach RAG Ltd., Challenge House, 616 Mitcham Road, Croydon, Surrey CR0 3AA, UK*

ALAN CRAIG MBCI
*Director, Survive! in Asia Ltd., 119 Soi 2, Sukhumvit Soi 22, Klong Tooey, Bangkok 10110, Thailand*

THOMAS DOEMLAND FBCI
*17240 Sarita Avenue, Santa Clarita, CA 91351, USA*

DENIS HAMILTON, FBCI
*CEO, Crisis Response Planning Corp., 78 Victoria Street, Milton, Ontario L9T 1S7, Canada*

Robert Heath, FBCI
*Managing Director, Crisis Corp. Ltd., Chesham House, 150 Regent Street, London W1R 5FA, UK*

Jayne Howe FCBI
*Partner, The Jayne Howe Partnership, 21 St Clair Avenue East, Suite 1400, Toronto, Ontario M42 2T7, Canada*

Peter Humpidge
*Consultant, Morton Hodson Management Consultants, Brakenhurst Farmhouse, Hoar Cross, Burton-on-Trent, Staffs DE13 8RB, UK*

Allen Johnson
*Risk Management Consultant, Safetynet PLC, 12–13 Bracknell Beeches, Bracknell, Berks RG12 7BW, UK*

Paul Kirvan FBCI
*Director, Telecommunications, Bellcore, 331 Newman Springs Road, Room # 2Z-162, Red Bank, New Jersey, NJ 07701, USA*

Simon Marvell
*Insight Consulting, Churchfield House, 5 The Quintet, Churchfield Road, Walton-on-Thames, Surrey KT12 2TZ, UK*

Bill Meredith FBCI
*Partner-Consultancy, Meredith Solutions, 5 The Maltings, Huntonbridge, Kings Langley, Herts WD4 8QL, UK*

Melvyn Musson FBCI
*President, Musson Consulting Group, 2001 Seckman Road, Imperial, MO 63052, USA*

Michael O'Hehir FBCI
*Director, Operational & Systems Risk Management, PricewaterhouseCoopers, 580 George Street, Sydney NSW 2000, Australia*

Geert Vancoppenolle
*Consultant, Arthur Andersen, Rue Montagne du Parc 4, 1000 Brussels, Belgium*

# Foreword and introduction

## Andrew Hiles—UK

Andrew is Chairman of *Survive!* The Business Continuity Group and is also a Director of the Kingswell Partnership.

Welcome to what we believe to be the most authoritative work on Business Continuity Planning yet produced.

*Survive!* was founded in 1989 as an international user group for business continuity professionals, with the objects of developing, encouraging and implementing best practice in business continuity planning. It saves expensive false starts in planning and helps members to improve the robustness and security of their critical business processes. Members share experience.

*Survive!* now has over 3000 members world-wide, a mix of public and private sector membership. These include leading banks, insurance corporations, government departments, local government, emergency services, utilities, manufacturers, distributors, retailers, computer manufacturers and suppliers, software houses, consultancies and service providers.

About 85% of the members are users of services: the others are suppliers. Members benefit from the expertise and experience of supplier members—the suppliers make a living from disasters, whereas the average member hopes never to experience one!

Our international conferences are discounted to members. We hold conventions and training events in the USA, Australia, New Zealand, South Africa, Thailand, the Philippines, Hong Kong, UK, The Netherlands, Belgium and Germany. International speakers are invited and delegates hear actual case stories from organizations which have experienced—and survived—disasters. Some of the conferences have associated expositions where delegates can compare services from different vendors.

There have been over 40 free events during the last year for members. These include Workshops that attract up to 120 participants who share experiences in lively discussions and hard work which provides a fertile ground for developing improved contingency plans.

Members may also create special interest subgroups: for instance, there is a Public Sector Special Interest Group; one for the Financial Industry; one on salvage; and another which recently produced a report on software tools for business continuity and disaster recovery planning.

Our database of case studies is often used by members (and the media) to point up the real risks. Other databases include one of suppliers of disaster recovery services and one of members' systems to enable members to contact others with similar problems.

A video library is maintained for education and training—it includes videos of disasters as they happened.

Recent disasters world-wide have emphasized the truly international impact of apparently local disasters: during dramatic Chicago floods, the occupants of the upper floors of an office tower were working away unaware that lower floors were being evacuated—until advised by their London office! Terrorist explosions in London affected the international operations of some of the organizations situated in the area. A few years ago telecommunications down-time in the USA caused problems for the US subsidiaries of overseas companies.

The magazine, *Survive!*, is available to those with a special interest in risk management and business continuity and is free to members. The magazine provides advice, surveys, advance information, case studies and best practice to make sure readers stay on top of an increasingly complex but vital subject. Surveys help readers to select the services or products most suited to their needs. Book reviews keep readers informed of new ideas and best practice. And advertisers welcome the focus of the magazine, too.

The industry has come of age, and increasingly organizations have been demanding a clear demonstration of the competence of its practitioners. Through *Survive!*'s initiative, the Business Continuity Institute (BCI) was formed in 1994 as the professional body for practitioners, with examinations in 10 core competencies. These are shared with the Disaster Recovery Institute International (DRII). *Survive!* runs a comprehensive professional development programme to prepare professionals for professional certification. All in all, we believe that Survive! represents the truly professional approach to business continuity planning.

This book represents the fulfilment of an ambition we at *Survive!* have held since it began: to document the skills of leading practitioners and to make those skills available to the widest possible audience.

This introduction provides an overview of business continuity planning, and subsequent chapters deal with specific topics in depth.

The authors' experience of business continuity planning totals some 350 years and each of them is a distinguished authority on the subject. Increasingly business continuity planning is a global issue calling for global solutions. The author list also is truly international in its expertise.

For those of you new to the subject, their expertise is now yours! For those who are more experienced, we hope and expect that you will gain from the latest thinking, and challenging ideas presented to you.

## An introduction to business continuity planning

What is business continuity planning all about? Fundamentally, it seeks to mitigate the impact of a disaster by ensuring alternative mission-critical capability is available when disaster strikes. Business continuity planning seeks to preserve the assets of an organization in the event of a disaster: its capability to achieve its mission; its operational capability; its reputation and image; its customer base and market share; its profitability.

Most organizations are totally reliant on just a few key facilities: a head office building . . . a sophisticated production plant . . . a computer or telecommunications room . . . a Call Centre . . . workflow management software or financial systems . . . they simply cannot operate without them.

All too often computers are the focus of disaster recovery planning—but it is no use recovering a stock control system if the warehouse has been destroyed, and it is no use catering for hardware failure if software problems deny access to Electronic Point of Sale systems and close shops down. IT recovery remains important, but the growth of PC and distributed client–server computing has simply complicated the issues. It has led to a situation where, in many organizations, deployment of additional equipment has been a reaction to an immediate problem rather than a carefully planned strategy to improve resilience; where the real location of data is unclear; and where applications are so tightly integrated that it is extremely difficult to prioritize in a recovery situation. In some cases, loss of a single PC has caused bankruptcy.

While commercial recovery services are available for computing and administrative work positions, there are virtually no parallel services for warehouse or production facilities.

Business Continuity Planning requires a structured, methodical and comprehensive approach.

Buy-in is critical—from the most senior level possible. Awareness needs to be raised and commitment sought from all those likely to be involved in developing procedures or participating as team members. Senior managers need to allocate appropriate priority to the project—otherwise, the project will develop its own specific gravity: it will never rise to the top of the priority list, and never quite sink completely! Day-to-day business pressures have a habit of taking over and the project may never be completed. Realistic scope and deadlines are essential.

So, the project needs to be scoped. Is it to be a full crisis management plan, covering reputation management, together with contingency plans such as product recall, hostage, extortion, kidnap, attack on branches? Is it to cover all branches, or just the top ten? Is it to cover all customers, or just the 20% who generate the 80% of profit? Is it to cover all sites, or just Head Office?

Next we need to identify and validate the assumptions which are being made. For instance, do we assume our own skilled personnel are going to be available in a disaster? Many plans, perhaps a little rashly, assume this will be so. But if we do not assume our skilled staff will be available, many more detailed procedures will be required—the resulting plans will be a lot thicker and heavier!

Having scoped the plan and defined assumptions, we can develop the project plan. Business continuity planning is initially a project and needs to be handled with appropriate project disciplines until the project is signed off into the maintenance phase.

A Risk Review will identify the key threats to a specific organization and the likelihood of them occurring. A Critical Component Failure Analysis will define where resilience is weak. Recommendations for reducing risk may result.

Sometimes the risk analysis will identify issues of information security and integrity. The reliability of management information is a key factor to business success: often material errors exist and information integrity is compromised without the organization being aware of it. A review of information security procedures against international codes of practice can protect companies from major financial loss—especially when it comes to electronic trading opportunities.

Sometimes risk can be substantially reduced just by taking procedural action. In other cases, risk reduction may simply be included as a consideration in the capital programme. As the plant and infrastructure require renewal, it may be appropriate to reduce risk—often at little or no additional cost—for instance, by buying two lower capacity pieces of equipment rather than one high-capacity item.

An insurance review may also be undertaken to establish areas which are, and which are not, covered. Insurance, however, does not buy back the business: it only provides money. And in some cases, the money comes later rather than sooner, with adverse implications for cashflow. We find that, for a variety of reasons, insurance typically only covers about 60% of the actual loss. Moreover, business interruption and loss of profits insurance eventually stops—depending on your cover, this could be after six months.

In order fully to understand the impact of loss of service, a Business Impact Analysis can be undertaken. This establishes, in cash and non-cash terms, the value of IT services to the business. It also identifies the time window in which recovery has to take place before loss becomes unsustainable.

The Business Impact Analysis and Risk Analysis together provide an understanding of:

- The critical functions of the business
- Crucial dependencies (including people, resources, skills and knowledge)
- The potential loss, in cash and non-cash terms
- The time window in which recovery has to take place before losses become unsustainable

A full understanding of risks and impact will help in defining Business Continuity Strategy and may result in changes to the scope of the Business Continuity Plan. For instance, should the plan also cover critical research or development work?

During the Business Impact Analysis we may also conduct a preliminary Resource Requirements Analysis, which establishes when standby facilities and items of equipment are required, and in what timescale, following the disaster.

The risk and impact analyses, together with the resource requirements, help to identify and justify an appropriate Business Continuity strategy. This strategy may be a "mix and match" of various options, amongst them:

- A "fort" approach, seeking to strengthen facilities to make them less vulnerable
- Business process re-engineering or process improvement, to reduce risks or to make the organization more resilient
- Standby facilities, either in-company or commercial, ranging from immediate availability ("hot") to longer term ("cold");
- Quick resupply of equipment
- Working from home
- Maintaining buffer stocks to cover the period during which production is lost
- Outsourcing or buying in goods or services normally produced in-company
- Insurance

Basically, the quicker and bigger the restart capability, the more expensive it is likely to be in terms of capital or annual cost, or both. The cost of the recovery option has to be weighed against the impact of loss of service on the business.

Whatever the strategic restart option selected, the Business Continuity Plan is likely to comprise several elements:

- Immediate reaction procedures (disaster declaration, evacuation, damage assessment and limitation
- Provision of emergency facility
- Resumption of business production under emergency arrangements
- restoration of the permanent facility

One of the key factors in determining whether an organization recovers from a disaster is the effectiveness of its back-up arrangements—regular, off-site back-up is essential for effective recovery. Frequently vital paper documentation is not backed-up, sometimes because it simply cannot be. The solution may lie in business process re-engineering, to computerize some of the paper-based operations so they can be backed-up, or using a fire-protected and waterproof vault. Equally, there may be other vital materials that should be replicated off-site—for instance, tools, jigs, patterns or samples.

Backlog management is also an important consideration: the longer the period of unavailability and the higher the transaction level, the greater is the possibility of accumulating an irretrievable backlog. Backlog planning and management are therefore vital to recovery.

A company can still go bankrupt following a successful recovery—if customers, stakeholders and influencers think the recovery has been a failure. Media and reputation management therefore plays a vital role in the Business Continuity Plan.

Plans must be tested—and the more defects that are discovered, the better the test! Most plans "fail" when first tested—there is always something that has not been considered. An effective testing programme therefore needs to be put in place, both to improve the plan and to exercise team members in their roles. Plan tests could include "desktop tests", walk through, and role-playing rehearsals against a scenario. Testing should be conducted to verify the effectiveness of each component of the plan, and to check that all dependencies have been covered. However, it is important not to be over-ambitious—the business must be protected during testing. Testing the Business Continuity Plan should not cause the disaster! A review after each test will provide valuable feedback to improve the plan.

Whenever there is any change—in business emphasis, new products or services; in organization; in locations; in key personnel—its impact on the plan should be assessed and the plan updated if necessary. It pays to be prepared—disaster can strike in any form, at any time. No organization is immune from a disaster—not even the best-run ones. But experience has shown that those with effective recovery plans are likely to survive, while those without do not.

# Introduction: how to read this book

## Peter Barnes—UK

Peter is General Manager of Survive! The Business Continuity Group.

It is more than 15 years since the concepts upon which the modern approach to business continuity management is based were first documented—a very short time in which the business world has seen the emergence of disaster recovery strategies for computer departments and their evolution into the current idiom of enterprise-wide continuity planning. It has been 15 years in which strategies for the safeguarding and security of mission critical computer data have developed into a respect for the true value of the total asset inventory of the corporation. Furthermore, experienced business continuity management professionals recognize that such inventories encompass physical and logical assets as well as less tangible and more complex possessions—data and information, high-value physical items, people and their experience, knowledge and commercial contacts and, ultimately, corporate reputation.

Many attempts have been made to define Business Continuity Planning and, in truth, we have probably yet to arrive at the perfect, succinct definition. The task of definition is made more difficult as a result of the wide range of different terminology used, either in different parts of the English-speaking world, or by professionals operating at different levels of development (because this management practice, like so many others, takes its lead from the USA and has evolved at different speeds, and for different reasons, around the world).

Try as we must to determine the definition upon which this book is based, we would present the following for your consideration—more wordy than some but, hopefully, sufficiently clear that all readers will be able to understand, without difficulty, the purpose of this book.

Business Continuity Management is the development of strategies, plans and actions which provide protection or alternative modes of operation for those activities or business processes which, if they were to be interrupted, might otherwise bring about a seriously damaging or potentially fatal loss to the enterprise.

Business Continuity Planners deal with the consequences of the business-threatening "what-if" scenario—what if our operations are destroyed by fire or flood? what if a negative media story drives our clients to our competitors? what if the database upon which we depend for our sales is stolen or attacked by a virus? what if our offices are innocent victims of a terrorist attack? . . . the list of potential threats is unending!

The aim of this book is to tackle the principles of business continuity management from two perspectives. Section One provides an Executive Overview: a detailed discussion of the concepts, value and role of business continuity discussed by leading experts from around the world. It includes more detailed definitions of the kinds of events which can interrupt businesses with often disastrous consequences; a high-level view of a business continuity strategy; the issues to be faced within today's multicultural, multinational business environment; relationships with other flavours of risk and crisis management and some simple tips on how to avoid having a crisis or disaster in the first place—as avoidance will always be a better option than sound disaster management!

In Section Two we tackle the more practical issues in a "How to" guide which deals with many of the commonly accepted components of a comprehensive approach to business continuity management.

Throughout the book you will encounter a variety of styles as this volume is the work of many practitioners. Each of the contributors is regarded as an expert and is greatly experienced within the business continuity management world; few would necessarily regard themselves as expert writers but it is our hope that, with the guidance we have received from our publishers and the efforts of the editors we have arrived at a consistently readable and interesting style.

Each contributor is an individual who has shared his or her experiences in the past: some are consultants who are in the business of exchanging and promoting experiences through many organizations; many have been involved in training of fellow professionals; almost all have spoken publicly at conferences or group discussions.

Contributors to this book have been drawn from all corners of the English-speaking world and their writing is often complemented by examples and experiences from their own countries. When reading their work we recommend that you try to disregard the geographic issues and apply the most open-minded approach and evaluation to their ideas and comments. For example, simply ask yourself, continuously—could this or something similar happen to my organization? We may well associate earthquakes with California and terrorist bombs with London but the issues of a wide-scale disaster scenario and of employees preoccupied with ensuring the safety of their family rather than the business can be applied to many events.

The editors are sincerely grateful for the time and thought which each of the contributors has given freely in the development of this book. Our hope is that you, the reader, will benefit significantly from the many hundreds of hours of effort which have gone into passing on their skill and knowledge through the medium of the written word.

# Section One

Achieving and maintaining business continuity:
an executive overview

# What are we planning for?

## Geert Vancoppenolle—Belgium

Geert heads the Business Continuity Management practice of Arthur Andersen in Europe.

## Introduction

Imagine that you have been asked to rebuild the business of the company that you work for in the immediate aftermath of a major disaster. Perhaps there has been a serious fire and you cannot make use of the existing IT infrastructure or of any other infrastructure elements within your current premises.

It is your responsibility to ensure that it should be possible to take orders within two hours. Customer deliveries must be possible within five days, except for your two most important customers for which it must be possible to deliver within the same day.

An immediate suggestion is that you will have to source your company's products from alternative plants within your company. These plants are not aware of the situation, moreover they may not have the capacity to modify production to cope with the scenario.

The customers, who are waiting for delivery, will flood you with questions regarding the affirmation of quality, accuracy and punctuality. Those who want to place orders will request guarantees of delivery. In the meantime, a number of suppliers will be waiting to deliver their goods, at the exact location that is unavailable to you.

Are you ready for it?

The example above might be what you are expected to do when your company is involved in a disaster. The event that caused the disaster could be anything: fire, power failure, unavailability of the IT infrastructure, evacuation of the installation and so on.

How long did it take to build your current business organization, providing customer service as it is doing today? The fact is that you have to plan to avoid or mitigate disasters before the event. Under extreme time pressures and the scrutiny

*The Definitive Handbook of Business Continuity Management.* Edited by Andrew Hiles and Peter Barnes. © 1999 Arthur Andersen.

of shareholders you must deal with all this in a crisis situation. I bet you wish you had prepared for this scenario!

This chapter poses the problem: What are we planning for through Business Continuity Management? It not only defines "disaster", but also explains outcomes and implications to our business organizations. The chapter is composed of four parts. The first part discusses the inherent dependencies and vulnerabilities of our business organizations. The second part discusses how unexpected events can lead to disaster and interrupt our business operations. The third part takes a look at what these disasters can do to our business: the damage, the impact and the business risks from operational interruptions. The last part asks the question about the objective of Business Continuity Management: what should you expect to achieve through your business continuity plan?

## Vulnerability of today's business organizations

### Business organizations: who should plan for business continuity?

By "business organizations", we do not only mean commercial organizations that manufacture and sell products or which provide, for instance, financial services. A business organization in this context is any organization that provides services or goods, either to individual customers, to other business organizations, or to the public.

Examples of such business organizations include manufacturers, distribution companies, sales organizations, transport organizations such as railroads or airlines, utility companies such as electricity production and distribution, water, gas and telecommunications, and community services such as tax services, justice, emergency services, government, and so on. Although not all these organizations are established to make profit, they all provide some service to somebody else, and have all built an operational structure to enable them to do so. In the context of this chapter, they are all called business organizations.

As all these organizations are equally at risk from the effects of a disaster that interrupts their operations, they should consider Business Continuity Management if they are to optimize their chances of successful resumption of business following an interruption.

### The business organizations of today

Driven by short cycle times, increased pressure to cut costs and to increase efficiency and customer orientation, today's organizations are organized around business processes to a greater extent than ever before. To deliver a product or a service to a customer, a chain of activities has to be performed. This chain of activities is called a business process (see Figure 1.1). Although in many organizations there is still a division into departments with a formal hierarchy, the actual business operations are typically organized and executed across departments, through these business processes, which are driven by information flows.

For the same reasons of efficiency and increased business value, companies are focusing themselves more and more on their activities where they can differentiate themselves in the market. For the other activities required to deliver the product or the service, many companies enter into partnerships with other organizations or outsource some of their activities. This means that the activities executed to deliver a product or a service to the customers extend beyond the boundaries of the company. Considering business processes, we have to look at the "extended enterprise".

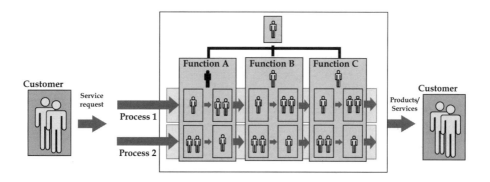

**Figure 1.1**—The business process

## Integrated organization

Each business organization always consists of three components (see Figure 1.2):

- Business processes—how products or services are delivered to the clients
- Participants—who participate in the execution of the business process
- Infrastructure and resources—used in the execution of the business process

These elements of the organization are integrated through information flows.

Because of the high level of integration of business operations and information flows, it is difficult to separate any of these elements from the others. It is these elements together that allow an organization to execute its business operations. Also, when you think about how you will bring about the resumption of business

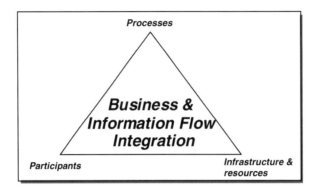

**Figure 1.2**—Elements of a business organization

after a disaster, you cannot separate any of the elements of the organization from the others. For instance, if you consider only IT, or just a single department, then you will probably not achieve business resumption, because you are overlooking the integration of dependencies throughout the organization.

## Business dependencies and vulnerabilities

Each business process depends on a number of critical elements. In a business process a number of persons or departments are involved, who execute one or more activities and pass the resulting information on to the next participant in the business process.

A first dependency is human resources, where a minimum number is required with the appropriate skills and knowledge to be able to execute the business activities. Other dependencies are resources and infrastructure elements. These can be logistical resources, utilities, office infrastructure, manufacturing infrastructure, information technology or financial resources. Examples of logistical resources are loading and stocking areas, transport facilities, weighbridges and so on. The extent to which business operations depend on these critical items means that there is a higher vulnerability to business interruptions. These vulnerabilities include for instance single points of failures in the IT architecture and network. When such a component becomes unavailable, many or all of the critical information flows to support business operations are interrupted.

Within each business process, there are a number of key activities. When such key business activity can no longer be executed because of an unexpected event, the result could be an interruption of the business process that is part of the value chain to the customer.

To illustrate this, let's take the example of the replenishment cycle of a supermarket chain (Figure 1.3). In this case there is a complex information flow that

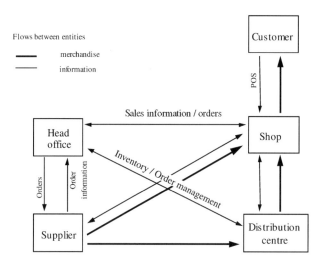

**Figure 1.3**—Retail replenishment

starts from the POS terminals in the shops. Each shop sends daily information on the local stock levels to the head office. The information from all shops is consolidated and processed to issue orders to the suppliers. A second information flow provides input to the distribution centres, allowing them to plan the distribution to the shops. For each group of products, there are different supply cycles and deadlines within this replenishment cycle.

Continuity of the replenishment depends on this complex activity chain, where there is an integration of information flows and merchandise flows. Throughout the chain, several departments and locations interact on a regular basis. Within the chain, there are a number of subprocesses, each with their own dependencies and vulnerabilities, for example reception and transfer of goods for transport to the stores. The information flows go through a number of servers and networks.

Within Business Continuity Management it is impossible to duplicate every process—this would be too expensive. Nor is it sufficient just to provide back-up for one or more elements; as discussed above, due to the interdependencies, this would be insufficient to effectively recover the full process.

To be able to provide continuity of this complex cycle when an unexpected event interrupts the chain, the business continuity plan will have to organize the business process differently by using a limited alternative infrastructure and by temporarily redefining the cycle times and deadlines.

## External dependencies

Business organizations are not only dependent on elements within the company. No business organization is an island. Each depends on a number of external

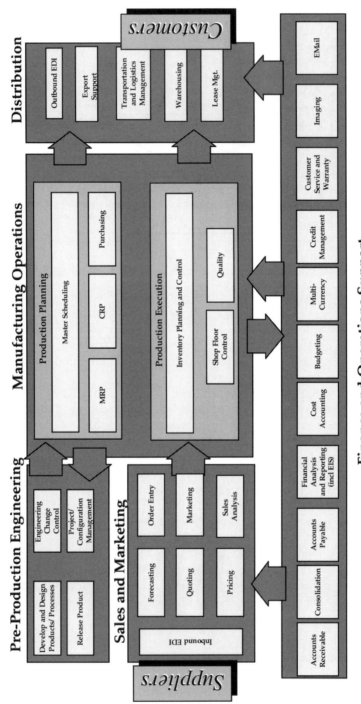

Figure 1.4— The complex business activity chain

resources and outside organizations. These external resources are often beyond its immediate control. Examples are electricity, water, telecommunications and so on. Although your organization cannot control the delivery of these services and therefore cannot prevent interruptions, it is your organization alone that can and will have to manage the impact on your business operations should these external dependencies fail. Likewise, the participants in the business processes are both internal and external to the company. Examples are suppliers, business partners, agents, banks and public authorities.

The business activities that provide customer service extend beyond the company boundaries. The concept of "extended enterprise" is very applicable. This means—again—that you are dependent on elements that are beyond your immediate control. You will have to handle the consequences to your business when they become unavailable.

These external dependencies are very critical for any company participating in a supply chain (Figure 1.4). These companies are for instance particularly dependent on a number of external information flows. Examples are order-entry and delivery notes, reception of invoices, payments to and from the bank, and ability to ship.

Companies are also dependent on the execution of business activities outside their own organization. This is especially true with the increased level of outsourcing and business partnerships. Examples are transport, distribution, packaging and financial services. Although these external companies are responsible for their own Business Continuity Management to resume their business, you are responsible for managing the impact on your business operations of a disaster within these companies.

## Disaster can strike, within your organization as well

### Unexpected events and incidents can become disasters

When one thinks of disaster, such examples as fire, flood, terrorist action, hurricane and so on immediately come to mind. Although there are regions where some of these threats are more real than elsewhere, the reality shows us that disasters come in a variety of guises. It does not have to be a large-scale event to mean disaster for your company. Neither does it have to be an event that causes extensive damage to the infrastructure.

Imagine, for instance, an event in your neighbourhood (your industry park or in the city centre), that requires an evacuation of the whole area until the problem is solved, which could be hours or even days. Your computers will still run, your telephones will still ring, and your business infrastructure will be unharmed. But you cannot use it. You cannot answer the telephone. You cannot enter the building. Such circumstances can be disastrous to your business.

Or consider a utilities company that starts a new service. But demand is so unexpectedly high that there is insufficient capacity to support the demand, and the service is reduced to the point of a business interruption. Is this a disaster? Probably, because the image will be damaged such that it will be extremely difficult to restore it.

Even small incidents, over only a short period, can create a disaster if they affect a key dependency. Consider the example of a fish farm, where an electricity failure of very short duration disturbed the temperature of the pools, causing the death or contamination of much of the stock. The effect was the loss of a breeding cycle of three years. Plenty of additional examples of events causing business interruptions can be found in the appendices at the end of this book, demonstrating that disasters do come in all shapes and sizes.

## Classification of disasters

A possible classification of disasters can be according to the type of event. Such classification includes the following groups:

- Acts of nature—e.g. hurricane, flood, . . .
- External man-made events—e.g. terrorism, evacuation, security intrusion . . .
- Internal unintentional events—e.g. accidental loss of files, computer failure, . . .
- Internal intentional events—e.g. strike, sabotage, data deletion, . . .

Such classification has its merits in driving emergency plans and crisis management, where the event itself must be managed in order to protect people and assets, and to mitigate damage. When it comes to Business Continuity Management, where the objective is to resume business operations, a different classification of disasters is more effective.

Some companies ask themselves if they should include the loss of the head office in the scope of the business continuity plan, especially as the probability of events leading to the destruction of the head office is considered to be low. Basically, this is the wrong, or at least an incomplete question. Your Business Continuity Management should not be driven by eliminating risks according to (only) probability of events, but rather by considering what would be the effect and impact on your business if an unexpected event were to occur, whatever the event. In that sense, for Business Continuity Management as a method of achieving business resumption, potential events and disasters would be better classified according to their business impact. Such classification according to effect could be:

- Failure of an individual infrastructure element, including single points of failure
- Longer term interruption of a critical information flow
- Longer term interruption of a critical business activity chain or business process

- Local longer term business interruption
- Complete business interruption

Experience shows that, in many cases, the effect of an unexpected event cascades into larger impact levels. This again underlines why, for Business Continuity Management to be effective, it must be driven in terms of managing the business impact, rather than handling the event. Many examples of this are to be found in the Appendix section of this book.

## Disasters do happen

It is still a widespread belief that disasters only happen to others, and that the probability of a disaster is so low that investment in Business Continuity Management cannot be justified with ease. However, statistics show that disasters do happen, and you could be the unfortunate victim today!

For instance, a survey conducted by Comdisco during 1995 shows that as many as 19% of companies have reported an IT unavailability of more than 24 hours. This is one in five organizations. And this is just IT. As organizations have many more key dependencies that are not IT, the probability of business interruptions is in reality much higher. And when your organization is larger, you will have more key dependencies and vulnerabilities, hence it is more probable that your organization will suffer a business interruption at some point in time. Although smaller organizations have fewer dependencies, they are usually more important, hence an occurrence of a disaster here usually has a higher impact.

Another myth is that when a disaster happens, organizations are flexible enough to survive, even without a business continuity plan. On this topic, there is some variance in the statistics. But all mention a figure between 60% and 90% of companies that find themselves out of business within 24 months of a disaster. And those that do survive typically never reach the same level of business that they would have obtained without the disaster occurring.

# The business risks of unexpected events interrupting operations

## Consequences of unexpected events interrupting operations

The immediate consequence of an unexpected event is the damage that it generates. This is the area where insurance can assist you in managing a disaster. In terms of business continuity, immediate physical damage is not the most important concern. Of greater importance is the impact on business operations, and how this can be overcome in order to resume the business and survive as a company.

## Damage, impact and long-term effects

An unexpected event can cause damage to infrastructure elements and resources supporting business operations. Examples can be buildings, computers, networks, machines, . . . The damage can be such that the infrastructure element is destroyed or unavailable for an extended period of time.

The direct consequences of such events can be twofold:

- Unavailability of infrastructure elements or resources
- Loss of information

In terms of Business Continuity Management, it is important to make the distinction between damage caused by the event, and the impact on the business because of the unavailability or the loss of information.

Next to the impact on business operations, one must also consider the long-term effects of such unexpected events. These are business impacts that are still felt long after the business has been resumed and operations have returned to normal. Loss of market share, lower share price, company image are examples. All these elements must be considered and will drive the Business Continuity Management.

## The direct impact: unavailability and loss of information

### Alternative business operations

Unavailability of IT infrastructure has always been the focus of the traditional IT Disaster Recovery Planning, which focused mainly on replacement or switching to alternative infrastructure. It is clear that it can rarely be cost-justified to duplicate all your resources—priorities must be identified. It is often very difficult to decide how far one should go in these arrangements.

As it is rarely possible to duplicate the complete business infrastructure after a disaster, business operations will have to be organized with only limited infrastructure available. Executing the most critical business activities with this limited infrastructure and personnel, is one of the fundamental challenges of Business Continuity Management.

Very probably, given the limited infrastructure and resources, the information flows and the business operations will have to be reorganized in order to meet the business objectives at a minimum acceptable level.

## *Loss of information*

After a disaster, one will typically restart from the last available back-ups (which have hopefully been stored off-site!) (Figure 1.5). If you can restart from back-ups (many do not), this means that all transactions that had been entered since the back-ups were taken will not be on the system after the restore. This information may well be lost. Also one must consider the synchronization of the data restored from different back-ups taken at different times. For instance the back-up of orders entered can be taken later than the backup of the financial systems, including the accounts receivable. It is as if your organization has gone back in time, but each system to a different time zone, and you have to match between time zones.

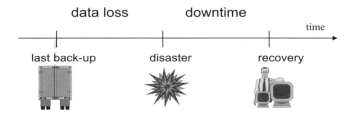

**Figure 1.5**

In addition to the time mismatch, the business events associated with the lost transactions will have been executed. For instance, invoices will have been sent out, goods will have been shipped, payments will have been made, but there will no longer be a trace of these events in the information systems.

When analysing the impact of information loss, one must consider how that lost information can be retrieved. Would you be able to reconstitute this information within your organization (the paper audit trail could be burnt in the fire), or will you have to ask your customers, suppliers, trading partners, banks for assistance? Will that affect your reputation? How much effort will this information retrieval entail? In the meantime, can you continue your business operations? How can you integrate the retrieved information in your information systems, without re-executing the associated business events? Can you guarantee the integrity and completeness of the retrieved information?

Consider for instance an air cargo company, where there was a tracking of the parcels by a computer system. Restarting after a disaster from the last back-up, in the worst case 24 hours old, means that information on all parcel movements since the last 24 hours would be lost. On top of that there is no way of knowing from internal sources which parcels had been transported in that timeframe. The company either had to recompose all transactions by manually collecting information from its world-wide agents and partners (nearly impossible to achieve complete-ness), or it had to perform a total inventory of all its warehouses and stop business operations until completion of the inventory.

Loss of information due to a disaster is not limited to data on computers. What about all the information stored in binders, agendas (with, for instance, customer information), the archives, the legally requested vital records, the paper client files, the business knowledge spread over the place, . . . Depending on the event, part of this information can be lost too. You must also consider the potential impact on your business of losing this information.

## The indirect impact: rippling effects on business operations

Each business process consists of a chain of activities that are executed typically by different departments. An unexpected event can interrupt a business activity, and/or interrupt an information flow supporting a business process. If the event is such that the business activity (or several activities) can no longer be executed, the impact could stretch out towards the entire business process.

Consider, for instance, in the process of handling requests for loans, that the business activity of checking the credit position of the requester can no longer be executed. Either, the loan is granted without the credit verification, which creates a financial risk, or the entire business process is halted, which will increase the risk of losing business opportunities (the customer will go elsewhere). The business impact of unavailability of key supporting infrastructure or resources can have chain effects throughout the process and even on other business processes. An example is the case of a distribution environment, where the goods tracking is done through bar codes. If the scanning of incoming goods is not possible for a certain period of time, there will be an impact on the full process. Either the process of transfer of incoming and outgoing goods is continued, with risk of losing track of goods, or the goods transfer process is stopped, with all the consequences of shortage of storage capacity for other incoming goods and of not being able to deliver the goods in time. The business impact will largely increase, as soon as external parties become involved. The higher the external visibility of the event, the more considerable and long lasting the business impact will be.

The effect of an unexpected event impacting business operations can easily ripple through the company. Even a relatively small event in an environment where many activities depend on each other, can have a tremendous impact. Consider for instance the replenishment process for a supermarket chain. A WAN failure at a bad time, that lasts long enough, can in the end create a logistical nightmare, impact customer satisfaction because of empty shelves, and create a large financial impact in an industry where net margins are already slim (Figure 1.6).

As no organization is an island, the rippling effects of a business interruption can even go beyond the company's boundaries. This is particularly true for companies which are an integral component of a wider supply chain—that is most of us! If, because of a business interruption, you deliver late, your reliability may well be

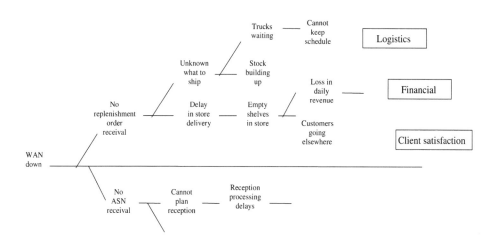

**Figure 1.6**—Effect diagram

brought into question for a considerable period of time—often well after the actual crisis.

In some cases, when a company participating in a supply chain is hit by a disaster, this could ripple down throughout the supply chain. Each company within the chain will have to deal with the impact of this on its own business operations through its Business Continuity Management.

## The long-term impact: image, market position, growth or decline

Even long after you have recovered from a disaster, and have returned to normal business operations, you will feel long-term impact. Depending on how good your business continuity plan has proven to be, you will suffer some long-term impacts, that can in the worst case even drive you out of business. These long-term impacts can include:

- Loss of customers
- Weakened financial position (for instance cash flow)
- Lost market share
- Loss of investor confidence
- Liabilities
- Eroded public image
- . . .

Your share price is a good indicator of the degree of long-term impact. Typically, shortly after a disaster, as your shareholders learn about the disaster through the media, share price will drop. Depending on how positive the perception is of you coping with the disaster, the share price will rise again. Whether it ever reaches the level it would have had without the disaster, is a good indication of the long-term impact. This means that it is not only important to have an effective business continuity plan, but also that you must handle the outside world perception of the effectiveness of your plan. You will have to include media management and public relations as an integral component of an overall business continuity management strategy.

The importance of the public image of your company cannot be stressed enough. Even with the most effective and successful business resumption plan, if the public, investors, shareholders and so on get a negative perception, it could ruin all your efforts. Sound communication management, coupled with an effective crisis management, is essential for survival beyond a disaster. For a company whose success is heavily dependent on its share price, the above-mentioned effect on share price alone should create a strong justification for investment in Business Continuity Management.

In industries with intense competition, loss of customers or loss of market share might be something you will never recover from. Typically, this will generate a downsizing, and dependent on the flexibility of your organization, can even mean that you are pushed out of the market.

## The business risks of an interruption in operations

A 1998 survey executed by The Economist Intelligence Unit in cooperation with Arthur Andersen, indicates that loss of integrity and availability were the risks having the highest impact on business operations, for over 70% of the companies participating in the survey.

An unexpected event interrupting information flows or business operations can be considered a risk to the extent that it would create a material business risk for your company. A business risk is a threat that an event or action will adversely affect your organization's ability to successfully achieve its business objectives and execute its strategies—in other words the achievement of business mission. This implies that you have to look at IT interruptions or business interruptions in the context of the key business risks for your company.

For example, a key business risk in the automotive components industry can be "not being able to deliver parts where they are needed at the exact time they are needed". In this industry, price and effectiveness are critical drivers that have enforced short cycle times through integrated logistics. Any disruption in business operations that would result in late delivery or loss of efficiency, is a key risk that subsequently must be covered in the Business Continuity Management for such companies.

When going through this exercise, it is important that you use a reference framework of business risks, specific for your business environment. Such a framework allows you not to dwell on symptoms or the obvious, but to focus on what is essential for your business success. An example of such framework is the Business Risk Model™, developed by Arthur Andersen for each industry segment (Figure 1.7).

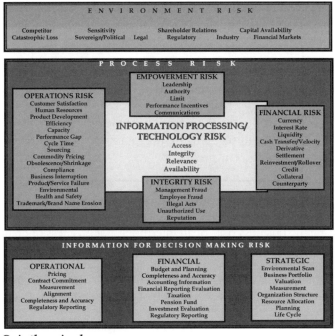

© **Arthur Andersen**

**Figure 1.7**—The Business Risk Model™

Analysing your key business risks and performing a gap analysis with your current protection will allow you to set priorities. It also allows you to focus your investments towards those areas where you have the most benefit, namely covering the largest business risks for your company of an interruption in business operations.

## Risk management: gamble or hedge?

Business Continuity Management is in the first place more about management of business interruption risks than about shopping around for solutions. The largest mistake one can make about Business Continuity Management is thinking "I have a Business Continuity Plan, nothing can happen to me". Every Business Continuity Management is based on assumptions, and on risk management decisions. These include items such as maximum allowable downtime, disaster scenarios to include single point of failure assumptions, acceptance of certain risks and finding a balance between cost and benefits.

No Business Continuity Management will ever cover all areas and all risks. The target is to cover the business risks that are key for your company, and to cover the business processes that are most critical for your business success. To reach that target, basically each Business Continuity Management exercise is a risk management exercise, which is always based on the "five As" of risk management (Figure 1.8).

---

✔ Assess risk
✔ Accept or reject risk
✔ Avoid risk, transfer risk or
   reduce risk to acceptable level
✔ Analyse performance gaps
✔ Act to improve

---

**Figure 1.8**—"The five As" of risk management

By analysing the business risks of an interruption of business operations and the business impact, decisions can be made with regard to what level of risk can be accepted and what risks must be reduced to an acceptable level through Business Continuity Management. It is important to realize that, when agreeing to accept a risk, this decision also includes acceptance of the consequences in the event that the worst happens.

Before going into defining solutions within a Business Continuity Management, it is important that you do not make assumptions "with a wet finger approach". To return to the air cargo example, IT had assumed within its disaster recovery planning that restarting from yesterday's back-up would be sufficient. We have discussed before what that meant in terms of loss of information and what would be the business impact.

It is important that risk management decisions are taken on an informed basis. Only in this way can a business continuity strategy be defined that will meet the business requirements and will cover the key risks. This is the difference between hedging and gambling: you gamble when you make assumptions, for instance, purely based on the probability of an event or based on "gut feeling". You hedge when you take risk management decisions based on a careful analysis of the business risk, on the potential business impact and on the key dependencies and vulnerabilities in perspective of your business objectives. Hedging is assessing the magnitude of the risks and taking informed and balanced decisions.

Business Continuity Management is about hedging the business risks of operational interruptions, deriving a business continuity strategy from this that meets the business objectives, and implementing this strategy.

## Business continuity: what does survival mean to you?

So, you need Business Continuity Management. It is a question of business survival. You want to manage the risks of a business interruption due to an unexpected event. But your business organization is complex. You cannot duplicate it all; this is just too expensive. Even duplicating only the most critical infrastructure is probably still very expensive and difficult to justify. Besides, what is critical and what is not, and to what level? Not all elements in your business organization are equally critical, yet they are interdependent because they are part of these activity chains.

What do you have to protect your business against? You can not foresee all possible events. How far do you need to go? Where will you start? More important, where will you stop? How do you identify your priorities? How do you ensure that you invest in the right places? Could it be that you spend more than you should?

Before you actually start your Business Continuity Management project, there is an important question to ask yourself: "What is your objective, what do you want to obtain from your Business Continuity Management?" At first sight, the answer is obvious: you want to be able to continue doing business after a disaster, to resume business activities and continue to serve your customers.

Consider the approach to Business Continuity Management that you intend to take, and the project organization you intend to establish to build the plan. Compare the focus areas of that approach against what your objectives of Business Continuity Management are.

Considering the different approaches to Business Continuity Management that we see organizations apply, there are basically three kinds of objectives, each matching a different approach:

- Rebuild the infrastructure: Where the focus is on alternative facilities and sites and on solutions to minimize downtime of key infrastructure and systems
- Resumption of business activities: Where the focus is on setting up an organization and the required facilities to enable key staff to resume their activities
- Continuity in customer service at an acceptable level: Where the focus is on defining what level of customer service must be maintained throughout a disaster, and what is required to achieve that level of customer service

The following sections discuss each of these objectives and approaches. They describe what are the benefits, what are the outcomes and what are the pitfalls or potential shortcomings of each of these.

### Rebuilding the infrastructure

The objective in this approach is to rebuild the critical infrastructure that has been damaged in a disaster. The idea is that as soon as the damaged infrastructure is available again (albeit in a different location), the business activities can be resumed as before because the required infrastructure is the same.

Lists are created of critical computer systems, networks, manufacturing infrastructure, call centres, dealing rooms, office space and any other essential infrastructure elements. The selection of these critical infrastructure elements is based on a business impact analysis and a risk analysis. The maximum allowable downtime is defined, when required differentiated per group of infrastructure elements. With this list in hand and the determination of the maximum allowable downtime, alternative solutions are considered and a cost/benefit analysis is made. The critical success factor in this approach is to have sufficient critical infrastructure duplicated that business activities can be resumed in a similar way to how they were executed previously.

Once the solutions are selected, plans must be built to bring them into action. This is the mechanism to switch on these alternative systems and infrastructure elements. Because of cost considerations, we see the list of critical infrastructure elements very often trimmed down to the very essentials, for which the least costly option is chosen.

Although the thinking process in the beginning is business-oriented through the business impact analysis, we very often see a too intense focus on systems and office space without sufficient verification as to whether business activities in the end can effectively be resumed. What we also see happen too often is that a reduced version of this approach is chosen to create a feeling of safety. Very often it is only the central IT system which is considered within the scope of Business Continuity Management, the concept being that without this system the company would not be able to survive a disaster. Consequently, the lowest cost options are considered in respect of hot-site or short-term delivery of a replacement system in the mistaken belief that this solution will ensure the company's survival. An example illustrating this is the replenishment cycle mentioned before, where the concerned company decided to duplicate, through server mirroring, only the most critical within the chain of systems and networks supporting the replenishment information flow, without considering how the replenishment process would be resumed with only this single server available.

A further problem which follows this narrow vision of protection of only the most critical infrastructure elements is in the testing component of the process. In many instances, testing focuses on making the alternative infrastructure available but too rarely considers the practical application of critical business activities based upon this limited infrastructure. Although the intention is correct, the outcome of this approach is infrastructure replacement, not necessarily business continuity. Extremely few companies can afford such an extensive duplication of infrastructure.

When a disaster does occur, we very often see these limited investments prove to be ineffective in providing business resumption. Stories abound of companies which went bankrupt even though their central computer system was recovered within hours of the disaster.

## Resumption of business activities

Having witnessed the pitfalls of a purely infrastructure-oriented approach to Business Continuity Management, many organizations have added the dimension of resumption of business activities to their approach.

Another key driver in the approach focusing on resumption of business activities, is the awareness that central systems are only part of the infrastructure supporting the business activities. PC networks and client/server architectures have created critical dependencies throughout the enterprise. In this approach, the activities of the employees are considered. A list is made of what the critical activities are and what is required to be able to execute them. Again, a business impact analysis and risk analysis are instrumental in determining the level of criticality of these activities.

The result of this analysis is typically a scheme of what number of staff (and the associated office space and infrastructure) is required by what day after a disaster. The idea is to gradually resume the business activities elsewhere, starting with the most critical ones, until full business resumption or until the return to the old facilities is possible. The benefit of this approach is that it links business activities to required infrastructure, providing a much better guarantee for effective business resumption in the case of a disaster. The critical success factors of this approach are the criteria that are used to prioritize business activities.

The most important pitfall of this approach is that it very easily results in building departmental recovery plans, where each department within the company will build its plan to resume the critical business activities executed within its department but in isolation of the whole. What is missing here is business integration. For instance, one department is dependent on being provided with input from another department to execute one of its key activities. Perhaps the provision of that input is considered non-critical by the provider department but is absolutely crucial to the operation of the receiving department. Very often, departmental recovery plans lack a business process orientation, where business processes cross over a number of departments.

Another pitfall is that the criteria to define business criticality of the activities are not uniform over the departments, and/or are not linked to the business objectives or the key business drivers of the company. We often see business continuity plans using this approach focus much more on the business activities as objectives on their own, instead of focusing on the resumption of the key business activities to enable continuity in service delivery.

## Continuity in customer service at an acceptable level

Considering the fact that it is rarely justifiable to duplicate all critical infrastructure, that infrastructure alone does not provide business continuity, and that it is very difficult to obtain integrated business resumption through a mere resumption of individual business activities, it is clear that selections will have to be made and that a structured approach to make these selections is the key to success. Making these selections is essentially business risk management, and is an executive level responsibility. It concerns the management of business interruption risks in the context of reaching the business objectives and safeguarding the key business drivers.

Typical management objectives of Business Continuity Management are: to provide continuity in customer service at a minimum acceptable level and to limit the impact on the financial position of the company. Defining what is the minimum level of customer service that is to be maintained throughout a disaster is critical in this approach. This requires a top-down analysis of business drivers and objectives, the key business processes supporting these business drivers and their key dependencies and vulnerabilities.

The goal of the business continuity plan is to build the business operating frame to reach these service levels. These will eventually include provision of alternative key infrastructure, resumption of key business processes and associated business activities, organization measures to execute the business resumption and many more.

## Conclusion

Business Continuity Management is about being prepared to rebuild your business organization after a disaster in order to provide continuity in customer service at a minimum acceptable level, to limit the impact on the financial position, and in the long term to survive as a business organization.

Today's business organizations are driven by business processes, which are chains of activities that are executed across departments. Each organization consists of an integration of business processes, the participants in these processes and the infrastructure and resources supporting these business processes. Within each business process, there are a number of critical dependencies, which can include: human resources, logistical infrastructure, information technology, key activities, and dependencies beyond the organization's boundaries. Unexpected events can at all times interrupt business operations. These do not have to be large-scale events or do not even have to cause extensive damage to mean a disaster to an organization.

Because unexpected events do come in all shapes and sizes, and considering the objective of Business Continuity Management of being able to resume business operations, potential events and disasters can better be classified according to effect, rather than type of event. Statistics show that business interruptions do occur, more frequently than one would expect. They also show that you should be prepared if you want to optimize your chances to stay in business.

The impact of a disaster is not limited to the damage that it causes. It also includes the business impact of unavailability and loss of information. The business effects and losses associated with extended interruptions of the critical business activities can be very high. Even after the resumption of business, the impact of a disaster can still be felt through loss of customers, a fall in the share price, in an erosion of the organization's image, perception and credibility in the marketplace.

An unexpected event interrupting business operations can be considered a risk to the extent that it would materialize a key business risk for the organization. A business risk is a threat that an event or action will adversely affect the organization's ability to successfully achieve its business objectives and execute its strategies.

No Business Continuity Management will ever be able to cover all business areas and all risks. The target is to cover the business risks that are key for your organization, and to cover the business processes that are essential for your business success. To reach that target, basically Business Continuity Management is a business risk management exercise. It is important that risk management decisions are taken on an informed basis. Only in this way, can a business continuity strategy be defined that will meet the business requirements and that will cover the key risks.

Business Continuity Management is about hedging the business risks of operational interruptions, forming a business continuity strategy from this that meets the business objectives, and implementing this strategy. Finally, it is very important to clearly define your objective: rebuilding the infrastructure, resuming business activities, or providing continuity in customer service at an acceptable level. Having defined your objective, you have to apply an approach that meets that objective, and stay focused on that objective, throughout the Business Continuity Management project.

# What is a Business Continuity Planning (BCP) strategy?

**2**

## Mike O'Hehir—Australia

Michael O'Hehir is Director, Global Risk Management Solutions, for PricewaterhouseCoopers in Sydney, Australia.

## Introduction

The process of business continuity planning can be both time-consuming and expensive. As a result, management will expect tangible benefits to be achieved by the process.

Corporate Governance is the system in place to balance risk and entrepreneurial energy with appropriate internal control procedures to manage that risk. Directors and management are under increasing pressure to provide assurance on Corporate Governance standards both to organizational stakeholders and to regulatory authorities and must remain informed on the organization's risks and obligations. They will rely on processes and controls to ensure strategies are implemented to mitigate their exposures.

## Business continuity planning defined

BCP is defined as:

> the identification and protection of critical business processes and resources required to maintain an acceptable level of business, protecting those resources and preparing procedures to ensure the survival of the organisation in times of business disruption. (*System Management Methodology—Disaster Contingency Planning*, 1992, Price Waterhouse)

*The Definitive Handbook of Business Continuity Management.* Edited by Andrew Hiles and Peter Barnes. © 1999 John Wiley & Sons Ltd.

A business continuity plan is a business management plan rather than a technical plan. Hence, contingency planning is based on the understanding of the organization, the tools that support the operations of the business, evaluating the loss of such tools, knowing who will handle a crisis situation and how they will do that.

It is essential in today's business environment for an organization to consider what should be done if a disaster were to have an impact upon the organization's normal business environment, as a minor, major or catastrophic disaster could bring substantial losses to any business. The issue of disaster recovery and business continuity planning must be addressed through the preparation of a Disaster Contingency and Recovery Plan.

The ongoing business is based on the assumption that the improved services, productivity and opportunities for growth provided by the current technology implemented within the organization will not decline. It is therefore important that the dependency of the organization on technology be considered by the organization in identifying the critical portions of the business.

Managers of the business are custodians of the business interests and responsibilities. They must practise good stewardship, which includes operating in a way that preserves profitability, stability and quality and advances the interests of customers, employees and investors. Management cannot be said to be fulfilling this duty if an unplanned event can jeopardize the survival of the organization. In addition, some legal mandates may have been issued, demanding that records of an organization be available at all times, regardless of the situation.

The following risks and issues are raised in the absence of effective BCP:

- Business interruption resulting in inability to serve the current customer base, erosion of customer base, lost opportunities, loss of goodwill, and inability to compete
- Financial loss due to inability to process receivables, late payment penalties and missed discounts, inability to update account balances and lost or unrecorded sales
- Legal liability resulting from failure to satisfy contractual obligations
- Going out of business

Just having addressed the issue of business continuity planning is not enough. A BCP project must involve the entire organization. Time and resources must be provided by management for the development, initial and ongoing testing and ongoing maintenance of the plan. Unless management commitment is displayed, the whole organization is involved and the plan development project is given a high priority, the project is likely to fail.

**Disaster contingency plans in the past have generally addressed only computer-related disasters. However, this is too narrow a focus and all of the related activities must be addressed to ensure business continuity, including manual records and information.**

It must also be decided how large an event the plan is to handle. If the organization is in an area where a regional disaster is likely, for example Southern California, which is subject to earthquakes, or central London, subject to terrorist activities, the plan should incorporate procedures to cope with loss of utilities and other outside services. If the organization is in an area where regional disasters are unlikely, the organization may choose to limit the plan to facility-related disaster planning. When a disaster is limited to a facility, help may be available from suppliers, authorities and the community.

The scope of the business recovery plan within the organization must also be determined. This will depend on the structure of the organization, such as a multiple or a single facility. The most important aspects of a successful approach to business continuity planning are paying attention to detail and addressing small sections at a time.

## Objectives of a BCP strategy

The overall objectives of a business continuity project are to:

- Establish a framework for evaluating business processes which allows a focused approach to develop a business continuity plan through a well-structured and comprehensive methodology
- Develop a pragmatic, cost-effective and operable recovery plan which enables an organization to complete the critical business processes in the event of a major disruption to its business operations
- Minimise the impact of a disaster on an organization

An effective recovery plan is a relatively inexpensive form of insurance and a necessary cost of doing business for prudent organizations in today's environment.

## Effective risk management and the drivers of BCP: shareholder value, risk, reward and control

Increasing shareholder value emerged as the key corporate requirement in a study amongst the *Financial Times* top 500 companies, commissioned by Price Waterhouse and carried out by the Harris Research Centre.

Opportunities to enhance shareholder value exist in almost all companies. New tools and methodologies are now available to identify where these opportunities are and how they can be used to achieve sustainable increases in shareholder value. For instance, market analysts and institutional investors are increasingly adopting cashflow valuation approaches in making key investment decisions.

There are two sorts of mistakes a company can make: to destroy value by bad decisions and to miss the opportunity to create value by not making good decisions. Whilst internal control is often better at preventing crisis than in guaranteeing long-run good performance, a balance of driving value and mitigating risks can satisfy shareholders.

## Risk and reward

Shareholders understand value—that is, reward. Do they understand risk? Mr Paul Barrett, the Executive Director of the Business Council of Australia, wrote in the July 1995 *Business Council Bulletin* in his paper on Corporate Governance:

> As shareholders and lenders we entrust our capital to companies and their boards because we seek a higher return than we could achieve from a "risk free" investment in Commonwealth securities.
>
> This implies that we expect boards and management to demonstrate entrepreneurship and dynamism, that is to take risks. What we expect is that the risks will be well considered and well managed and that the risk profile of the enterprise will be widely understood.

There is clearly a much greater awareness today of the need to manage both the drivers of risk and the drivers of value.

## Risk and control

In the past decade the global corporate landscape has been littered with the debris of risks that have gone awry: defaulted real estate loans; unsafe work practices; environmental disasters; failed contracts; millions of dollars of losses from imprudent investments in derivative exotica; and recently, the loss of power to the City of Auckland. The pendulum appears to be swinging towards more control. How much is enough? Too much control will restrict an enterprise; conversely, without appropriate business controls, an organization may be exposed with devastating results. Paul Barrett also stated:

> The worst possible outcome from the current focus on corporate governance would be if boards and management were to become risk averse.

## The need for a structured business risk management process

Complementing the *management* of shareholder value is the *management* of risk. Risk management has become a widely used term for a commonsense approach to the decision-making process concerning resources to avoid "intolerable" outcomes. It depends on an assessment of risks and their associated probabilities, which in turn, depends on experience, knowledge, value judgements, intuition, and attitude to risk.

Risk management is now understood to encompass much more than just insurance. In wider terms, it translates into: *are the costs incurred by additional management controls worth the avoidance of potential losses and costs?* In the past risk management has been undertaken on a project basis. However, the combined effect of organizational, commercial and legislative changes means that this approach may no longer be adequate. Moreover, what is adequate to address the risks faced by the business today, may not be so tomorrow.

For most organizations the need for a coordinated risk management capability has only become apparent in the past few years, and the techniques to manage this change are still in their infancy. Successful organizations recognize the importance of developing a coordinated risk management programme and acknowledge that risks occur and must be addressed.

## Managing the exposures

A research report prepared by Price Waterhouse for the American Institute of Internal Auditors Research Foundation, titled *Improving Audit Committee Performances: What Works Best*, provides a useful summary of the source of risks.

> Business risks occur because of the volatile environments in which businesses operate and the nature of their operations.

Risks are diverse and arise from both external and internal sources. The research report cites external risks as including "*such matters as the state of the economy, or of the company's industry, and the legal and regulatory environment*". Internal risks include "*such factors as the nature of the company's operations and products, the control environment within the company (tone at the top), the adequacy of control systems, the financial strength or weakness of the company, the quality of the organization's accounting policies and procedures, and the quality of management.*"

The multitude of risk areas where active risk management is necessary is illustrated in Figure 2.1. The challenge is to control risk within acceptable limits without constraining operational effectiveness, business development opportunities or entrepreneurial spirit.

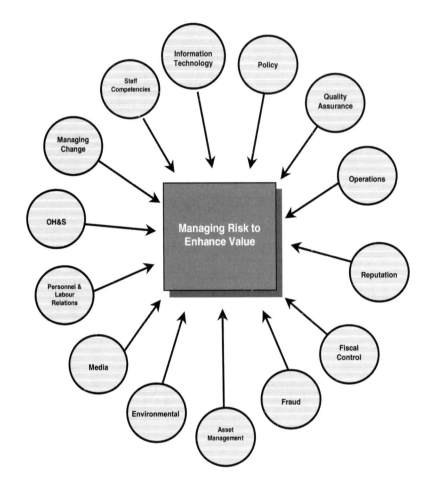

**Figure 2.1**—Areas where active risk management is necessary

## What is management control?

The elements of management control are as follows. The *control environment* provides an atmosphere in which people conduct their activities and carry out their control responsibilities. IT serves as the foundation for the other components. Within this environment, management *assesses risks* to the achievement of specified objectives. *Control activities* are implemented to help ensure that management directives to address the risks are carried out. Meanwhile, relevant information is captured and *communicated* throughout the organization. The entire process is *monitored* and modified as conditions warrant.

Management control is thus the process of establishing controls to mitigate business risks.

The key elements of risk management comprise:

- The attitudes and attributes of the Board or CEO (the "tone at the top") which establish the overall risk control environment
- Analyses of external and internal risks which potentially affect the achievement of objectives
- The controls established throughout an organization to mitigate risk
- The monitoring process, both in respect of the controls and the control system itself, which ensures that the system remains effective and dynamic

These are demonstrated in Figure 2.2 which integrates risk management into the overall management process.

## Classification of risk

> Risk management has moved up the corporate management agenda. A growing multiplicity of business risks pushes multinationals to find more comprehensive approaches to managing them.
>
> But what is business risk? Risk is a matter of perspective. Finance and operational managers, institutional and speculative investors, all see risk differently. It can mean any impediment, inside or outside the organization, to meeting business objectives. One report concludes: "Business risk arises as much from the likelihood that something good *won't* happen as it does from the threat that something bad *will* happen." (*CFO—Architect of the Corporation's Future*, Price Waterhouse Financial and Cost Management Team, Wiley, 1997)

The population of risks that an organization is exposed to can be divided into five core groups (Figure 2.3). These can be used as a starting point and over the course of the risk management measurement process should be further developed.

- **Strategic:** the risk of plans failing or succeeding
- **Financial:** the risk of financial controls failing or succeeding
- **Operational:** the risk of human error or achievement
- **Commercial:** the risk of relationships failing or succeeding
- **Technical:** the risk of physical assets failing/being damaged or enhanced

Risk groups are not mutually exclusive. For example, human factors—prime drivers of operational risks—are significant in many strategic and financial risks. Also, companies carry their histories with them: a business may have accumulated

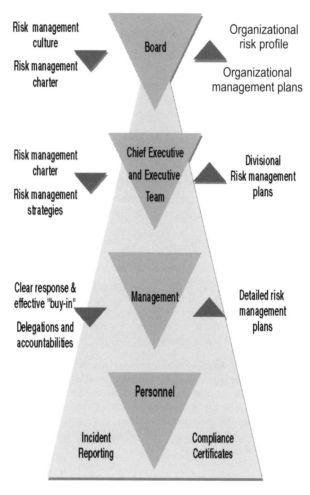

**Figure 2.2**—Risk management key roles and components

liabilities or assets, bad or good practices, weak or strong relationships. Consider how past risks influence current exposures—and how risks of all types affect strategic direction and, ultimately, the company's ability to generate shareholder value in future.

Until recently, companies managed risks largely in terms of possible solutions. An insurable risk might be the insurance manager's responsibility. If a risk seemed a financial control matter, the treasurer might deal with it. Risks touching on consumer relations might be managed as part of sales and marketing.

Today, functionally segregating risk management seems dated. The CFOs and other senior executives of many multinationals are learning to take a more integrated view of business risks and business risk management.

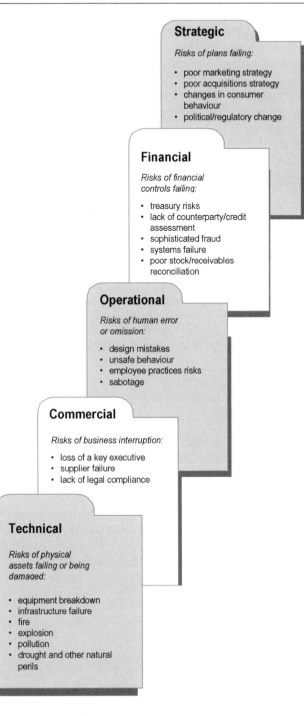

**Strategic**

*Risks of plans failing:*

- poor marketing strategy
- poor acquisitions strategy
- changes in consumer behaviour
- political/regulatory change

**Financial**

*Risks of financial controls failing:*

- treasury risks
- lack of counterparty/credit assessment
- sophisticated fraud
- systems failure
- poor stock/receivables reconciliation

**Operational**

*Risks of human error or omission:*

- design mistakes
- unsafe behaviour
- employee practices risks
- sabotage

**Commercial**

*Risks of business interruption:*

- loss of a key executive
- supplier failure
- lack of legal compliance

**Technical**

*Risks of physical assets failing or being damaged:*

- equipment breakdown
- infrastructure failure
- fire
- explosion
- pollution
- drought and other natural perils

**Figure 2.3**—Five core groups of risk

## Management response to the risk profile

Management action will need to be taken to reduce the risk levels where they have been deemed unacceptably high, or alternatively to remove constraints where they are preventing the department from pursuing opportunities. Management responses need to be developed to improve the current processes and close the gap between the risk profile and the company's "appetite for risk". This action will be formulated into a risk management response in a framework which ensures a disciplined approach to the future management of the risk as outlined below.

Embedded in the framework are some key issues as follows:

| | |
|---|---|
| Policy | • A policy statement authorized at an appropriate level, should codify the company's attitude to a particular risk. |
| | • This policy statement should also prescribe the objectives of the company's risk response. |
| Accountability | • Individual accountability for the management of the risk should be clearly established. |
| | • The nominated person should have the appropriate technical expertise and authority to effectively manage the risk. |
| Current business process | • A description of the management processes that are currently employed to manage the risk. |
| Future actions | • Recommended business processes that are to be implemented or refined to reduce the residual risk to an acceptable level. |
| | • Responsibility and milestones are assigned. |
| Performance measures | • Key measures used by management to enable them to assess and monitor the effectiveness of the risk. |
| | • The measures may be proactive or reactive. Proactive measures are best as they tend to monitor risk preventive actions rather than risk detective actions. |
| Independent expert | • If appropriate, a suitably qualified independent expert (internal or external) assesses the adequacy of the risk response. |
| | • The frequency of the review will depend upon the nature of the risk. |
| Contingency plan | • If appropriate, develop plans to manage or mitigate a major loss following the occurrence of an event. |

# BCP strategies for managing risk

## The BCP process is as important as the plan itself

The process of building a business case for implementing business recovery plans is critical to the success of the process. The soundness of the Business Impact Analysis methodology is characterized and supported by the following critical components:

- **BIA business case**—the Business Impact Analysis or Risk Assessment processes are critical in building the business case to progress to future stages. Without a rigid methodology to gather the data to assess the risk environment, it may be difficult to get commitment to proceed.
- **Management support**—in the absence of management support for recovery planning, the project may stall, or at worst not even get off the ground. Ownership of the BCP process should rest with the senior executive levels of the organization and not in the domain of individuals whose main aim in life is an expansion of their empire. It is not a project for project's sake.
- **Enterprise-wide versus IT**—be clear on the scope of the project. The continuity of business operations may be reliant on a range of dependencies, not just IT: e.g. manufacturing plant and equipment, key suppliers, personnel, vital records, operational systems.
- **Be realistic—risk versus cost**—management may be prepared to accept certain levels of risk. The business case should be conscious of this and build a business case to progress to further stages based on a risk of occurrence versus cost of implementation of selected strategies.
- **The soundness of the financial impacts**—data gathered during the BIA in the event of a loss or outage of business functionality can bring your business case undone. It is critical that user management provide written agreement and sign-off to the financial impact data they have provided, e.g. the impact on the business from revenue deferral after a disaster, as opposed to lost revenue, is significantly less. Be sure of the facts.
- **Formal sign-off and agreement** to findings from the BIA provides support from the business to the process. The business must own the process and recommendations. It must not be seen as a "consultant-inspired" exercise.
- **Internal Audit involvement provides an independent assessment**. An often quoted description of an auditor is: *"An auditor is the person who comes in after the war is over and bayonets the wounded"*. However, contrary to the myth, Internal Audit can be an ally in raising business continuity planning to the level of importance required within the organization. Often the Internal Audit Department will have significant influence with management through regular reporting and meetings at Board of Director and Audit Committee level.

## Adherence to legislative requirements

Is your organization adhering to the myriad of legislation which requires your Board of Directors and management to identify and address the risks they face ? Some of the more well known UK and Australian regulatory and legislative requirements include:

- COSO—internal controls model
- Cadbury Commission on Corporate Governance
- Australian Stock Exchange listing 3C(3)(j)
- Finance Regulations
- State Emergency and Rescue Management Acts
- AS/NZS 4360 and 3931
- Local Government and Planning Acts
- Insurance and Superannuation Commission
- Aust. Institute of Co. Directors 1994 Guidelines on Due Diligence
- Public Service and Audit Acts

## Plan for a worst case scenario

If a disaster is going to happen it will more than likely occur at the worst possible time for an organization. Two recent Australian examples include:

- Victorian TAB (TabCorp) system crash on Melbourne Cup day 1996. "The system crashed when the volume of transactions generated by cup bets, peaking at 300 a second, exposed faults in the disk logging. . . . As a result, TabCorp's earnings were down about A$2 million from 1995" (MIS February 1997).
- "A major disaster with the Australian Stock Exchange's SEATS computer trading system dampened the financial euphoria over the Coalition victory and overshadowed a strong rally on the bond market. The sharemarket failed to trade at 10.00 a.m. and was down for two-and-half hours due to the breakdown in the electronic trading system" (*Sydney Morning Herald*, 5/3/96). "Macquarie Equities' managing director . . . said the meltdown would cost his company thousands of dollars because of settlement problems" (*Australian Financial Review*, 5/3/96).

In developing a scenario around which an organization's Business Impact Analysis and Risk Assessment will be performed, it is important to consider a range of scenarios. These should include incidents as well as a worst case event. This will provide management with the basis upon which to assess the risks and the likely impacts should an incident or disaster occur.

## The plan should reflect the changing business environment

If the plan is not up to date and does not reflect the current business environment then you might as well not have a plan. The plan should allow for changes in the business environment, and procedures should be in place to ensure it is updated in a timely manner.

Responsibility for ensuring the plan is up to date should be assigned. This should include:

- Issuing updated versions of the plan
- Maintaining a record of who has copies and for retrieving outdated versions
- Implementing mechanisms to facilitate maintenance of the plan whenever the business environment changes

The contingency plan must be updated regularly in order to reduce the risks associated with disruptions. The contingency plan should contain sufficient update procedures to ensure that any changes to the organization or its information systems environment are accurately and promptly reflected in the plan. Specifically, mechanisms should be in place for:

- Changes of personnel—particularly changes to management, user and information systems personnel
- Systems changes—including changes to hardware, software, telecommunications equipment, and security requirements
- Consider including business continuity in all due diligence assignments
- Key support services—are they still available?
- Has the business been involved in mergers, acquisitions, divestments which may impact the plan?
- Have new processes and operations commenced or some ceased?
- Have customer commitments and supplier relationships changed?

## Adequacy of insurance coverage

Does your organization have adequate business interruption insurance and if so does it:

- Incorporate adequate indemnity periods?
- Allow for future business growth?
- Consider the nature of the disaster on all business components?
- Consider the contractual arrangements with customers and suppliers?
- Provide for loss of physical access to the business?

The *Insurance Broker*, March 1992, cited that underinsurance averaged around 30% for commercial properties damaged during the Newcastle (Australia) earthquake.

## Document management and control

Procedures should be established to ensure all changes that affect the operation of critical and necessary business processes are communicated for inclusion in the Plan document. The steps involved in maintaining the Plan should be documented, including any approval and logging procedures required.

To keep the information in the Plan current, it will be necessary to continually incorporate alterations into the Plan. It may be best to schedule regular updates to the distributed copies of the Plan while having an on-site and off-site copy (both in hard and soft copy form) that incorporates all changes as they are made.

Once any alteration is made to the Plan, those involved in that aspect of the Plan must be notified and all copies must be updated and distributed. Any old procedures must be destroyed to ensure there is no confusion.

The key components in ensuring an up-to-date and controlled document are:

- Identify triggers for planned and unplanned maintenance, e.g. new business processes or acquisitions, personnel changes, new technology, etc.
- Prepare procedures for notification from critical departments in the event of changes in their business processes
- Prepare a schedule for regular review of the Plan. This may encompass a re-evaluation of the risks and threats to the organization, random samples of adherence to procedures, etc.
- Document procedures for incorporating new business processes into the Plan
- Prepare procedures to incorporate alterations into the Plan. This must be performed in a structured fashion and all copies should be version and number controlled
- Determine a distribution list for the Plan. Plans should be issued with an identifying code to ensure all copies have been updated and distributed
- Prepare procedures for distribution of Plan alterations to ensure all appropriate sections are replaced and distributed
- Prepare procedures to ensure that the Plan is independently reviewed on a regular basis. This can be conducted by auditors and/or senior management to ensure the Plan is relevant and accurate.

### Identify and evaluate all threats

There are many threats which can disrupt an organization's business operations. The identification and evaluation of threats is necessary to prepare prevention and recovery procedures. Threat identification also provides a number of other advantages including:

- Identifies where preventive measures are required
- Highlights previously unnoticed susceptibility that needs to be addressed by plans and procedures
- Can increase the awareness of staff to threats and evidence of those threats becoming problems
- Can also provide a stronger sense of purpose in staff related to the preparation of the continuity plan as they realize the importance of such a project
- Can highlight interdependencies between departments and result in better interdepartment cooperation to protect shared vulnerabilities
- Identifies where cost-sharing is possible for threat prevention systems

Threats can be categorized under the following headings:

- Water
- Fire
- Service failure
- Mechanical breakdown or software failure
- Accidental or deliberate damage to property and assets
- Personnel problems
- Environmental/facility-wide damage

A common threat to an organization's information systems assets may come from inadequate protection of company data and information. The risks associated with unauthorized activity of this nature and the potential impacts are often not considered in the development of recovery plans.

The Business Impact Analysis/Risk Assessment phase provides an excellent opportunity for an organization to also evaluate its logical security environment. The loss, destruction and/or disclosure of company data and information may have far more significant consequences and should be included for consideration in the continuity process.

## Recurring themes from major disasters

Key lessons learned from recovery attempts during recent disasters demonstrate the importance of the human element in continuity planning. Other lessons "relate to the absolute necessity of realistic testing of recovery plans, the need for clearly articulated communication links, and the need for explicit knowledge of environmental dependencies. Each of these was a recurring theme among the experience of several South Florida organisations during Hurricane Andrew" (*Information*

*Systems Audit & Control Association Journal*, **1**, 1994). The four recurring themes they identified were:

**Recurring Themes in Hurricane Andrew Disaster Recovery**

1. *Human Element*
   - Establish payroll policies for period of disruption
   - Establish policies to assist employees' families
   - Plan to proceed with recovery efforts without some personnel as a result of personal losses experienced by employees
   - Plan to locate key personnel before, during, and after disruption

2. *Testing*
   - Must be realistic.
   - Must be recurring/ongoing
   - Must acknowledge all dependencies on external support or environmental constraints which might be affected by widespread disaster

3. *Communications*
   - Access to public service announcements as a means of communication may not be feasible
   - Reliance on radio broadcasts may be dependent on existence of radio towers
   - Plan structure for communications—pre-numbered memos and dated voice mail
   - Do not rely on cellular phones—land lines were more stable during Hurricane Andrew

4. *External Dependencies*
   - Consider possibility of limited access to assets and business due to road and/or waterway damage/blockage
   - Reciprocal agreements should consider the likelihood of shared loss experiences among participants
   - Set realistic expectations of access to common carriers for transport of key personnel and data
   - Do not rely on delivery of services such as water, sewer, power and gas.

## Training is not the same as testing

This is often the most overlooked component of business continuity planning. Much effort is put into developing, testing and maintaining the plan but often personnel are not adequately trained in all aspects of plan activation.

Significant business disruption can be caused by overreaction to an alarm. Staff should be appropriately trained to recognize and discern between incidents and disasters, enabling them to make rational decisions. It is not unfeasible to imagine a diligent employee triggering the fire suppression system, after an alert, resulting in the dumping of litres of water over critical IT components. Appropriate training would however enable the employee to identify the real urgency of the situation and therefore make rational decisions regarding alternative actions to be taken. An incident of this nature recently occurred in Australia, resulting in a A$90 million ambit insurance claim for damages, business interruption and so on.

## Fail-safe systems are a myth

In most cases (perhaps with the exception of defence systems) there are no regulations on how computer software systems should be specified, developed, implemented and controlled—even though lives and economies increasingly depend upon them. Consider the following (*Sydney Morning Herald*, 18 May 1996):

- The pilots of a Boeing 747 began their descent into Seattle Tacoma airport on 11 August 1995. Checking their instruments, they notified the control tower of their position. Then . . . nothing. A computer software failure knocked out the radio communications facilities of US air traffic control across an area of more than 500 000 square kilometres, leaving all commercial aircraft above Washington State . . . flying in complete isolation for more than a minute. Those who could not contact a military air base fell back on "visual systems"—i.e. looking out of the window to see if any other planes were about. The software in this incident was part of a state-of-the-art system, just two months old, which cost US$1.4 billion.
- During the filming of *Babe* in the Southern Highlands of NSW, the animatronic pig, which was being operated by radio in the middle of the field, suddenly began behaving strangely, its legs kicking and jerking. Next day the Bowral police arrived. Every time the pig was operated, police radios were blacked out in an area of 120 square kilometres.
- At Melbourne's Tullamarine Airport, police thought a professional hacker must be blocking pilot communication channels. When they identified the source of the interference it turned out to be an ordinary VCR in a home beneath the flight path.
- Although other engineers—mechanical, electrical, civil—operate under much more onerous regulatory constraints, anyone can develop a computer system regardless of experience, competence or resources.

How much of our lives is dependent upon computer systems. Consider:

- Nuclear power plants
- Air traffic control
- Traffic light grids
- Train networks
- Freeway fog and speed limit signs
- Hospital drug administration
- Patient monitoring
- Braking systems on some cars
- Weather forecasting
- Stock Exchanges

*Have you included Business Continuity planning as a mandatory phase of your organization's Systems Development Life Cycle ? If not, then you should.*


## Conclusion

**Effective contingency planning requires the commitment of significant financial and human resources for situations that may never even occur. Nevertheless, prudent management recognizes that preparatory measures can make the difference between business survival and business failure.**

# A crisis management perspective of business continuity

## Robert Heath—UK/Australia

Dr Robert Heath is an internationally respected counselling, organizational and managerial psychologist. Australian born, he is Managing Director of Crisis Corp Ltd based in London.

In a survey undertaken by *The Corporate Response Group* of Fortune 1000 companies in 1997, some potential crisis situations were identified as being workplace violence (55%), kidnap (53%), terrorist action (51%), fraud (35%), product tampering/recall (34%), ethics (30%), CEO succession (28%), racism-sexism litigation (26%), and take-overs (20%). The survey respondents thought that areas in which their organization still needed to improve included internal awareness (50%), communications (45%), exercises and training (37%), vulnerability/risk analysis (35%), information technology (32%), planning (31%), and business continuity (24%). Given the specific and general natures of some of these findings, we need to clearly understand the current concepts involved in what is termed "business continuity management" and "crisis management".

Business Continuity Management (BCM) has a number of equivalent titles—the key ones being Business Recovery Management, Business Recovery Planning, and Business Continuity Planning. The names suggest the central concern: *planning to recover from a disruption to the normal function of an organization.* Consequently, conventional BCM processes involve **reacting** to the consequences of a given situation. This reaction can include a range of approaches from seamless recovery (developing ways in which processes, information systems and facilities may be recovered with imperceptible disruption) through to rebuilding (planning for detailed reconstruction activities that may take months or years to complete). Traditional BCM emerged from Information Technology concerns regarding failures in computer and information management systems. As a result, the focus of attention was firmly placed on:

- Reacting to failure or loss of system
- Physical and tangible events
- Returning any disruption or failure or loss to a normal function as soon as possible

*The Definitive Handbook of Business Continuity Management.* Edited by Andrew Hiles and Peter Barnes. © 1999 John Wiley & Sons Ltd.

This conventional approach involved undertaking risk and impact analysis, developing reactive recovery strategies, and training staff to implement these strategies when needed.

Traditionally, Crisis Management (CM) also involved reacting to a critical situation. In conventional crisis management, this reaction placed most attention on responding to the stimulus event (onset management) and dealing with the impacts on people and resources inflicted by that stimulus event (impact management). Many of these early approaches placed some emphasis on pre-crisis planning and post-crisis recovery management, with an even smaller emphasis on any form of reducing exposure to crisis situations. CM emerged from general situation management requirements—mainly drawn from military applications (battlefield and campaign management) and community disaster responses from paramilitary organizations (police, fire fighting, and paramedic). Consequently, traditional crisis management involved:

- Response (onset and impact) management of the crisis situation as the crisis unfolds
- Tangible and intangible situations
- Recovering an organization to pre-event levels of functioning

This conventional approach involved undertaking risk and impact analysis, developing reactive response and recovery strategies, and training staff to implement these strategies when needed.

This evolution of BCM and CM shows two clear differences. These were:

1. Where BCM primarily waited until the situation consequences were known, CM was involved in dealing with the situation as it emerged (response management).
2. Where BCM had a specific focus on planning for, and managing, recovery from tangible and physical disruption, CM had a broader design that included response *and* recovery management.

As these points indicate, BCM fits under the umbrella of CM activities as the important component called Recovery Management.

Links between BCM and CM are more complex than this look at their traditional and conventional forms suggests. Both approaches now involve more detailed attention to searching for sources of risk, threat and hazard (and the consequent impacts on an organization) and greater emphasis on risk management and organizational resilience. Both approaches accept the need for greater pre-disruption management and preparation or readiness. Many BCM practitioners have realized that the conventional BCM approach does not cover less physical situations such as action by pressure groups, assaults on an organization's image and reputation, or the effects of "white collar" crime.

CM practitioners now place greater emphasis on the areas of crisis reduction, improving preparedness, and on recovery management. In this sense, BCM still fits under the broad umbrella of CM activities. Moreover, CM more easily addresses the different skill demands made by the less tangible situations to which organizations and their management may be exposed. Contemporary CM is likely to adopt an even-handed approach to pre-crisis, crisis, and post-crisis management in what can be seen as a RRRR (or Four R) action approach:

- Reduction
- Readiness
- Response
- Recovery

As a result, CM seeks to eliminate, modify, or reduce exposure to crisis situations as much as developing response management and recovery management plans.

Within most CM approaches, however, is an understanding that three transition points exist in the CM domain. At each of these three points, the personnel (and even overall management) may transfer from one set of people to another. The three transition points are:

1. From pre-crisis to crisis management.
2. From crisis onset to crisis impact management.
3. From crisis impact management to recovery management.

In pre-crisis management, CM activities are focused on prevention and preparedness activities. Consequently, many people involved are engineers and other specialists, planners, project managers, and trainers. While many respondents may assist in planning and participate in training, the activities involved differ from those activities required to deal with an actual crisis.

Within crisis response management there may exist two different clusters of management activities. The first cluster of activities involves confronting the emerging crisis situation in an effort to resolve the crisis before any significant damage arises. The second cluster involves dealing with the impacts of the crisis on the organization and people, so that the damage sustained is minimized.

The third transition point involves transferring emphasis from dealing with the crisis and crisis impacts to recovering from those impacts. In most cases, this transition involves very different skills, personnel, and management.

Two examples can illustrate these transitions. First, take a passenger aircraft. Those undertaking pre-flight safety inspections of the aircraft and training of aircrew in dealing with in-flight situations are unlikely to be involved in managing such a situation. When a crisis situation arises, the flight and cabin crews (along with air traffic controllers in some circumstances) try to regain control over the aircraft in order to avoid significant damage (a crash). When an aircraft does crash, these onset response personnel are unlikely to be involved in dealing with the impacts of that situation, as fire fighters, police, paramedics, and associated response personnel manage the site. Once the fires are out, victims are dealt with, and the site is made safe, a different set of people take over. Air crash investigators and clean-up personnel examine and remove the debris, and reconstruction crews move in to restore the site.

Second, in most business settings those responsible for establishing response and recovery plans and for providing the training involved in being ready for crisis situations may not be those who have to undertake the response or recovery tasks. When a critical situation emerges, those trying to resolve or contain the situation before significant damage occurs are likely to be a different set of people to those handling the impact damage. In tangible situations, this may mean on-site organization personnel give way to off-site professional personnel from police, fire fighting, and paramedic organizations. In intangible situations on-site personnel may try to contain the crisis until more specialized trouble-shooters arrive and take over. In tangible situations, the impact-managing professionals are likely to depart once they believe the site is safe for others to enter. Here, those recovering the site, facilities, and personnel for the resident organization are likely to be different from those responding to the situation itself. In intangible situations, the specialized respondents are likely to hand over to other specialized recovery personnel who try to rebuild the intellectual and perceptual (or image) components that were damaged during the crisis.

Effectively, BCM still fits under the CM umbrella. This is especially true for most businesses moving from a BCM approach into a broader contingency management or CM strategy. Given that recovery management usually involves different skills and personnel, BCM activities can be linked into the broader CM design while retaining some independence. Such linked independence can contribute four advantages. These advantages are:

1. **Greater ease in dealing with tangible and intangible situations**. Intangible situations can be handled by CM-sourced teams, allowing BCM teams to remain focused on their more tangible concerns.
2. **The response management component of the CM approach is able to handle non-recovery activities and is able to alert the BCM team on the need to stand-by**. Moreover, the CM team can provide information to the BCM team on what is happening and thus on what may need to be recovered.
3. **The use of CM and BCM approaches means that both operations can activate at the same time**. While the Crisis Response personnel are dealing with the emerging situation and the impacts arising from that situation, BCM personnel can alert service providers to possible need, call in specialized personnel (from insurance loss adjusters to engineers), and even transfer the operations of the organization to a pre-selected recovery site. This saves wasted time and loss of business function.
4. **The CM structure can coordinate and support the various pre-crisis, response, and BCM teams so that transitions between these activities are smooth and resources are efficiently managed**. By providing "host" support when BCM is needed, the CM management can remove obstructions

and delays that may arise when BCM activities interact with non-BCM activities within an organization.

As a consequence, BCM and CM efforts can be complementary.

Most BCM activities are triggered by some crisis situation. As CM activities involve dealing with the crisis before recovery management becomes involved, a clearer picture of what constitutes a crisis and what is involved in CM helps delineate the similarities, differences, and links between BCM and CM.

## So what is a crisis?

Crisis situations appear to happen *suddenly*. Four key elements indicate the presence of a crisis situation. These four elements are:

- Missing or uncertain (unreliable) information
- Little time in which to act (or respond)
- A threat to people or resources valuable to people
- The resources required to resolve the situation exceed the available resources

These four factors illustrate the difference between problem situations, critical problem situations, and crisis situations. A problem may have missing or uncertain information, and may have a specified period of time in which the problem has to be solved. A critical problem has missing or uncertain information, appears to have very limited time in which to solve the problem, and poses a threat to people or to resources valuable to people. A critical problem can appear to be a crisis to those involved in managing the situation. A real crisis situation, however, has a fourth factor added—the situation seems likely to overwhelm those involved. Put specifically, a crisis is a critical problem that has a demand for resources that exceeds the resources available.

This sense of information uncertainty, very limited time, threat, and of being seemingly overwhelmed can be seen in most definitions of what constitutes a crisis situation and thus what is involved in crisis management. Note that most definitions use different terminology to describe the same aspects—emergencies, disasters or crises.

- Foster (1980, p. 217) finds that *"emergencies are characterised by four distinguishing features, an urgent need for rapid decisions, accompanied by acute shortages of the necessary trained personnel, materials, and time to carry them out effectively"*. As a working definition of a crisis, the ideas of "an urgent need for decisions", "acute shortages of personnel", "acute shortages of material", and "acute shortages of time" point to fundamental aspects of a crisis situation.

- Rosenthal and Pijnenburg (1991, p.3) outline a broader concept of crisis wherein *"the concept of crisis relates to situations featuring severe threat, uncertainty, and sense of urgency"*. Crises can be threatening situations that stress urgency in response and which are uncertain in the nature and impact of the crisis.
- Barton (1993, p.2) finds a crisis to be *"a major, unpredictable event that has potentially negative results. The event and its aftermath may significantly damage an organisation and its employees, products, services, financial condition, and reputation."* In this statement, Barton points out that there can be tangible and intangible effects from the impacts of a crisis situation.

A crisis can cause other crisis situations (or critical problems) to emerge. This knock-on effect of a crisis situation is termed a **ripple effect** because these crises seem to fan outward like ripples after a stone is thrown into a pool of water. Mitroff and Pearson (1993) note this ripple effect as a chain reaction that may be caused by poor management of the original crisis situation.

Crisis situations can cause ripple effects in organizations and communities. A physical accident drains money from an organization, puts people out of work, and may cause further damage to the surrounding community system through loss of resources or pollution. In Seveso (Italy, 1971), the accidental release of dangerous chemicals from a factory led to long-term pollution of surrounding farming land and communities. This necessitated the relocation of those living in the area. Similarly, the meltdown of the nuclear reactor at the Chernobyl nuclear power station (USSR/Ukraine, 1986) made large areas of land uninhabitable through radioactive fall-out.

Some ripple effects may cause crisis situations larger than the initiating crisis. Once wild fires ignited among communities in Oakland (California, 1982) or country Victoria (Australia, 1989), crisis impact management sought to prevent greater loss of resources and life until the fires were brought under control. Once the fires were out, a crisis ripple effect emerged—families disintegrated and communities found recovery difficult. In Oakland, half the residents and businesses did not return to the community, which caused a critical impact on the ability of Oakland to repair and recover its infrastructure through its local taxes. In major community crisis situations such as fire, flood, catastrophic windstorms (tornadoes and hurricanes) and earthquakes, just over one-in-four small businesses (around 29%) will exist within two years (Stuart, 1993).

## So what is involved in CM?

CM covers all aspects of what may precipitate a crisis situation through to recovery from that situation. This means assessing, reducing, and managing the risks, threats and hazards that can promote crisis situations, as well as planning and preparing to respond to—and recover from—crisis situations.

Effective CM means seeking to:

- Mitigate or reduce the sources, size, and impacts of a crisis situation
- Improve crisis onset management
- Improve crisis impact management when responding to a crisis
- Enhance the recovery from a crisis situation through effective and rapid recovery management action

As a result, effective CM means acquiring skills and task management capabilities across a number of dimensions—from dealing with processes and structures to managing (and communicating with) people.

In many ways, communication is a central and essential set of tasks for crisis managers. Without reliable information exchange within the CM (and particularly within the Crisis Response Management processes) and effective image management with stakeholders, media representatives, and the outside public, CM activities are likely to fail and be seen to fail. Communication tasks include:

- Developing secured communications within the crisis situation
- Acquiring good communication skills—from developing and using patterned communication protocols to dealing with emotionally upset outsiders
- Media management
- Debriefing skills for gaining information from witnesses and respondents
- Image management

Such tasks are covered in some form in books on crisis management. *Crisis Management for Managers and Executives* (Robert Heath, 1998, Pitman) has three chapters entirely focused on these areas, along with other chapters presenting information on effective communication of risks and warnings. *Crisis in Organisations: Managing and Communicating in the Heat of Chaos* (Lawrence Barton, 1993, South-Western) presents a chapter on crisis communications along with a number related issues throughout the book. *Crisis Management: What to do when the unthinkable happens* (Michael Regester, 1989, Business Books) also considers crisis communications, referring to the author's experience in dealing with some petrochemical crisis situations in the United Kingdom.

Crisis management involves five core activity clusters:

1. Crisis managers work to **prevent crisis situations from arising and to minimize crisis impacts**.
2. Before crisis situations arise, crisis managers **plan response and recovery activities and rehearse organizational members in doing those activities** so that organizations and communities are prepared in some way to deal with future crisis situations and crisis impacts.
3. When a crisis situation arises, crisis managers **deal with the crisis onset** in the available time.

4. When the crisis threat or threats begin to affect the situation, crisis managers **deal with any crisis impacts**. This may mean using different resources, personnel, and management approaches from those used in dealing with the crisis onset period.
5. After a crisis, crisis managers can be involved in managing **recovery and restoration** programmes. This may mean using different resources, personnel, and management approaches from those used in dealing with the crisis onset and crisis impact periods.

Again note that the recovery core cluster may equally be managed by any existing BCM arrangement. The key point is to link such efforts into the surrounding CM structure so that both BCM and CM operate effectively and efficiently.

## Managing in crisis settings

Managing crisis situations generates feelings of pressure. These feelings of pressure can be eased by using stimulus-response "breakers" (called "stoppers" in psychology). One technique is the PBR (Pause–Breathe–Relax) method (Heath, 1994). Managers need to find ways in which they can systematically get more time and more information and to efficiently use resources. One way is *CrisisThink* (Heath, 1995) which involves mentally recycling three key questions while operating in a crisis situation:

- *How can I (or we) gain more time?*
- *How can I (or we) gain more information?*
- *How can I (or we) reduce the loss or cost of resources?*

These questions help managers focus on the means to reduce the feelings of pressure and resolve the crisis situation. The focus on preserving or reducing the costs and losses in resources also helps in presenting a positive image.

## Developing the CM team

Most people involved in crisis management have some ideas on building a Crisis Management Team. Key features usually include:

(i) a desire that the crisis manager is as senior as possible,
(ii) a need for the crisis manager to be able to manage the crisis,
(iii) the need for the Team to have fixed membership so that the Team's roles are known by all,

(iv)   the need for the Team to be flexible or adaptable because of the different requirements of different crisis situations,

(v)    a need to centralize command and control structures, and,

(vi)   a need to coordinate and delegate responsibility to different groups who often have specialized knowledge and skills.

Unhappily, these features are often in conflict with each other. Seniority, for example, does not necessarily mean ability to manage crises. Likewise, flexibility and adaptability may be lost if the Team membership is fixed (or the "wheel has to be reinvented" if Team members have to be assigned roles each time a crisis situation arises). Many managers with command and control backgrounds— military, law enforcement, fire fighting, paramedic—can be weak coordinators and tend to command and control the response. In most community and business organizations, management by command and control alone is likely to fail. Too many independent and loosely structured groups are involved.

CM often demands quick and decisive action. Such action rarely occurs when consensus and cooperative management are used. This is a core problem as fast decision-making usually needs single decision-makers working in centralized structures. This suggests that a senior manager using a command and control structure provides the best crisis management.

Most crisis situations, however, cannot be managed by a single person. Many crisis situations need responses from different groups of specialists who are likely to resent command and control from someone outside their group. These groups are often more motivated when they provide input into the decisions that involve their actions. This suggests that a crisis manager using decentralized and consultative decision-making and coordination will promote a more motivated effort and thus provide the best crisis management.

In reality, crisis management needs highly motivated respondents operating in a decision structure that uses both authoritarian and participative processes. Crisis managers have to find a balance between speed of decision and involvement in the decision by all involved. We can achieve this by using participative management in the reduction and readiness stages of the RRRR CM Model—the pre-crisis components of crisis management. By involving response personnel in planning and training for crisis management, the response and recovery activities become coordinated clusters of pre-selected and agreed tasks that accept the direction and support of command and control teams.

# Crisis management and humans

Early crisis situations were either caused by people or by natural disasters within the surrounding environment. Solutions to these crises were very simple until the last two centuries. People *fought* other people or *ran away* and either *fought* wild animals or *ran away*. Natural hazards such as quicksand and falling rock were **avoided**. Fighting or fleeing were two basic human responses to sudden events that we still display. These responses are called the **fight or flight response.** These responses can reduce the effectiveness of CM and BCM activities, and may incapacitate victims, bystanders, and respondents within a crisis situation should such actions lead to inappropriate behaviours.

Natural weather and geological disruptions (such as volcanic eruptions and earthquakes) were seen as beyond human control and understanding, and thus were caused by some "godlike" beings. Volcanic activity, earthquakes, floods, droughts, and huge storms were seen as caused by some specific god who became displeased with the humans in her or his domain. Crisis management actions were thus quite simple—placate the specific god with some form of ritual offering (worship, gift giving, and sacrifice of living animals or humans).

Many of us still react superstitiously to crisis situations. We feel guilty at having survived or express beliefs about our sins catching up with us because of some negative impact. Feelings of discomfort and guilt lead us to find ways to settle our disquiet. Most crisis situations feel threatening, and often leave us feeling powerless. The feelings of being powerless can often lead us to try to identify guilty people so that we can blame them for exposing us to the feelings of threat, guilt, and being endangered.

People are core to crisis management and business recovery. Without people (and their valued resources) there would be no crisis situations. Without staff, shareholders, suppliers, and customers, there would be no exchanges of labour and resources that generate business and wealth for organizations. We thus need to look after people who are involved with our organizations. We call those involved with an organization its **stakeholders** (as they each hold a "stake" in that organization). This term covers all of those people who have a direct or indirect investment in an organization and may include customers, creditors, staff, suppliers, product users, shareholders, owners, and government regulatory agencies. Each of these groupings needs careful management during response and recovery periods should we wish to accomplish a positive and effective crisis management.

Crisis management can thus be seen as having four faces or "sides". These sides are:

- Managing the processes involved in developing and preparing for crisis management
- Dealing with the crisis situation
- Looking after the stakeholders of an organization
- Managing the communication processes involved (particularly those with the outside world through enquiries from the general public, media interactions, and the protection of community or business images)

On looking at these sides, a similar structure is apparent for BCM—manage the BCM process, undertake actual BCM, look after the stakeholders, and manage appropriate communication and public relations programmes.

## BCM and CM management

Good CM and BCM work toward removing any sources of crisis situations and business disruption that can be eliminated, transformed, or avoided. The remaining sources are then managed in some way—regulation and careful containment actions; developing plans for responding to an emerging situation and dealing with the impacts of that situation (Crisis Response Management) and recovering from the damage caused by that situation (Business Continuity or Recovery Management). All of these elements can be efficiently managed under an organization-wide CM approach. These plans are then regularly re-hearsed and tested so that those involved in a response or recovery activity gain the necessary skills and understanding to be able to perform their task effectively and quickly. These common areas of interest link the broad area of managing crisis situations with the more specific skills and actions involved in recovering from crisis situations that is the central goal of Business Continuity Management.

## References

Barton, L. (1993). *Crisis in Organisations: Managing and Communicating in the Heat of Chaos.* Cincinnati, Ohio: South-Western.

Foster, H. D. (1980). *Disaster Planning: The Preservation of Life and Property.* New York: Springer-Verlag.

Heath, R. J. (1994). Integrating crisis management: Some principles and practices. *Abstracts from the First International Congress of Local Authorities Confronting Disasters and Emergencies.* Tel Aviv: IULA, pp. 45–53.

Heath, R. J. (1995). The Kobe earthquake: Some realities of strategic management of crises and disasters. *Disaster Prevention and Management,* 4(5), 11–24.

Mitroff, I. I. and Pearson, C. N. (1993). *Crisis Management.* San Francisco, CA: Jossey Bass.

Rosenthal, U. and Pijnenburg, B. (1991). Simulation-oriented scenarios. In U. Rosenthal and B. Pijnenburg (eds), *Crisis Management and Decision Making: Simulation Oriented Scenarios.* Dordrecht, Holland: Kluwer, pp. 1–6.

Stuart, H. (1993). The Newcastle Earthquake: Local Government Response. *The Macedon Digest,* **7**(4), 17–21.

# Multilateral Continuity Planning

**4**

## Dennis C. Hamilton—Canada

Dennis is CEO of Toronto-based Crisis Response Planning Corporation and is an internationally recognized expert in Crisis Management and Business Continuity Planning.

For many years now the most progressive of organizations have been addressing the need for Business Continuity Planning (BCP). For the most part they have done an adequate job of dealing with all the known issues and problems that could arise from a disaster situation affecting their technologies or their organization as a whole.

For many organizations their Business Continuity Plans were based on a worse case scenario, meaning the loss or inaccessibility of their primary location for an extended period of time. While this approach is fundamentally sound, it does not go far enough. When executive management and stakeholders directed the implementation of a disaster recovery capability for the business, they did not expect the planning process to stop midway through the exercise.

A few simple questions may bring some perspective to what is without question one of the most important, yet commonly disregarded issues in BCP:

- What happens if one of your *key* customers has a disaster? What is the impact on you? What must or should you do to support their recovery efforts? What can you do to ensure a minimal disruption to your organization?
- What happens if one of your major suppliers of product, raw materials or information has a disaster? What is the impact on you? What must or should you do to support their recovery efforts? What can you do to ensure a minimal disruption to your organization?
- What happens if one of your business partners, distributors or resellers has a disaster? What is the impact on you? What must or should you do to support their recovery efforts? What can you do to ensure minimal disruption to your organization?
- What is the impact on your customers, suppliers and business partners if you have a disaster? What would you want them to do to support your recovery efforts?

*The Definitive Handbook of Business Continuity Management.* Edited by Andrew Hiles and Peter Barnes. © 1999 John Wiley & Sons Ltd.

The answers to these questions are remarkably similar to those that were first used to justify most Business Continuity Planning, including;

- Customers cannot take delivery of your products
- Customers cannot pay invoices
- Contracts could be postponed or terminated
- Suppliers cannot deliver critical products and services
- Sales projections cannot be achieved because business partners, distributors or resellers cannot meet their commitments

These are just a few of the reasons why continuity planning must go beyond the corporate borders; why a full operational recovery capability will not exist until the recovery issues surrounding Key Customers, Primary Suppliers and Principal Partners have been addressed.

The need is growing . . .

The business community is not only internally dependent on technology, all external communication is being performed electronically as well. This growing level of ***technological interdependence*** further increases the bilateral and multilateral affect of technology failure. In today's business environment, the concept of "just-in-time" affects absolutely every one of us, not just the manufacturing sector, who are normally associated with "just-in-time" inventory management techniques. In fact, the first and currently the largest application of "just-in-time" principles is for the provision of **information**, a delay or absence of which could be devastating.

In the name of "productivity", "partnerships", "cost sharing" and "cooperation", business-to-business integration has grown and will continue to grow to meet these operationally and politically sponsored relationships. Interdependence amongst organizations has in many situations ensured that when one has a crisis, others who are not affected physically, will suffer to the same extent or more as the organization having the disaster.

We must not only view Crisis Management and Business Continuity Planning inwardly. We must be proactive and embrace **Multilateral Continuity Planning** as a mandatory component of Crisis Management. We must extend our planning endeavours to our partners, suppliers and customers.

Obviously, you start by understanding the impact on your organization if one of your key customers, primary suppliers or principal business partners has a disaster and conversely what the impact could be on them if you have a disaster. A high-level understanding of this impact will probably determine the extent that Multilateral Continuity Planning (MCP) is required. Most of the impact (tangible and intangible) will be relatively evident from discussions with senior and middle management throughout the organization.

Once you have determined that there is sufficient concern to further your investigations, consider a controlled and proven approach. Articulate your concerns and the issues facing your organization to your customers, suppliers and business partners. If they don't share your concerns or if they have not effectively addressed Business Continuity Planning internally, you (or they) may just be out of luck. In order to find solutions you must first have cooperation, understanding and a willingness to participate. If you have been able to achieve this somewhat daunting task, further identification of problem areas and impact is required. Discussions will result in multiple alternatives that all organizations must consider. As is often the case, the final solutions may be totally dependent on cost. In fact, they may be rejected based on cost or the perceived effort required on the part of the participants. If no action is taken, you can at least know that an attempt was made and that the company is fully aware of the consequence.

Contingencies, alternatives and interim solutions during a crisis will ultimately impact all areas within your organization as well as vital operations within your customers, suppliers and business partners. Consideration will need to be given to a large number of operating functions in order to ensure coherence within all affected organizations. These will include:

- extended payment terms
- direct assistance through MCP support teams
- interim or emergency policies, standards and guidelines
- interim line of credit support/receivables financing support
- collective bargaining unit emergency agreements
- alternative transaction processing methods
- alternative forms of communications to customers/end-users
- cooperative competitor programmes
- alternative sourcing of supplies/raw materials/finished goods
- alternative finished goods production/manufacturing
- standard inventory level adjustments
- alternative warehousing of materials and products
- shared cost on technology back-up/recovery solutions
- mutual personnel support programmes

# MCP approach

Multilateral Continuity Planning can be a time-consuming and costly process without a well-defined and orchestrated plan. The actual project steps and time required to complete the process will of course be dependent on the availability of internal resources, the scope of the project to be defined by the participants and the priority established within each organization.

The following steps are based on the CRPC methodology for Multilateral Continuity Planning (MCP).

1.  **Conduct Awareness Presentation(s)**. The first step is to ensure company management are aware of and appreciate the need for continuity planning with customers, suppliers and business partners. Through a presentation, the management team, representing all business units (functions) should gain a sufficient level of understanding as to the need, objectives, approach, benefits and deliverables of Multilateral Continuity Plans. The primary objective is to receive approval to proceed with this critical project.

2.  **Establish an internal MCP Project Coordination Team(s)**. An MCP Project Coordination Team will be required from the onset of the project. It is necessary to determine who will be the Project Director; whether or not there will be an external Project Facilitator and which business units will be represented on the Project Team. While this is only a part-time role, it is paramount that the representatives are relatively senior and very knowledgeable in terms of their business unit's operation.

    The Project Director should be your senior BCP practitioner, Crisis Manager, Technology Recovery Planner or a business manager having significant knowledge of all major operations within the company. If the Project Director does not represent the Information Technology division of the company, a senior IT person is to be appointed to the Project Coordination Team.

    It may be necessary to establish an MCP Project Coordination Team for each of the three major impact groups, Key Customers, Primary Suppliers and Principal Business Partners. This will be dependent upon the size of your organization and the probable number of external participants.

    In addition, the overall MCP Project Coordination Team will have a general responsibility to address issues not covered by the three major groups, including; interaction with regulatory bodies, environmental agencies and government departments.

3.  **Conduct an Internal MCP Think Tank**. Multilateral Continuity Planning is a relatively new discipline and as such may require explanation and promotion within the organization. An "MCP Think Tank" should be conducted and include senior representation from all major business functions having a direct interface with customers, suppliers and/or business partners. The "MCP Think Tank" would consider a number of the "what if" disaster scenarios previously discussed. Through interactive discussions, the participants would identify every major issue that must be addressed within Multilateral Continuity Planning. The process is based on an analysis of a disaster scenario; concluding with identification and agreement as to the bilateral and multilateral issues to be subsequently discussed with the respective external participants. This key step provides not only the identification of the organization's main issues and concerns, but establishes a framework on which to initiate similar discussions with suppliers, customers and business partners.

    This internal process is key to identifying all potential problems that could arise from any one of the disaster scenarios. Representation is required from all business functions in the discussion of each business area. Interrelationships between business functions will have a bearing on subsequent strategy development.

4. **Prepare an MCP Strategy Statement**. Based on the conclusions established through the internal MCP Think Tank, an MCP Strategy Statement should be prepared identifying each potential problem area (for all disaster scenarios); a strategy (or options) of how to address those problems caused by a disaster within the organization; and a strategy (or options) of how to address problems created as a result of a disaster at a customer, supplier or business partner location.

   As an example, if your organization has a crisis that prevents processing of customer orders electronically, your choice would be to process orders manually. However, the advanced systems of your customers may not provide for one-off manual order processing. Alternatives would be required. Additionally, your own internal systems may not be able to support a manual transaction.

   The MCP Strategy Statement, to be prepared by members of the MCP Project Team, should consist of summary documentation only and consist of as many workable options as can be determined. It is important to remember that the alternatives or options devised by your MCP Project Team may not be acceptable to your customers, suppliers or business partners, respectively.

5. **Obtain MCP Strategy Approval**. The MCP Strategy will be the basis for all external discussions in order to complete the subsequent Multilateral Continuity Plans. It is imperative that organizational management understand and support the strategies and alternatives that will be presented to your customers, suppliers and business partners. A formal review and approval is required of the MCP Strategy Statement prior to disclosure of proprietary information external to the organization.

6. **Prepare an MCP "Participant Discussion Paper"**. Although the MCP Strategy was developed to provide alternatives of business-to-business processes in the aftermath of a crisis, the MCP Strategy document itself would not necessarily be provided to all or any external organizations. As an example, it is reasonable that only those issues relating to Supplier interaction would be provided to your Suppliers. As well, there may be unique alternatives that will be made available to a specific Supplier, while other, more general solutions will be provided to the balance of the Suppliers identified. This process would also apply to customers and business partners.

   Therefore, it will be necessary to prepare a "Participant Discussion Paper" for distribution to the respective organizations. The discussion paper should provide an overview of the need for Multilateral Continuity Planning, your suggestions as to how the issues should be addressed and your recommendations for collaboration on finding workable solutions.

   The discussion paper would suggest conducting an MCP Think Tank, similar to the internal Think Tank previously used to identify the potential problem areas and resolutions (alternatives) available. These documents would be presented to individual organizations where a private MCP Think Tank is required or to a number of organizations where a collective MCP Think Tank is appropriate.

7. **Identify External Participants**. Careful consideration must be given to the selection of customers, suppliers and business partners that will be asked to participate in the Multilateral Continuity Planning process. Every business function within the organization is to be asked to identify external organizations that:

    (i)    would be detrimentally impacted should your organization experience a major crisis or disaster impacting its ability to carry-on normal operations (a worse case scenario should be applied) or,

    (ii)   would detrimentally impact your organization should they experience a major crisis or disaster impacting their ability to carry-on normal operations (a worse case scenario should be applied).

A clear and precise analysis should be provided for each organization or groups of organizations in terms of the impact considered. A standard list of quantifiable and intangible impacts should be created and applied to the analysis. Impacts will vary with each organization and should minimally include:

    (i)    loss of sales/marketshare,
    (ii)   inability to provide products or services,
    (iii)  significant effort required to alternative source supply,
    (iv)  detrimental impact to organization's image/reputation,
    (v)   loss of customers to competition.

8. **Conduct MCP Think Tanks for Key Customers, Primary Suppliers and Principal Business Partners**. Multilateral Continuity Planning may be a new discipline for many of your customers, suppliers and business partners. As such, it will be necessary to conduct an MCP Think Tank with each group or individual Think Tanks for specific organizations. The MCP Think Tanks conducted at this stage are similar in approach, scope and objectives to the internal MCP Think Tank conducted earlier.

The primary purpose of the MCP Think Tanks is to generate interest in dealing with the joint issues of Multilateral Continuity Planning. It is not likely that every organization asked to participate will attend; nor is it likely that every organization which attends will continue through the entire process. However, the majority of organizations will understand the issues and potential problems and support the need to address all joint concerns through formal Multilateral Continuity Planning.

9. **Determine Project Participants**. While each organization will determine whether or not they will cooperate in subsequent Multilateral Continuity Planning activities, it is in your best interest to ensure those organizations most important to your operations become active participants. Ensure that

you have pre-qualified those customers, suppliers and business partners who will provide the greatest value to you through their participation. Unique Multilateral Continuity Plans may be required with specific external organizations, depending on the impact that would result from a disaster on your or their operations.

10. **Establish MCP Project Teams**. Each of the participating customers, suppliers and business partners needs to determine who, from their respective organizations, will be their representative(s) on the MCP Project Teams to be established. Understandably, there needs to be a limit established as to how many representatives are assigned to the overall MCP Project Team.

    In those unique situations where Multilateral Continuity Planning will be conducted exclusively with specific organizations, the number of participants may be inconsequential. However, where the MCP Project Team is to be made up of many organizations (i.e. Suppliers), a limit of one representative from each supplier is not unreasonable.

    In theory, you should have no more than one MCP Project Team for each of Key Customers, Primary Suppliers and your Principal Business Partners. The exceptions would be where your organization found it advisable to create an MCP Project Team with a specific Customer, Supplier or Business Partner, or where the number of organizations participating warrant multiple teams.

11. **Conduct Interdependency Review**. Although your organization has a complete understanding as to the bilateral impact of a disaster, the other participants (your customers, suppliers and business partners) may not. It is necessary for each of them to obtain a clear understanding of the impact of a disaster from their perspective.

    Using your Internal Think Tank, Strategy Statement and Participant Discussion Paper as guidelines, provide a framework on which you suggest each participant conducts their own internal impact assessment from all of the disaster scenarios presented. Clearly, your suppliers would only be in receipt of your analysis for suppliers; customers for customers, and so on. You are not encouraging them to conduct a complete Multilateral Continuity Planning project, such as yours, but rather to participate in your process, learning from that experience and applying the new-found knowledge internally at a later date.

    Although their conclusions will differ from yours in terms of impact, there should be a correlation between what problem areas must be addressed by both of your organizations. This step is necessary if their management are expected to accept and adopt the recommendations made through the overall Multilateral Continuity Planning process.

12. **Conduct MCP Resolutions Workshops**. Resolution Workshops will provide the informal and interactive process required to effectively analyse and determine which alternatives will be acceptable to all participants. In many cases, it will only be a single organization or related group that decides, while in other cases the ramification could be in multiple organizations therefore requiring a collective decision.

Each potential problem area must be dealt with independently, alternative resolutions/options discussed and selection be made of the most effective and acceptable solution to all participants.

It is likely that separate workshops will be conducted with customers, suppliers and business partners. Rarely will they have the same issues as the other groups. Further, it may be necessary to conduct private workshops with specific organizations due to the unique relationships that exist.

The Project Manager or Project Facilitator has the primary role of ensuring that the appropriate amount of time is applied to each issue; that a common solution is adopted where possible and that the workshop concludes with all problem areas resolved.

13. **Prepare Multilateral Continuity Planning Implementation Plan**. All resolutions agreed to in the MCP Resolutions Workshops are to be scheduled for implementation concurrently at each of the affected organizations. In some cases it may be necessary to establish joint implementation teams to ensure a timely and accurate completion of the tasks.

14. **Conduct Presentation to Management for Review and Approval**. Each participating organization will be required to approve the implementation of the recommendations being made by the MCP Project Team(s). A summary presentation should be provided to ensure senior organizational management have a sound understanding as to the importance and implications of this cooperative effort. Management must recognize that there must be an ongoing commitment to support these endeavours through general maintenance of the strategies developed and for testing appropriate resolutions.

15. **Implement, Install and/or Document Multilateral Continuity Plans**. Implementation of the Multilateral Continuity Planning resolutions may very well be the easiest step in the overall process. It is not likely that the accepted resolutions will be complex, costly or disruptive to day-to-day operations. However, it is most important that all participants adopt a common implementation schedule; conduct regular reviews through the implementation step and keep their own management informed as to the project's status.

Complete and thorough documentation must be prepared for all implemented resolutions. The documentation amongst all participants should be common in structure and content. This will provide for an easier change transition within each organization and subsequent MCP reviews.

16. **Perform Test and/or Verification on all Strategies Implemented**. Although most of the implemented resolutions will be on a contingency basis only, testing and verification of applicability is mandatory if any reassurance is required in terms of their workability.

All procedural strategies should be reviewed at least on an annual basis and preferably twice a year. Technological resolutions should be tested twice yearly or on the same frequency as the organization's technology recovery plan tests.

As with all contingency and recovery plans, testing is critical to ensure the plans reflect the organization's current requirements. Multilateral Continuity Plans are even more vulnerable to change due to the multiple sources of change.

Although the tasks presented above are shown and numbered consecutively, it is reasonable to conduct several activities concurrently, particularly once the external organizations are on-side with the MCP process. The actual tasks performed will be dependent on the size of the organization, number of Key Customers, Primary Suppliers and Principal Business Partners.

## Project success factors

Multilateral Continuity Planning can be extremely rewarding to the organization or it can be a frustrating, counter-productive process. The level of success achieved will be dependent on a number of major "success factors".

These are:

1. While the solutions to Multilateral Continuity Planning will be implemented by various Business Units within the organization, it is necessary to maintain participation on the part of Executive Management. The fact that multiple independent organizations will be jointly developing continuity and contingency plans in case of a crisis or disaster, dictates the understanding and approval of the organization's senior Executive Officer. It may be necessary to obtain Board of Director and/or shareholder approval under the organization's by-laws. It can be a political decision based on the relationship between the organizations for other, non-public reasons. The most compelling reason to maintain executive participation is the value that can be derived by having the support and participation (reviews and approval of plans) at the highest level.

2. The scope of Multilateral Continuity Planning can easily be drawn into a number of operational issues, and yes, it will take forever to find solutions that meet the approval of a number of parties. A degree of focus is initially required. It is likely that the technology-based interfaces between any two organizations represent the most critical of interface activity. This is the most appropriate place to begin. Not only is it likely to be the most important, it is probably the most defined and manageable. Once Multilateral Continuity Planning has been established in and around the technologies being employed, other interface processes can be evaluated in a like fashion.

3. We all know how difficult it can sometimes be to get the productive participation of a number of people in the same organization. The complexity is

ten-fold when attempting to conduct Multilateral Continuity Planning. Not only are you dealing with different corporate cultures, you are working with a wide-ranging group of personalities who are all unknown. The primary success factor here is basically to maintain a mindset of cooperation and compromise. While somewhat obvious and simply stated, its lack is nonetheless the main reason why the process will fail.

4.  Depending on the number of Key Customers, Primary Suppliers and Principal Business Partners it may be advisable to prepare Multilateral Continuity Plans with a single organization from each external group. The option is to develop the one plan from each group as a working model that can be applied to all other participants within the same group. This approach is strictly dependent on the number of participants within the respective groups.

5.  The end result of Multilateral Continuity Planning will be a series of agreements on procedures, cooperative activities, contingency steps, bilateral support and emergency policy interpretations to be applied at time of crisis to all parties to the agreements. All participants are stand-alone entities and, other than through Multilateral Continuity Planning, have little or nothing to do with each other on a day-to-day basis. As such, each participant will continue to go through change within their organization and will be under no obligation to inform signatories to Multilateral Continuity Planning agreements. Changes in personnel, organization structures, physical locations and internal systems and procedures can all impact on the Multilateral Continuity Planning that has been established. Therefore, it is necessary that Multilateral Continuity Planning be completed and documented at a high level only. The probability of maintaining the agreements decreases proportionally with the level of detail within the agreements themselves.

6.  While general cooperation will superficially be maintained by all participants, the overall priority of the Multilateral Continuity Planning project will fluctuate on a daily basis. Maintaining a common priority within all organizations on a consistence basis is impossible at best. The operative word in Multilateral Continuity Planning is *patience.*

7.  In order to achieve the many benefits that will result from Multilateral Continuity Planning, it will be necessary to test and review the resulting plans on a scheduled, but periodic basis. Not dissimilar to Business Continuity Plans and Technology Recovery Plans within your own organization, Multilateral Continuity Plans must be tested to ensure they perform as and when expected. The obvious difference will be the degree of testing necessary to the level of planning performed, or even possible given the organizational autonomy of the participants. Testing of technology-based processes is unquestionably possible and necessary on at least an annual basis. Twice per year testing should be acceptable to most organizations. Procedural-based continuity plans should be reviewed once or preferably twice per year. Any new personnel should participate to ensure they are aware of the content and expectations of the Multilateral Continuity Plans.

8. In order to maintain an objective and unbiased acceptance of the project plan, project activities and the conclusions/plans to be implemented, it may be prudent to recruit a *project facilitator.* This person would ensure all participants are treated equally and that the conclusions drawn do not necessarily favour one over another. The Project Facilitator would also function as the overall project manager, providing a higher likelihood that project assignments are completed as planned and that status reports are prepared and distributed on a regular basis. Fees of the Project Facilitator would be shared amongst all participants, making the costs relatively minor to each organization.

9. Keeping expectations in perspective can be difficult in dealing with such diverse and sometimes, what seem to be, opposite requirements. It is very important for every participating organization to remember that each and every one of you is also a Customer of someone, a Supplier to someone and probably a Partner of sorts to someone else as well!

As with any multilateral project, there will be those who are interested and even excited about the prospect of Multilateral Continuity Planning and those who just can't place its importance as a priority to solving today's problem. Multilateral Continuity Plans will not be developed with everyone on your wish list. Start with those most enthused, the probability of success increasing proportionately to their level of concern and commitment.

# Benefits of Multilateral Continuity Planning

Multilateral Continuity Planning may very well make the difference between recovery and bankruptcy as a result of a disaster. Regardless of your internal state of preparedness, much of your recovery success will be based on the actions initiated at the time of crisis with your key customers, primary suppliers and principal business partners.

Multilateral Continuity Planning has a number of benefits that have a far reaching impact not only in your organization, but equally with all participants. The benefits of Multilateral Continuity Planning are many, including:

- An advanced level of preparedness with critical external stakeholders will significantly increase the probability of a fully successful recovery effort
- Integration of emergency response and recovery efforts with key customers will promote an interdependent relationship; thereby protecting those customers from competitor advances
- Multilateral Continuity Planning will enhance the functioning relationship with the organization's key suppliers, creating stronger assurances of continuous supply of information, material product and services

- The promotion and provision of Multilateral Continuity Planning services to prospective customers will provide a measurable competitive advantage
- Cooperative planning with business partners, distributors or resellers will establish a stronger foundation on which to enhance business relationships
- Extended influence and support external to the organization will provide an immeasurable level of goodwill value, significantly bettering the organization's image and reputation
- Interaction with customers, suppliers and business partners by many management and staff will provide a much improved understanding of their operations, priorities and the issues that are most important to them. This provides an opportunity to enhance the operational interface between organizations

You may also find that you or your customers and suppliers may find marketing opportunities or a competitive advantage through your Multilateral Contingency Planning efforts. Your success will be dependent on a number of factors, not the least of which will be intra-company politics and everyone's willingness to cooperate.

## Conclusion

Multilateral Continuity Planning is not an exact science nor can the CRPC Methodology presented here apply to every organization. Individual organizational needs, and the needs of their customers, suppliers and business partners vary depending on a number of factors, including: their industry, business type, business size and the level of technology employed throughout their organization. However, the approach presented does provide a proven road-map of how to address what can be a complex and difficult problem to address. Apply the CRPC Methodology as you would utilize any procedural approach, learn from it and customize it to fit your needs and method of operation.

The primary consideration in what has been presented is recognizing the critical importance of your continuity planning to a variety of external organizations. Virtually every organization has suppliers and customers of some type. Many of them will have business partners, resellers, distributors, representatives, agents, brokers, regulatory agencies or other types of organizations requiring regular communications and the exchange of information or the physical transfer of assets.

It is necessary to understand the impact your organization has on another and how they may impact on you in a disaster situation. Until Multilateral Continuity Planning is addressed as a component of your overall Business Continuity Planning process, full restoration is not attainable; at least not without severe consequences to your own organization and to the detriment of those you rely on.

# Marketing Protection: a justification for funding of Total Asset Protection programmes?

**5**

## Andrew Hiles—UK

Andrew is Chairman of Survive! The Business Continuity Group and is also a Director of the Kingswell Partnership.

Two new concepts could ensure the survival of your organization. The first is Total Asset Protection. What is Total Asset Protection and why should we fund it? Protecting the enterprise has previously been a piecemeal activity. Disaster Recovery Planning ensures the recovery of IT systems and telecommunications capability. Business Continuity Planning is designed to ensure the continued viability and operation of an organization in the event of a disaster resulting in the major loss of product or denial of access to mission-critical facilities. Crisis Management Planning goes one stage further, and covers contingencies such as product recall, kidnap and hostage or branch hold-up—it includes issues such as adverse publicity. Other related issues include Health and Safety, Environmental Protection, Security and Insurance. Often there is no coherent escalation process from customer complaint or operational incident or quality defect through to invocation of disaster recovery, business continuity or crisis management procedures and to the declaration of an emergency or a disaster. We are just beginning to see the emergence of convergence of these piecemeal elements into a coherent whole under a single umbrella, which we call Total Asset Protection. Without a Total Asset Protection Plan, the organization is in peril. There is an 80% mortality rate for organizations that are without contingency plans and which experience a disaster.

An Information Technology Disaster Recovery Plan alone is not a substitute for Total Asset Protection, since the computers, although fully functional, will be useless if the production system they control has just disappeared in flames. A Total Asset Protection Plan will therefore cover all key facilities, such as office buildings, computers, communications, production capability and warehouses.

But, according to a joint DTI/APR report, the proportion of companies' intangible assets (essentially goodwill) to tangible assets has grown over the last 15 years to represent, on average, 70% of their balance sheets during mergers and

*The Definitive Handbook of Business Continuity Management.* Edited by Andrew Hiles and Peter Barnes. © 1999 John Wiley & Sons Ltd.

acquisitions.[1] A Total Asset Protection Plan therefore needs to cover all other situations from which an organization can lose its goodwill, image and reputation.

Around 43% of companies suffering a disaster never reopen and a further 30% go to the wall later as a result.[2] Businesses can be destroyed by the loss of a critical resource for more than 10 days.[3] Nearly three-quarters of businesses hit by serious fire end up closing.[4]

An example of a business disaster will illustrate the point. Ronson, the lighters and pens group, has international brand recognition. A fire destroyed their Newcastle warehouse. Their insurance claim was £10m. In May 1997, only 60% was being settled. The company faced additional costs from reorganization following the blaze. The result of the fire meant an overall pre-tax loss for the year of £1m, a dramatic fall in Ronson's share price and severe long-term costs in re-establishing its business.[5]

The second concept, Marketing Protection, delivers the justification for Total Asset Protection. To justify the extent of funding for any of the elements of Total Asset Protection (TAP) for any organization, Business Impact Analysis is undertaken to identify the impact on an enterprise, in cash and non-cash terms, of a disaster. Typically it examines loss of market share, loss of product, cost of restoration (including extra cost of working), cost of fines or other penalties. In addition it will weight "non-cash" losses such as loss of image, regulatory non-compliance or political impact. Using this standard approach, it is frequently difficult to justify spend on consultancy, services and products for business continuity, crisis management or other activities within the Total Asset Protection Programme. This is because:

- Some of these costs may be covered by insurance (although in practice insurance usually only covers some 40–60% of the real loss following a disaster)[6]
- The cost of the project usually has to be covered from the budget of an administrative department which has been pared to the bone by downsizing and which is seen as a target for further cost reduction

The traditional Business Impact Analysis tends to look at short-term costs and too frequently fails to quantify longer term costs (e.g. lifetime value of customers; cost to regain market share and image). The concept of Marketing Protection takes the argument into a different dimension. It looks at the whole value of the business at stake from a marketing perspective and looks to the techniques of the worlds of advertising and brand management to demonstrate loss potential and justification for spend on BCP.

Seven out of the top ten brands in the UK in the 1930s remain in the top ten brands in 1998.[7] Brands and companies have outlived nations. Smirnoff, the Grand Metropolitan vodka brand, has survived the reigns of the tsars, Marx, Lenin, Stalin, Gorbachov, and Yeltsin. The USA beer Budweiser is some 130 years old. The brand has value outside of any single product: Persil, originally a soap powder, was relaunched as a detergent, followed by an automatic version, followed by a low-temperature product, followed by Persil liquid and by washing-up liquid.

Keith Holloway of Grand Metropolitan[8] says "we know from recent experience, particularly the Nestlé episode, that the richest companies are prepared to buy other companies for brands that they own for a multiple of 20 or 30 times their annual earnings (perhaps 40 to 50 times their annual marketing costs)." The episode Holloway refers to was Nestlé's purchase of Rowntree in 1988 for £2.55bn. Tangibles on the balance sheet were worth only £409m. Even if you added up 10 times Rowntrees' profits the total only comes to about half what Nestlé paid. Since Nestlé was capable of manufacturing anything that Rowntrees could, it meant that they paid £1.25bn for the brands and the strategic value that went with them.[9]

Since 1988, there has been continued debate about brand valuation and whether or not brand valuations should appear on companies' balance sheets. Reckitt and Coleman, and Grand Metropolitan have both put acquired brands as assets on the balance sheet since 1988. Rank Hovis McDougal declared, in the same year, that the development of Mr Kipling, Hovis and Mother's Pride was worth £678million.[10]

It is no coincidence that, as soon as Grand Metropolitan proposed the merger with Guinness on 22 May 1997—a merger which would put the new £24bn operation sixth among the world's food and drink companies, just behind Nestlé and Unilever—they announced the proposed new name: GMG Brands (subsequently changed to Diageo). Grand Met's price immediately rose 76.5p to 591.5p and Guinness's climbed 86 to 602.5p—the first time they had been above 600p since 1992.[11] GMG was expected to capitalize its brands, which included Johnnie Walker and Gordon's Gin: the brands' stated value could rise from £5.7bn to £12bn.[12]

So brands and the goodwill associated with a company name have a real value—capable of being destroyed by a disaster and resulting adverse publicity. That value is created by many years of advertising and good experience by the consumers of the product or service. Another way of approaching the value of a brand is to assess the amount that has been invested in creating it—the advertising and public relations spend over many years.

There are formulae for spend on advertising, market share or sales volume and product profitability and highly sophisticated ways of analysing the effect of advertising after a campaign has finished.[13] Fundamentally, the more that is spent on effective advertising, the more volume that is shipped and (assuming product pricing is correct) the more profit that makes. The more profit that is made and the bigger the turnover, the more the company is worth and the higher the share price. It follows, therefore, that any disaster which adversely affects the attractiveness of the brand or of the goodwill associated with a company's name, regardless of its impact on production capability, will impact turnover, will impact profit and will impact the value of the company and hence its share price.

Weight tests have been introduced to test the impact of advertising. These are usually evaluated by comparing the cost of more or less advertising with the estimated change in sales volume times the marginal revenue per case. There is new evidence that successful weight tests can show more sales in the years after the test finished than during the test—that is advertising impact has its own momentum after advertising spend has stopped.[14] In one case, sales volume was up against its neighbours 28% in the second year after the campaign and 8% in the third year. In a summary of 44 BehaviorScan tests, it was found an average increase of 22% in year one was followed by year two sales 14% above average and year 3 sales 7% up.[15] And these effects may spin off on to other "sister" brands.

So, what sort of money is invested in creating brands? An examination of some of the best recent campaigns will illustrate the large sums of money involved.

- Orange, as a newcomer in "wire-free" telephony, invested £26.3m directly in advertising for its launch alone: it generated £300m of sales[16]
- Daewoo's launch in the UK cost £22m in advertising and generated £190m in revenue
- Between 1989 and 1995, £17m spent on advertising increased the sales of Felix cat food by £108m
- Reebok spent £2m on advertising in the UK alone in 1994–95 to generate a £2.2m–£2.8m incremental gross profit
- BT regularly spends over £6m a month on advertising. BT's "It's Good to Talk" campaign cost £44m between May 1994 and June 1995, with a payback of six times that. It spent £23m on TV alone in 1995 on Bob Hoskin's domestic consumer advertising. One campaign, "Working Smart Not Just Harder", achieved a 67% return on media spend
- The Automobile Association's "4th Emergency Service" campaign cost £16m— something over £5m a year for a benefit of up to £50m
- Nescafé Gold Blend advertising runs at £5m a year and delivers £50m a year sales
- De Beers global diamond advertising campaign was designed to maintain sales during recession. De Beers spends around 0.4% of the value of world diamond jewellery sales on marketing (4% of rough diamond sales). In 1995 alone, diamond jewellery sales world-wide increased by 5%
- Luxury goods advertisers spend 1–15% of revenue on marketing, while perfumiers spend up to 25%[17]
- Barclaycard's advertising campaign from 1991 to 1995 featuring Rowan Atkinson as a bungling secret agent cost £40m, stimulating 3% extra card usage and increasing its share of new card users from 15 to 25%
- Renault Clio's "Papa, Nicole" advertising campaign took Renault UK sales from an all-time low in 1991 to almost double in 1995 and has sustained the Clio's success at a higher level and for longer than could reasonably have been expected, as well as creating a "halo" effect on other Renault models
- Stella Artois invested £14.2m in advertising to deliver incremental net returns on that investment over a decade of £70m

The "halo" effect of the reputation of one brand can be passed on to another: Virgin, which started as a record company, opened music megastores; moved into airline, cola, insurance and pensions and banking. From March 1995 to October 1997, over £1bn has been invested in Virgin Direct's savings and pension products. Sainsbury's and Tesco stores have both moved to banking. One of the most important factors in this is that: "As popular trust in institutions declines and individuals feel they are faced with ever more choices and even less time to make them, consumers are seeking new partners to help them confront, share and manage the risks they face in their everyday life. In this situation, brands are ideally positioned to fill the vacuum."[18] Researchers discovered that, over the last three years, confidence in Sainsbury grew from "a great deal" or "quite a lot" score of 59% to 74%; in Marks & Spencers from 73% to 83%, in Tesco from 52% to 71% and in Boots from 78% to 83%. Other scores include Kellogs (83%) and Heinz (81%). Brands score higher than the police (62%), the judiciary (43%), a local council (24%) and, oddly, a multinational (13%).

The corollary of this is that, in the event of loss of image or reputation through a disaster, market share losses from "negative advertising" could be equally as dramatic and these sums of money would have to be spent *in addition* to the normal ongoing advertising which has to continue merely in order to *preserve* market share. These days, volume is often the key to viability: lose volume, and viability is lost. The loss of a brand could mean the extinction of a company. Moreover, the "halo" effect could work in reverse: like guilt by association. Using the argument of Marketing Protection, the justification for spend on BCP becomes immediately obvious and immensely strengthened. When the Mercedes A Class small car proved unstable in 1997, it cost some $900m and 2000 cancelled orders to recover the position.

Advertising agencies always consider the up-side of the advertising message, rarely the down-side. If the company fails to deliver against the expectations set by that advertising message, the message will work just as powerfully against the company. For instance, advertising for banks which stresses warmth, compassion and humanity is largely counter-productive because it does not match with customers' experiences and consequently they feel such advertising is an attempt at cynical manipulation: this merely reinforces their antipathy to the bank. "Let the train take the strain" backfired as thousands of passengers waited for an uncertain, unreliable, dirty and crowded train service. Arguably Kinnock lost the election against Major because the soft focus promotion was simply not credible. All these are inadvertent examples of advertising backfiring.

How much worse the situation could be in a disaster. Commercial Union's slogan "We don't make a drama out of a crisis" was replayed to brilliant effect when their offices were devastated in April 1992 by the IRA bomb at St Mary Axe in the City of London. Their Business Continuity Plans worked—but what if they had not? What if they had made a drama out of a crisis? A software company has the slogan "The Integration Company". What if, in a disaster, they failed to deliver—and the message became "The Dis-Integration Company"? What if the Automobile Association, "The 4th Emergency Service" could not cope with its own emergency?

An example of such an impact can be seen from the Perrier water benzene contamination incident in 1990. In 1989, Perrier was the market leader in bottled mineral water, its name synonymous with purity and quality. Perrier water was on the tables of virtually every high-class restaurant around the world; sales peaked at 1.2 billion bottles a year. The plant at Vergèzem, near Nîmes, was tooled up for 1.5 billion, with capital investment and personnel to match. After recalling 160 million contaminated bottles and mishandling the publicity, Nestlé took advantage of the drop in share price, fought off Giovanni Agnelli's Fiat-based group and in 1992 paid £1.6bn to buy Perrier, giving Nestlé 40% of the French mineral water market. In 1991, Perrier production plunged to 761 million bottles a year, heading downwards: the plant was uneconomic, making heavy losses. Perrier was effectively dead in the USA and in the UK; the French mineral water market, having grown by 10% a year up to 1990, stagnated for over three years.[19] A lifetime investment in promoting the images of purity and quality was effectively written off: all had to be started again from scratch.

Moreover, this sort of damage could be inflicted by a third party: Rolls-Royce has a name synonymous with engineering quality—an almost priceless reputation. However, this hundred-year image was threatened in May 1997 when Airbus A330–300s powered by Rolls-Royce Trent engines suffered from inadequate lubrication of gearboxes, allegedly through defective parts supplied by a French sub-contractor. It cost one airline alone, Cathay Pacific, between US$15.5m and $19.4m from withdrawn flights.[20]

When viewed against an advertising budget rather than against the budget of a single administrative department, the sums involved in Crisis Management Planning and BCP seem almost trivial. Product recall plans are readily justifiable to protect reputation and brands and are in place amongst all major companies. Why should any of the elements of Total Asset Protection be any different?

When considering advertising campaigns, how many agencies consider the downside of the advertising slogan? How can the slogan be turned against the company by a ruthless journalist? Should not that be part of a risk analysis of the campaign? Before the disaster and during each advertising campaign, should not some creative thought go into how that campaign would be developed to mitigate the results of a disaster?

The Marketing Protection approach brings a new dimension, a new urgency and a new justification for a coherent programme of Total Asset Protection. Every Finance Director, every Marketing Manager, every Advertising Agency should be aware of the twin concepts of Marketing Protection and of Total Asset Protection. Every Security Manager, Risk Manager, Disaster Recovery Planner, Business Continuity Planner and Crisis Manager should be aware of these concepts and apply them to their own (or their client's) organization.

# Notes

1. Tim Sutton, CEO of Charles Barker plc, in *Finance Director Europe* (March 1998), p. 34.
2. IBM and Cranfield Management College survey, *A Risk too Far,* 1993.
3. University of Minnesota and SRI International survey, reported in *Internal Auditing* (March 1993).
4. Tony Pilkington, NatWest Insurance Services, quoted in *Financial Mail* on Sunday, 24 September 1995.
5. *Daily Mail,* Thursday, 6 May 1997.
6. The Kingswell Partnership.
7. Tim Sutton, CEO of Charles Barker plc, in *Finance Director Europe* (March 1998), p. 34.
8. *A view on the financial valuation of brands*—2 in *The longer and broader effects of advertising,* IPA (March 1990).
9. *A view on the financial valuation of brands*—1 by Stephen King, WPP Group, in *The longer and broader effects of advertising,* IPA (March 1990).
10. *How advertising affects brands—an overview,* by Simon Broadbent and Leo Burnett in *The longer and broader effects of advertising,* IPA (March 1990).
11. Nils Pratley and Kate Rankine, *Daily Telegraph Business News,* 13 May 1997, p. 23.
12. *Daily Telegraph, City Checklist,* 19 May 1997, quoting *Sunday Business.*
13. Vide *Accountable Advertising,* by Simon Broadbent, published by IPA.
14. *Are our ways of evaluating advertising too restrictive?* by Simon Broadbent and Leo Burnett in *The longer and broader effects of advertising,* IPA (March 1990).
15. Ibid.
16. This and subsequent examples are taken from *Advertising Works* **9**, edited by Gary Duckworth, IPA.
17. *Economist,* January 1993.
18. Henley Centre, *Planning for Social Change,* May 1997.
19. *After the Perrier bubble burst,* by Anthony Peregrine, *Weekend Telegraph,* 23 January 1993.
20. *Financial Times,* 2 June 1997.

# Why have a disaster if you don't have to?

## Peter Humpidge—UK

Peter is a highly experienced management consultant who is highly respected within the UK business continuity management community.

On the whole, suffering a disaster to your business is not much fun. Particularly if you have not planned in detail how to respond to the particular disaster, which is seldom the one you expected, the result can be all the things which managers are advised to avoid—stress, tension, loss of sleep and even redundancy. Yet, when managers are asked to consider the threats to their business continuity, very few will seriously attempt to use their imagination and figure out what could halt their operation. The favourite chestnut is the Boeing 747 scenario, where a large aeroplane crashes into the facility, wiping out most of it and the staff working there. The fact that the building is miles away from any flight path only makes this scenario more popular—it is so unlikely that it can safely be ignored.

A common response to risk analysis is that the issues are often considered to be either too trivial to bother about on the one hand, or outside the responsibilities of the particular manager on the other. "*Let's get on and talk about recovering from the disaster*", is the response and not worry about taking common-sense precautions which could reduce the chance of a disaster in the first place. The main problem with identifying threats to one's own organization is simple familiarity. Threats seem to be rather like patterns on wallpaper—after a while, they are no longer noticed. There is also a failure of imagination, in the words of the Duke of Wellington, "*an inability to guess what was on the other side of the hill*". Particularly where threats are posed by a third party, this means putting one's self in the position of someone seeking to do mischief and seeing how it could be done, in order to guard against it occurring.

From a consultant's point of view, the most encouraging part of starting a new assignment with a client is the certainty that one will uncover a whole range of realistic threats to the business, which have not been recognized by the client's own personnel. To identify many of these threats does not require highly sophisticated techniques, months of carrying out a CRAMM methodology or access to actuarial tables. The strange thing is that the threats have often already occurred

*The Definitive Handbook of Business Continuity Management.* Edited by Andrew Hiles and Peter Barnes. © 1999 John Wiley & Sons Ltd.

before but adequate steps have not been taken to prevent them happening again. A few examples from recent projects will suffice:

1.  A computer room, situated immediately below a shower room, where the ceiling tiles were hanging down after a shower had overflowed and poured water into the room, narrowly missing the computer equipment. Management were reluctant to agree to the suggestion that either the showers or the computer room should be moved.
2.  Inadequate security of a fire exit, which made forced entry very easy, was identified. Inquiries found that computers had been stolen only a few weeks before by this route, yet no effort had been made to increase the security of the door.
3.  A high-security consumer electronic facility, where all entrances were controlled by swipe cards, but the Facilities Manager knew that almost twice as many cards had been issued as workers on the site. In spite of this, no action had been taken to reprogram the locks and issue fresh cards.
4.  An office block which had recently lost computers through a break-in, where bars were fitted to the actual window used but not to the rest of the ground floor windows because of the effect on the appearance of the building.
5.  A drugs company which shared its reception area with the Crown Prosecution Service and considered it necessary to install CCTV to monitor visitors but which did not bother to put film in the camera.
6.  A financial securities company which suffered failure of its telephone switch due to a spike through the electricity supply, preventing trading taking place. Eighteen months later it had taken no steps to guard against a repetition of the incident.
7.  A University Hospital Trust where the Computer Centre was in the basement of a building which announced in large letters that it housed a research laboratory. The building had been previously occupied by students protesting against the use of laboratory animals, giving the opportunity for unauthorized access to the computer centre. No action had been taken to remove the name from the top of the building.

This list could be much longer. The conclusion which can be drawn from it is that in today's business climate, management prefers to ignore threats to business continuity, even when the threat has been proved. Partly, this is due to the cumulative effect of downsizing over the last ten years. In the past, in many organizations, a post of Security Officer, or some similar title, would be given to a middle manager approaching retirement. He would take pride in ensuring that precautions were tightened up and that risks in general were guarded against. The slimmer, more efficient organization of today gives such a person early retirement and subcontracts security and facilities management. As a result, Senior Management is often isolated from the housekeeping issues which are at the heart of so many risks, in order to concentrate on business issues. The contradiction is that these same risks, if ignored, can have a serious effect on the continuation of the business itself.

## Facing a disaster

The list of threats to business continuity are well known and the frequency with which they occur is measured in many different surveys. Figure 6.1, from a survey by Survive! of 12 000 incidents shows the frequency by cause. What the figure is telling us is that disasters do occur as a result of a wide range of threats. Survive! estimate that 7.5% of organizations suffer a disaster each year. Clearly then, threats to business continuity should not be ignored by managers of organizations. In order to avoid disasters, precautions fall into two phases:

- Minimizing risk
- Planning to deal with irreducible risks

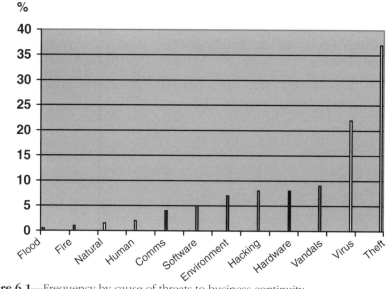

**Figure 6.1**—Frequency by cause of threats to business continuity

## Minimizing risk

### General issues

Figure 6.1 showing the frequency of disasters by risk can only give a broad indication of what might happen. To be effective, any risk analysis has to focus on the local specific issues relating to the particular organization. Before looking at other issues, consideration needs to be given to the environment in which the organization operates. This can cover issues such as:

1.  **The Type of Business**—different types of organizations are subject to different threats, for example fraud in financial institutions; product recall due to quality problems in manufacturing; product tampering in food manufacturing for purposes of extortion; unauthorized access in any organization visited by the general public and fire where inflammable materials are handled.

2.  **The Location of the Organization**—risks associated with location vary depending upon whether it is situated in a city centre, on a trading estate or in an isolated rural location. Not only direct threats to the organization but wider issues such as site exclusion and threats posed by neighbouring organizations need to be considered. The location will also influence the potential for recovering on-site following a disaster—the availability of space, such as parking lots, for positioning mobile computer rooms and other temporary buildings will influence the recovery plan or the availability of other buildings on a large site, where recovery could be planned.

3.  **The Construction of the Building**—this will have a major influence on risks, in particular:

    (i)    Potential fire hazards: the age of the building and materials used in its construction.

    (ii)   Resistance to explosion: for example vulnerability of windows to being blown out.

    (iii)  Site security: the number of entrances; number of ground floor windows; existence of perimeter fencing.

    (iv)   Multiple occupancy: if the organization occupies only part of a building, risks posed by other tenants needed to be considered.

To a great extent these general risks are beyond the control of the organization in the short term unless it changes the business it is in or relocates its operation. This does not mean that the risks should be ignored but rather that they need to be considered when preparing a business continuity plan.

## Ranking the threat

In order to minimize the chances of a disaster occurring, detailed consideration needs to be given to what threatens business continuity in the organization and taking steps to eliminate or minimize the risks. In reality, it is optimistic to think that time and resource will be available to eradicate every single threat, however remote. With limitations on management time and budgets, it is necessary to focus on the issues which are important to survival by producing a ranked list of actions. There are many ways of doing this but simplicity is often the best method and the following can provide a clear priority list:

- Consider each specific risk and rank the likelihood of it occurring on a scale 1–4, with:

    1—very unlikely
    2—possible
    3—probable
    4—very likely

- Consider the potential impact on the organization if the risk actually occurred on a scale 1–4, with:

    1—minimal impact
    2—significant impact
    3—serious impact
    4—catastrophic impact

By multiplying the two factors together, a ranked list in order of importance will be produced. From practical experience, any risks scoring six points or more should be dealt with and steps taken to reduce the likelihood of them occurring.

## Specific issues

In reviewing the risks, the best way of identifying specific issues is to consider them under individual headings and have a checklist of particular issues. The approach needs to be that of a person deliberately seeking to threaten business continuity: "*How could I cause the maximum damage to this business?*" A particular issue to look for is any single point of failure—it could be a piece of equipment, a communication link or a key document, which if lost, would cause key business activities to come to a halt. Once this is identified, consideration can then be given to providing an alternative to, or back-up for, the equipment or record.

Considering the threats listed in the Survive! ranking in Figure 6.1, there are issues which should be reviewed to reduce the chance of a problem occurring.

### Flood

Although statistically floods occur rarely, the experience of providers of business continuity services shows that the effect of flooding can be major and can take surprisingly long to recover from. There are a number of factors to check. Usually, the computer room itself is most vulnerable to damage due to flooding. It is necessary to check what is installed above and adjacent to the room:

- Service pipes in the roof void
- Water-based functions directly above on a higher floor

- A flat roof or valley immediately above
- Service pipes, for example obsolete central heating junctions, in the room
- Sinks or water taps (faucets) adjacent to the room, which if they overflowed could flood it
- Sprinklers fitted in the room

The problems are made worse if the computer room is situated in a basement or the equipment is standing on the floor.

Four examples of flood threats will demonstrate what can happen:

1. A National Charity situated in a Georgian terrace in central London and which located its equipment in the basement, with hardware standing on the floor, had a water main burst in the road outside and water flowing into the area yard outside. Because it was a working day, a disaster was averted by sandbagging the entrance and calling the Water Company, but if it had occurred at a weekend, severe damage would have been caused.
2. A company occupying a modern high-rise office facility where the air conditioning header tank, on the roof, burst and flooded the computer room two floors below.
3. A customer of a business continuity contractor whose processor was damaged by a sprinkler leak and who was advised by the insurer to have a specialist company dry it out. Although the computer powered up, the hardware supplier would not support it and a three-month fight ensued with the Insurance Company over whether or not to settle a claim for a replacement.
4. An Insurance Company which located its computer room in the basement immediately below an ornamental pond.

## Fire

Fire is the threat which most readily comes to mind. As the statistics show, it actually causes a disaster rarely, but when it does occur, the effects can be catastrophic. In considering the threat, it is important to recognize that about half of fires in commercial premises are caused deliberately. There is no shortage of well proven precautions to minimize the chances of a fire breaking out. These include:

- Smoke detectors
- Sprinklers
- Inert gas systems
- Fire extinguishers
- No-smoking policies
- Fire doors

It could be assumed that the more recent the building or refurbishment, the better the fire precautions which will be in-built. Surprisingly, this is not always the case and it is not unusual to find a modern facility with few or no fire prevention precautions and no clear allocation of responsibility for them.

Examples of poor fire precautions include:

- Highly flammable materials, for example paper packaging materials kept in the computer room
- Smoke detectors fitted but not routed to external communications outside working hours
- The marketing function of a consumer electronics company, with a significant amount of packing material around the work area, which had a no-smoking policy during normal working hours but which allowed employees to smoke after 6 p.m. when they were often working alone
- No-smoking rules which encourage staff to go outside, using fire doors as access, which are wedged open to allow re-entry. This can lead to increased risk of unauthorized entry

There is of course a major link between fires and flood, and consequent water damage on lower floors can often be as serious as the damage caused by the fire itself. To minimize the chance of fire occurring and the resulting damage, efforts need to be concentrated on reducing the risk and increasing the chance of discovering the fire before it gets out of control. This includes ensuring the Fire Service can easily gain access in the event of a fire. Other precautions can sometimes hinder this:

1. An aerospace company which suffered regular break-ins to steal waste aluminium built a strong steel gate at the entrance to the site. As there was no on-site security, this would severely hamper access of the Fire Service if, in the event of a fire breaking out, they had to await arrival of a key-holder.
2. A pet food distributor which made its office block a virtual fortress at night, with steel shutters on windows and doors, with similar problems of access by the Fire Service.

## Natural disasters

In some areas of the world, the risks from natural disasters can be significant, in particular:

- Extreme weather conditions—wind, snow etc.
- Floods from rivers overflowing
- Earthquakes
- Lightning strikes

These can cause a number of threats to business continuity: damage to the facilities, inability of staff to get to work or inability to receive supplies and dispatch goods. Since many of the events occur only rarely, it can be difficult to take precautions, other than making plans should one occur. These threats are best evaluated before a decision is made to locate there in the first place. Once located, many precautions may be considered too expensive to justify in view of the perceived risk. The main exception to this is protection against lightning strikes. Unless these are adequately guarded against and precautions regularly tested, vulnerable buildings can be affected, resulting in failure of computer and communications equipment and damage to networks.

## Human error

Although scoring quite low in the Survive! rankings, many problems can be put down to human intervention. Indeed, some surveys suggest that the biggest single threat to business continuity is from people. They, of course, are behind many of the other threats, such as theft, hacking, fire and virus attacks. What are needed are enforceable policies towards people which are aimed at minimizing the threat from both staff and subcontractors.

There are a number of different aspects which need to be considered:

1. Staff training—to reduce threat to equipment, computer systems, product and data caused by incorrect handling.
2. Comprehensive recruitment checks on new employees who have access to confidential systems or data.
3. Similar checks on subcontract staff. This is nearly always delegated to the Agency supplying the person and which may not be as stringent in selection as the in-house procedures.
4. Regular review and update of building access authorization systems.
5. Uniform disciplinary codes to ensure that access to systems is withdrawn promptly.
6. Adequate cover for personnel with business critical skills and knowledge.
7. Formal procedures so that those responsible for critical systems and processes are promptly notified of staff leavers (particularly following disciplinary/dismissal cases) so that access rights can be removed in time to prevent unauthorized removal of data, harm to systems or other acts of a disgruntled ex-employee.

## Communications

The dependence of organizations and the impact of losing communications links is growing all the time. The ability to access data and pass information remotely is critical to many organizations and the common existence of single points of failure often results in multiple threats, such as:

- Loss of the telephone switch
- Damage or loss of communication equipment
- Damage to cables either internally or externally
- Damage to external telephone exchange

Strangely, though few would question the importance of communications, it is often given less priority than the computer installation in risk reduction measures. However, consideration both of the likelihood of failure of communications and the likely impact on the business normally shows that the development of a resilient network should have high priority when considering risk reduction steps:

1. Although loss of computers is routinely covered by a disaster recovery contract, far fewer organizations cover their telephone switch in a similar way, although their business depends on the telephone communications to maintain contact with customers. In surveys, recovery of telephone communications is usually considered to be more urgent than access to computer systems.

2. Far less security is often provided for communication equipment cabinets than for computer installations. Often they are situated in vulnerable positions in accessible areas where malicious damage could easily be carried out with potentially disastrous consequences. In one Drugs Company, the communication cabinet was situated on an open office floor next to an almost identical cabinet containing a confectionery vending machine. The main difference between them was that while the vending cabinet was locked, the communications cabinet was not.

3. Because networks tend to grow in an unplanned way, insufficient attention is often given to providing alternative routing in the event of failure of one part of the network and avoiding the single point of failure of a central hub controlling the whole network. Particularly when planning the recovery of the computer configuration following a disaster, it is necessary to identify an alternate node on the network where the computer systems can be installed.

4. Where a wide area network is critical to operations, ISDN can provide a low cost back-up for use in a disaster and should be installed as a fall back for key communications.

## Software

The software industry has worked hard to provide safeguards in its system to prevent unauthorized access and, human nature being what it is, users have worked equally hard to minimize their value. Proper use of these safeguards will help reduce risks to data and systems. Policies need to be in place to provide a firm foundation for the use of systems:

- Specifying adequate security features at the same time as specifying the contents of a new system
- Providing adequate time to test new systems before going live
- Ensuring that users have adequate training on new systems
- Providing and policing a policy of regular password updates, with approved composition and ensuring they are kept confidential
- Only allowing access to key levels of the systems to approved staff and reviewing the approval list regularly
- Providing a central point to which systems security issues can be referred and recorded, for example using a help desk
- Insisting on the use of realistic systems time-outs for users accessing confidential levels of the system.
- Limiting access time to key systems to eliminate unauthorized access out of normal hours

The information held on organizations' computer systems is usually critical to business survival and yet in many cases, senior management give very little attention to ensuring its security. The adoption and maintenance of a clearly defined security policy and procedures goes a long way to minimizing the threats to key systems and data.

## Environment

Loss of environmental controls within a computer room can be an immediate threat to the maintenance of computer systems. In particular, these relate to:

- Temperature and humidity control
- Electricity supply

In both cases there are acceptable limits set by manufacturers and it is necessary to ensure that they can be maintained by:

1. Providing sufficient air conditioning capacity to cope with extremes of temperature, with two stand-alone units in each computer room to provide some resilience.
2. Connecting each piece of key equipment to an uninterruptable power supply (UPS) in order to ensure that data are not lost in the event of a loss of external power. Too often, organizations only cover part of the total configuration, thus defeating the object of the exercise.

3.  Where 24-hour operations are run and the business impact of loss of systems is high and immediate, it may be necessary to install a back-up generator.

Precautions against loss of power are not infallible and there are plenty of unfortunate incidents reported:

- A UPS unit that overheated and caught fire, damaging the computer room
- One which boiled the acid in the battery, which damaged the computer mother board
- Stand-by generators which did not start when required but the IT department were told too late to close down systems before the UPS batteries ran out

## Hacking

The threat from hacking is considered by many organizations to be remote, in spite of evidence to show that it is on the increase and can cause major damage both to systems and commercially. The real problem for IT managers is that as the threat grows the demand increases for external access to data and systems. The rapid increase in the need for access to e-mail and web services means that if defences are not developed in parallel, the threats to systems can become serious. An insidious threat is where individual users on a network gain direct external access and by-pass any firewalls that may have been installed to control entry.

Constant attention by IT management both to the latest developments in firewall technology and to potential weakness in the network is needed if this risk is to be minimized.

## Hardware

### Computer room

If key hardware and communications equipment are to be safeguarded, it is important that they are housed in a secure environment. Yet a review of many computer rooms leads to the conclusion that when organizations plan their facility, siting of the computer room comes very low as a priority and it is often in an unnecessarily vulnerable position. The issues which should be considered before siting a computer room in order to minimize risks, are:

- An inconspicuous site, preferably without windows or external access
- Not in a basement, in order to minimize the risk of flooding
- Constructed for at least one hour's fire resistance in an office environment
- Fire and intruder alarmed

- Solid entrance door with electronic lock to monitor those entering
- Power isolator at the door

The issue of securely fastening the door to the computer room is strangely often ignored. A random visit to many computer rooms will find the security door left open to provide "ease of access" to transient staff. Alternatively the quality of locks is so poor as to provide almost immediate access to a determined thief or undesirable individual. A popular arrangement is a card swipe lock system accompanied by effective emergency access systems. It is easy simply to break the glass and press the door release button just inside.

Examples of insecure computer rooms include:

- One shared with an administration function, requiring regular visits by non-IT staff
- One in a hospital situated in the basement, directly under the Children's Ward, where periodically lavatory bowls were blocked and overflowed into the floor below
- One with large openable windows on two sides, situated on the ground floor, adjacent to the parking lot
- One with glass panels in a partition next to the door. These could be easily removed by lifting the rubber seals
- One situated remote from the IT department, where the inert gas systems for fire prevention needed to be turned off manually before entry. Because of the lack of direct supervision, this system could be left turned off after the visitor left the room.

## Computer equipment

The aim of any risk reduction exercise, when considering hardware, is to increase the resilience provided by the configuration; even where two computer rooms exist, for administrative convenience, it is often found easier to keep all similar equipment in the same room. By splitting this across two rooms, business continuity can often be provided if disaster strikes one. Priorities must change to make continuity more important than convenience. It is not uncommon to find organizations with a significant number of similar platforms, which keep them together in one computer room rather than dispersing them.

Consideration needs to be given to the correct siting of systems and data back-ups. Even today, it is not uncommon to find back-ups stored in the same building as the hardware and no copies held off the site. The risks caused by site exclusion under these circumstances can be catastrophic. Even in quite sophisticated organizations, back-ups are routinely taken home by the IT manager, while back-ups of C drives are kept (if at all) in the user's desk drawers. To ensure that back-up routines are adequate, they should be tested against accepted disaster scenarios to see whether they are adequate.

## Virus

Every organization has, or claims to have, an effective policy to guard against virus attacks. On examination, they are not always adequate. The main questions relate to:

1. Frequency of update of the anti-virus software. Some organizations depend on a three-monthly cycle, which could potentially allow a significant number of new viruses to pass unidentified.
2. Ability to by-pass the virus checking process—perhaps via e-mail. Does the system cover all possible points of access?
3. Senior management disregarding the policy: with many senior managers using lap-tops off-site and then connecting to the network and loading floppy disks, do they always follow the procedures?

## Theft and vandalism

There has been a significant increase in the frequency of disasters occurring due to theft or vandalism, particularly of computer equipment. This risk can only be controlled by:

- Reducing visibility of valuable assets
- Controlling access to vulnerable areas

The siting of computer rooms on the ground floor of a building with picture windows and easy vehicular access is still a common practice, thus increasing risks under both of these counts. Where ever possible, computer rooms should be located discretely away from prying eyes, without internal or external windows and in an area where the entrance is under supervision. An intruder alarm should be fitted and set out of normal working hours.

Increasingly, organizations are using badge systems to recognize visitors. This is rather a strange approach to risk control unless staff also wear an identity badge. It is not always true that staff in a large building will invariably recognize each other—yet the theory is that individuals who do not have a badge must be all right. Even a card-swipe system on all major doors is not foolproof: people will frequently hold the door open if you follow them.

## Loss of key documents

In this age of the paperless office, it is remarkable how often business continuity is dependent upon records held only on hard copy. Because effective protection of paper records can be expensive and inconvenient, many organizations prefer to ignore the risks associated with loss of access to this data. One of the main problems is that responsibility for the security of these documents usually belongs to the department using them. Yet a disaster which destroys such data may be catastrophic, for example:

1.  An electronics company that kept all personnel information in hard copy alone—if the building were affected by a fire it would not know how to contact its staff.
2.  A finance house that kept all specimen signatures in a filing cabinet—in a disaster, under Regulators' rules, it might be prevented from accepting instructions to sell securities.
3.  A property-selling company that held all disputes files in hard copy and would find great difficulty in resolving them if the files were lost.
4.  Organizations that keep current project files in hard copy and would experience serious business impacts if these were lost. This applies to the majority of businesses.

## Avoiding that disaster

An incident only becomes a disaster if it has a serious effect on business continuity. Therefore disaster avoidance should be approached as a two-stage process.

● **Reduce the Risks**

Once threats to business continuity have been identified and ranked, a programme of risk reduction can be carried out so as to eliminate the unnecessary disasters. It may not always be possible to carry out everything immediately and changes may need to be incorporated into future plans, for example resiting the computer room as part of a wider office replan. However, a firm timetable needs to be established, budgets obtained and progress monitored. As time passes, the threats will need to be revisited to ensure that other changes have not produced new risks.

● **Plan to Overcome Irreducible Threats**

Some threats will still remain after the most rigorous risk reduction exercise. Plans need to be developed to deal with the consequences so that in business continuity terms, no disaster occurs. This involves planning in detail how each resulting disaster scenario should be dealt with and identifying:

- Recovery resources which need to be provided and when to recover key functions
- Where these resources will be obtained from
- Where recovery of key functions will be located
- What management structure will oversee the process
- What external bodies will need to assist
- What timetable is needed for recovery to achieve acceptable levels of business continuity

If the plans are realistic and are rehearsed, there is no need for any organization to suffer a disaster.

. . . **Why have one if you do not have to?**

# Section Two

Planning for business continuity:
a "how-to" guide

# The business continuity planning methodology

## Malcolm Cornish—UK

**7**

Malcolm is a widely experienced and highly regarded consultant employed by Comdisco in the United Kingdom.

## Introduction

In this chapter we provide an overview and introduction to the business continuity planning methodology advocated by the Business Continuity Institute and the Disaster Recovery Institute International. It is based on the input and experience of countless business continuity planning professionals over the last 20 years. The methodology provides a structured approach to tackling business continuity planning in a logical and proven manner.

## What is business continuity planning?

Section One has explored the concepts and principles of business continuity planning and provides the full answer to this question. But how many times have those involved in the industry been asked this simple question at a cocktail party or similar social gathering and been stumped for a simple answer. In essence: "business continuity planning is the process that every organization should go through to ensure that it continues to provide an acceptable level of service to its clients, customers and other business partners regardless of any events or incidents that occur."

The methodology outlined in this chapter and enlarged on in the ensuing chapters has been proven to provide the required information and result in the successful development of business continuity plans. However, many organizations that adopt this proven methodology, fail to meet the deadlines they set themselves for producing effective and workable plans. This chapter also identifies some of the reasons for failure and suggests ways around them.

*The Definitive Handbook of Business Continuity Management.* Edited by Andrew Hiles and Peter Barnes. © 1999 Malcolm Cornish.

## A structured approach

In line with most other aspects of business that involve the introduction of significant changes to attitudes and processes within an organization, the overall framework for tackling business continuity planning can be regarded as being fairly simple:

1. **Assess** your organization's current situation—from a business continuity planning viewpoint: how does it compare with other organizations in the same industry? Are there any particular threats or vulnerabilities that make it more or less vulnerable? If there were to be a major interruption, how long would it be before your business really started to suffer? Which of its business activities are the most sensitive and vulnerable? What can you do about it? What are the costs and implications of the different options available to you? What are the realistic options? Which options should be implemented and why?

2. **Implement** the chosen solutions for your organization: make arrangements for the new facilities required; improve security and protection; sign contracts with those organizations that can help you deal with a disaster; document the new procedures that have to be implemented; train your staff in these new procedures; document precisely how your organization will respond to a disaster in a manner that is clear, unambiguous and will work.

3. **Manage** the entire process and the new regime into the future so that it does not become outdated or even obsolete.

It is not surprising that many organizations throw in the towel at the assessment stage because the more you start to think about business continuity planning and all the various and interrelated issues, the more frightening and difficult it becomes. The methodology outlined below and explained in more detail in later chapters, tackles all of the above phases in a logical and structured manner that addresses the issues of concern.

## The assessment phase

The Business Continuity Assessment commences with project initiation and management and concludes with the development of the business continuity strategies. The key stages outlined in Figure 7.1 are as follows.

# Business Continuity Assessment

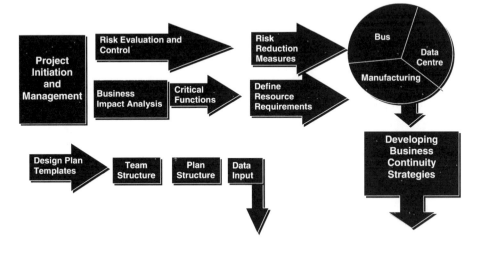

**Figure 7.1**—The assessment phase

## Project initiation and management

As a result of reading Section One, you will appreciate that business continuity planning is not just a once-off project. It requires continuous update and assessment as the business environment that your organization operates and the technology that it relies on change with frightening rapidity. Nevertheless, there is a project element that requires careful planning and execution. This project involves raising awareness and changing attitudes within the organization. It requires valuable resources to be allocated for specified periods of time and clear commitment from management. This phase should also include an audit of existing business continuity and disaster recovery arrangements. At the conclusion of the phase, a detailed project should be drawn up for the business continuity planning work to be undertaken. Key objectives should include the following:

- Create awareness within your organization
- Identify individuals required to participate
- Develop customized questionnaires
- Establish interview schedule
- Conduct survey and audit

- Report to management
- Draw up project plan

Chapter 8, by Jayne Howe, provides detailed guidance on the project initiation and management.

## Risk evaluation and control

Risk evaluation and control involves identifying the major threats and exposures and evaluating the overall risks that your organization faces. A clear objective is to determine cost-effective measures that can be implemented to reduce specific risks and mitigate their impact. Chapter 9, by Alan Craig and Ian Charters, provides detailed guidance on how to tackle risk evaluation and control.

## Business impact analysis

The primary objective of the business impact analysis is to identify those functions that are essential to the ongoing survival of the business and would cause the most impact if they were to be disrupted. The analysis must take into account financial and other impacts (e.g. customer service, ability to comply with legal requirements) and identify the timescales within which non-performance of these functions becomes critical. Chapter 10, by William Meredith, provides detailed guidance on how to conduct a business impact analysis.

## Develop business continuity strategies

Once the risk evaluation and control and business impact analysis stages are complete, the next step is to develop the business continuity strategies that will provide the recipe for successfully facing the demands of a major incident. These strategies must balance the value of the business and its assets against the cost of guaranteeing continuity of the critical business functions. Providing answers to the following questions will form the basis of the strategy:

- What can we do to reduce the risk of the disaster happening in the first place?
- What are our absolute minimum requirements and how quickly do we need them?
- How much can we afford to spend, bearing in mind that faster speed of availability almost always means increased cost?

The purpose of this phase is to define the resource recovery requirements and confirm the business strategy that will support business operations at an alternate facility. Data determining the exposure of your organization to different outages will be consolidated and evaluated against the cost of recovery alternatives, risk reduction and insurance.

By the end of this phase, there are a number of other issues that will also need to have been addressed:

- Appointment of an overall Plan Coordinator
- The recovery team structure that will be needed and the roles and responsibilities of each team and department
- Appointment of Plan Administrators to manage the development of individual plans
- The underlying structure of the business continuity plans to be written so that there is consistency and coordination between them.
- The locations from which recovery can be undertaken and managed, including initial assembly points, Command Centres, temporary office space and computer back-up sites
- The timeframes within which relocation must be completed
- Minimum resource requirements of each department for which a plan is needed and the teams that will support them

Chapter 11, by Neal Courtney, provides detailed guidance on developing business continuity strategies. Chaper 12, by Melvyn Musson, outlines strategies for manufacturing and logistics, and Chapter 13, by Paul Kirvan, covers strategies for communications.

# The implementation phase

As presented in Figure 7.2, the implementation phase involves commissioning the recovery facilities; negotiating the required insurance cover; instigating risk reduction measures; documenting business resumption and disaster recovery procedures; implementing an exercise and maintenance programme; conducting exercises; and providing the basis for review and continual improvement of your organization's business continuity capability.

## Implementing the continuity strategy

During this phase, the recovery facilities including the physical locations, computer and other equipment, communications and office infrastructure will be

# Business Continuity Implementation

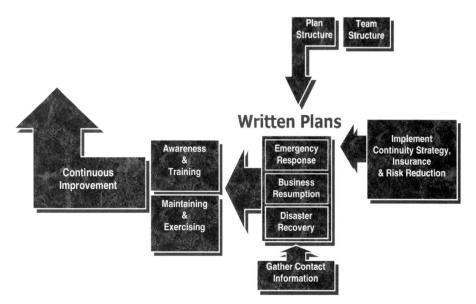

**Figure 7.2**—The implementation phase

commissioned; insurance provisions will be finalized; and risk reduction measures will be put into place.

Service providers should manage and implement all aspects of commissioning the recovery facilities. Regardless of the source of the recovery solution, one company should act as lead contractor to ensure that all interrelationships between the various elements of the recovery solution are addressed. Implementation issues are addressed in Chapter 14, by Gregg Beatty.

## Developing and implementing the written plan

Developing the written plan involves two key stages. Firstly, creating plan templates for the teams needed to recover your organization's business in the event of a major incident. Secondly, gathering the necessary data and including it in written plans that dictate clearly and precisely what needs to be done following a disaster. This should include steps to determine the effect of the incident on the business and the action needed to recover lost transactions and work-in-progress. Department personnel must participate in the writing of the plan, since they are going to have to implement it when it is needed. The data to be gathered include contact details of critical employees and external organizations and details of the minimum resource requirements of each department and team.

Plans that need to be written include:

- Emergency Response that identifies the immediate action following a disaster including the establishment of a Command Centre and Crisis Management
- Business Resumption plans that identify clearly and precisely the action that will be taken to resume the critical business activities identified during the Business Impact Analysis
- Disaster Recovery plans that identify clearly and precisely how the technical and office infrastructure will be recovered to support the business

Chapter 15, by Andrew Hiles, provides guidance on the development and implementation of the required plans.

## Maintaining and exercising plans

The process does not end once the plan is written. It must be kept up to date and exercised to make sure that it will achieve its objectives. The best way to prove that the business continuity plan will work when it is needed is through regular exercising. Consideration must therefore also be given to a strategy for ongoing plan maintenance and exercising.

During this phase, the accuracy and completeness of the plans and supporting documentation are verified. Involving team and department personnel in exercises raises awareness and they will become familiar with the plans and the procedures that they will have to follow at the recovery locations. The recovery locations and the facilities that they provide will also be assessed for adequacy.

Chapters 16, by Thomas Doemland, and 17, by Tim Arnit, address the issues of awareness and training and how to maintain and exercise the written plans.

## Key elements of business continuity

Drawing up plans and implementing a true business continuity capability involves addressing many issues and concerns. This book addresses the following key elements:

- Public Relations and Crisis Coordination (Chapters 3, by Robert Heath, and 14, by Gregg Beatty)

- Coordination with public authorities and relationships between the public and private sectors (the need for such partnerships is illustrated through many of the case studies contained in this book)
- Selecting the right tools to support the process (Chapter 18, by Lyndon Bird)
- The role of the external consultant (Appendix 2E)
- Coping with people during the recovery (Chapter 19, by Allen Johnson)

Chapter 20, by Andrew Hiles, provides a round up of all the key elements that must be addressed.

## Coordination and management of the process

If an organization is to be successful in developing and then maintaining a business continuity capability, it is essential that there is clear management commitment and support for the process. To ensure that the plans and procedures that are implemented will be effective, there must be overall as well as individual ownership. There must be a plan coordinator with overall responsibility for managing and coordinating the entire business continuity planning process described above. That plan coordinator must have the visible support of top management and the necessary authority to make things happen. To spread the workload, individual plan administrators should be appointed to manage the development and maintenance of individual plans.

## So what's the catch?

Many organizations have adopted the methodology outlined above and been successful in implementing a true business continuity capability. Of those, many have met with disaster and emerged intact. Research by Oxford University has demonstrated that organizations which manage a disaster effectively emerge stronger than they were before the disaster. There are, however, too many companies that have tried to adopt the methodology but have failed miserably to complete even the Assessment Phase.

The most common reason for failure is undoubtedly lack of true management commitment. However, there is a way of making real progress and securing the management commitment needed for success.

A major problem is the time it takes to produce the written plan. If you follow the methodology strictly and have dedicated resources, the first plan will be produced after approximately seven months. What usually happens is that failure by key managers to support the initiative delays the project for months. By this time, management, who expected you to produce a plan in a matter of weeks, have become disillusioned, business managers still don't understand what is required of them. No one has any idea what the plan they are meant to produce for their business unit should look like and the likelihood of getting a plan out in the next decade looks very remote.

The solution is simple. Produce template plans containing basic contact information and resource data quickly, preferably within a month of starting. You will then have something to show management and business managers and to educate them in their role. Education should involve walk-through tests using the template plans. This enables business managers to begin to understand the issues involved and the input that is needed from them.

# Getting ahead of the game

The key steps to producing template plans prior to completing the entire assessment phase are outlined below.

## Appoint overall plan coordinator

A vital first step is to appoint a senior manager to be responsible for driving the project. Without such a focal point, the project will never gain sufficient momentum and is likely to lose direction well before any plans are produced. The main responsibilities of the plan coordinator are to:

- manage and coordinate the whole plan development process
- provide advice and guidance to all personnel involved
- assure the quality and consistency of plans developed by each department

On an ongoing basis, the plan coordinator will be responsible for:

- managing the ongoing development and enhancement of the plans
- coordinating plan maintenance and testing
- contract management and liaison with the third party service suppliers
- initiating periodic risk reviews and managing risk reduction projects
- assessing the impact of any changes to the business and IT infrastructure

### Identify critical functions

Regardless of any other considerations, the development of business continuity plans must have focus. If you spread available resources too thinly, you will inevitably fail. The first step is to determine which functions are critical to the ongoing survival of the organization and which departments will therefore need business continuity plans to carry on those functions following a disaster. The primary objective of the business impact analysis (BIA) is to do this. An alternative is for senior management to decide what is critical without going through an analytical process.

The plan coordinator should initially draw up a list of business functions within the organization and present these to senior management for ranking according to criticality. The process is primarily intuitive but key criteria should be developed prior to examining the functions to establish a consistency to the ranking process. A review of Chapter 10 may be helpful in identifying key areas of concern. The prime benefit of this method is the time that can be saved at the start of the project. Overall time-savings will only be achieved if senior management participation proceeds without any problems. The major disadvantage is that the list is based solely on intuition and does not provide any basis for documenting the reasons for the ranking of functions.

If you have time to perform a full BIA at the outset or wish to revisit the BIA once the first draft plans have been developed, refer to Chapter 10 for detailed guidance.

### Draw up a list of departments for which a written business continuity plan is required

Identify the departments that will be responsible for undertaking the critical business functions following a disaster and for which a written business continuity plan will be required.

### Draw up a recovery team structure

Following a disaster, the key objective is to ensure that critical functions are recovered before their non-performance threatens the ongoing survival of the company. In all likelihood, the personnel responsible for performing these functions in a normal business environment will be called upon to perform them following a disaster, albeit in a different location. To provide overall coordination and management of the recovery and to establish the necessary infrastructure for performing the critical functions requires the formation of special teams.

Team structures are considered in Chapter 15.

## Appoint plan administrators

A plan administrator should be appointed for each team and department with responsibility for:

- liaising with the plan coordinator
- managing the development of the team or department plan
- developing team or department-specific plan contents
- briefing and training those involved in the development of the plan
- acceptance testing of the plan
- ongoing review and maintenance of the plan

## Decide on the roles and responsibilities of each team

Roles and responsibilities (in no particular order) that may need to be considered include:

| | | |
|---|---|---|
| • Overall Command and Control | • Finance | • Property |
| • Insurance | • Transport | • Office Services |
| • Security | • Legal | • Public Relations |
| • Personnel | • Purchasing | • Buildings |
| • Building Services | • Damage and Salvage Assessment | • Computer Hardware |
| • Software Applications | • Data Communications | • Peripherals |
| • Cabling | • Voice Communications | • PC Networks |

## Decide the underlying plan structure of each team and department plan

An underlying structure is needed to ensure that all plans are coordinated and consistent. Chapter 15 identifies possible plan structures.

## Identify Command Centre and other recovery locations

As a minimum, draw up a list of potential locations for the following:

- Office Recovery Locations
- IT Recovery Locations
- Command Centres

A primary site for each type of location should be identified. In most cases, this will need to be fitted out with the necessary utilities and services before the disaster occurs. Other options for dealing with protracted or large-scale disasters should also be considered. Each location can serve multiple purposes. For example, a general conference room could serve as the Command Centre, depending on the scope of the disaster. The Command Centre could also be located in the same building as the recovery location. When choosing any location, as with all decisions with the plan, allow common sense to be the predominant factor. For example, in the case of a bomb explosion, any area within half a mile of the blast is likely to be cordoned off and inaccessible.

For guidance on choosing recovery locations refer to Chapter 14.

## Identify minimum resource requirements of each department and team

The plan administrator for each department must specify the minimum resources needed by the department to continue the critical functions for which it is responsible. Team plan administrators should specify the minimum resources required to discharge the team's responsibilities. The most efficient method of gathering this information is to use data collection forms.

## Gather contact details of all critical personnel and external organizations

One of the key requirements during a disaster is to be able to communicate with your own staff and external organizations. A vital part of any plan is to have up-to-date contact details within it. There are at least three different categories of contact information—namely, personnel, recovery services and vendors (suppliers)—that need to be collected.

## Allocate personnel to teams

Identify a manager, deputy and members for each of the teams.

### Create templates that are specific to your organization

Using other plans as a model, create templates for each of the teams and a master template for all departments.

### Create team and department plans

Create plans for each of your teams and departments.

### Conduct walk-through tests

Using the "first draft" plans, conduct walk-through testing.

## Summary

Business continuity is a very wide-ranging and interesting topic. However, like a snowball that grows and grows as you push it along, you will encounter many diversions, challenges and issues that need to be considered. By adopting the approach described in this section, you will be able to tackle them in a logical and focused manner that will enable you to stay on track and achieve your objectives.

# Project initiation and management

## 8    Jayne Howe—Canada

Jayne is a consultant with wide experience in business continuity management within Canada and the USA. She also coordinates the Canadian membership of the Business Continuity Institute.

## Project initiation

Business Continuity Planning projects, as well as projects for Disaster Recovery capability, are initiated, or "born", from many different sources. The most common scenarios seem to be when a corporation is told that possessing a demonstrable business continuity capability has become a requirement because of:

- an outside auditor's report
- the regulatory bodies which govern their industry that have deemed it to be a requirement for membership or compliance
- the companies "stakeholders" (those with vested interest in the company, such as shareholders, owners, insurers, employees and investors) who are demanding it
- the company (or a competitor) having in fact experienced an "event" which opened their eyes to their own vulnerability in not having a continuity capability in place

But whatever the reason that upper management is now talking about business continuity within an organization, it is still a long way from having them commit funds, resources and time to activating a business continuity project and understanding the ongoing corporate cultural change that will become an integral part of their day-to-day business long term.

One of the most effective methods used to "sell" business continuity to upper management, is to approach it with the appropriate corporate "hot button". Corporate hot buttons can be any one, or a combination, of several different critical mandates. It is, therefore, important to find out what upper management really cares about in running the business and which elements are vital, in their minds, to

*The Definitive Handbook of Business Continuity Management.* Edited by Andrew Hiles and Peter Barnes. © 1999 John Wiley & Sons Ltd.

keeping the business doors open even in the face of a disaster. Some examples of corporate "hot buttons" are listed below.

- Protecting revenues—ensuring profits
                                    —minimizing losses
- Retain marketshare
- Corporate image
- Customer service
- Satisfy "stakeholders"
- Auditors
- Product delivery

Although a company may sell a product or service as their business, their immediate concern may in fact be continued customer service capability or protecting their corporate image rather than ensuring production. It's important to know which "angle" to use when approaching management for business continuity project approval and support. Therefore, if building a business continuity capability can ensure protection and continued availability of the true critical mandate, from management's point of view, there is a better chance of success in obtaining appropriate funding and resources.

Timing can also become a critical factor when the reason for initiating a business continuity planning project comes from regulatory bodies which have compliance deadlines or from an auditor's report which will have an annual review. Projects which have critical time factors are usually more expensive to execute and involve more internal resource effort.

Once the appropriate hot buttons have been identified, a cost/benefit analysis should be prepared which demonstrates the benefits to the company of ensuring the protection and ongoing availability of those critical mandates. A cost/benefit analysis isn't always just about hard cost.

## Project costs—start-up and ongoing

There should be fairly accurate costs associated with the resources, time, effort and third party contracts to be created in the business continuity planning project phase. But be sure to add in ongoing annual costs for plan maintenance/administration, training/awareness, testing and plan updates. These figures should be a very small fraction of the projected rebuild cost figures.

## Projected rebuild costs

It should be possible to create a scenario of rebuild (with projected costs) if the company does not develop a business continuity capability. Although these costs are estimates, the majority of them would be one-time costs with a smaller component of ongoing costs. Be sure to include new, concentrated marketing efforts, potential employee recruitment and new hire costs, technology replacement and potential moving costs. Some of these figures can be obtained from past records.

## Projected potential savings

Fortunately, developing a business continuity capability doesn't necessarily always just cost money. There are opportunities for corporate savings as well. In some countries and in some industries, there are discounted insurance premiums available to corporations which possess demonstrable business continuity capabilities. Depending on the technology recovery strategies that are developed, there can be opportunities to outsource technology maintenance, support and/or upgrades, which can be more cost-effective than providing those services in-house. Off-site vaulting can also be more cost-effective than providing the appropriate environmentals and structure on-site. These estimates can also be included in the cost/benefit analysis.

Too often well-intentioned business continuity initiatives are not "sold" effectively to upper management and only receive funding to perform a disaster recovery planning project or, more commonly, just a technology recovery planning project.

Often a half-day senior executive workshop is useful to build business continuity awareness and generally educate management on the various components of business continuity planning and the overall size of the undertaking. It is also true, unfortunately, that "scare tactics" sometimes work to drive the message home. There are all kinds of smoke and rubble videos available as well as world-wide statistics on companies without proper continuity plans in place, that experienced some form of physical disaster (or even bad press) and did not survive.

Once the corporate decision has been made to pursue business continuity planning as an initial project, and hopefully, as an ongoing corporate process, it is critical and beneficial to disseminate this information throughout the organization. Every employee as well as appropriate third party suppliers and support organizations should be informed that developing business continuity capabilities has become a priority mandate to the organization. Building employee awareness and keeping them informed throughout the process is key to building corporate support for the efforts. Everyone is already busy performing their daily job functions and if upper management is not clear on helping to "sell" the business continuity planning project as a priority mandate, then resources throughout the firm will eventually just add it to the never-ending list of "other" things to do when they have time. Management must be seen as visibly supporting and endorsing the continuity efforts of the project throughout the entire process.

# Project management

Creating comprehensive continuity plans and ongoing processes for an entire organization is a large and daunting undertaking. Trying to grasp all components of the project and plan development process at the same time can become quite intimidating when trying to figure where to begin. Business continuity planning is managed much more successfully if it is broken into sections with go-forward decisions acting as milestones at the end of each section.

Generally, a business continuity planning project can be broken down into manageable thirds or phases. The first phase is Information Gathering and is comprised of risk evaluation and control, beginning to establish appropriate corporate support recovery teams, conducting a business impact analysis and using the information learned from the business impact analysis to develop appropriate continuity strategies. The second phase is Plan Development which includes developing emergency responses and procedures to ensure the life and safety of employees and visitors, as well as controlling the initial corporate response or reaction to an "event". This phase also includes development of the plan itself, as well as implementation and documentation of the plan. The third phase is a true transformation when a business continuity planning project becomes an ongoing corporate-wide process, where internal training and awareness programmes are developed, plan testing is scheduled and ongoing administration/maintenance of the plans begin.

In order to successfully manage each and every phase of business continuity planning, it is critical to create and install appropriate project-reporting relationships throughout the life of the project and on an ongoing basis as an integrated, corporate process. Overall, the project should report up to a small Executive Committee where the members are the most senior executives in the organization. (Ideally, these would be the same executives who approved the project budget and sent the corporate message to all employees in the first place.) These could include the Chief Financial Officer or Senior Vice-President of Finance, the Chief Executive Officer or President, and the Chief Information Officer or Senior Vice-President of Technology. Although it is not always necessary to utilize their time throughout the project, a reporting structure should be set up which makes it mandatory to give the Executive Committee some kind of project status update at least every two weeks.

Members of the working committees will change as the project advances through its phases, however, the onus should rest with the Project Manager to ensure that project status reports are timely and complete for every reporting period.

## Phase One—information gathering

### Structure

For the first phase of business continuity planning, the project team should consist of:

- A Project Manager who coordinates the activities of the team, manages time-lines and budget, and reports to the Executive Committee
- Enough resources who understand the "business" of the company and what information is needed to be acquired through the Business Impact Analysis process
- One or two key resources from technology who understand the underlying technical issues as business units prioritize their recovery requirements
- A Project Liaison who will be responsible for gathering together all the required company documentation such as:

  (i)      any third party contracts,
  (ii)     insurance policies,
  (iii)    technology topology schematics,
  (iv)     employee organizational charts,
  (v)      corporate phone lists, fax and modem numbers,
  (vi)     end-user workstation configurations,
  (vii)    computer inventory lists,
  (viii)   LAN server configurations,
  (ix)     building cabling and electrical drawings, etc.

Comprehensive business continuity planning projects should include not only gathering information for the technology systems and business functions of a corporation, but also reviews of such things as:

- current insurance policies
- technology maintenance/support contracts
- physical premises review
- surrounding geographic review
- corporate conformity and liability concerns
- voice recovery requirements
- paper-based vital records review
- third party contract review for suppliers, off-site storage providers, etc.
- human resource recovery requirements
- premises (office workspace) recovery requirements
- incoming feeds/deliveries review (electronic incoming feeds, mail/courier delivery, etc.)

### Budget

The one-time costs incurred here should have been the closest to "true" costs which were included in the cost/benefit analysis. This phase of the project should have a definite start and end date with, at least, an upper limit on cost. Since it is always better to be seen as coming in under budget, rather than over budget, be sure to add in a 5–15% buffer into the timelines and costs before they are submitted for approval, in order to accommodate unforeseen delays and expenses. Adding in a small overrun buffer, should apply to every phase in project management.

## Timelines

This phase of the project is the time to maximize on the employees' new awareness and management support which has freshly made its way throughout the organization. This phase involves the most effort that will be required from the general employee population and it's important to meet with them and acquire the needed information while they are still aware and supportive of the initiative. If resources are available, several information gathering methods should be going on at the same time since it is not always necessary to finish interviewing or getting recovery information from one department or business function, before another one is started.

## Milestones

There are many opportunities within the first phase of a business continuity planning project to identify milestones or successes to show to management. It's always helpful in assisting ongoing project awareness throughout the organization if the project team does a bit of "flag waving" now and then. Milestones during Phase One can include:

- Publishing the establishment of the corporate support teams and informing employees who those teams' members are and what their responsibilities are
- Finishing the risk assessment and analysis and internally publishing the results to management
- Establishing the critical corporate support recovery teams (see section "Continuing visible support")
- Completion of the business impact analysis and reporting appropriate recovery strategy alternatives to management
- The last milestone in this phase which is when management decides which recovery strategy will best suit the recovery requirements, budget and disaster recovery time period of the corporation

## Phase Two—plan development

### Structure

Once an appropriate disaster recovery strategy has been chosen by management, the project team members will change somewhat. In addition to a Project Manager, the team will also require the services of:

- Corporate legal counsel to complete third party contract negotiations
- Senior management with signing authority for third party contracts
- Technical writers to assist in plan documentation
- Internal/external assistance from Human Resources, property management and the local emergency authorities to document emergency response procedures
- A corporate communications representative with media training to develop corporate first response scripts
- Lots of resources from technical support to assist in the technology recovery plan development

This group will be working in isolation from most other company employees until some of the contracts are signed and some of the documentation is completed.

## Budget

Budget approval may be necessary if any of the project team members in Phase Two are outside consultant or contract resources. There may also be expenses incurred if media management and communications courses are required for those executives who have been appointed as spokespersons for the corporation. Additional expenses may include recovery plan documentation software and training. The largest budget item in this phase (besides the resource time utilized during plan development) will be the costs of activating any third party contracts for off-site recovery capabilities and/or off-site storage requirements. (Initiation or contract costs to third party recovery providers are included in this budget. However, monthly subscription fees to the providers should become a line item within the company's appropriate department or division.)

## Timelines

It is unique to each corporate environment and business continuity planning project whether the proposal evaluations from third party recovery providers is included as the end of Phase One or set up as the opening step within Phase Two. Once a recovery strategy has been decided upon, an RFI (Request for Information), an RFQ (Request for Quote) or an RFP (Request for Proposal) must be written and submitted to those third party providers who have been deemed as being most appropriate to have the correct "fit" of recovery capabilities for the corporation. Then, time must be allocated in order to give these companies enough time to respond (two to three weeks is usually acceptable). They may wish to give presentations and/or site tours of their facilities to company management and technical support staff in order to properly explain and demonstrate the configurations and capabilities of their facilities.

Plan development, implementation and documentation always take longer than can be originally estimated. Be sure to allow enough time for plan documentation which should include a draft version that is reviewed not only by the employees who have to work from the plan during recovery, but also reviewed with "fresh eyes" by someone who would only have to use the documentation if the allocated resources were not available for recovery. It is important to remember that the procedures and language used within the plan documentation must also make sense to someone who didn't write it, or doesn't do these activities as their day-to-day job.

### *Milestones*

This phase of the project seems to hum along in isolation within the project team and the outside support providers, without much involvement from other members of the organization. It's important, therefore, to continue to make every effort to keep corporate management and employees informed of small successes and completed targets within this phase. In addition to regular status reports up to management (even if management is currently involved "hands on" with third party contract negotiations), the project team should publish, or at least make public, certain milestones as they occur within each phase. Some of these milestones can include:

- Completion of third party recovery provider contracts
- Announcing the completion of each business unit's plan
- Completion of each technical component recovery implementation
- Completion of the establishment of all corporate support recovery teams (see "Continuing visible support" section)

## Phase Three—business continuity process

### *Structure*

Activities during this last phase, as well as those on an ongoing basis, will again shift around to involve more internal staff. It is also this third phase where there will in fact be several different project teams and ongoing process tasks assigned to permanent employees and embedded into daily and annual business functions. Initially, the project team, under the direction of the Project Manager, needs to stay focused on two main components:

- Developing initial awareness and recovery training for all employees
- Coordinating and scheduling the first recovery "test" for the organization

While the project team should still be forwarding status reports up to the Executive Committee on a regular basis, the frequency of those reports may drop down to once per month while training programmes are developed internally (or purchased from recovery training organizations and modified). It also takes many weeks, or in some cases, a few months, to schedule and properly prepare for technical or relocation recovery tests. The project team for employee training should consist of:

- The Project Manager who coordinates the activities of the team(s), manages timelines and budget, and reports to the Executive Committee
- Representation from Human Resources or the internal Training Department
- Representation from one or two key business units to review the appropriateness of training materials
- Outside resources (if necessary) which specialize in employee awareness and training for business continuity issues

The other set of activities that will be happening at the same time is for a team to develop a test plan, script and schedule for an initial restoration/recovery. Although some organizations try to test system recovery as well as resource relocation and voice restoration at a recovery site, it is advisable not to try all these recovery components at the same time, especially for an initial test. It is still critical to have demonstrable successes, especially at this stage when the organization has now invested large sums of money and effort into building plans. So try an initial test that is not too big to manage and has the greatest change of success. A single system restore test is often a good starting point. Or, redirect only a percentage of incoming calls to a recovery call centre. To accomplish this, a project team needs to be assembled which includes:

- A Project Manager (probably the same one) who coordinates the activities of the team, manages timelines and budget, and reports to the Executive Committee
- Representation from Technology Support who will be involved in the test
- Representation from a business unit which will be involved in the test
- Representation from the recovery site provider

## *Budget*

Estimating costs for internal training and awareness programmes is dependent on whether the programmes will be developed in-house or purchased from outside training organizations and modified. Be sure to include the costs of software and/or training materials, internal resource effort, workshop costs, consultancy fees (if applicable), printing materials, and so forth into the budget.

Creating a budget for recovery testing is more difficult. There may be hard costs associated with using "test time" at a third party recovery facility; however, the internal effort to prepare, plan and script for a test, as well as the internal resource effort to conduct and post-test audit, is ALWAYS underestimated. Be sure to allow lots of time to prepare for a successful test, as well as the time that will be spent afterward performing a post-test audit.

### Timelines

Since this phase of the project melds over into an ongoing corporate process, the timelines are, ultimately, never-ending. However, an end date or milestone could be determined to, for example, complete a first session of recovery training to all employees. After that, the process of training each new employee or each employee transfer, takes over.

A target date, or end date, can also be established to set up a test schedule. And it is true that if a third party recovery facility is to be involved, a test date and time will have to be scheduled and reserved with them. This is most often at least two months in advance. Add into the timeline, a completion date for the post-test audit work as well. Then the ongoing process will take over for plan updates, maintenance and redistribution to affected business units. In the meantime, activities for the next test and test date should be under way.

### Milestones

This phase of business continuity planning has the most visible milestones of all phases. The obvious first milestone will be the general announcement after all employees of the organization have completed their first series of recovery training.

The second milestone will be the general announcement of the first successful recovery test. After that, the company needs to focus on successes every year as business continuity becomes an integrated, corporate process.

# Continuing visible support

## Corporate recovery teams

During recovery from a disaster or event, the business units within an organization will need to concentrate on restoring their own environment and becoming productive again. The technology support staff within an organization will be focused on providing a restored technical environment so that the business units can access their systems and data and become productive again. Therefore, it will be necessary to create overall corporate recovery support teams that are activated during recovery procedures. These teams are comprised of the company's decision-makers who have the authority to declare a disaster status on behalf of the organization, as well as the authority to release funds from the organization, deal with insurance companies, the press, and process any employee personal claim or pay issues. For organizations who have the internal resources available to create separate support teams, the following suggestions are made.

## Crisis Management Team

The Crisis Management Team consists of selected senior management personnel who will be responsible for making all significant decisions regarding the response to a crisis situation. Only specified members of this team are authorized to declare a disaster, after analysis of the preliminary damage assessment when they determine the appropriate course of action. All significant notifications will disseminate from this group. This group will be responsible for addressing the longer term recovery issues once the immediate emergency response strategy has been activated, and as more detailed damage assessment information becomes available.

Key responsibilities include:

- Activating the contingency plan
- Initial notification of recovery team leaders
- Analysing the preliminary damage assessment reports to determine whether a disaster declaration will be necessary
- Determining appropriate emergency response strategy, identifying which components of the recovery arrangements are to be activated under the circumstances
- Determining Corporate level communications strategy, including external and internal actions to be undertaken by the Corporate Communications Team (external) and the Administrative Support Team (internal)
- Initiating the disaster notification (alert/declaration) procedures if required

## Administrative Support Team

The Administrative Support Team consists of representatives from Distribution Services, Corporate Purchasing, Facilities, Human Resources, as well as Administrative Support staff. Their main responsibility is to provide ongoing support to meet the needs of the Crisis Management Team and other teams if a recovery process has been initiated. They are to set up the alternative office strategy and provide all necessary forms for insurance and expense claims.

Key responsibilities include:

- Establishing the Emergency Control Centre (Command Centre) and ensuring that ongoing requirements of the Crisis Management Team are addressed
- Ensuring that key administrative support activities have been addressed (e.g., mail, couriers, etc.)
- Coordinating all internal disaster notification of technical and user personnel, including preliminary notification and ongoing status updates
- Procuring forms and supplies required for disaster recovery processing as detailed by the recovery teams and business units

### Damage Assessment Team

The Damage Assessment Team consists of representatives from business units. Depending on the physical location of the damage or disaster, these team members are best qualified to perform a preliminary assessment based on the usability of the premises and equipment. They are responsible for preliminary damage assessment activities to determine the extent of damage to the affected premises, and whether worker health and safety would be at risk in using all or part of the existing premises. This team should also be able to make a "first guess" on how long the site will have to remain uninhabited.

Key responsibilities include:

- Conducting a preliminary assessment of damage to the following entities:

    (i)    structures (e.g., buildings, rooms, offices, furniture),
    (ii)   environmental support equipment (e.g., air conditioning, chillers, power supply),
    (iii)  environmental protection and security equipment (e.g., access control devices, fire/smoke detectors, alarm systems),
    (iv)   computer hardware, software, data communication capability, and other specialized equipment.

- Estimating the usability and time to recover critical resources
- Reporting assessment and recommendations to the Crisis Management Team for evaluation and selection of the appropriate recovery and restoration action plan

### Recovery Coordination Team

The Recovery Coordination Team consists of those members of the company who are most familiar with the Disaster Recovery Plans, having assisted with the development and maintenance of them, and who are able to advise staff of their roles and responsibilities in a disaster recovery situation. Once a disaster has been declared, this group will access the plan and issue internal notifications, then ensure that steps in the plan are being followed.

Key responsibilities include:

- Coordinating all activities and communication between the technical areas and the user areas
- Coordinating the activities of the recovery teams and monitoring all planning, back-up, recovery, restoration/construction, and support department activities
- Conflict/resolution at time of disaster
- Assisting the Crisis Management Team with details of the plan or in formulating alternative actions if needed
- Timely updates of recovery plan progress, conflicts/issues that the recovery team cannot resolve
- Receipt and updating of disaster recovery logs from corporate team leaders

## Corporate Communications Team

The Corporate Communications Team consists of Marketing and Human Resources representatives who have had formal media training and are best suited to script and disseminate all media management, and all internal and external communications issues. They will act as a central dissemination point for all media management, external communications out to shareholders, stakeholders and the press, as well as monitoring/controlling corporate policy statement and status announcements to key customers, suppliers, employees and their families.

Key responsibilities include:

- Assisting Crisis Management Team in finalizing Corporate communications strategy
- Initial public/shareholder/stakeholder/market communication
- Key customer contact notification
- Executing competitor response if required
- Activation of internal call trees
- Set-up of internal status notification process

## Human Resources Support Team

The Human Resources Support Team consists of representatives from Human Resources and Legal Counsel who are trained, knowledgeable and have approval authority for dealing with employee insurance claims, payroll continuance, and coordination of temporary staff requirements. This team provides support and direction of employee/family trauma counselling, sick leave claims, payroll at times of crisis, personal injury and loss claims, extended family care and day care, shiftwork for employees, coordination of temporary staff requirements and family enquiries.

Key responsibilities include:

- Dealing with all employee-related issues on a timely basis
- Scheduling personnel during recovery activities
- Acquiring additional temporary staff as defined by authorized team leaders/ resources
- Activating family care centre plans
- Dealing with situations as they arise
- Coordinating with Corporate insurance and/or legal representatives

## Site Restoration Team

The Site Restoration Team consists of representatives from Facilities and Purchasing, as well as representatives from Physical Security. Some of the members on this team may be carried over from the initial Damage Assessment Team. This team in fact, follows the Damage Assessment Team to ascertain whether salvage operations are possible, and to coordinate efforts to return business units and/or technology groups/operations to the primary or alternative permanent site.

Key responsibilities include:

- Conducting a comprehensive assessment of damage to structure(s), environmental support equipment, and supplies that results from a disaster
- Coordinating salvage efforts related to structure(s), environmental support equipment and supplies
- Providing comprehensive damage assessment information to the Crisis Management Team to support longer term recovery/restoration strategies
- Upon direction of the Crisis Management Team, obtaining new facilities (temporary or permanent) in the event the primary facility is beyond repair
- Coordinating the repair/replacement of environmental equipment, security devices, alarm systems, furniture, etc.
- Ensuring security at damaged facility and at alternative processing facilities
- Working with technology recovery teams to ensure proper environmentals and power are in place to accommodate incoming replacement equipment

## Transportation Support Team

The Transportation Support Team coordinates travel arrangements/accommodation for personnel as well as for delivery of equipment and supplies, as well as printouts where necessary, at the alternative site. This group will also facilitate the delivery of meals to the alternative site if necessary.

Key responsibilities include:

- Coordinating travel arrangements for all personnel, including activating corporate accounts with several taxi companies, bus rentals, etc., if necessary
- Coordinating with Customs Brokers (if necessary)
- Coordinating arrangements for delivery of equipment, computer tapes, supplies, and communicating modified instructions to suppliers
- Coordinating meals for personnel
- Accepting travel requests from the Crisis Management Team and all team leaders

## Legacy System Restoration Team

This team is primarily responsible for re-establishing key information resource systems operations. The steps to initially condition the hardware will largely be done by a hot-site provider. All subsequent tasks related to the installation of the operating system, the database and application programs along with the establishment of the point of restart, will be done by this group. Members of this team will also assess the damage and coordinate any salvage effort, as well as complete insurance forms and provide equipment specifications to the vendor.

Key responsibilities include:

- Assisting in the recovery and maintenance of operating system software, application software, and databases at the alternative processing site(s)
- Establishing and monitoring production operations at the alternative site(s) and the restored/reconstructed primary site
- Coordinating salvage efforts related to computer hardware
- Coordinating the acquisition, delivery, installation, testing, and turnover of the equipment at any alternative processing site(s) and the primary data centre

## Voice Recovery Team and End-user Technical Support Team

These two sets of responsibilities are often combined into one team. The End-user Technical Support component of this team is responsible for the restoration of all data communications such as modems and routers for external communication. It is also the responsibility of this team to recover the network operating system(s), applications, and configuration of desktop computers and network servers.

The Voice Recovery component of this team is responsible for the re-establishment of all telephone services; these would include the redirection of call centre calls, recorded messages on major advertised numbers where necessary, workstations for the processing teams, and providing all technical support for them. All tasks related to voice communications, from cabling and equipment installation, to ensuring the proper functioning of telephone services through testing and monitoring, are performed by this group.

Key responsibilities include:

- Activation of interim voice message intercept and assistance in starting up the call centre, if necessary
- Assisting in the recovery and maintenance of network operating system software, application software, and databases at the alternative processing site(s)
- Establishing and monitoring network processing operations at the alternative site(s) and the restored/reconstructed primary site
- Coordinating salvage efforts related to telephony, PC, and data communication equipment
- Coordinating the acquisition, delivery, installation, testing, and turnover of the telephony, PC and data communication equipment at the alternative site(s) and the primary site

## On-going support from upper management

As the business continuity planning project winds down, the corporate business continuity processes take over. Part of the changes in corporate culture will include ongoing support from management in continuing to build and reinforce employee awareness and training, and actively participating in recovery simulations, exercises and tests through their corporate recovery support teams. In addition to ensuring that all members of the various corporate teams understand their roles and responsibilities during disaster recovery, it is critical that key back-up personnel be trained as well as secondary back-up personnel to cover off-staff availability (for whatever reason) during a disaster and general staff turnover as time passes.

## Employee BCP awareness

The Human Resources/Personnel/Training Departments of an organization must play key roles in installing appropriate training programmes for employees of an organization. Initial awareness workshops or seminars should be incorporated into part of all new hire and employee transfer processes as well as assisting with the ongoing maintenance of up-to-date employee notification lists.

# Risk evaluation and control:I

## Alan Craig—Thailand

**9**

Alan is Managing Director of Survive!'s operations throughout South-East Asia and brings to the book a wealth of experience in risk management and business continuity gained through active senior management and executive roles in this dynamic region.

> "It was the best of times; it was the worst of times"
> (Risk Management—a 1990s perspective from Asia)

## Introduction

Charles Dickens's memorable opening lines from *A Tale of Two Cities* epitomize the economic fluctuations in the Asia of the 1990s. The full quotation gives even greater insight and emphasis to the phenomenon of the soaring of those high-growth economies followed by the hardest of landings:

> It was the best of times, it was the worst of times; it was the age of wisdom, it was the age of foolishness; it was the epoch of belief, it was the epoch of incredulity; it was the season of Light, it was the season of Darkness; it was the spring of hope, it was the winter of despair; we had everything before us, we had nothing before us; we were all going directly to Heaven, we were all going the other way. (Charles Dickens, *A Tale of Two Cities*)

Other than perhaps the insulated and somewhat politically isolated country of Myanmar (Burma), countries within Asia have been deeply touched by a turn-around in economic fortunes that devastated both the macroeconomy and business performance alike. Currencies fell dramatically and in many cases verged on collapse. Non-performing loans in the banking sector reached staggering proportions of total business. Loans denominated in overseas currencies caused many businesses and state-owned enterprises to haemorrhage cash to meet interest and repayment burdens (much of the debt ultimately being rescheduled or

*The Definitive Handbook of Business Continuity Management.* Edited by Andrew Hiles and Peter Barnes. © 1999 Alan Craig.

even cancelled). Dependence on support from the IMF became commonplace, thereby placing further strains on the international support system itself. Consequent upon the economic crises, political and social upheavals placed further strains on both government and business revenue and costs. Finally, the effect of the Asian "bust" reached out to touch the world, with few economies avoiding some negative effect.

The management discipline and the business processes represented within the concept of Risk Management have been less widely practised in Asian economies and businesses than might be expected, given the volume of inward investments from countries in which Risk Management is a discipline not only seen as worthy but often enshrined in law or regulation. It will be useful to look at the reasons why, within the context of both local and foreign investment and business operations.

## Is there a single Asian perspective?

Asia is the most populated and arguably the most highly differentiated region in the world. Look at the billion plus populations of India and China, and the other densely populated countries of Japan, Indonesia and Korea, for example. Consider also the sheer size of and differences within the landmass and the myriad island communities that constitute the geography of Asia. Compare the relative sophistication of the Japanese, Singapore and Hong Kong economies to many of the others. Religion, culture, language, politics, economics and even geography—the wide variety would ordinarily dispel any idea of a homogeneous region. However, the economic crises of the late 1990s have certainly emphasized what common aspects do exist among Asian nations, especially the "Tiger Economies".

In the context of this work, the term "Asia" is intended to refer to those sub-regions and countries that comprise the geopolitical zones of South Asia (India, Pakistan, etc.), South-East Asia (Thailand, Philippines, etc.) and Far or North-East Asia (China, Japan, etc.).

## The principles of the management of risk

Risk Evaluation and Control are the fundamental components of risk management, which concerns itself with the prevention or the minimization of loss. In the wider context, Risk Management can be seen as comprising the following.

## Risk assessment

The identification, analysis and evaluation of risks to the business. Risk assessment allows businesses to formulate strategies that will allow them to manage risks in an economic manner, within the resources available. The main risks are to the critical and other assets of the business. These assets can be human, physical, cash or income based; and intellectual, such as company reputation or a brand name.

Due to the very powerful effect that economic and financial risks could have on businesses wherever they are based, there are standard methods and instruments available to managers to identify, evaluate and offset such risks. Exposure to foreign currency loans is a major example. It is a relatively simple matter (and within the experience set even of middle-managers) to calculate the impact on the "bottom line" if currency rates were to fluctuate. That a currency has not fluctuated before is no reason to assume that it will not fluctuate in the future. This was one simple and fundamental point missed or ignored by companies in Asia, both local and multinational. If business plans look five years or more out, then so must your risk assessment.

There are other risks that must be identified and the potential impact explored. The very real political and social risks that exist, for example. However, apart from these very high level and country-wide risks—and as part of the standard approach to business operations, organizations must analyse a broad range of risks and their implied impacts. Fires, terrorism, access denial, industrial action, natural disasters—in fact, the whole range of potential interruptions to business operations must be assessed. Often the potential impact may have to be calculated as more severe due to the lack of infrastructure available in the overseas country to avoid or overcome a risk, such as fire.

The problem is that just as companies were ill-prepared for the economic crises that beset Asia in the late 1990s, the chances are that they are just as badly prepared to face other risks and interruptions. Business Continuity Planning—if it exists at all—is often a document in a binder sent out from Head Office, reflecting Head Office requirements and culture and its success as a Business Continuity tool may even depend on a Head Office infrastructure! So, in general—throughout Asia—there is a lack of formal processes where such risks to the business are recorded and assessed. This will mean that the management of the risk will become difficult at best.

## Risk financing or risk transfer

Making provision for the financial consequences of loss. Insurance coverage has been the traditional vehicle for this but most companies operating to international standards of best practice now consider Business Continuity Planning (BCP) as a basic requirement also. Additionally, companies are looking to fresh ways of risk financing, such as Alternative Risk Transfer.

Insurance will remain for a long time as the tool of choice for businesses that need to cover the cost of lost or damaged assets and lost business revenues, for example. In most situations, some form of insurance is compulsory. But insurance has its limitations. Not all business losses will be covered—e.g. loss of market share—and there may be delays in obtaining payment, while the losses are investigated.

The investment in a sound, professional Business Continuity Plan can pay an excellent dividend for a company. Just as Risk Management concerns itself with the avoidance or minimization of loss, a BCP is one of the most effective tools to achieve this, by providing the methods and tools whereby a business can protect itself and then quickly recover if a problem should occur.

Thus a company—especially one operating in an unfamiliar geopolitical environment—should look carefully at using some investment or recycled profits to protect its business on a long-term basis. Insurance must be taken out but structured Business Continuity Planning must also be undertaken and implemented.

## Risk or loss control

Loss prevention and loss minimization. Again, the BCP is the essential tool for risk control, with respect to both the safeguarding of assets and business revenues. Many of the methods and techniques of loss prevention and loss minimization will be articulated in the Plan, which will include sections covering (for example): fire prevention, detection and fighting; how to salvage assets; planning for and the selection of alternative sites where your business operations can be quickly re-covered; restoring normal business operations.

A key concept is that of the alternative site. Many risks if experienced will lead to the loss of access to the place of business, whether on a long- (e.g. a major fire) or short-term (e.g. access denial) basis. Insurance may cover some of the costs and missed income associated with the associated disruption but such recompense is unlikely to maintain your business operations if you are denied access to your place of work for more than a few days. It is vital for most businesses that an alternative site of some kind is planned and organized before risk and loss occur.

## Risk monitoring

Are risk financing and risk control cost-effective? Also, are all known risks still being considered or covered? One of the problems about insurance as the main, or only, method of Risk Management, is that, for the multinational company at any rate, the insurance is most often arranged on a global policy basis through Head Office. Thus the need for the regular discipline of re-evaluating risks over time—perhaps the general business or economic environment changes or there has been a significant internal change, such as a merger—is not required for the business manager operating in the overseas company. However, the regular review of the risks, the potential losses plus planning and remediation techniques, should be a fundamental part of management activity. It is not just an insurance issue. It is an issue about the continuation of the business even after a serious interruption.

We have seen that risk assessment should include potential loss-making situations such as loss or damage to property and physical assets; cash and income streams; reputation, brand name and image. The first priority, above all, is the protection of people. The monitoring of some of these key aspects of business operations and development on an insured basis only, may well miss some of the other risks and threats that might manifest themselves.

The methodology of maintaining, updating and testing Business Continuity Plans will help ensure that all potential risks and losses are identified and updated, on an ongoing basis.

# Risk Management in Asia

For most companies based in Asia—whether local or multinational—the questions of risk, its management and the reality of major losses have become overwhelming, forcing many organizations to make sweeping changes to the shape of their operations. Managers have been compelled to identify and manage political, social, economic, financial and business risks all at the same time: a skill set complex enough for managers to acquire; and both time- and resource-consuming to perform in a competitive business environment. This applies to both local and multinational company managers although the multinational usually has the resources of Head Office to call on for specific areas of risk management, especially financial risk. In fact, Head Office Treasury functions will often assume control of some aspects of financial risk best managed from the core, where currency consolidation techniques can reduce the overall exposure.

Some of the reasons for the "boom to bust" scenario of most Asian economies demonstrate the need for, but a lack of, application of classic Risk Management concepts. There are several reasons as to why this should be but the situation is summarized by Chris Panes, Managing Director of Cunningham International of Thailand, a major regional loss-adjusting company:

> Risk Management has certainly not been a priority during the rapid growth of Asian economies. The focus has very much been on business growth with little or no attention given to risk evaluation and control.

> This situation has been exacerbated by a relative lack of Statutory Regulations addressing fundamental issues such as occupational health and safety and an absence of Agencies—with authority—to enforce what regulations do exist.

Nigel Smith, Director and General Manager of Royal and SunAlliance, underscores this view: "Broadly speaking, risk evaluation and control in the region is a management discipline whose time has yet to come."

On the other hand, in many ways it is not surprising that such economic problems existed, problems that highlight the lack of application of Risk Management and other disciplines, as Chris Panes pointed out earlier.

Spectacular economic growth started in the mid to late 1980s, depending on the country. Prior to that period, there were few signs of non-agrarian economic development and the working populations were still mostly involved in farming or small community-based industry. There was no business management culture to speak of, even less management training. Economic growth quickly fuelled a rapidly increasing need for resource, at all levels of the organization. Employment grew like crazy, and universities and technical colleges expanded quickly. Getting a job often depended only on just being available, existing skills or experience were not required (they were not readily available anyway!) and would be taught in-house. Few, neither managers nor staff, understood or had even heard about such concepts as recession, economic crisis, downsizing and the like. A whole employment culture had grown up solely in boom times and there were no background skills or experience in-country to manage the major risks that were growing darkly in the background. Even some seasoned multinational managers—having moved around the world from growth region to growth region—had little experience of the severity of an economic crisis or of risk management techniques.

Those agencies that did have in-depth knowledge and experience about the potential weight of such problems looming—bodies such as foreign governments, aid agencies, multinational head offices and banks—unfortunately did not place sufficient emphasis in applying the risk management disciplines they would normally apply elsewhere. The sweeping enthusiasm for growth, for high returns with low (even seemingly non-existent) risks—these factors helped set aside the prudence and due diligence that the situations required. Where wise counsel was indeed given, the short-term and almost rollercoaster effect overwhelmed the argument.

## Risks of and from natural disasters

Asian nations and their island counterparts who share borders with the Pacific Ocean suffer more than their fair share of natural disasters, for many reasons. In the 1990s there have been many natural disasters: major examples include earth-quakes (Japan), volcanic eruptions (Philippines), tsunami (Papua New Guinea), floods (China). Even the smoke haze that affected Indonesia, Singapore and Malaysia so severely in 1997 and 1998 can be regarded partly as a "natural disaster"—although the hands that lit the forest fires were very human indeed.

The effect of such natural disasters is broadly three-fold. Firstly, the loss of human life is often very substantial and leads to widespread tragic consequences for families deprived of their loved ones. In a business context, such disasters quite clearly have the potential to become major business interruptions. From an economic perspective, natural disasters usually mean that the already beleaguered resources of the nation involved are stretched even more thinly to cope with the disaster and its outcomes—both economic and human. One set of almost inevitable outcomes is that capital projects are cancelled or delayed and business expansion plans are also set back. However, in comparison to the tragedy of the loss of human life, such matters come a poor second.

There is no doubt that the managers of companies based in Asia have to implement Risk Management and Business Continuity principles vigorously in order to obviate the threat from natural disasters.

## Year 2000—another major regional headache?

As the whole world prepares for Year 2000, the question must be asked in what way the Y2K phenomenon will affect Asia and to what extent. There seems to be little doubt that Asian governments, state-owned enterprises and companies in general are lagging behind their North American or European counterparts, with respect to Year 2000 issues. This situation covers the risk assessment aspect of Y2K plus the skills and resources available for both the preparedness and the remediation aspects of Y2K.

There are additional complexities: many Asian governments feel "cheated by the West" because they have purchased software with sparse foreign exchange funds and now have to spend more to make the software fit for its purpose. This is a very strong perception in certain government and local business circles. Also, there is a general lack of skills to both perceive and quantify the potential scale of the Y2K problems or to do anything about them. Tackling Y2K problems would mean hiring "expensive foreign resource" using foreign currencies that are already in seriously short supply.

One possibly important Y2K risk management aspect of doing business in Asia is that in many countries, the extent of computerization is still relatively low. For many government Departments and for businesses, the threat of Y2K to the continuation of their operations is not as great as it might be where fully computerized systems dominate the day-to-day operation of the business. Manual procedures are still very much a major part of working life in many Asian countries, with computers used frequently only as a convenient way to store and retrieve information that is on hand anyway in hard copy format. However, this does not apply to advanced multinational companies, sophisticated industry sectors (such as telecommunications) or more developed regional economies, such as Japan or Singapore. Companies must still make a full and detailed analysis of all YEAR 2000 issues, including those involving leap-year assessments.

# Summary

Risks of doing business can be greater in Asia than elsewhere, because of major risks associated with natural and other disasters. In addition, most of the staff in companies, governments and state-owned enterprises in Asia have never been taught about, or experienced before, the range of economic, financial, business and other risks that can affect their businesses and their lives so fundamentally. Regrettably, YEAR 2000 may become a problem that appears just too quickly after the last crisis.

On the upside, doing business in Asia can be a real pleasure. Profits can be generated on a very long-term basis for the firm that is both prudent and aggressive in its plans. However, part of such profits should be reinvested in the business to support the Risk Management and Business Continuity Planning infrastructure that has been so sadly absent in the past. A relative lack of computerization will help overcome the YEAR 2000 issues while offering opportunities for productivity increases.

The lesson of the lack of prudent risk management will ultimately be one painfully learned for many in the region. However, Asian business managers and the working population will quickly come to terms with the risks of actually doing business—and as the universities and other learning institutions start to promote training and awareness opportunities about Risk Management and Business Continuity. Such pain and the need to learn quickly are not unknown concepts within many Asian countries. Therefore, it is possible to state with some confidence that the professional management of Business Risks will be a basic component of doing business in Asia within a very short period of time.

# Risk evaluation and control:II Practical guidelines for risk assessment

## Ian Charters—UK

**9**

Ian is consultant with Continuity Systems Ltd in the UK.

## Introduction

We spend most of our lives making risk decisions and becoming so adept at it that we rarely analyse how we came to a decision. For example, deciding what time to leave for work will involve many implicit decisions about the chances of delay at various points, applied experience of past journeys and an assessment of the consequences of being late. It is just as well that we do make these decisions intuitively otherwise we would spend all the time trying to assess the risks and never setting off.

However, when we are charged with evaluating risks to our business we must be more explicit in assessment, both because we will need to convince others to take action through our reasoning and because the consequences of getting it wrong may be more serious for ourselves and our colleagues.

There are some fundamental problems when you assess business risks:

- You are responsible to others for managing these risks yet the factors that can affect them are numerous and few may be directly under your control
- Statistics on catastrophic events are difficult to apply to a single location and type of business
- We rarely let unlikely events affect our decisions—yet these could have a disastrous effect on our business

Risk control in many businesses consists of a kneejerk reaction to near misses and press scare stories. This chapter offers some techniques and strategies to assess risk in a more systematic fashion.

---

*The Definitive Handbook of Business Continuity Management.* Edited by Andrew Hiles and Peter Barnes. © 1999 John Wiley & Sons Ltd.

# Objective of risk evaluation and control

The Business Continuity Institute states that the objective of risk evaluation and control, within the context of business continuity management, is:

> To determine the events that can adversely affect an organization, the damage that such events can cause, the timescale needed to restore normal operations and the controls that can be implemented to reduce the probability of impact.

Five stages are identified in reaching this objective:

- Understand the Loss Potentials and Vulnerability to such Losses
- Evaluate Risk Analysis Tools and Techniques
- Define a Risk Evaluation Strategy
- Select a Process to Evaluate Risk
- Establish Risk Avoidance Measures to Prevent or Minimize the Effect

## Threats and vulnerabilities

Some of the many threats to which a business is exposed are fire, flood, power failure, air conditioning failure, lightning strike, industrial action, terrorist activity, malicious damage, contamination, legal action, fraud, theft, software virus, Legionnaires' Disease. . . .

The specific nature of the threat could be one of an almost infinite list of potential causes and may come from the most unexpected source.

Consider perils:

- From natural and man-made sources
- Having accidental or intentional causes
- That are internal or external to the organization
- Causing material damage, financial loss or damage to reputation
- Resulting from a combination of unlikely circumstances

## Assessing the risk

How do we assess the probability of being struck by a disaster as a consequence of an almost infinite list of threats? There are many surveys and lists but the majority focus on a particular region or industry and will be of little direct relevance to the international readership of this book. You should therefore seek advice from your insurers, local trade associations or business continuity user forums to assess the likelihood of specific threats in your particular location.

The following points illustrate the difficulty of assessing specific threats:

- Certain perils are more prevalent in certain geographic/climatic regions—e.g. tornadoes are more likely in the southern states of the USA but even in the UK we occasionally experience severe storms
- Earthquakes can occur in any part of the world though they are concentrated on tectonic plate boundaries. Their effects can be felt thousands of miles away—Hawaii was struck by a tsunami caused by an earthquake in Japan.
- Prevalence in the news would lead you to believe that the risk of terrorism in the City of London outweighs the risk of fire. However, statistics show this is not the case
- Most computer software failures are caused by inexperienced users—they are rarely intentional
- Employees know how to hit a company—Ernst & Young found 84% of the worst frauds were perpetrated by company employees
- Most computer fires start outside computer rooms
- Air conditioning can duct toxic chemicals way beyond their source
- Floods can occur at almost any height—most high-rise blocks have large water storage facilities on their upper floors
- Police Forces in many parts of the world have considerable powers to declare an area a "scene of crime" which enables them to deny access and may also prompt a media invasion which can raise security and reputation issues
- Security companies market their products on saleability and profitability, not on a balanced assessment of the individual company's risk profile. Many of the most crucial security issues cannot be solved by a purchase but are best addressed through staff training, awareness and job satisfaction.

## Why undertake risk analysis?

There are no laws in the UK that require institutions to have off-site Disaster Recovery by name but there are a number of other directives that can be interpreted as a requirement. For example, in the UK financial markets the Bank of England is responsible for Banking regulations in the UK. The **Blue Book** (*Security and Control in Computer and Telecommunications Systems*) published in 1985 as a guide for licensed Deposit Takers and Banks advises:

> Banks must protect their computer resources effectively against physical threats and have adequate recovery procedures or standby arrangements in place and levied to call on when events occur which cause systems to fail.

The **Banking Supervision Division**—BSD/1987/2, published in 1987, provides guidance on the Bank of England's interpretation of the Banking Act. The section entitled "Controls in a Computer Environment" was revised in July 1992 under the new heading of "Controls in an Information Technology Environment" and includes the following key phrases:

> Particular consideration should be given to . . .
> Business interruption planning, which should address the way in which business critical electronic systems are to be maintained in the event of fire, flood, power failure or other physical damage. It might also be appropriate to consider the provision of other resources, e.g. staff accommodation, in order to take a wider business perspective. Plans should be agreed, documented and regularly tested.

The Financial Services Act 1986 set up a self-regulatory structure to administer non-banking financial markets in the UK under the umbrella of the Securities & Investment Board (SIB).

The **Act** itself allows member institutions to claim *force majeure* (very loosely translated as Act of God) if, and only if, they can clearly demonstrate that the cause of failure was beyond their control and that all reasonable efforts were made to alleviate the effect of failure.

In other words, a securities firm must have examined the effect of disruption to dealing and either have taken all adequate measures to minimize such disruption or be able to show that failure would not materially affect the business. Alternatively, the institution needs to demonstrate that it was beyond its powers to make back-up arrangements. Given the existence of commercial DR services, this is becoming ever more difficult to prove.

There are, as yet, in the UK no other statutory requirements for risk analysis. However there are other pressures that encourage organizations to practise risk evaluation and control.

- Quality standards required of suppliers by their major customers
- The desire of businesses to adopt best practice
- Companies seeking BS7799 certification
- Personal liability of directors shown to have been negligent (by not controlling risks)
- Appreciation of the cost to business of disasters and near-misses

The last point should be the most effective spur for businesses to manage risks. In a competitive environment the loss of reputation or a major customer could be business-threatening.

## Risk evaluation

A structured approach to risk evaluation involves four steps:

1. Asset and threat identification.
2. Quantification of potential losses.
3. Assessment of vulnerabilities.
4. Evaluation of solutions.

Some pointers to the scope of these steps follow.

1. **Asset and threat identification**
   Assets:

   (i)    list and categorize your corporate assets,
   (ii)   consider both tangible, intangible (e.g. reputation) and transient (e.g. technological lead) assets;
   (iii)  ensure you have identified all of them.

   Look at areas of risk:

   (i)    policies and procedures,
   (ii)   manufacturing processes,
   (iii)  physical access security,
   (iv)   personnel issues—recruitment, induction and discipline,
   (v)    computer systems and networks,
   (vi)   communications,
   (vii)  marketing and customer interface.

   Assess the risks identified:

   (i)    through interviews and observations
   (ii)   through structured walk-throughs and "what-if" scenarios,
   (iii)  then relate these back to your key assets.

2. **Quantify your potential losses**

   (i)    use company accounts,
   (ii)   let marketing assess the cost of finding new customers or restoring a tarnished reputation,
   (iii)  explore the effects on stock market valuation,
   (iv)   look at recent events in your company and others in your sector,
   (v)    seek outside opinions from insurers, lawyers and consultants.

3. **Assessment of vulnerabilities**

   (i)    use appropriate historical data,
   (ii)   apply formulae commonly used in your industry,
   (iii)  make subjective estimates,
   (iv)   agree and apply a risk weighting system (there are many of these which you can adapt or develop your own),

(v)     conduct simulation or scenario analysis
(vi)     . . . then calculate:

**RISK = IMPACT × PROBABILITY**

which should enable you to rank risks from the most serious to the most trivial in terms of their overall impact on the business.

4.  **Evaluation of solutions**

    Risk control measures fall into one of four categories:

    Accept, Manage, Reduce, Plan

    The types of risk to which each is an appropriate reaction are shown in the following table.

| Probability \ Impact | LOW | HIGH |
|---|---|---|
| HIGH | Manage | Reduce |
| LOW | Accept | BC Plan |

(i)     Accept the risk—if the impact of a rare event is low it may be reasonable to accept the risk, such as the occasional theft of company property which is unlikely to jeopardize the business. Some risks fall outside your control, such as government policy, and so must be accepted by default.

(ii)    Manage the risk—for frequent low impact risks the most sensible strategy is to monitor and seek to reduce the risk. An example is the development of procedures to reduce operator error.

(iii)   Reduce the risk—a frequent potentially damaging event is a target for risk reduction measures. The hazardous procedure should be re-engineered or carefully monitored to reduce risk. An example in manufacturing could be changing from solvent-based to water-based paints. Alternatively you might outsource the risk—giving it to someone else better equipped to manage it. Insurance can be viewed as an example of outsourced risk.

(iv)    Business Continuity Planning addresses risks which are of low probability, such as fire and flood, but whose potential impact is business failure.

It is unlikely that you can remove all risk entirely—any enterprise must involve risk almost by definition. However, by concentrating on their core business many enterprises fall victim to damaging impacts from risks which they had not identified or sought to control.

## Is Risk Control worth doing?

A Risk Control programme is not a substitute for a Business Continuity Plan. This is because there are serious weaknesses in the various risk analysis methods. They were developed to address wide portfolios of risk, to analyse accidents after the event or to apply quantifiable failure rates in simple engineering systems. When applied to a complex organization at a single location at a particular time they fail because:

- The probability of occurrence for rare events is always a guess
- Mathematical analyses methods may give a pseudo-scientific exactitude to the results which are only based on guesswork
- The least expected can happen—and it is no comfort or assistance to the business that it failed due to a rare event
- Many disasters happen due to a complex sequence of circumstances which cannot be modelled in advance
- The reduction of one risk may increase another—a retaining wall can prevent a flood but it can also cause a flood if there is a water leak within the building. Outsourcing risks in particular tends to create other, less obvious, risks elsewhere in the organization
- The analysis of risk is a means to an end not an end in itself—without action it is pointless.

However, Risk Control plays an important part in Business Continuity Planning because:

- There is a statutory need for controlling specific risks—especially in the chemicals and financial sectors
- The control of obvious risks raises awareness and can prevent disasters
- A risk analysis can support the business case for Business Continuity at a Board presentation

## To finish . . . some ideas to make a success of Risk Control

- Many problems happen because "everyone thought that someone else would do it" so make named individuals responsible for each specific risk
- Make measures appropriate and realistic

- Use external help from outside (much of it free), from brokers, consultants, fire officers and the police
- Involve everyone in the evaluation process—education and raising awareness are as important as implementing procedures.

# Business Impact Analysis

## William J. Meredith—UK

Bill is Chairman of the Advisory Board of the Business Continuity Institute and the Continuum Forum.

"What is a Business Impact Analysis?"

"Well, it's part of the process used in a Disaster Recovery Plan."

"What part is that?"

"I think it's the phase that comes after Risk Analysis."

"I see, but what does it do?"

"I think it provides an analysis of the impact on the business."

"What sort of impact?"

"Any sort of impact I suppose."

It is frightening to think that conversations like the above actually take place but they do! Even some of the more enlightened individuals in our business do not fully understand the purpose or the importance of a Business Impact Analysis (BIA). Consultants even sell a BIA module without knowing how important it is or how useful it can be.

The following is a personal explanation of what Meredith Solutions uses a Business Impact Analysis for and why it is so important. Let's start again at the beginning with the original question. "What is a Business Impact Analysis" and why is it so important to your company in the quest to build a Business Continuity Management (BCM) plan for your business?

The Business Impact Analysis is the backbone of the entire business continuity exercise, or at least it should be if it is handled correctly. Even so, it cannot stand alone and you should not let anyone persuade you otherwise. It has to co-exist with the "awareness programme" which is always the first stage of the BCM programme. It is necessary to make the highest level of management aware of the need for BCM and for them to understand that without their approval, backing and direction, the exercise will not achieve its full potential.

*The Definitive Handbook of Business Continuity Management.* Edited by Andrew Hiles and Peter Barnes. © 1999 John Wiley & Sons Ltd.

Angela Robinson, FBCI, in *Continuity*, **1**(2), under the heading "The business case", emphasized "the need to approach the highest level executive within the organization to gain approval to proceed with the business continuity planning project". She went on to remind us of "the need for planning across the whole organization, or at least across a self-contained business unit".

I fully concur with Angela's comments and would expand them only by saying awareness must be raised from the chief executive right down to the shop floor or office. The senior management must be aware of the need for Business Continuity Management and give the exercise the direction and leadership it deserves. An organization I worked with recently gave equal credence to Year 2000, the Euro and Business Continuity Management even though, with all the work involved in the first two programmes, it would be far simpler to leave the latter until after the millennium.

The Planning Team or Steering Committee need to be aware of the importance of BCM so that they understand their responsibilities and take full ownership of the programme. Similarly the people who are to be actively involved in the BIA module have to fully understand the extent and purpose of the analysis, where it fits into the whole BCM exercise and what the results of their due diligence will produce. They should be actively encouraged to pass the word to their colleagues and subordinates, about the importance of BCM and how the resultant organization, together with appropriate contingency plans and procedures, will protect their very own livelihoods.

I said earlier that a BIA cannot stand alone and I think I have said enough about preparing the ground (awareness). I also firmly believe that Risk Analysis follows naturally on from a BIA although it is not absolutely essential.

My recommendation however, is that Business Continuity Awareness fronts the exercise, Business Impact Analysis comes next with Risk Analysis following on closely behind. In fact I propose all three to my clients as the first module in a Business Continuity Management Programme. Some learned individuals in our business will recommend that Risk Analysis comes before a BIA but I strongly disagree and I will explain why as we proceed.

As Angela Robinson says "get a clear definition of the project first of all" which brings us neatly back to where we began. What is the BIA being carried out for? What are the terms of reference (TOR) and what are the specific requirements of the Project Sponsor? The real point is that the BIA exercise can be adjusted to cover additional ground or be slanted towards a particular aspect of the BCM programme. Therefore we need to understand if this is the first BIA ever conducted in the organization and if it will be used as the very blueprint for the eventual contingency plans. Is it simply a refresher exercise to check the validity of existing arrangements? Is it to question the appropriateness of existing arrangements and perhaps prompt a complete change to current contingency policy, that is self-provision to third party provider or a shared responsibility?

The most important detail is to have agreed a signed terms of reference with the Project Sponsor who would usually hold a key role on the Planning or Steering Committee. Once the terms of reference are agreed the BIA can begin but remember to refer back to the TOR regularly because a one degree (1%) deviation on day one has a nasty habit of becoming a one hundred and eighty degree (180%) deviation after six months.

Having said the BIA can be adjusted to cover any specific client requirement, it does have a fundamental theme at its very core. This purpose is to identify the effect of many different external and internal impacts upon the various parts of your organization in times of crisis. These different impacts, which I will describe later, when analysed, will show us which parts of your organization will be most affected by an incident and what effect that will have upon the company as a whole. In other words, we will use the BIA to establish which are the most critical business functions to your company's survival. Each organization has thousands of operations in its overall business but only a percentage will be key to survival and it is these we need to build business continuity arrangements for. Of course we will not ignore the remainder, but because they are less important we can prepare recovery plans for them instead.

In our opening conversation we talked about Disaster Recovery and I would counsel you to discard those words once and for all. They are associated with failure, the need to recover from a disaster because of a lack of planning. In a Business Continuity Management Exercise when we have carried out our BIA and we know what is key to our Company, we are able to prepare our contingency plans accordingly. We may have "Hot" provision for the critical business functions, "Warm" for the next level of importance and a "Cold" provision for the rest. The point being that, even if we have decided to do nothing because the risk does not warrant the expenditure, **we are prepared** because **we are aware**. It will not be a disaster because we have considered the cause and effect and decided our policy accordingly as part of our Business Continuity Management Exercise.

Now I can explain why I believe Risk Management comes after the BIA. Surely it is better to consider the internal and external risks to our business when we know what the critical business functions are. We will have a much more focused investigation if we know beforehand which functions are the most important to us.

Let's get down to the BIA exercise itself and make the point, right at the start, that this is probably the one and only occasion when you will get to sit down with all the function heads in the organization. These are busy people so make sure you use the opportunity to the full. I prefer to adapt my BIA forms to reflect the exact terms of reference and to cover as wide a spectrum as I can. Furthermore, I always have these forms completed and analysed before I speak to the individuals concerned. Other practitioners I know complete the form during the interview but I consider this cuts down the actual discussion time. I find it difficult enough to cover all the ground I want to in an hour without having to complete the very considerable detail required in my BIA forms. I prefer to explain the forms carefully at the start of the exercise so that everyone knows what to expect and how to fill in the questionnaire. Then I am in a position to understand the participants' responses before the interview and have relevant questions available. I want to know, apart from anything else, what is key in their operation and what impact, financial or otherwise, an interruption will have on the business as a whole.

We can now begin to look at the programme of events in more detail.

## Introduction

It is necessary to speak to each member of the team who it is intended will be part of the BIA exercise. Effectively we are looking to interview line, product or function managers, who are the middle management of the firm. Those who understand the objectives of the company but also have a good understanding of the operations they are responsible for. Assemble the whole group together to discuss the BIA process but be sure to position it with regard to the rest of the BCM programme. Stress the need for BCM, continuation of the business, the requirements of regulators, shareholders, and so on, the effect of an unscheduled incident for which one is not prepared. However, do not dwell on the negatives but stress the positive—key business functions can continue whatever the event, client confidence is maintained, competitive advantage if others are affected too—but stress particularly the personal level of self-preservation and continued livelihood. Of course BCM is about the long-term preservation of the Company and its reputation, profitability and growth but it is also about the continued employment and development of its employees.

At this inaugural meeting of the BIA participants give out your draft forms which cover all aspects of the module, including any special aspects requested by the Project Sponsor, who definitely should be present. Explain to them that they have been selected to fulfil a very important role, that of identifying the critical business functions of the firm. Their returned forms and subsequent interviews will provide the blueprint for the eventual contingency arrangements that will protect the good reputation of the firm, enable continued profitability and make sure their and their colleagues' livelihoods are protected whatever crisis may beset the company.

Explain that the BIA forms are intended to provide all the detail required as far as you have been able to ascertain. However, the content is flexible and can be adjusted should any individual feel there are further aspects to explore and the Project Sponsor agrees. These are forms developed over several years but they often need adjusting for specific assignments. Explain each part of your set of forms and then ask them to consider their suitability in this particular exercise and let you have their comments over the next three days. The amended set of forms should be circulated within one week of the inaugural meeting, with a further week given for completion. It is important to keep this timespan short in order to avoid any loss of purpose instilled at the outset.

The BIA forms used by different practitioners vary widely and in fact, some use no forms at all. I believe they are an integral part of the module, particularly as they are completed and signed by each participant. There can be no confusion then about what detail was provided as is the possibility when only an interview takes place.

# BIA forms

I do not pretend to have a set of BIA forms that is a panacea for all requirements, and in fact they are developing all the time as part of a structured BCM methodology. All I can suggest is that you should include the following items and at least cover these issues during your interview. The level to which you drill down into the organisation's operations will also shape the format of your forms, i.e. will you stop at function level or delve deeper to examine the processes in these functions.

## Part 1. Impact section

Make sure that everyone is considering the impact to the business from the same level of severity. We have to overcome the problem where some managers will gloss over the impact, for example, "I will send my salesmen to work from the Paris office so the effect is minimal"! Similarly, we have to ensure everyone is working to the same timeframe otherwise some departments will assume normal working is possible after only a week.

I get around this problem by asking them all to assume the most serious incident which simply no one can trivialize. I use the example of an aircraft crashing into their building. This is unlikely to happen I know, but at least it means all the participants are starting from the same point of view. Their likely continuity and recovery criteria will be based on the same level of understanding.

Explain that your forms, and the associated interview, set out to achieve the following:

1. To understand what the operational and financial impacts and exposures are to THEIR PARTICULAR BUSINESS FUNCTION should a serious disruption occur.
2. To be able to define the critical business functions that must be able to continue, more or less uninterrupted, should an incident occur.
3. Similarly to define the priorities for the resumption of the remaining business activities.
4. Produce a blueprint of the requirements (personnel, equipment, services, etc.) to enable continuity and a phased recovery as appropriate.
5. Identify the present level of preparedness to deal with an incident should it occur.

6.  Highlight areas where operational practice can be improved to give greater operational resilience.

Make sure your audience understands how these forms will help to achieve the above objectives because:

1.  You will ask the respondents to categorize the severity of operational impacts on a scale of 1–5 over a timeframe from the day of the incident up to the end of a six-month period. Clearly some functions will need to be continuous but perhaps others could be left for up to six months to recover. Your category of impacts will vary for different organizations but should probably include some or all of the following from an operational stand point: Cash Flow, Public Image, Financial Reporting and Control, Client Service, Competitive Advantage, Industry Image, Legal and Contractual Violations, Regulatory Requirements, Third Party Relations and Employee Morale.
2.  Then you will turn specifically to the Financial Impacts and ask the respondents to attempt to put a developing cost figure for each category over the six-month period. Explain that these, when collated, will provide a picture of the likely financial impact to the company, if a serious incident occurred for which they were not prepared. It is not unrealistic for it to take a company six months to start operating again if their operation was completely destroyed and they had no contingency plans.

In the financial categories you should probably include some or all of the following: Inability to Complete Current or Outstanding Business, Loss of New Business, Loss of Existing Business, Cancellation of Existing Sales, Compensation Payments, Contractual Penalties/Fines, Availability of Operating Funds, Drop in Share Value, Lost Interest on Incoming Monies or Cost of Borrowing Expenses, Lost Productivity, Extraordinary Expenses, and so on. Clearly your categories will vary according to the business you are working in and the above is by no means a comprehensive list.

N.B. It is important to stress that you need details of all financial impacts even though they may be covered by insurance.

**Be sure to stress how important it is to respond to the questions only from their own department's viewpoint rather than that of the company as a whole, otherwise you will experience double counting.**

## Part 2. Impact profile

In the earlier sections we attempted to gain information on the Operational and Financial Impacts following an incident. Now we want to ascertain whether there are particular times when these impacts are more severe than others. For example, if a department shows it can lose £1m in a period of six months it is particularly relevant to know that the actual loss occurs only in the month of June and not at any other part of the year.

Probing into the impact profile provides us with the information we require to understand whether a company or department is more vulnerable at one time than at another. Your BIA forms, therefore, should cover Daily, Weekly, Monthly and Annual Impacts, again using a 1–5 categorization. The returns from the forms will allow you to understand the crucial times in the company's key procedures and allow you to build appropriate contingency plans accordingly.

## Part 3. Recovery

In this section we assume that the incident has occurred and facilities are available to recover. What we are aiming to ascertain is how long it will take the department to recover from the disruption given their current level of preparedness. There will be a backlog of work and we need to know how long it will take to get back up to date again, if indeed that is possible, or whether it is feasible that the department has to start from scratch.

The particular importance of this section is not only to understand how long it takes to catch up but also whether or not other functions or indeed the department's own work, can start afresh beforehand. Furthermore, it is not simply about the function itself but it also gives us an insight into the possible staffing requirements.

For example, consider a Premises Department. They could find themselves securing and salvaging at a damaged site, managing a contingency site, looking for an alternative site and preparing to repair the damaged site. It is very unlikely that the existing complement of staff could cope under these circumstances and this emphasizes the need for "additional cost of working" insurance to pay for the additional staff required.

## Part 4. Losses

In a major incident companies will lose all sorts of vital information and equipment. This section is an attempt to gain information about the significance of those losses.

In the industry I work in, the majority of loss revolves around the loss of information and my forms reflect that fact. I attempt to ascertain how long it would take departments to reconstruct that information if it were even possible. In other industries it may well be key equipment or processes which, if lost, would take time to replace and we need to know these facts in order to establish a pattern for continuity or recovery.

This is the first part of the BIA form that addresses the present level of preparedness and allows us to understand where we might suggest improvements to existing operational practice.

## Part 5. Work-arounds

Heading on directly from loss of information, equipment or processes is the section on work-arounds. Here again we are looking at the present level of preparedness. How far have the individuals concerned thought about what they would do if there was a serious interruption to their function?

For example, in Banking if we lost access to our computer systems we could not settle outstanding transactions, could we? Well, if we had copies of yesterday's computer printouts, yesterday's deal tickets and access to a phone, we could probably make a jolly good try! This example is oversimplified of course, but I hope it gives the general idea. Similarly, if you were working on a complex legal transaction it would make sense to go to your lawyers, who would undoubtedly have all the relevant papers anyway.

Once again we are also trying to ascertain how long it would take to put the work-arounds in place following an incident and how long the department could continue to function with them once they were in place. Furthermore we need to know whether these are simply ideas or practised and tested emergency procedures.

It is often useful to refer back to this section of the BIA forms when planning desktop exercises to test the practicality of individual department's contingency plans at a later stage in the BCM programme.

## Part 6. Computer access

Nearly every company now has access to computers in some form or another and they become more and more reliant upon them as each day passes. It does not really matter whether we are talking about access to mainframes, midrange or PC (networked or standalone). What we are trying to establish is how dependent they are upon them and how prepared they are to deal with a disruption to their availability. We trust in the case of mainframes and midrange that the IT department will have set the necessary level of contingency arrangements, security, access criteria and back-up programme. However, in the case of PCs certain functions are available, even on networked machines, which can cause a glitch in the company procedures.

We need to know what the back-up procedures are and whether this responsibility lies with IT or the individual. If the individual uses the local hard drive and floppy disks, what are their back-up arrangements and where is the resultant media stored? Once again this section is all about understanding the level of preparedness, the likely effect of an impact and the likely recovery time, if that is even feasible.

I make two recommendations. Firstly, I tell my participants **they** should decide how often their data are backed up and they should not leave it to IT to decide as they have no knowledge of its actual importance. Secondly, always interview IT last of all in the BIA exercise because by then you will have a pretty good idea what the overall situation is and what is important at departmental level, rather than what IT considers it to be!

## Part 7. Continuity and recovery requirements

By now we should have made each respondent aware of the Operational and Financial Impacts caused by an interruption to their functions, when it would have most effect, how long recovery might take, what losses would be suffered and how prepared they are for such an event. What better time than to ask them to consider what they require to continue the key business functions and recover the remainder? We need to understand what they currently have in place to carry out their operations and what they will require from the time of the incident through to normal operations again.

I use a varying timescale showing requirements immediately after the incident (1 day, 2 days, 3 days, 4 days and a week) and then less frequently (1 week, 2 weeks, 3 weeks, 1 month) and finally three months and six months. This gives the opportunity for the respondents to show their requirements in the first few days for the continuity of essential functions, then as they bring the next most important aspects of the operation back into being, and then finally the slower recovery of the less important aspects.

We will need to know how many people are required, what equipment they will need, what software is necessary, what computer printouts will be needed, what critical business records, what raw materials and external services, what data and information, and so on. In fact we are aiming to provide a blueprint for the overall requirements needed to continue the company's key business functions and recover the remainder in a phased but controlled manner.

There is a tendency today, particularly in the Financial Sector, to provide a three-stage contingency arrangement. First are "Hot" facilities which are immediately accessible with mirrored systems and applications for those critical business functions which cannot afford to experience an interruption. This facility usually covers the requirements from the day of the incident through to the end of the first week. Next, a "Warm" facility, often occupied by staff who do not have to be in the main business offices, equipped with the requirements for the recovery of functions that must be operational again within one month. In a crisis the normal residents will be moved elsewhere and the systems realigned to cope with the requirements of the new incoming operatives. (The key critical functions are protected by the "Hot" facility and we have up to a week to make the "Warm" facilities operational.) A "Cold" facility or service will be available to cope with operations that can wait for longer than a month before recovery is necessary. This may involve empty space with simply the required infrastructure in place and the equipment will either be purchased in the preceding month or be on contract delivery from a Disaster Recovery Firm. The important point, however, is that they are only able to be this precise about their requirements because a BIA has identified what processes are key to their business and the departmental management has specified their continuity/recovery requirements.

## Part 8. Dependencies

There is also a need in a BIA to understand the relationship between departments and functions: how dependent one area is upon another and how the functions fit together. This part of the BIA is important for two reasons. Firstly, to ensure that in their recovery requirements departments consider their relationship with others, and secondly, to make sure the eventual contingency facilities allow for the interaction between related functions. There is no point one department having comprehensive contingency plans if another on whom they are totally dependent has nothing.

It is interesting to note that, particularly in the retail sector, major companies are insisting on seeing and understanding their suppliers' contingency arrangements. Similarly major Pension Fund Companies are telling the organizations, whose shares make up their funds, that they will sell the holding unless they can prove they are year 2000 (Y2K) compliant. Just two examples of good BCM practice related in this instance to Dependencies.

# The BIA report

I have now developed my BIA procedures to such an extent that when my interviews are complete the only thing that remains to be completed in the final BIA Report is a Management Summary (Introduction, Conclusions and Major Recommendations) and the Findings and Conclusions section.

I write up the departmental notes as I go along and list the recommendations at the same time. By this time you will be very familiar with the overall operations of the company, but remember that anyone reading your report in six months time will not have your experience, so make sure the document can survive the passing of time.

Make sure your report is positioned by the inclusion of the background as to why the BIA was conducted, what the objectives were, the scope of the exercise and the approach you used. If you follow this methodology you will undoubtedly produce a large and detailed report, particularly if you use graphs, tables and diagrams to stress the impacts and contingency requirements. However, very few people need to read it all. You should have a management summary for the executive, individual sections for the departments and proposals for those in quality assurance and those whose responsibility it is to introduce the contingency plans.

I would always recommend that a draft report is submitted to the Planning or Steering Committee for their perusal and ratification. There is nearly always a need for someone to critique and rationalize the departmental content, that is the training department may insist they are back to 50% strength in a week but senior management may well take a different viewpoint. During interviews you can only suggest the returns and requirements seem unrealistic but if the respondent insists you have to include their detail, hence the importance of rationalization.

Once the BIA report is complete it will highlight which are the critical business functions where the impact of an incident has most effect. You will have indicated the current level of preparedness, made recommendations for improvement in normal working practice and in emergency, and provided a blueprint for the continuity and recovery of the functions making up the entire company.

## Risk Analysis

At this stage I would conduct a Risk Analysis because I know which functions are critical to the company's survival and reputation. Therefore, I know which areas to concentrate upon specifically when I conduct my analysis.

Remember we are concentrating on Operational Risk but this is not simply about premises, facilities and systems, it involves people too! No contingency plan, no matter how well defined and practised, will work without the essential people, so do please look at such important aspects as depth of knowledge and training. Does the company have "succession planning" in place?—because the loss of key personnel can be just as big an interruption as a fire. Operational Risk is a vast subject covering premises, facilities, location, services, suppliers, utilities, systems, people and procedures, but that will have to be the subject of another article.

## Conclusion

I hope I have at least been able to give you a flavour of the importance and depth of a properly conducted BIA. How, if you get the structure, purpose and scope agreed, it will become the very backbone of your Business Continuity Management Programme and provide the blueprint for survival. Furthermore, you will have collected a great deal of the information required to populate the individual departmental plans (people, equipment, applications, market data, etc.). You may also be able to transfer this information to these plans from the various BIA spreadsheets, electronically.

Finally I would leave you with these thoughts:

- Disaster Recovery is a term of the past, an admission of failure. Yes, some of you will experience serious disruption but if you are aware of the consequences it will not be a disaster
- Business Continuity Management is the process to ensure your critical business functions continue in a crisis and the remainder are recovered in a controlled and phased manner
- Business Continuity Management and Maintenance do not belong with IT or Premises but with the business itself. If responsibility cannot reside there then Internal Audit is the obvious choice
- It is easier to teach someone to carry out a BIA than it is to teach someone your business. Make sure at least some of your people are involved first hand in the BIA or that the consultant comes from a relevant background.

# Developing business continuity strategies for the business or work area

## Neal Courtney—UK

Neal is an active writer, speaker and commentator on business continuity management issues and is a senior executive with international disaster management specialists Belfor Imbach Ltd.

When a business or organization chooses their business continuity strategy it
should best reflect the required recovery requirements within the corporate policies of that organization. Ideally it should be the most cost-effective solution
although this may not always be possible within the practicalities of day-to-day
business. In order to arrive at this preferred strategy several alternatives, which
provide a range of times and certainty of recovery at different costs, should be
presented for consideration by the board or senior management. It is recommended that there should be at least three options, each providing a complete
solution to the recovery requirements.

The chosen strategy must be complete and homogeneous in itself. That is, it
must meet all the recovery requirements to management's satisfaction without any
gaps or weaknesses, such as reliance on a non-contracted verbal assurance of an
outside supplier. Any strategy for recovery will always be a balance between
acceptable expenditure to the organization versus the peace of mind it provides
for those who are charged with running and progressing the organization. It is
therefore appropriate to conduct a risk analysis of each alternative strategy and
present the logical conclusions of these findings in summary form so that senior
management has a real understanding for their key decision-making. This will then
ensure that if the chosen strategy is not the preferred strategy senior management
are aware of the shortcomings and can address these through other means, that is
risk transfer.

The rule of thumb for Business Continuity is that the less it costs then potentially
the greater the risks and the less the speed and certainty of recovery, and vice
versa. It is essential that the organization's senior management take on board the
full cost implications of their preferred strategy choice. It is not appropriate or
indeed a viable approach to select the recovery results of a strategy without
accepting and then implementing the full resourcing requirements with the

*The Definitive Handbook of Business Continuity Management.* Edited by Andrew Hiles and
Peter Barnes. © 1999 John Wiley & Sons Ltd.

supporting financial budget. Usually a chosen strategy will lie somewhere between the cheapest and the most expensive alternatives, with perhaps some modifications structured by senior management to reflect the corporate policy for
recovery. Such modifications must be examined however, to ensure that any
changes in resource requirements and implied costs are picked up.

Any strategy should demonstrate a clear understanding of the recovery planning
objectives and truly reflect what the business needs to be able to continue trading
profitably, or however it is judged in terms of its viability. It is therefore essential
that there is utmost confidence in the Business Impact Analysis which will have
been completed to identify the critical functions that must be recovered, their
minimum levels of activity that they must be recovered to, and the maximum
acceptable outage time for each function. These are the targets that the strategy
must meet in order to be certain that the organization stands the best chance of
survival following a disaster. It is important that the board or senior management
also takes into account the strategic direction and initiatives of the organization in
their final strategy decision as only they are likely to be aware of these. Should
these not be taken into consideration then it could well be that the organization's
recovery is jeopardized, or at best confused and therefore delayed, when the
disaster strikes and the continuity plan is activated.

An essential aspect of the business continuity strategy is to ensure that appropriate and timely contingencies and other resources are provided or available,
such that the critical functions can be promptly and successfully restarted under
the guidance of the Business Continuity Plan. Contingencies refer to planned
replacements for any resources which may become unavailable in an unexpected way or at an unexpected time. These resources would normally be those
required to support the organization's critical functions. For instance a resource
could be a service such as the telecommunications infrastructure or a facility
such as fully equipped and ready to occupy office space. Any contingency
should be suitable for the required purposes. Furthermore, it should be available
at a cost that is reasonable for the circumstances and maintainable by the
business.

If existing contingency arrangements have been entered into, or contingency
plans have been prepared, these should be reviewed for their suitability or content. If their functionality is relevant then they should be included in the appropriate strategic recovery option for consideration. However, simply because they are
currently available does not mean that the strategic recovery options should be
compromised just to ensure that they can continue to be used. Such a policy could
seriously undermine the process of selecting the best recovery solution for the
organization. It must also be said, however, that pragmatism may be necessary.
For instance, if an in-house mirrored mainframe computer facility has been invested in it would be inappropriate to suggest that this should not underpin any
recovery strategy! However, usually existing contingencies and contingency plans
are for specific, local situations whereas what is now required is a location-wide or
company-wide approach.

There is obviously a risk that any existing contingencies may be unsatisfactory for the new approaches. For instance if there is a computer facility of a specific type at one of the company's locations it may already have its own contingency in place. This contingency arrangement should be checked to see that it meets the recovery needs of each of the critical functions at that location, but equally should be considered in relation to the other locations of the organization where this is appropriate. It is, after all, quite possible that another location could provide a contingency service for this first location without continuing with the third party arrangement, thus saving costs which could then be reinvested in other aspects of the preferred recovery strategy.

Additionally, where an outside supplier provides computing or other services then that supplier's contingency arrangements need to be examined to see if they meet the organization's needs. Where the strategy determines that moving location is necessary in the event of a disaster, then it is also important to establish whether this supplier's services can be provided at the contingent location within the recovery time limits.

# Business/work area recovery

It is a reasonable assumption that in many instances the major contingency likely to be required is for the place of work. This type of contingency is usually referred to as "work area recovery". Its specifications need to be decided before the method of contingency provision can be selected.

## Requirements for work area recovery

In conjunction with the recovery requirements for the critical functions which have already been established, it is also necessary to consider the following:

### Time

There are two aspects in relation to time. The Business Impact Analysis will have established the time by which work must be restarted. However, it must be borne in mind that there is a time required to get the work area recovery facility operational and then a time which is required by the business activity such that they are operational at the predetermined level at that facility. This overall time should obviously not exceed the original time determined by the critical function to re-establish operations to avoid business losses.

## Period of occupancy

A further consideration is the period of time over which the recovery area will be required for occupation. This is obviously dependent on the nature of the event and the extent of damage to the normal place of work, and can range from a few days to many weeks. It is wise to plan for a stay of 60–90 days at the very least, as this will provide the required time to procure any alternative contingent arrangements, should they be necessary, before returning to the normal place of work. As a further contingency it is also perhaps diligent to have reviewed what internal arrangements may be necessary in the event that the original premises is too seriously affected to return to at all.

## Geography

It is important to consider if there are any business or social reasons which necessitate the locating of the work area recovery in a specific locale. For instance, if the business customer base is within a specific catchment from the existing location then it is most likely that the business will need to remain in that locality. Secondly, it is of paramount importance to consider how employees, and perhaps customers, would get to, or access, any contingent recovery area. If this is not reasonably near the normal location of the business then transport or hotel accommodation may be required for employees and communications will need to be made effectively to customers so that you continue to receive their custom.

## Size

The size of the work area facility is obviously largely dependent on the numbers of employees requiring accommodation immediately. This number will in turn be dependent on the recovery requirements determined by the critical business functions, as well as the management's policy. It is less common to expect the recovery area to accommodate all employees and more reasonable that only a proportion of them (typically between 20 and 30%) are immediately accommodated.

Where the numbers of employees are initially small and the stay in the recovery area becomes extended, management may wish to increase their numbers and thus return to a more normal work output, using the contingent site. If this could be a requirement of the contingent facility then consideration should be given to this aspect beforehand so that the necessary preparations can be completed.

*Assets/facilities*

The work area recovery site will need to contain all the assets/facilities, in the required quantities, to enable the work of the critical functions to be restarted and continued within the specified timescales. Such facilities are likely to include the following at the very least:

Desks and chairs
Telephones, photocopiers, fax machines, etc.
Storage for working papers and reference items, i.e.: filing cabinets etc.
Employee welfare facilities
Toilet facilities

Depending on the nature of the critical functions to be recovered, other resources, for example PC network systems or information feeds such as Bloomberg and Reuters, may need to be made available.

*Computing and other activities*

Many organizations rely on computing services provided by in-house facilities. Some organizations have manufacturing, assembly, warehousing or other activities that are, or have, critical functions for recovery. These are covered in the next sections of this chapter. The point to be made here is that it may be desirable, for reasons of economy or convenience, to include these other activities within the same recovery area as the clerical business functions. In such a case, all the recovery requirements will need to be taken together.

From the above considerations the list of requirements, and therefore selection criteria, for the recovery area can be made. If the organization has an individual responsible for the premises, it could be advantageous to draw on their expertise and involve them in the selection process for the recovery area.

# Types of contingencies

In brief, selection of any contingency is a balance between the cost the business can afford to sustain and the degree of risk it is comfortable to incur. Access to a contingency, such as a mainframe computer facility or a work recovery area, can only be guaranteed when it is owned. If any other alternatives are selected then it is essential that wherever possible written contracts or SLAs (service level agreements) are entered into to guarantee provision of the facility. Anything less than this will introduce a degree of risk and whilst this uncertainty may be acceptable where the impact of the threat is low, it could make the difference between surviving or failing if the impact is clearly of a substantial magnitude.

There are principally four contingency types that can be used by a business continuity strategy.

## In-house

The least risk option, and invariably the most expensive, is to acquire or set-up an in-house contingency. Such a facility could be put *in situ* for almost anything from offices to warehouse or production facilities. The limiting factor is the cost of these facilities and the additional assets which are then depreciating and will require maintenance and update. The main advantage of course is that these facilities are to the exact specification required by the business, potentially without compromises, and additionally these facilities can be accessed at any time without time constraints on occupation. Furthermore, the organization is able to test the contingency at any time or at any level of activation.

In view of these advantages and disadvantages such an approach is only usually adopted where facilities must be on stand-by for immediate use or where equipment is unique or difficult to obtain within acceptable business timeframes. A perfect example is a financial securities trading floor where seconds or minutes lost may amount to substantial financial losses if positions remain open. In certain circumstances a business will make use of a contingent site as an overflow facility or as a research and development facility to absorb some of the extra costs. The problem with this is that, more often than not, as business increases the requirement to maintain this facility as a true contingency becomes less of a priority as cost savings accrue through not having to create new facilities to accommodate the increase in trading activity.

## Third party contracts

Where the contingency is secured through an outside supplier this is known as a third party contract arrangement. Usually this facility is sold several times to different organizations to cover the supplier's start-up and maintenance costs. The advantage of this over an in-house facility is primarily one of cost as any owned facility is likely to be far more expensive to set up at the outset, with a considerable outlay for ongoing maintenance. Various different types of contingency are available from third party suppliers, most commonly IT-related. For instance:

1. Mainframe computing facilities—these could be of a "warm start" type, i.e. capable of being up and running typically within 24 hours, or of a "cold start"

type where temporary "portacabin"-type units are transported to the recovery location and equipment is installed to be running typically within 7–14 days after invocation. Usually any planning permission requirements are addressed by such suppliers as part of setting up the contract.

2. PC networks—a number of companies now specialize in providing considerable quantities of pre-configured PCs such that a company's computer networks can be replicated within 24 hours.

3. Telecommunications—contingencies range here from delivering a replacement PABX through to providing complete operational call centres. Times for delivery can range from virtually instantaneous for the latter to most typically within 24 hours for the former.

4. Work Area Recovery—perhaps the newest of the contingency types available; there are now several providers who effectively span conurbations within the UK and are starting to address the requirement for contingency centres within continental Europe. Time from invocation to achieving a working environment can vary considerably, depending on client requirements. A subdivision of this is dealing room workstation recovery centres which are very often available on a "hot start" basis to meet the financial loss implications of being unable to trade for even a matter of minutes.

The overriding advantage of any third party arrangements is the redundancy factor. If a company owns its facilities then it has to maintain the currency of the equipment. With the acceleration of development on computing and the inherent redundancy of equipment, within months now not years, this can become a considerable extra financial burden for a company. Conversely, any external arrangements by their very nature are more risky than an in-house controlled solution. Other potential disadvantages are the time allowance on or using these facilities before they must be vacated or high rental penalties are applied, which may not be covered by increased cost of working insurance.

With most of the suppliers a degree of testing is factored into the annual contract fee to ensure the facility will operate to client expectations if it is invoked in anger. The supplier should be able to integrate the contingency activation details into the BCP and the contract should state categorically what are the exact deliverables upon invocation. It is however, essential that the client then confirms that all items and facilities do exist and can operate as required.

## Reciprocal arrangements

If an organization enters into an agreement to assist another part of the organization or a totally separate organization then this is termed a reciprocal arrangement. Such agreements for reciprocal recovery ensure that should one site be affected, the facilities of the other become available to the agreeing party. However, when one business relocates to another the impact of the disaster is invariably exported to that second business. Reciprocal arrangements are often feasible and cost-effective in theory; however, unless there is existing spare capacity in the receiving premises which matches the requirements of the displaced personnel, then further disruption will ensue in trying to accommodate them, especially if employees then have to share equipment and other necessary facilities. One resolution to this problem is to utilize parts of the premises or indeed alternative premises where the space is not currently in use as workspace. Examples of this would be an in-house restaurant facility or an off-site training centre. A change in work patterns could also be used to accommodate two streams of employees during partly extended working hours.

Although reciprocal arrangements incur minimal cost they require considerable thought to ensure the recovery of the affected organization is not compromised. For this reason, wherever possible, such agreements should be written and not left as verbal "gentlemen's agreements". This is especially the case where the reciprocal organization may have competitive aspects of the other party's business.

Additionally, it is important to recognize that where the reciprocal arrangements include use of computing equipment, what may start as two similar organizations when the agreement is initiated, can rapidly diverge as the technology requirements of the individual organizations develop.

## Reactive

There are numerous examples where a business will secure a replacement at the time of a disaster and this is frequently done for minor events which occur, such as hiring a piece of presentation equipment if the in-house one fails. However, specialist items, say a video conferencing facility, may not be readily available. Normal office equipment is usually available off the shelf but larger quantities of electronic items such as laptops and desktop PCs may take days to obtain, particularly if they must have particular specifications. Also it is important to be aware that, since product design and specification usually change over time, it may not be possible to replace the existing equipment with identical items. In many instances this may not be a problem, but if it is perceived this could be an issue, then periodic checks with the suppliers may be advisable to understand what exactly can be supplied at short notice.

For replacement premises this approach assumes that a suitable property can be obtained and made ready within the predetermined restart time constraint. A list of property agents, or even a list of suitable properties, could be maintained for immediate use. With the exception of maintaining the list, the cost of this option is low, but it has the inherent risk that no suitable properties will be available when needed. Issues which may delay finding a utilizable premises include, for example, cabling infrastructure requirements, air conditioning, location, lease/occupancy contract arrangements and intended usage versus permitted use.

## Organization, administration and support issues

Any business continuity strategy requires a distinct infrastructure to ensure that the recovery is effectively managed. The recovery organization need not be the same as that in daily use, in fact it is more often preferable to select a unique and specific structure consisting of suitable individuals who are capable of implementing the BCP. Such individuals will need to be organized into teams with specific responsibilities for certain actions of response and recovery. Throughout the recovery the organization would operate under this structure, thereby ensuring that only individuals required for the organization's timely recovery are present and organizing the relevant actions and activities. At the end of the recovery period the organization can then return to its normal management infrastructure.

It is important to recognize that there is a requirement usually for two recovery teams or two tracks of recovery activity. Firstly, the recovery at the contingent site which obviously takes priority if business is to be resumed as quickly as possible. Then secondly, the activity which must occur to address the potential damage at the original site to understand the extent and ramifications of the damage such that plans can start to be assembled to return to pre-incident levels of activity. Each of these teams would have differing concentrations of expertise reflecting the main actions and issues which need to be addressed.

For instance at the contingent site it will be necessary for an "Administration Team" to oversee that everything required for the office functions is in place and working—that is desks, chairs, telephones, stationery, and so forth and that employees can reach the site without undue inconvenience and that rest and eating facilities are available to them as necessary. Additionally an "IT Recovery Team" would ensure that the hardware was operational and that individuals were able to access their relevant software applications and data when required.

## Vital records and paper documentation issues

Even in our present technological era we are all still heavily dependent on hard copies of information and data. There are moves in many larger organizations towards the paperless office via the use of microfiche and now, increasingly, document imaging systems. However, for a large number of companies the need for paper records of work in progress is still a reality. Such paper documentation is particularly susceptible to damage from fire, flood, and other physical disasters. Clear-desk policies are commendable in principle but notoriously difficult to enforce or maintain. It is better to encourage employees to safely store essential documentation in closed drawers or filing cabinets and archive records off-site or in fireproof cabinets if they are of a critical nature. Comprehensive duplication is not practicable in the majority of instances but for some essential records may be a viable alternative. Where possible, review how essential documentation could be replicated if it became necessary to do so, and if this process then highlights which documents are more difficult to obtain this will provide guidance on what to keep protected.

With regard to computerized data and software this should have a program for frequent, automatic, backing-up with the back-ups being taken immediately off-site for safekeeping. Any such system should be designed so that the back-up procedures are not onerous on the business and consequently recovery is simple to either the existing or contingent sites.

The business continuity strategy should have helped to determine which assets, including documents, are essential for recovery and therefore require protection. It is then relatively straightforward for the recovery team using the BCP to collect these and deliver them to the contingent site. (If any backed-up data is recalled from off-site storage for the computer recovery, remember to return this to the off-site storage as soon as possible.)

If there are any items which are not possible to guarantee being available, but which are essential to the continuation of the business, then these must be detailed beforehand and "Workarounds" considered to negate the effects of such unavailabilities.

## Restoration

Restoration should be an essential aspect of any recovery strategy, although many aspects of the restoration programme can only be determined once damage occurs and the effects are assessed. There are nevertheless a considerable number of preparative measures which can be planned beforehand. These will ensure focused and effective actions are taken in the very early stages of a recovery, which can dramatically reduce the impact of a disaster and the overall time it takes to get back to pre-incident status.

Such preparations include bringing together the right skills base to accurately assess the damage to the premises and assets so that the options for recovery can be rapidly and objectively assessed. With this reliable and substantive information available, decisions on short, medium or long-term displacement can be reviewed and any requirements to escalate procedures can be taken in good time to reduce any additional disruption which might otherwise result. Conversely, it is also possible that, by knowing quite soon after the event that a return to the existing premises may be possible, this could prevent the second wave of employees needing to go to a contingent location, with all the associated disruption.

Furthermore, just as with data, the strategy should record which assets are essential to support the critical activities and their location as this will assist in the damage assessment and recovery process. If such assets, as is often the case within manufacturing environments, are on long lead times or are unique and no longer manufactured, then restoration may be the only assured strategy for recovering the business operations. In such circumstances a business may find it necessary to outsource aspects of their production process while the equipment is restored. Investigating how this could be fulfilled before the need arises should precede any such strategy.

## Salvage considerations

Although the companies operating in the salvage and restoration industry can often achieve wonders with what at first may appear irrecoverable it is still preferable to ensure that critical items receive adequate protection. In the immediate aftermath of a physical disaster there are two major activities:

- How serious is the damage?
- How can we stop the damage getting worse?

In all instances, therefore, part of the recovery strategy should address the coordination of skilled personnel to ensure the damage is quickly quantified and qualified so that time for recovery and the extent of remedial activity can be determined. Secondly, there needs to be coordination of the activities to stabilize the damage so that the initial losses do not escalate further and cause unnecessary additional activities which could divert other essential resources. An example of this is the rapid freezing of water-saturated documents to prevent further deterioration, or the reduction of humidity to reduce the corrosive action of the products of combustion of PVC cabling combined with water.

There are firms offering salvage and restoration assistance with priority site attendance for a small annual retainer. The business continuity strategy should include a salvage and restoration contract as part of the overall risk management of the business. The BCP should then detail when and how to call out these contractors and ensure that liaison with them, insurers and loss adjusters is integrated within the actions of an appropriate recovery team.

# Business continuity strategies for manufacturing and logistics

**12**

## Melvyn Musson—USA

Melvyn Musson is President of the Musson Consulting Group of St Louis, MO, and a Principal of the Recovery Facilitation Network.

## Introduction

Recovery planning in a manufacturing environment encompasses many different issues and different types of planning than those found in work area and data processing recovery planning.

Since manufacturing can involve business, data processing, production and distribution functions, the question is often: "Where should we put the emphasis for recovery planning?" The emphasis can be put on the business and data processing utilizing specific recovery strategies. However, if the production/distribution are unavailable, the company will be unable to provide the product it is selling after recovering its business functions. The other question often raised is: "If the business and data processing functions are not available, can you still provide product?" The company may be able to, but with difficulty. The increasing link between all these functions means that manufacturing recovery plans should cover all of them, but possibly as separate sections involving different methodologies and strategies.

Manufacturing recovery also provides challenges often not found in other areas. These range from the increasing globlization, including component manufacture in third world countries, to just-in-time (JIT) inventory systems, the use of EDI and e-commerce to determine actual production needs and scheduling or the unavailability/delays in equipment availability. Government regulations or recertification requirements are another factor.

As a result, recovery planning and recovery strategies for the manufacturing environment must consider and accommodate:

- A plan that will cover differing areas and functions ranging from office/work area, to data centre, to manufacturing and the related supply chain and logistics functions

*The Definitive Handbook of Business Continuity Management.* Edited by Andrew Hiles and Peter Barnes. © 1999 John Wiley & Sons Ltd.

- The links between manufacturing and business/data processing functions., e.g. CAD/CAM or CIM
- The greater impact that changes in a company's business environment have on the manufacturing operations. This will affect the determination of the actual recovery strategy to be used at the time of the disaster
- Multiple strategies to be considered at the time of the disaster
- Lack of actual fixed recovery locations
- Recovery strategies which are more business-related than technologically related
- Impact of circumstances at locations in other parts of the country or the world
- Impacts of incidents affecting the community infrastructure (e.g., transportation, utilities)
- Dependency on outside sources (e.g., raw material or component supplies)

One other factor that has to be considered and allowed for is what one might call the "manufacturing approach". Firstly, it should be realized that manufacturing facilities handle emergencies on a daily basis (e.g., equipment breakdown, the quality of components not up to standard). The facilities handle such emergencies as a part of their daily work. Secondly, the approach for handling problems is often "put enough engineers in the room and they will take care of it". While a recovery plan should never be based on a strategy utilizing such attitudes, the plan should accommodate them to help determine whether the situation is an emergency or a disaster, and to help deal with problems that occur in a disaster and which were not considered or planned for during the plan development.

Another consideration is whether the company manufactures final products or components. With component manufacture, the need for and extent of recovery planning and determination of recovery strategies should be agreed between the companies. However, the final product producer does have the opportunity to work with alternative suppliers, although that may be affected by business-related decisions. Another consideration will be whether both companies can be affected by the same hazard (e.g., flooding, earthquake, hurricane).

# Developing strategies

The key is to know the hazard, exposure and the potential impact. This includes consideration of:

- Primary hazards and their impact
- Secondary/collateral hazards and their impact

This can be achieved by completion of a Risk and Business Impact Analysis (RBIA). This must be an in-depth analysis and must determine:

- What can happen (Risk Exposure Analysis)
- What will be affected (Damage Potential Analysis)
- What will be the impact (Impact Analysis)

The RBIA should cover:

- The main facility
- Other company-owned facilities producing products/services for the main facility
- Suppliers and other non-owned facilities providing products/services
- Site/Community infrastructure (utilities, etc.)
- Logistics involved with moving materials in and product out of the facility

The RBIA provides details of:

- The maximum allowable downtime of individual product lines
- The criticality of product lines and their priority for reinstatement
- Key equipment and supplies and their anticipated replacement times
- Critical utilities and other resources
- Suppliers and vendors
- Interdependencies between individual manufacturing operations and possibly individual facilities/locations
- Logistical needs

An important consideration is that whilst this information is current at the time of the analysis, product changes can render it obsolete very quickly. It is therefore important that the information be reviewed both periodically and whenever product changes are being considered.

The RBIA should also detail the extent of the damage that an event can cause to the facility, the employees, the locality and the region. For this reason, the use of Scenario Based Analysis can assist companies in evaluating the potential damage from each type of event. In addition, Scenario Based Analysis can assist in determining possible actions which could reduce the impact and form the basis of recovery strategies.

Irrespective of whether a standard RBIA or a Scenario Based Analysis is used, the overall result should be to provide information which forms the foundation of the recovery plan and the development of the recovery strategies.

# Types of recovery strategies

Unlike work area and data processing recovery plans, hot and cold sites for manufacturing operations are not available as separate commercial operations. It is possible that there may be some internal arrangements that can be made relating to spare capacity or changing marginal product lines, but companies cannot maintain production facilities sitting idle, waiting to be used in a disaster situation.

There are two types of recovery strategies:

- Pre-incident
- Post-incident

and three main categories:

- Specific
- Mitigation
- Procedural

All three can be either pre- or post-incident or a combination of both.

The use of two types and three categories emphasizes that:

- Consideration should be given not only to the future actions at the time of the event, but also to what can be done now to reduce the impact
- It is necessary to consider a broad range of strategies and customize these to a company's individual needs

Pre-incident strategies are those implemented before any disaster situation to miti-gate the likelihood or impact of an incident or minimize the downtime. These strategies include risk control/loss control actions, vital record procedures, back-up arrangements for utilities and other services, special contractual arrangements, and so on.

Examples of pre-incident strategies include:

- Mitigation recommendations
- Spare equipment availability lists from internal and/or external sources
- Buildings and equipment drawings and specifications maintained off-site
- Tool and die drawings off-site
- Contractual arrangements for back-up boilers, generators, compressors, etc.
- Arrangements (possibly contractual) with alternative fuel suppliers, rental unit suppliers, potential subcontractors
- Contractual arrangements with specialist salvage/restoration companies
- Load-shedding procedures for potential electrical outage situations
- Special arrangements with specialist contractors for building services
- Alternative operating procedures for key production lines

Post-incident strategies (whether developed pre or post incident) are implemented after the disaster to maintain partial or total product supply. They can include:

- Use of spare capacity within the organizations
- Shutdown of marginal product lines and transfer of key products to those production facilities
- Assistance from competition
- Outsourcing to subcontractors, job shops, etc.
- Relabelling of competitors' products (after consideration of all legal implications)
- Establishment of temporary facilities when production capabilities can be established with "off the shelf" or secondhand equipment

A company may incorporate several potential recovery strategies in its plan. This results from the continually changing nature of products. The timeframe between major changes of products is often twelve months or less. New products often supersede existing products within similar timeframes. This means that major damage to a production facility may result in recovery of the facility for production of a new product or a new version, rather than recovery of the existing product. For such situations, the decision on what will actually be done will be decided at the time of the disaster.

This emphasizes the need for the plan to include procedures for a detailed situation analysis immediately after the disaster. Such an analysis will include not only a damage assessment but also a review of the business environment for the products involved.

Companies may also utilize periodic scenario analysis prior to the disaster utilizing "what-if" situations to consider what they would do should certain events occur during various business environments. The results of such analysis are then incorporated in the recovery strategies section of the plan.

Within the pre- and post-incident classification, there are three main categories of strategies—specific, mitigation, and procedural. It should be noted that differentiation between the categories may be a grey area, with certain strategies being considered combinations.

Specific strategies are those which are determined before the event and which are detailed in the plan. These can include:

- Use of specific hot/cold sites for work area and data processing functions
- Use of specific spare production capacity elsewhere
- Mutual aid arrangements
- Use of specific contractors, job shops, etc.
- Discontinuance of specific marginal product lines and transfer of key products to those production facilities
- Closure of the facility and transfer to a new or alternative facility (access to this strategy information should obviously be tightly controlled)

Although most specific strategies will relate to the reinstatement of a production capability, they can also relate to the utilization of a different course of action. An example of this would be to specify that there would be increased marketing/ advertising of similar alternative products rather than attempts to reinstate some form of temporary production capability. This strategy may also be linked to procedural strategies to reduce the time needed for reconstruction or repair of the facility.

Mitigation strategies are actions taken beforehand to eliminate or reduce the likelihood and/or mitigate the impact and downtime. Many mitigation strategies can also be considered as risk or loss control actions. The strategies may be specific actions taken or contractual arrangements made and maintained before the events.

Mitigation strategies include:

- Seismic design/retrofitting of buildings
- Installation of sprinkler systems
- Compartmentation of buildings to prevent fire spread
- Anchoring of equipment to prevent damage in an earthquake
- Employee disaster preparedness education and training
- Contractual arrangements for back-up generator, boilers, air compressors, etc.

Procedural strategies are procedures developed and incorporated in the plan to:

- Provide limited operational capability at the damaged facility or another location
- Facilitate reconstruction, repair and/or reoccupancy of the facility
- Maintain credibility with employees, the public, customers, regulators and the investment community

Procedural strategies can include:

- Alternative means of operating. This may involve additional manual handling or use of simpler equipment
- Use of equipment on a more continuous basis (e.g. 3 shifts over 7 days instead of 1 or 2 shifts over 5 days)
- Accelerated building inspection procedures
- Coordination with local authorities regarding building access, building inspections, construction permits, etc.
- Use of special construction techniques to facilitate reconstruction/repair

Development of a Crisis Communications Plan may also be considered a procedural strategy.

## Conclusions

Recovery strategies for manufacturing operations can be multiple and varied. In addition, unlike those for work area and data processing functions, they may not be as clear cut and are often dependent upon the circumstances at the time of the event. This means that the recovery plans that are developed must be flexible to accommodate the actual circumstances and changes that are needed and which result from such new circumstances. Therefore a manufacturing recovery plan format should place emphasis on the recovery organization, responsibilities and information database together with recovery support documentation such as checklists, action plans, and so on, rather than describing specific detailed procedures based upon a single recovery strategy.

In developing both the recovery strategies and the recovery plan, the planners should follow several basic rules:

- Don't confine yourself to traditional ways
- Be adventurous in your thinking—use creativity and common sense
- Use group thinking to develop and review strategies
- Infrastructure, support functions and interdependencies are major considerations
- Know the hazard exposures and their potential impact. Mitigation is an important recovery strategy
- Strategize but don't become committed to any one recovery strategy
- In a recovery mode, you can't do anything until you know the type and extent of the damage and the business environment.
- Educate, train, exercise, educate, train, exercise.

# BC strategies for communications

**13** ## Paul Kirvan—USA

Paul is a highly respected writer, practitioner and presenter who is well known throughout the international community of business continuity management professionals. Paul occupies a senior management postition within Bellcore Inc.

Communications and information systems managers in the 1990s are responsible for providing a broad range of facilities and support systems to keep their operations—and their companies—in business. Their responsibilities extend beyond simply providing communications services; they are directly linked to the firm's ability to compete effectively in its chosen markets.

Numerous trends can be identified in communications today that are critical to business success. These include, but are certainly not limited to, the following:

- Higher transmission speeds, e.g., 1.544M bps (T1) and 2.048M bps (E1) to 34M bps (E3) and 45M bps (T3); local area networks (10M to 100M bps)
- Increased use of digital transmission circuits, e.g., T1/E1 and T3/E3 channels, fractional T1/E1
- Dramatic increase in use of the Internet, and new technologies spinning off from it
- Extensive use of stored-program computer-based systems
- Greater focus on network management and control
- Increased decentralization of business functions

Each of these is a significant factor in business success today, and into the next century. For example, the push for higher transmission speeds, particularly for data, has grown steadily over the past five years. While this is important for business, it also has a downside. Specifically, the use of high-capacity digital transmission circuits forces communications managers to place a greater percentage of their information processing needs into a smaller number of facilities. This of course creates a higher risk of network failure, with potentially disastrous consequences to the company.

The use of digital facilities, for example, is easily justified from cost and business perspectives. However, increases in the risk of network failure also exist if (i) the

*The Definitive Handbook of Business Continuity Management.* Edited by Andrew Hiles and Peter Barnes. © 1999 John Wiley & Sons Ltd.

facility fails, (ii) the hardware associated with it fails, or (iii) the site where the facilities are connected fails.

IT departments have long recognized the importance of contingency planning and disaster recovery for their computers and related subsystems. This typically includes activities such as:

- Backing-up data files
- Off-site storage of critical company records
- Duplication and redundancy of critical processing elements
- Creation of corporate disaster recovery teams
- Establishing system security practices
- System/network diagnostic and trouble-shooting procedures
- Use of emergency computer operation sites during emergencies

But for communications professionals, contingency planning and disaster recovery activities are much more recent. The notion of rapid communications system/network recovery and restoration has taken on new significance. Events of the current decade have spurred interest in protection of corporate communications and network facilities. Further, senior management recognition of the importance of communications to business success has helped increase corporate interest.

Protecting a company's investment in information systems is costly—and essential—to survival. As companies become increasingly dependent on information systems not only to conduct business, but also to remain competitive, the stakes involved in a communications system outage have risen.

# Business continuity strategies

Communications is increasingly recognized as a key element in business success. Many users now think of their PBXs, key systems and analog and digital transmission circuits as corporate assets. Access to the Internet is increasingly a strategic part of business as well.

The principal strategy regarding this position results from the recognition of two points:

- Communications is essential for the company to remain in business
- Loss of communications could put the company out of business

Perhaps the most important user strategy for dealing with disasters is common sense. Users must think carefully about the role a communications system or network service plays in a company, and what would happen if that service was disrupted. This should be done before anything is designed, planned, ordered or installed.

The following are several broad-based user strategies:

- Establish plans and strategies for dealing with the overall issues of contingency planning
- Create decision guidelines to decide whether a contingency plan is appropriate for a company
- Develop hardware strategies for getting the best recovery arrangement for communications systems
- Develop software strategies to protect an extremely important part of a communications operation
- Define transmission facility strategies to ensure the network components that link applications to users are maintained
- Provide off-site storage facilities to ensure that critical data are properly protected
- Develop strategies for reducing personal liability, assuming communications managers are corporate officers and, as such, are potentially liable for lost or damaged network resources
- Encourage use of common-sense strategies to make sure very little falls "through the cracks"

# Importance of common sense

While a technology thrust for contingency planning is assumed, one cannot forget simple common sense as a key strategy. Suppose common sense, for example, suggests relocating a PBX away from an overhead water pipe. The answer is simple: move the switch. However, in a crowded equipment room with minimal extra space that may not be possible. Again, common sense suggests installing something that shields the PBX from water leaks. Options could be plastic covers or even a trough suspended under the pipe to catch drips, routing them to a drain.

Common sense dictates that unauthorized people should not be permitted in an equipment room. So identification badges are required; visitors are signed in at a reception area; entry control systems are installed.

Connections between a mainframe and some remote terminals are based on dedicated private circuits only. Common sense suggests a back-up of some kind, such as dial-up service, in case the private circuit is disabled.

Most of the recommendations found throughout this book are based on experience and common sense. Communications professionals already use many of these techniques in daily operations. What is unfortunate is that most users do not identify these practices to management as part of contingency planning. This approach needs to change.

## General strategies

Users can develop contingency plans for communications based on the following primary guidelines:

- Obtain continuing senior management support
- Make sure the plan reflects the importance of communications to the business
- Define hardware, software and facility requirements for business applications needs
- Identify time business can survive without communications service
- Make sure primary systems have back-ups (e.g., redundant CPUs, spare parts) both on-site and at alternate locations
- Make sure primary facilities and communications systems have back-ups available if primary network paths are disabled
- Test contingency plan elements regularly; test the entire plan at least once a year
- Document plan elements; establish plan updating procedures and follow them regularly
- Train and retrain contingency plan members
- Never assume a network is 100% safe

## Hardware strategies

The following hardware strategies are recommended for communications professionals:

- Use systems from known manufacturers that offer warranties and recovery options; contact other users of the same products for their experience
- Use installation and maintenance sources whose skills and performance are professional and dependable
- Install duplicate, or redundant, processing elements where appropriate, to ensure uninterrupted processing; install back-up power supplies, cable routes
- Use quality parts and supplies, cables, connectors, etc.

- Install and test equipment according to manufacturer specifications
- Provide proper environment for equipment, e.g., raised floors, proper temperature/humidity range, sufficient power
- Provide proper equipment security to prevent damage, theft or vandalism
- Follow building and construction codes, follow electric codes for wiring and electrical systems
- Invest in spare components, terminals, circuit boards; store these in protected areas both on- and off-site
- Conduct regular tests of system performance, following manufacturer's recommended test and maintenance procedures

## Software strategies

The following software strategies are recommended for communications professionals:

- Maintain back-up copies of all critical software: operating systems, applications, utility programs, databases
- Have multiple back-up storage, both on-site and off-site
- Keep special databases as current as possible; make sure back-up copies are no more than one to three days old, unless more recent updates are indicated
- Use proven software products for major systems, rather than untested items; check product's customers
- Analyse software performance regularly; vendor and/or distributor can support this activity
- Update software documentation regularly as changes come on line; update contingency plan as well
- Install software patches as soon as they are received
- Make sure back-up copies of primary applications are the same release level, or generic, as operating versions
- Make sure vendors have emergency back-up copies of system software and special programs available
- Make sure software can be used by communications staff as well as vendors

## Network service strategies

The following network service strategies are recommended for communications professionals:

- Identify and pursue (if appropriate) local access alternative routing options
- Identify and pursue alternative routing options from customer site to long-distance operators
- Use multiple long-distance carriers
- Use multiple local access providers and Internet Service Providers (ISPs)
- Identify carrier network routing paths; look for possible overlapping transmission paths across multiple carriers that could represent disaster risk points
- Mix transmission facilities, e.g., 64K with fractional T1/E1, to obtain best overall price/performance
- Mix switched access services with dedicated circuits to obtain hybrid configurations, spreading risk more evenly
- Use alternative transmission services, e.g., cellular, radio paging, two-way radio, microwave, satellite where needed
- Deal with carriers who are committed to supporting customer contingency plans; check with other users for input
- Deal with carriers who have circuit assurance plans, a demonstrated commitment to network survivability, and who have demonstrated a desire to work with users

# Off-site storage facility strategies

The following strategies are recommended for communications professionals who plan to include off-site storage and electronic vaulting arrangements:

- Make sure physical layout of facility is conducive to rapid movement of materials
- Make sure facility uses fire-resistant construction
- Facility should have fire detection, suppression and alarm connections to the local fire department
- Facility should have proper temperature/humidity monitoring and control
- Security and access control systems should be available and linked to local police department or other appropriate organization
- Ensure availability of back-up power for user systems, security, fire and environmental systems
- Ensure convenient and rapid access to records within required recovery time frames; open on weekends, holidays, etc.
- Facility location in non-hazard or minimal hazard geographic area, e.g., periodic flooding, earthquakes, power fluctuations, etc.
- Ensure availability of bonded transport services
- Storage flexibility for various media types in addition to magnetic tapes, such as printed matter and diskettes

# Call centre strategies

If your company has a call centre, the following strategies will help ensure its continued availability:

- Use incoming routing service arrangements from local and long distance carriers
- Ensure that all call centre systems, e.g., automatic call distributors (ACDs), have redundant components, back-up power, and back-up copies of the system database
- If your company has more than one call centre, configure network services to easily route incoming calls from a disabled system to working call centres
- Ensure availability of alternate call centre staff (e.g., using temporary placement firms) in an emergency
- Arrange for call centre staff to work at home if access to call centre is denied
- Arrange for rerouting of incoming calls to call centre staff working at home
- If using computer telephony integration (CTI) as part of the call centre, ensure that CTI hardware and software are backed up, and emergency copies stored in a safe location

# Year 2000 strategies

Communications can be at risk when the Year 2000 date change takes effect. To ensure that critical systems and network facilities are protected, the following strategies are recommended:

- Remember that Y2K affects all software-based systems. In addition to IT/IS applications, that means voice and data network devices and their management systems are at risk as well. It is just as important to assess the Y2K risks in your networks as it is in your business systems
- Prioritize efforts to obtain Y2K compliance by focusing on the most critical communications hardware and software. Convert as many systems as possible
- Cut back or defer non-critical production as much as possible to provide additional Y2K compliance testing time
- Verify Y2K compliance for specialized systems, e.g., HVAC, lighting, alarms, and environmental control, to ensure they function properly
- Make sure that all critical communications systems and files are backed-up as close to the Y2K deadline as possible
- Look into sharing network services, e.g., mutual aid agreements, with other companies that have obtained Y2K assurances from their vendors and carriers

- Establish emergency arrangements with all equipment vendors, network service providers, and other key suppliers
- Notify all key customers, suppliers, shareholders and other important organizations in advance about your plans to deal with Y2K compliance
- Pursue carriers and equipment vendors diligently to ensure their products and services will be Y2K compliant
- If it is unlikely you will complete all Y2K conversions in time, focus on noncompliant mission-critical devices, determine the impacts of Y2K failures, and build contingency plans

# Strategies for communications products and services

Communications contingency planning and disaster recovery products are generally designed to provide the following:

- Alternative sources of power
- Alternative communications paths
- Fire and smoke suppression
- Back-up for critical computer/communications applications
- Testing and diagnostics of critical network elements
- Rapid replacement of failed or damaged hardware components
- Rapid repair or replacement of damaged transmission circuits

Communications equipment vendors, such as PBX manufacturers, now actively market PBX back-up and restoration services. The same is true for most service providers, with the possible exception of ISPs. These options are currently available to users, and are worth the investment of time and financial resources.

Instituting a communications contingency plan will help ensure the availability of communications hardware and services. It will help minimize the chances of a network disaster occurring. And it will minimize the impact on the company if a disaster occurs.

# Emergency response and operations

## Gregg C. Beatty—USA

**14**

Gregg is Senior Vice-President of The Darien Group, Ltd of Glenn Mills, PA.

## Identify potential types of emergencies and the responses needed

Emergency response is that period of time during which your adrenaline is flowing, some events seem to be happening in slow motion while others are going by at the speed of light, and you keep having the nagging feeling that something is being overlooked. Decisions come more quickly for some people and others freeze when having to make a quick decision. The future of organizations, structures and people is hanging in the balance. How confident are you in your ability to recognize the situation and make the correct decisions? In another day or another week you will be able to provide an accurate evaluation of how well you performed but you need an answer now. Preparation is the key.

If this chapter were organized like a Hollywood movie, the opening scene would focus on you in the midst of an emergency (fire, flood, building collapse, physical violence, hurricane, etc.) giving orders and wondering if you are making the correct decisions. The future of people and your company at stake. Then the camera would fade and in a series of flashbacks we would all have the opportunity to see how you, and your company, prepared for the emergency. We would see you and your planning group trying to identify just what is an emergency. After hours of conversation, citing examples to support various positions, stories of known emergencies, and the retelling of actual experiences, you would have reached the conclusion that an emergency isn't just one single type of event but that they are wide-reaching and a composite of many different elements. You decide to use the definition of an emergency that is used by the Federal Emergency Management Agency in its publication, *Emergency Management Guide For Business and Industry* which states that:

*The Definitive Handbook of Business Continuity Management.* Edited by Andrew Hiles and Peter Barnes. © 1999 John Wiley & Sons Ltd.

> An emergency is any unplanned event that can cause deaths or significant injuries to employees, customers or the public; or that can shut down your business, disrupt operations, cause physical or environmental damage, or threaten the facility's financial standing or public image.

This definition opens the door to considering many different types of events which could have a negative impact on your people and your business. And the question it raises is: "How do we identify the types of emergencies that we are most likely to experience and what will be the impact on us?" This two-part question then leads you to design a simple, effective matrix system for identifying, estimating the probability, anticipating the potential impact and recognizing existing internal and external resources to respond to the emergency.

Such a matrix is shown in Figure 14.1 and is referred to as a Vulnerability Analysis. One of its strengths is that it is simple to use and simple to understand. The key to the use of the Vulnerability Analysis is the recognition of the many types of emergencies which could affect you, the projected impact of the emergency, and the resources that are available to respond to the emergency. From this beginning you are now in a position to begin the process of allocating resources to minimize or even prevent some emergencies, determine what elements of your organization and facilities are at greatest risk and how you want to spend your limited resources to prepare for the various emergencies. The Vulnerability Analysis becomes a very valuable planning tool to help you prepare, respond and recover from an emergency.

When you start the process of completing the Vulnerability Analysis, one of the questions you will raise will be, "Where do I find information about past emergencies and potential emergencies?" so you can complete the first column. The knowledge of long-term employees will be a rich resource of emergencies, and near emergencies, that have occurred in the past. The actual emergency experiences at other locations of members of your planning group will also assist you. Local newspaper and magazine records are a source of information about previous emergencies. And then there are the community emergency response organizations.

The community emergency response organizations include fire, law enforcement, medical response, rescue, Red Cross, Emergency Management (Civil Defence) and others. They know what types of emergencies are most common, which ones they are prepared to respond to, and what potential emergencies worry them the most. Establishing a rapport with these organizations before any emergency occurs is extremely valuable in ensuring an effective response on their part to your emergency. Having these organizations work with you as you develop, test and maintain your emergency response capabilities is a win-win situation for everyone.

Many local governments, probably under the auspices of the local Emergency Management Agency, have developed Hazard Analysis or Risk Assessments for their jurisdiction. In the United States the Army Corps of Engineers have

| Type of emergency | Probability<br>High — Low<br>5 ←→ 1 | Human Impact<br>High Impact | Property Impact<br>5 ←→ 1 | Business Impact<br>Low Impact | Internal Resources<br>Weak 5 Resources | External Resources<br>1 Strong Resources | Total |
|---|---|---|---|---|---|---|---|
|  |  |  |  |  |  |  |  |
|  |  |  |  |  |  |  |  |
|  |  |  |  |  |  |  |  |
|  |  |  |  |  |  |  |  |
|  |  |  |  |  |  |  |  |
|  |  |  |  |  |  |  |  |
|  |  |  |  |  |  |  |  |
|  |  |  |  |  |  |  |  |
|  |  |  |  |  |  |  |  |

Figure 14.1—Vulnerability Analysis chart

developed "Dam Failure" Studies for many of the dams and these studies are very useful.

Within your corporation you want to examine the experience of various emergencies, including the size and impact of the emergency, at locations throughout the company. The event that occurred in Great Britain in 1993 may in fact have some possibility of happening at your location and you will want to gain from their experience. One of the most difficult aspects of emergency planning is examining emergencies at other locations within the same company and learning the lessons. Most organizations tend to remain isolated within the various locations and not only are the lessons of previous emergencies not shared but the sharing of resources in responding to a future emergency is ignored or minimized.

For a Business Continuity scenario, make sure you look carefully at the issues of vital records, computer operations, hot sites, continued supplier operations, continued customer operations, death of the CEO/Founder of the company, and the negative news media reports based upon either fact or fiction. All of these events can have a very significant impact on your company and its very survival. The loss of electric power, telephone service, or other utilities can create a real time emergency that doesn't involve the loss of life or structural damage to the facilities. But it can have a very significant negative impact on your business operations.

# Identify the existence of appropriate emergency response procedures

Once you have determined what can constitute an emergency and established a framework for determining the impact of the various emergencies on your company, you can begin the task of determining what emergency plans and/or procedures are currently in place. This may seem to be a futile task as you either find that there are no plans/procedures which specifically address the various potential emergencies, determine that the plans/procedures were written ten years ago and won't work in today's environment, or find that there are too many separate plans/procedures which are very redundant. In some ways it is easier to start with nothing rather than to try to bring order out of the chaos of a dozen or more incident-specific emergency plans/procedures.

However, the collection of the numerous plans and procedures will provide you with an opportunity to create several matrices. On the first one, list the names of the various plans/procedures across one side of the matrix and on the other side list responsibilities, communication channels, notification systems, operational areas, equipment, and so forth. Each of these may be subdivided to permit you to list all of the information. For example, communications may have telephone (office, cellular, pager, power failure), radio (different frequencies), e-mail, Internet, commercial radio stations, and commercial television stations. Then in each box of the matrix identify the specific information from each plan/procedure. Usually you will see that a number of the plans/procedures use the same operational area, or the same position has the same responsibilities no matter what the emergency. A pattern will quickly develop along with empty boxes. This matrix will permit you to see how you can consolidate much of the common information into a single plan.

We will use the information from the first matrix to begin to develop a second matrix that will provide us with a clear picture of responsibilities. This will be a simple Primary and Support Matrix which will clearly outline the emergency response functions and the organizations or individuals who are responsible for carrying out those functions. Along one matrix list the organizations/department which might be involved in response and recovery to an emergency (management, human resources, maintenance, information systems, environmental, safety, production, public relations, communications, engineering, etc.) and on the other matrix list the functions that need to be performed (notification, direction and control, public information, hazardous materials response, medical response, employee notification, notification of next-of-kin, etc.). Then for each function place a P (for primary) in the box by the organization/department that has the primary responsibility and an S (for support) for those organizations/departments who will have support responsibilities. When this matrix is finished not every box will be completed. This matrix will identify for you, and your entire organization, who is going to be responsible for each function.

These two matrices will next lead you to determining what is missing. Is it a lack of communication systems, a central location for directing the response to the emergency, training for hazardous materials incidents, not having an organization identified to handle the news media, or whatever? Now you can begin to make assignments and allocate the necessary resources to ensure that the organizations and individuals are prepared to respond to an emergency.

As you continue the process of consolidating the existing documents into a single, effective emergency management plan, you want to determine how effective the current plans/procedures have been in past emergencies. This is best accomplished by talking with the individuals who have used the procedures. Ask questions such as: Did you use the procedure in response to the emergency? How effective was the procedure? What needs to be changed in the procedure to make it more effective? Did you have sufficient training on the procedure prior to the emergency? Is there equipment or facilities that need to be upgraded to make the procedure more effective?

If the procedure has never been used in an actual emergency, you can ask the same questions about the use of the procedure in a drill or exercise. Be very careful to identify the type of drill or exercise that was conducted and whether it really provided an opportunity to test the procedure in a situation very close to an emergency condition.

At the same time you are asking questions about existing plans/procedures also interview the key participants in your emergency response organization. They will be the individuals identified in the Primary and Support Matrix. You should interview them with the idea of picking their brains to identify good ideas and learn at first hand what each individual believes is the best way to respond to an emergency. You need to ask them about their perceived role and responsibilities in an emergency, what type of procedure they would most likely use/follow, what experiences they have had in actual emergencies (either at this location or at another company), what they think would be the worst emergency for their department and the company, and what they think can be done to make the emergency management programme better.

## Recommend the development of emergency procedures where none exist

When the emergency occurs we anticipate, and hope, that every employee will respond as they have been trained to. And for those individuals who have response functions to perform, that they will follow their training and their procedures. In the heat of battle, people won't turn to an extensive plan but will rely on a simple, concise procedure. And if one doesn't exist then they will respond by the seat of their pants. Thus every emergency response function must have a procedure detailing the activities that must be considered and/or taken in response to an emergency.

For the members of the Emergency Management Group (the individuals responsible for the overall response to an emergency) their procedures may be included in their Position Notebook (see below). Ideally, their individual procedures will be a checklist of actions to be performed and considerations that must be evaluated. For example, items such as determining the exact location of the emergency along with the number of injured and killed are recorded. And considerations for evacuating other areas of the facility, notifying customers of possible delays in product delivery and determining the message to be given to stockholders are also included.

For members of the Emergency Response Group (the individuals responsible for the immediate response and termination of the emergency—fire, medical, hazardous materials, etc.), the procedures will clearly identify actions for establishing triage areas, conducting hazardous materials response, and for conducting search and rescue. These procedures will help to ensure a safe response as well as to protect both the victims and the responders.

The format of the procedures is dependent upon company policy and usability. Whether the format is one with each sentence being numbered or merely a simple checklist, the users of the procedures have to be comfortable with the format. The format must encourage the use of the procedure, not restrict its use.

A good test of the usability and effectiveness of a procedure (short of use in an actual emergency) is how easily employees who are being trained on the function for the first time can understand and follow the procedure. If it takes hours and hours of training to be able to understand and follow the procedure then it is probably too complicated or confusing. You can test the readability and under- standing of a procedure by asking someone who has never seen the procedure to read it and tell you what they would have to do if they were asked to follow it.

Like the Emergency Plan, the procedures will go through a sequence of steps before being implemented. A standard sequence or cycle is a first draft followed by a review by a number of potential users. Then comes a consolidation of the comments and development of a second version. The second version should then be tested in a limited drill or tabletop exercise. This "testing" will highlight addi- tional changes and permit the issuance of the final version. Of course, over time the procedure will be updated and revised, based upon actual emergencies, new equipment and changes in personnel.

## Integrate disaster recovery/business continuity procedures with emergency response procedures

The transfer of emergency operations into recovery operations begins as soon as you know the location of the emergency and initial estimates, or perceptions, of damage. Knowing that a fire occurred in the main warehouse will have you thinking about the loss of product, delays in shipping, impact on customers, lost profits and other business concerns.

Therefore the emergency procedures must logically lead you into recovery and business continuity procedures and activities. One way to facilitate the transfer is to have representatives for business recovery operations as members of the Emer- gency Management Group. Some of these positions are naturally occurring, such as the Risk Manager, Production Manager, Maintenance, Public Relations and Engineering. They are present to respond to the emergency and their knowledge about the emergency will permit them to initiate recovery and business continuity activities very quickly.

One of the major concerns for any business will be the actual and perceived impact of the emergency on customers and suppliers. This concern is initially addressed during the emergency when the decisions are made about the content of press releases, the contact with customers by Customer Service or Sales, and what the Sales Department is told to tell customers when they call. Those first statements will have a dramatic impact on business continuity.

This is not to imply, or state, that you give false statements and mislead customers about the seriousness of the emergency. Or about the impact of the emergency on the customer. But it is the opportunity to put into place the back-up systems, operations and options that will allow you to continue to meet the needs of your suppliers and customers. In some cases the most immediate option available to you may be to supply your customer with products from one of your competitors. But you should plan that in advance.

Early in the emergency response phase you may be considering how to shift production to another facility or to use contract manufacturers. Or you may have to use back-up shippers to deliver products. But at the very least, you want to contact every customer who is affected by the emergency and inform them of how you are going to meet their needs. And then you want to contact your other customers and give them a status report. Customer service is still paramount.

The business continuity procedures should identify the back-up operational facilities, contract manufacturers, testing laboratories, shippers and suppliers. Have contracts in place to immediately activate their services. And include in the procedure the names, telephone numbers (24 hours-a-day), fax numbers, and so on for each back-up organization.

Before any emergency strikes, have a very candid conversation with your insurance carrier. Be very precise in determining what types of emergencies are covered, the amount of deductible, the percentage of loss covered, amount of business loss covered and for how long, and if the loss of potential new business is included.

At this point you will also want to develop a list of contractors who can be called upon to help restore, repair or rebuild your buildings. You can lock in rates and know in advance the type of work they can perform and the number of people they can provide.

## Identify the command and control requirements of managing an emergency

Who is in control of the emergency response and recovery? What are their responsibilities? Where do they operate from? Who reports to them? Who do they report to? How do they function? These are all essential questions and ones that will help to shape your emergency response organization.

There are two different organizations, or groups, who may be involved within your company. The first one, the Emergency Management Group, should be present in every company. The second one, the Emergency Response Group, may or may not be present in every company. Let's look at both groups, their roles, their composition and how they interact with one another.

The Emergency Management Group (EMG) is responsible for the overall big picture of the emergency and its impact on the company. They are responsible not only for identifying the location and source of the emergency but also for determining the emergency's impact on the rest of the facility, employees, visitors, contractors, surrounding community, stockholders, customers and suppliers. They will be responsible for coordinating with regulatory agencies, contacting family members of victims, interfacing with the news media, working with insurance companies, providing additional resources to resolve the emergency, and keeping control over the entire situation. They must be able to look at the big picture and make decisions that will have the potential for long-term ramifications.

So who makes up the EMG? For the most part it is senior management representing functions such as production, engineering, safety, environmental, human resources, public relations, risk management, accounting, information services, legal, records management, and management. They are supported by administrative staff who are absolutely essential to the successful operation of the group. The number of members of the EMG will vary depending upon the type of emergency, its location and consequences, but all members should be assembled at the beginning of the response so all potential aspects of the emergency are addressed and the best allocation of resources is accomplished.

The EMG is directed by an individual referred to as the Emergency Director. In some organizations the individual maintains his usual title, but for our discussion we will use the title Emergency Director. He is responsible for the EMG and for assuring that it has the information it needs to make informed decisions. He authorizes the individual members of the EMG to perform their responsibilities while creating teamwork among the members by having information shared, decisions arrived at jointly (where appropriate) and using all the necessary resources within the organization to limit and terminate the emergency and undertake the recovery process. He has the authority to authorize the expenditure of funds and to commit the organization to specific actions.

While the Emergency Director is normally the highest ranking company official, in some organizations this individual may want to play a different role. He/she may want to be free to go to the scene of the emergency, to be interviewed by the news media, to visit victims at the hospital, and to go where he/she believes he/she can have the greatest positive impact. If this is the case in your company, then the individual needs to be equipped with a radio/cellular telephone so you have constant communications with him/her (to keep him/her informed of changing situations and information) and someone else has to assume the role of Emergency Director.

The second group, the Emergency Response Group (ERG), consist of individuals who have been specifically trained to deal with one or more unique emergency conditions. They are prepared by training, organization, equipment and authorization to respond to fires, hazardous materials spills, medical emergencies and/or search and rescue operations. They are probably organized under the "Incident Command" system and are led by an Incident Commander. They have a very specific mission which is to report to the scene of the emergency and resolve the immediate issue. They are not concerned with notification of regulatory agencies, meeting with the news media, contacting family members or other actions being performed by the Emergency Management Group. The ERG has tunnel vision in terms of recognizing, responding and resolving the immediate emergency.

The ERG will have their own equipment, training programme, organization, and communications. They should be highly trained individuals who have the necessary physical and mental requirements to meet the immediate challenge. They will be organized under the concepts of Incident Command and understand the roles of Incident Commander, Safety Officer, Logistics Officer, Operations Officer and Scribes. The Incident Commander must have a secure means of communication with the Emergency Management Group since he will be required to keep the EMG informed about the situation and the progress that is being made. The EMG will also actively promote procuring additional resources that the ERG needs. These may range from additional personnel to drinking water. But it is essential that the two groups work together.

An additional key element in the command and control of the emergency response is the community emergency response agencies. Those companies that do not have their own Emergency Response Group will be totally dependent upon the community to provide fire, law enforcement, hazardous material, medical and rescue services. This will require the company to know the capabilities and individuals of these organizations and to actively promote the exchange of information between the two organizations. Tours of the company's facilities, joint training sessions and joint exercises will be the best way to build confidence in each other.

When an emergency occurs, the company should automatically provide the responding community emergency response agency with personnel to direct the response organization to the scene of the emergency, personnel to serve as a liaison between the company and the response organization, and technical support personnel to identify chemicals, shut-off valves for chemical process and/or electrical lines, the location of natural gas lines, the location of water and sewer lines, and other vital pieces of information. The company will also have to provide the number, names and last known location of missing personnel to the response organization.

So where do the EMG and the ERG operate from? The ERG will operate from a Command Post at the scene of the emergency. The Command Post may range from the front seat of a response vehicle to a mobile Command Post. The Incident Commander will operate from this location and will have his communication resources at this point. This is the location to which the company must send representatives to provide communication between the Incident Commander and the Emergency Management Group and to answer basic questions from the Incident Commander. If technical advisers from the company are required by the Incident Commander, the Command Post is where they will report.

The Emergency Management Group will operate from an Emergency Operations Centre (EOC). The EOC is a predetermined location that will be equipped to permit the EMG to operate 24 hours a day for as long as necessary. It should be equipped with tables, chairs, telephones, radios, television, commercial radio, clock, flip charts/white boards, computers, display boards, copies of plans/procedures, maps/diagrams of the facility, telephone directories (community and company) and other pieces of equipment that will permit the EMG to do their job. The facility is tested at least twice a year through exercises and should not take more than ten minutes to be made fully operational. There is also an alternative location either on site or at a location outside of the facility.

The EOC can be a conference room, training room, or some other location within the facility. It may also be a fully dedicated facility that is only used for this purpose. It should have nearby restroom facilities, eating area, sleeping area, duplication facility, and small rooms that can be used for private meetings.

You will also want to identify both a primary and an alternative Media Briefing Centre (MBC) for meeting with the news media. In today's society, you can never assume that the news media won't make an appearance when you have an emergency. Part of your planning process is to recognize the needs of the news media and how you can provide them with the information they need to assist you to transmit important information to your employees, customers, stockholders and the general public. One of your planning tools is the development of the Media Briefing Centre, where you can conduct press conferences.

The MBC will most likely be a multipurpose room such as a conference room, auditorium or cafeteria. It should be able to accommodate 20–30 members of the news media and provide them with seats, electrical outlets for their equipment, and refreshments. You will also need to equip it with a podium, television, VCR, clock, and audio visual equipment that you might need to use in detailing the emergency, its location and its consequences. The briefing and press conferences that are conducted in the MBC will reflect the decisions made by the Emergency Management Group in the EOC. Any news conference/briefing should be video-taped and the videotape played for the members of the EOC.

The last command and control component you will want to examine is dependent upon the size of your company and whether it operates from more than one location. If you do have multiple locations then you will carefully examine how the location directly experiencing the emergency can be supported by one or more other locations. From the perspective of a large corporation, you will probably want to create a Corporate Crisis Response Team (CCRT) who will be able to provide very specific support to an individual facility for a limited amount of time.

The CCRT usually provides unique skills/experience which the location experiencing the emergency either does not have or has expended. For example, the local facility may have one individual who can meet with the news media, but because of the duration of the emergency (or other reasons) this one individual cannot meet all of their demands. In this case the public relations member of the CCRT can be dispatched to the local facility to work with the local organization in responding to the news media.

The CCRT is not to take over or assume control from the local organization, unless that is the request of the local organization. The CCRT is there to provide support and fill in missing elements. Members of the CCRT may represent risk management, legal, engineering, environmental, safety, production, public relations, information systems, human resources, and management. Each company needs to examine their organization and determine who should be a member of the CCRT.

To be effective the CCRT must be capable of being activated and on the road to the location of the emergency within 90 minutes. It will take with it its own equipment such as: laptop computer(s), credit cards/purchase orders, cellular telephone(s), maps, plans/procedures, safety equipment (hard hats, safety glasses, hearing protection, steel tip shoes), paper, pens, portable printer, clothing and so on. If the emergency involves the entire community (hurricane, tornado), the CCRT will want to take extra clothing and perhaps bottled water and/or canned food.

# Recommend the development of command and control procedures to define roles, authority and communication processes for managing an emergency

The members of the Emergency Management Group, Emergency Response Group and the Corporate Crisis Response Team will all have their own procedures. The ones for the Emergency Response Group will mostly likely be a series of checklists to ensure they respond safely and effectively to the specific emergency. They will be based upon the Incident Command System and be very specific for the response to the specific emergency. These checklists may be laminated so they can easily be used and marked on with china pencils and then be cleaned and reused again and again.

The Corporate Crisis Response Team will have procedures that are more general in nature but will give them a checklist of issues and activities that must be examined to ensure that the local facility is effectively responding to the emergency. They will also have a site description for each of the company locations they may have to support. These site descriptions will include: brief description of the facility; local government officials; local news media contacts; directions from the airport to the facility; local hotels; and other information that will permit the CCRT to begin working immediately upon their arrival.

The Emergency Management Group will have simple checklists that will be a part of their Position Notebooks. Each position in the EMG will have its own customized notebook (probably a ¼ inch three-ring binder) detailing the activities they must execute or examine, resources that are available to them and any unique information that they want to have available to them. Each notebook may have a section of common information (emergency action levels, organization table, communication directory, etc.) but each will have its own unique checklists and support materials. A copy of each Position Notebook is always kept in the Emergency Operations Centre and each member of the EMG should also have their own second copy that they will keep in their office and/or briefcase.

The Position Notebook will permit each member of the EMG to quickly and effectively perform their responsibilities in an emergency. In those instances where a primary member of the EMG is not present, the Position Notebook will permit the replacement to easily determine what actions need to be considered or completed and to become an effective member of the EMG with a minimum of downtime.

The checklists within the Position Notebooks should be just that. A checklist of actions that should be considered, reviewed and/or implemented for each emergency. Not every action will be completed for every emergency, but each action should be considered. This approach will permit each member of the EMG to work both independently and jointly to achieve a quick resolution of the emergency. It eliminates having some individuals just going off to do their own thing (and perhaps working in a counter-productive manner) or relying on individuals to use their "best judgement" and the seat of their pants to respond to the emergency.

The basic section of the Comprehensive Emergency Management Plan will detail the roles, authorities, organization, operational areas and responsibilities of the Emergency Management Group and the Emergency Response Group. This basic section is not long (usually between four and fifteen pages depending upon the size of the organization) but gives a very precise overview of how the organization is structured and how it will respond to an emergency.

The roles and responsibilities identified in the Primary and Support Matrix earlier are detailed in the basic section. A brief listing of the responsibilities for each member of the EMG is given and an organization table clearly identifies both membership and organization. The location, layout and equipment needs for both the Emergency Operations Centre and the Media Briefing Centre are included. The basic section will also identify any Emergency Action Levels (EALs) that the organization will use to initiate automatic actions.

EALs are brief descriptions of trigger points that call for automatic actions to be implemented by the Emergency Management Group, the Emergency Response Group and general employees. They are usually based upon a combination of weather conditions, type of emergency, size of the emergency, number of injuries/deaths, off-site consequences or regulatory requirements.

Communications in any emergency is always the one topic that everyone afterwards agrees could be improved. Identification of existing systems is one of the primary functions to be accomplished when developing your emergency management programme. How many radio frequencies currently exist? Who can talk to whom on which frequencies? How many telephone systems exist? Are any of the telephone lines able to function when the basic telephone system is non-functional? Who has cellular telephones? What kind of information can be sent out over e-mail? Do we have an internal television network? If so, who has access to it? Are our fax machines on separate telephone lines?

The members of the EMG need to be able to talk to each other (usually face to face in the EOC), to members of their staff (telephone, radio), to the Incident Commander (radio or cellular telephone), the news media (face to face, telephone), customers/suppliers (telephone and news media), general public (news media, Internet), employees (telephone, radio, e-mail, news media), other company locations (telephone, cellular telephone, e-mail, Internet, satellite television broadcast) and Board of Directors (telephone, news media, e-mail, Internet).

The communication channels need to be identified and their reliability established. Back-up systems must be established and the limitations of the current systems understood. The types of information that can be transmitted over the various types of communication systems must be recognized. For example, you never want to transmit the names of fatalities or injured personnel over a non-secure radio frequency.

You also want to recognize that the news media can be a very valuable channel for informing employees, families, general public, customers, competitors and regulators about your situation and what is being done to relieve it. Knowing all of this in advance, will permit you to develop sample press releases, determine the types of messages that need to be prepared for the individual audiences, and be prepared to keep everyone informed about the situation.

At the same time, you need to be aware of the rumour and innuendo that may be being spread through gossip, the news media and/or the Internet. The Emergency Management Group needs to anticipate that this will happen and be prepared to respond to these false reports in a very positive manner. Facts and the method in which they are presented are essential.

## Ensure emergency response procedures are integrated with requirements of public authorities

While most emergency management programmes are developed to ensure the proper preparation, response and recovery to an emergency, some programmes are only developed because of a legal requirement. The occurrence of various emergencies (chemical releases, Three Mile Island, explosions, etc.) over the years has resulted in a wave of regulations from local, state and federal agencies. They are intended to protect workers and the general public but they place unique planning requirements on the specific industries or companies.

You need to identify the specific regulations that apply directly to you and determine how you are going to meet them. In some instances it may seem expeditious to merely write a plan that will follow the outline of the regulation and thus, one hopes, permit you to comply with the regulation. However, while this approach might get you an approval rating from the regulatory agency, will the plan permit you to effectively prepare for the emergency and, more importantly, effectively respond to the emergency? The plan and procedures need first to permit you and your organization to effectively respond to the emergency and then to address each of the elements of the regulation. This may require you to actually create another section at the end of your plan, identifying where in the plan you meet the regulation and/or address the remaining regulatory requirements.

You may also have to create a matrix to show where your one overall plan meets the requirements of several regulations. Creating a separate plan for each regulation is asking for a disaster. A multitude of plans will not only contain a great deal of repetitive information but will also confuse your people when they are trying to figure out which plan they should be following to meet an emergency.

You may also find yourself trying to meet the standards from some international organizations. Again, the key element is how usable the document is for your employees in an emergency. Required, standardized formats tend to create "cookie cutter" plans that look great on paper but are less than effective in an emergency. Discuss these issues with the regulators and try to find an approach that will satisfy both needs.

Finally, it is vital that all of your emergency planning efforts are coordinated with the organizations that you are relying on to help you respond to an emergency. As was stated earlier, share your needs, requests and resources with the local community emergency response organizations. Joint training and exercising will permit both organizations to develop a working relationship and test equipment, procedure and organizational coordination.

If they know your facility and your capabilities then they can respond more effectively. If you know their capabilities and limitations then you can plan accordingly. In either event, both you and the community response organizations are winners in this type of arrangement.

# Developing and implementing the written Plan

Andrew Hiles—UK

Andrew Hiles is Chairman of *Survive!* and a director of The Kingswell Partnership, an international consultancy specializing in business continuity, risk management and service delivery.

## Developing the Plan: scoping

### Where do you start?

What is the scope of the Plan? Will it cover all sites? Will it assume skilled people remain available after the disaster? How far will it go into the customer chain and the supply chain? Will it cater for multiple disasters—perhaps simultaneously at different sites? Will it cover just Information Technology disaster recovery, or all functions? Will it cover industrial relations issues? Will it cover a wide area disaster or just loss of company facilities? These initial scoping decisions are important and the decisions and assumptions made should be exposed.

The next step is to define what your recovery capability is going to be. Is it to be "business as usual" or simply operation in survival mode? Can you get by simply by supporting the 20% of customers who give you 80% of your profit—or the 20% of branches that provide 80% of your turnover? How long can you get by without serving your customers? Your Business Impact Analysis should have considered these issues and your recovery strategy should balance the potential losses against ongoing costs for business continuity and business recovery services. However, there are many ways of achieving your objectives, and a sound plan is usually a judicious mix of the strategic recovery options outlined below.

## Business continuity strategy: options

The best business continuity plans tend to take the worst possible case, on the basis that such plans are likely to cater for lesser events. They also split the

*The Definitive Handbook of Business Continuity Management.* Edited by Andrew Hiles and Peter Barnes. © 1999 John Wiley & Sons Ltd.

organization into two teams: one to manage the ongoing business activities, the other to handle disaster response and recovery.

The restart strategy is an important determinant of the costs. The options which follow are not necessarily mutually exclusive; they may be complementary.

Options are:

### Do Nothing

The "do nothing option" is to wait until a disaster happens and hope to acquire equipment and facilities at the time. This may be appropriate where an organization has a recovery window permitting restoration of services, without prejudice to the business, which can be met by the equipment and facility acquisition lead time.

### Fortress

A fortress approach will seek to limit risk to a level where management decides any further disaster recovery plan is unnecessary. A fortress can only protect what is inside it: the operation may still be vulnerable (for instance, through loss of external data or telecommunications or denial of access to the site). Moreover, in some cases buildings may be open to the public and in other cases may not be suitable for a fortress approach. In all cases, however, a degree of "hardening" will be possible.

### Continuous Processing

Continuous operation will provide continuous "shadowing" or "mirroring" of the production operation at an alternative site with adequate capacity and communications links to permit the production operation to be switched to the alternative site at minimal notice. One major bank, for instance, has an 8-minute recovery window. The cost of this option is high: it implies standby, installed and operational equipment waiting for a disaster.

### Distributed Processing

Distributed processing spreads the risk around different locations so that not all the corporate eggs are in one basket. Some production or operations may reside on dedicated equipment so that the loss of this equipment leaves other production unharmed and available. Alternatively, operations may be replicated at different sites in order to gain even more resilience. Distributed processing may be designed with disaster recovery capability in mind, so that there is excess capacity on which to rebuild the lost application. Recovery is facilitated by standardization of equipment.

### Alternative Site

An alternative site may be selected either from a commercial disaster recovery service supplier or from spare in-company accommodation. Standby workspace needs to be considered as well as standby equipment. Depending on the required recovery timeframe, the alternative site may be:

#### Cold

A "cold" site will provide an environment in which a new facility can be built from scratch.

### Warm
A "warm" site will provide an environment and basic infrastructure to enable the facility to be reinstated before its absence becomes critical to business survival. It may have most of the equipment required except, perhaps, for items that can be supplied quickly from stock.

### Hot
A "hot site" will effectively provide a duplicate facility in another location, with capacity to absorb the additional workload before its absence becomes critical to business survival. A hot site will have all the equipment and facilities required operationally and will simply require installation of systems, applications and data.

Cold, hot and warm facilities may be mobile (delivered in trailers with independent environment), portable (delivered in prefabricated form, with independent environment) or static (pre-installed at the supplier's or in-company premises).

Where an organization has more than one site, relocation from the stricken site to another site or sites may offer relief. While these might offer short-term havens for a few people, they may not offer a reliable site for relocation of all the essential work unless it was agreed that these premises would be evacuated in a disaster.

Commercial disaster recovery service vendors normally limit the period for which a warm or hot site can be used. This is typically six weeks—so in the event of a major disaster such as a fire or explosion, it may be necessary to move from the warm or hot site to a cold site and then back to the original premises.

### "Budge Up"
This is a variation on the Alternative Site option: it simply means optimizing the use of your own existing facilities. This may mean working weekends or shifts in office or production facilities where this is not normal practice—or it could mean sending non-essential staff home to make space for staff undertaking higher priority work.

### Quick Resupply
This approach depends on acquiring equipment, software and communications facilities when the disaster occurs. Equipment vendors or disaster recovery service suppliers may guarantee resupply within a specified timescale in return for a retainer.

### Off-site Storage
Commercial services are available for off-site storage of materials vital to recovery. These can range from storage of buffer stock, equipment, documents, tools, plant, samples, as well as computer tapes and discs. Computer data can be transmitted to on-line back-up to tapes stored in tape libraries or silos or to disc arrays.

Off-site back-up should aim to supply secure storage, with contents retrievable 24 hours per day, 365 days per year.

### Working from Home
Using PCs with modems, working from home may be practicable for some staff. PCs may be:

drawn from a quick resupply contract;
redistributed portable PCs;
salvaged;
obtained from PC superstores, some of which are open 6½ days a week.

Access can quickly be gained to the Internet for e-mail—subject to security constraints.

### Reciprocal Arrangements

Reciprocal arrangements tend not to work in practice. Frequently they are not adequately documented and supported by a contract or Service Level Agreement—this leads to conflicts of priorities, dispute and sometimes refusal to honour the commitment in a disaster situation.

### Stockholding

In some circumstances, especially where there is a long lead time on resupply of production equipment and where the product has a low unit cost, it may be practicable to maintain a buffer stock to allow customer supply in the interim. The extra cost of inventory needs to be balanced against potential loss of market share.

### Outsourcing Business Continuity Planning: Management and Maintenance

Disaster recovery planning may be managed in-house or outsourced. However, the development, ongoing maintenance and testing of any Business Continuity or Disaster Recovery Plan requires the active support and commitment of in-house specialist staff to provide detailed information on requirements and configurations and to supply appropriate technical procedures.

In-house staff need to take "Ownership" of the developed plan, and their ongoing commitment to training, plan testing and maintenance is essential if the plan is to be effective when implemented.

Staffing of recovery teams could be outsourced to some extent, although the substantial involvement of internal staff will be essential in the event of disaster.

**The effect of weekends, public holidays and transport disruptions on equipment delivery needs to be considered as well as the basic resupply timescale.**

### Lateral Thinking

By focusing on the deliverable of the operation, rather than on its existing processes, it may be possible to identify alternative ways of servicing customers. For instance:

- Could you outsource or subcontract the service to a competitor, or buy product from a competitor to maintain supply?
- Instead of calculating, could you estimate, negotiate or arbitrate?
- could you agree a procedural solution (e.g. for a government funding operation, could you simply agree "same as before" with the paymasters)?

## Insurance

Insurance is a critical part of the recovery plan. However, insurance in itself simply provides money if defined risks occur. It does not necessarily pay out immediately—in some cases payment can take years. Stating the obvious, it only pays for what it covers—which is why one financial institution received only half what it would cost them to restore a historic building to its former glory. Insurance by itself will not supply customers, nor will it guarantee recovery of market share. Moreover, the recovery plan should take into account that the insurer will have a major say after a disaster in decisions to replace or salvage equipment and in any actions which involve extra cost of working or which are intended to alleviate loss of profits. Issues of salvage and purchase of new equipment will need to be cleared with the insurers.

If the insurers do not like what you are doing, their payout may be reduced. Insurance of loss of profits and for extra cost of working only covers a specific time period—typically six or twelve months after a disaster. After that, you are on your own. And while self-insurance sounds like a good idea, in many cases any self-insured loss eventually comes back (in one way or another) to hit the bottom line.

To make an effective claim, you need to prove loss. This usually involves production of records and inventories of equipment, stock, software, data. A claim for loss of service at say $100 000 an hour is difficult to sustain—it has to be proved that such a loss has occurred. Insurers may claim for instance that it is not really a loss, merely a deferred sale. If a disaster happens just as a new product or service is about to be launched, it may be difficult or impossible to prove what the profit from it would have been. Insurers may look back at history rather than forward at plans.

However, appropriate insurance of assets, working costs and profits does provide a lifeline and should be considered as part of the continuity strategy.

## Options and Strategy Recommendations

The cost of the recovery option has to be weighed against the impact of loss of service on the business. Cost is usually related to speed of recovery.

The effect of weekends, public holidays and transport disruptions on equipment delivery needs to be considered as well as the basic resupply timescale.

Typically the strategic options outlined above are not mutually exclusive—the optimum solution may "pick and mix" from these strategies for individual business functions or combine several elements to form a comprehensive solution. A business unit may, for example, decide that it needs 100 workplaces available within eight hours followed by quick resupply of equipment for 25 people working from home within 48 hours and a cold site to house another 100 people within five working days.

# Option evaluation

Basically, the "hotter", bigger and more comprehensive the restart capability, the more expensive it is likely to be. It is therefore important to be realistic about the timescale within which recovery can physically be achieved, bearing in mind the specific nature of each organization's operations, and to keep the numbers of staff involved during recovery to the minimum required to maintain operations.

# How the Plan builds up

Figure 15.1 shows how the Plan is developed as the Business Continuity Project progresses. Existing Procedures, Asset Registers, Inventories and similar information can provide a starting point. The Business Impact Analysis helps to justify the Business Continuity strategy. Often the Business Impact Analysis overstates the timescale for recovery—few departments will admit to being unnecessary for days or weeks! It may also be used to:

- Identify materials vital to recovery which should be kept off-site
- Establish equipment and resource requirements over time
- Establish capacity requirements

A "sanity check" should be run on equipment and resource requirements—again, these may be overstated. Capacity requirements, however, are often understated. If there is a backlog of orders following a disaster, greater capacity than normal may be required to avoid an irretrievable backlog situation.

An evaluation of contracts may also identify exposure to vendors or customers which needs to be reflected in recovery strategy. Once the strategy has been defined, the requirements can be firmed up and arrangements made for their provision following a disaster.

## Service contracts

Depending on the strategy selected, contracts may need to be negotiated with vendors—for instance, for standby facilities and equipment or quick resupply of equipment. These contractual arrangements will need to be reflected in the Business Continuity Plan—they are not, by themselves, a Business Continuity Plan.

# Business continuity organization and roles

An effective plan needs an organizational infrastructure. Classic Business Continuity Plans divide the operational activities into two: one arm dealing with the

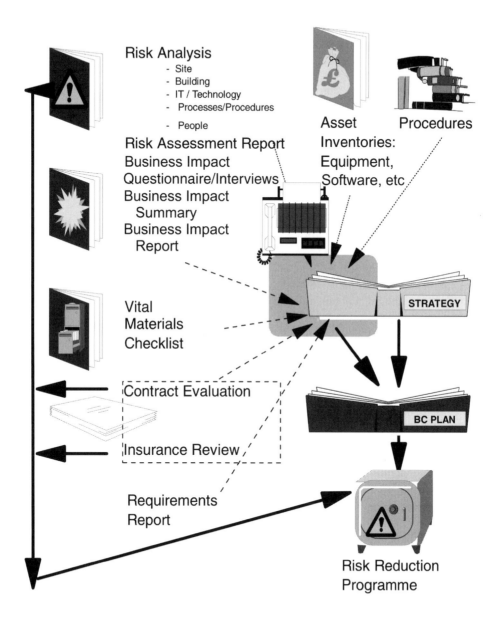

**Figure 15.1**—Plan build-up

ongoing operations unaffected by the disaster, and the other arm dealing with the consequences of the disaster and recovery from it. Typically an Emergency Management Team will be established, comprising key senior managers, public relations and marketing, and the Business Continuity Manager or Coordinator. This management team will have their own top level Business Continuity Plans which are integrated with subordinate Departmental or Business Unit recovery action plans (see Figure 15.2).

The role of the Emergency Management Team (EMT) is to take business decisions, assess and make judgements on business priorities and to facilitate and support the Business Continuity Manager. They also have an important role in marketing, public relations and media management issues.

Normally an Emergency Control Centre (ECC) has been established: this is a "War Room" that contains all of the technical infrastructure and documentation necessary to oversee the recovery effort. The loss of premises will have been considered as part of the planning and arrangements for an off-site ECC will have been made.

The Business Continuity Manager (BCM) is usually a member of the EMT and is effectively the project manager for the recovery operations, reconciling priorities and coordinating recovery efforts of the departmental or business unit recovery managers. The BCM ensures communication between Teams and to Public Relations, Marketing and the EMT.

In their turn, the departmental and business unit recovery managers manage the recovery in their own areas and ensure communication with other affected teams and with the BCM.

The Plan will have considered what staff are needed for the recovery effort and non-essential staff will have been sent home or found alternative accommodation.

The roles of departments will change fundamentally, for instance:

- Human Resources will not be involved so much in annual appraisals and training as in providing welfare and logistical support, particularly for members of the recovery teams, and possibly in arranging trauma counselling
- Internal Audit will be involved in policing *ad hoc* financial and procurement activity and may provide spare resource for the recovery teams
- Legal department may be involved in litigation rather than in contractual issues
- Sales may be trying to restrain customers from buying while maintaining customer confidence and market position

The Premises Management plan is crucial to effective and speedy damage limitation and restoration of the facility.

## The Plan

The Business Continuity Plan will have an incident escalation procedure that allows the incident to be compared to a definition of disaster. If the incident is, or

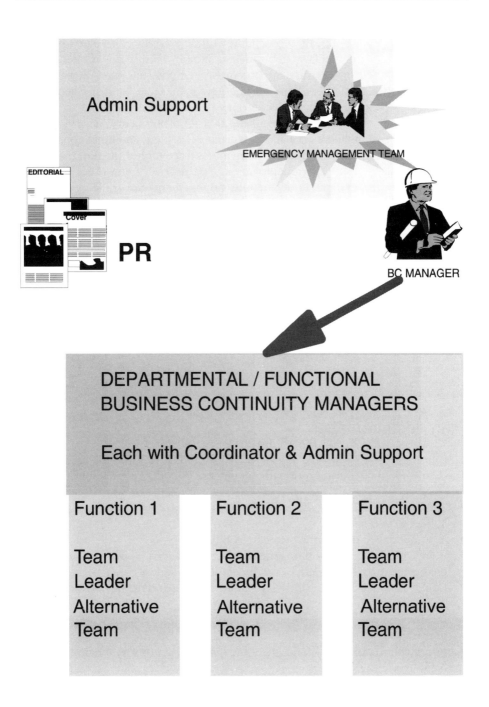

**Figure 15.2**—Business continuity organization

may be, a disaster, a decision is then made as to whether to alert teams or to mobilize the plan. A notification procedure will be established to alert and mobilize management and members of business continuity teams. This is often a documented calling tree or "cascade" arrangement whereby one person calls several others, who then call others, until all key personnel have been notified. If Call Centre-type technology is available, this may be automated.

The Plan will cater for all phases of the disaster. The initial Emergency Phase covers evacuation, incident escalation, damage assessment and limitation, disaster declaration, invocation of standby arrangements, recovery of off-site materials to the standby site(s) and staff redeployment. The Recovery Phase covers the re-establishment of operations under standby arrangements in parallel with restoration of longer term facilities. The Plan should also consider the move back from standby facilities to a permanent base. In the Recovery Phase, different procedures, practices, equipment and software may be involved. Change management and the audit trail of change is therefore crucial—otherwise the move back to permanent base may become a disaster.

The Plan should also cater for logging of actions to begin as soon as possible: this will be essential to provide evidence for insurance claims, for possible legal actions, and to keep track of spend (using predefined disaster account codes). If available, it may be possible to use existing Help Desk tools or to design a simple database for this purpose.

## Plan documentation

The Plan should be an action-oriented document. It needs to include:

- Title, document control, date and version number, confidentiality marking
- Table of contents
- Assumptions and known weaknesses of the Plan
- Alert, invocation, notification and briefing instructions (sometimes issued on a credit card-sized document or on the employee identity card)
- Contact lists for internal and external contacts including Business Continuity Team members
- Information on staff redeployment, standby locations and how to gain access to them
- Prioritized action plans and the time line for actions to be initiated and completed
- Lists of vital materials and instruction on how to obtain them
- Equipment and resource requirements necessary for recovery, the timescale in which they will be provided and how to obtain them

- Communication, reporting and logging requirements
- Instructions on media and reputation management
- All supporting detailed technical, operational and administrative procedures, plans, drawings maps, etc. (or references to where they may be obtained)

The plans should not include details of business impact analysis, risk assessments, tests, audit report, methodologies, detailed testing and maintenance instructions and other information not essential to the recovery effort. These should be kept separately to avoid cluttering the plan.

# Plan format

The Plan should be simple, clear, unambiguous and comprehensive. Plans based on different risk scenarios (e.g. fire, mechanical breakdown, etc.) are usually not effective: it is not usually the cause of the disaster that matters, it is the result. Whatever the cause, the result is usually damage to or loss of use of facilities. That becomes the starting point for planning. However, there may be different actions in the event of loss of facilities for say one day, three days or longer.

There are many different ways of designing the plan, including the use of:

- Specialist business continuity software tools (see Chapter 18)
- Project management software
- Database software
- Word processing tools

Selection of the right tool depends in part on who is going to become responsible for the Plan. If it is to become a line management responsibility, it is probably best to use tools for which the line manager is responsible—otherwise buy-in and maintenance of the plan may be problematic.

In a multisite environment, where departmental or operational functions span several sites, the structure of the Plan is extremely important. It may be preferable to have two views of the Plan: a site-based recovery plan and also an overall view of all recovery plans for the multisite department or operation. This can be done provided:

- A standard plan template is developed
- Terminology is absolutely consistent throughout each plan
- Each site plan has a section for each multisite department or operation which is structured so it can be collated into an overall plan for that department or operation

Annex 15.1 provides an example of a Table of Contents for one organization. Annex 15.2 contains an example of a simple plan for Media Management.

## The end—or the beginning?

A Business Continuity Plan is never completed. The more detailed the accompanying procedures, the more effective the Plan is likely to be. It is normal that, on handover, the Plan will contain less detail than is ideal and that further detail will be added during the life of the Plan. A schedule for Plan Enhancement is therefore a normal part of Business Continuity Planning.

One of the objectives of both initial and regular testing of the Plan is to find areas for improvement that can be included in the Plan Enhancement schedule.

Equally the Plan needs to be kept up to date. Clearly major organization, staff or equipment change will require revisions to the Plan. Plan maintenance therefore needs to be linked to Change Control procedure.

## ANNEX 15.1
## EXAMPLE OF CONTENTS PAGES FROM A
## BUSINESS CONTINUITY PLAN

Note

"TBD" identifies areas for completion (omitted to preserve client confidentiality).

# BUSINESS CONTINUITY PLAN CONTENTS

## BUSINESS CONTINUITY PLAN APPENDICES: CONTENTS

# ANNEX 15.2
# EXAMPLE OF A WORKING DRAFT
# MEDIA & PUBLIC RELATIONS TEAM
# BUSINESS CONTINUITY PLAN

## MEDIA & PUBLIC RELATIONS TEAM
## BUSINESS CONTINUITY PLAN

**WEAKNESSES OF THE PLAN**

1. This document is designed to develop a template and will be substantially changed as the disaster recovery project progresses. It has no pretensions to being other than a first working draft.

2. The Teams identified are examples only. They need to be amended in line with the organization's recovery structure.

3. The search string "TBD" identifies areas for decision or completion.

4. The following sections identify vital information that would be essential to ensure that the disaster recovery plans can be actioned. If the appropriate information is maintained elsewhere then simply give a reference (in the "Reference" column of the Action Plan at 9.5) to where that information can be found when required. Copies of all information must be maintained off-site so that it is readily available in the event of a disaster that prevents access to premises for an extended period.

**ASSUMPTIONS**

**TBD**

# CONTENTS

## Section 9: Media & Public Relations Team Plan

## 9.     Media & Public Relations Team

### 9.1     Media & Public Relations Team Role

To be the sole source of information to the media (directly or indirectly) from within TBD concerning the Emergency or disaster and progress of recovery

To ensure that, under *Emergency or disaster* conditions, positive media messages portray TBD as being:

- compassionate of their employees and any third parties affected by the *Emergency or disaster*
- in confident control of the situation
- able to service their customers as their customers expect
- able to retain market share
- uninterruptedly profitable
- able to meet their financial, legal and contractual commitments

To vet and approve any message to the public (through Marketing or other route) and to staff, suppliers, contractors, landlords, tenants or others which may get in to the public domain.

To establish Media and Public Relations functions at the Standby site or under Emergency conditions at *Base Site*.

To implement *Standby Procedures.*

To liaise with TBD Managers and Managers on Business Continuity arrangements.

To keep the EMT and BCM informed of actions and progress.

To maintain day-to-day contacts with TBD Managers and Managers.

To ensure timely and appropriate information is provided to stakeholders.

To maintain corporate reputation, image and credibility so as to preserve market share and managership value.

**9.2      Staffing**

Team staffing is at 9.7.1 and TBD.

**9.3      Standby Locations**

Standby Locations are detailed at TBD.

**9.4      Statement Template**

The team should be briefed on question evasion methods as appropriate. The statement should cover the following areas:

9.4.1    Concern for staff, stakeholders over death/injury and other disaster impact on them

9.4.2    Impact in perspective

9.4.3    Implementation of effective BCP

9.4.4    Confidence in ability to continue to meet client requirements/impact on customers

9.4.5    Recovery timescale

9.4.6    Impact on environment—reassure local population

9.4.7    The future—confidence

9.4.8    Next update—when and where

**9.5      Media & PR Team Action Plan**

| No. | Reference | Action | Timescale Hours 0 3 6 24 36 | Weeks 1 >1 | Contact | Y |
|---|---|---|---|---|---|---|
| 001 | TBD | Receive notification of Emergency from EMTL | X | | TBD | |
| 002 | TBD | Contact other team members | X | | TBD | |
| 003 | TBD | Arrange to meet at Control Centre | X | | TBD | |
| C04 | TBD | Get a Communications (i.e. Media and PR) Team member to Incident asap | X | | TBD | |
| 005 | TBD | Meet at Control Centre | X | | TBD | |
| 006 | TBD | Spokesperson to receive briefing from BCM Covering:<br>—Extent of loss or damage<br>—Anticipated duration of loss<br>—Anticipated recovery timescale<br>—Emergency contacts and telephone numbers etc. | X | | TBD | |
| 007 | TBD | Brief telephonists | X - X | | TBD | |
| 008 | TBD | Liaise with Marketing, HR, Procurement and EMT as necessary to ensure consistent positive message is delivered in all communications to stakeholders (other TBD offices, managers, employees, suppliers, customers, financiers etc.) | X--------X | X X | TBD | |

| No. | Reference | Action | Timescale Hours | Weeks | Contact | Y |
|---|---|---|---|---|---|---|
| 009 | TBD | Prepare statement from pre-defined template. Cover concern for people and stakeholders, nature of incident and steps for recovery; impact on business, customers and profit; time/plans for next briefing | X | | TBD | |
| 010 | TBD | Obtain EMT approval for statement | X | | TBD | |
| 011 | TBD | If possible issue statement on website with additional information (e.g. people profiles, company/site profiles, product profiles, annual accounts summary, corporate videos if relevant) | X | | TBD | |
| 012 | TBD | Release statement to media and list of stakeholders. Consider using fax bureau/call centre for contacting stakeholders and media | X | | TBD | |
| 013 | TBD | Arrange time and place for press conference | X | | TBD | |
| 014 | TBD | Contact TBD Directors and Managers and brief accordingly | X | | TBD | |
| 015 | TBD | Prepare staff and Customer communications, in liaison with Marketing, Human Resources and Finance, Facilities and Administration and IT | X----------X | X X | TBD | |
| 016 | TBD | Handle media enquiries | X----------- | X X | TBD | |

*mediaplan.doc*        *BUSINESS CONTINUITY PLAN*

| No. | Reference | Action | Timescale Hours | Weeks | Contact | Y |
|-----|-----------|--------|-----------------|-------|---------|---|
| 017 | TBD | Update statement prior to press conference and obtain EMT approval for revised statement | X----------- | X  X | TBD | |
| 018 | TBD | Identify spokesperson | X | | TBD | |
| 019 | TBD | Arrange time and venue or channel for partner and staff briefing | X | | TBD | |
| 020 | TBD | Prepare enhanced statement for staff briefing—cover: pay, expenses, relocation, job security as well as issues above | X----------- | X<br>X | TBD | |
| 021 | TBD | Hold press and manager/employee conferences | X----------- | X  X | TBD | |
| 022 | TBD | Contact key suppliers etc. in liaison with Marketing, Finance, Facilities and Administration and Production & IT | X - X | | Appendix A | |
| 023 | TBD | Ensure media handling procedures are in place | X - X | | TBD | |
| 024 | TBD | Create proactive PR campaign | X----------- | X  X | TBD | |
| 025 | TBD | When time permits, read the Business Continuity Plan. Be well informed about the current status of restoration work and client/public impact | X------- | X  X | TBD | |

| No. | Reference | Action | Timescale | | Contact | Y |
|-----|-----------|--------|-----------|-----------|---------|---|
| | | | Hours | Weeks | | |
| 026 | | Contact all TBD Managers, Managers as appropriate and other contacts according to Appendix A or other lists. Inform them about: *Your recovery situation: what services are available What services are not available When services will become available What this will mean for them (alternate methods for supply and other deviations from normal procedures).* | X -------- | X    X | Appendix A | |

*mediaplan.doc*                                  *BUSINESS CONTINUITY PLAN*

## 9.6     Key Tasks

**Departments/Areas**

**TBD**

**Secondary Department/Areas**
**TBD**

## 9.7     Contact Lists

### 9.7.1     Internal

The key internal interfaces and contacts for the department are provided in the following tables

| Media & PR Team | Members | Work Tel. | Home Tel. | Mobile Tel. | Pager |
|---|---|---|---|---|---|
| Leader | TBD | TBD | TBD | TBD | TBD |
| Alternate | TBD | TBD | TBD | TBD | TBD |
| Marketing Member | TBD | TBD | TBD | TBD | TBD |
| Member | TBD | TBD | TBD | TBD | TBD |
| Member | TBD | TBD | TBD | TBD | TBD |
| Admin Support | TBD | TBD | TBD | TBD | TBD |

### 9.7.2     External

The key externalinterfaces and contacts for the department are provided in the following table

| Company/Org. | Name | Telephone/e-mail | Position |
|---|---|---|---|
| TBD | | | |
| Journalists | TBD | TBD | TBD |
| Trade Press | TBD | TBD | TBD |
| PR Companies | TBD | TBD | TBD |

## 9.8    Vital Materials List

On activation of the department's Business Continuity Plan, one of the first activities will be to retrieve the Vital Materials from the salvage teams and/or the archive store and transfer them to the Business Continuity Site.

The Vital Materials required for the recovery of the department are stored at the following location(s):

| Vital Materials | Desk (specify) | Filing Cabinet/Firesafe (specify) | Archive Site | Network Backup |
|---|---|---|---|---|
| TBD | | | | |
| BRAD | TBD | TBD | TBD | |
| Stationery blank with TBD Logo only | TBD | TBD | TBD | TBD |
| Avery Labels pre-addressed to Corporate and customers | TBD | TBD | TBD | TBD |
| Pre-prepared faxes to other offices and customers | TBD | TBD | TBD | TBD |
| List of contacts (home and office) of managers | TBD | TBD | TBD | TBD |
| List of contacts (home and office) of customers | TBD | TBD | TBD | TBD |
| | | | | TBD |
| Business Continuity Plan | TBD | TBD | TBD | TBD |

## 9.9　　Equipment & Software & Timescale For Provisioning

| Equipment/software | 8 hrs | 16 hrs | 24 hrs | 32 hrs | 40 hrs | 48 hrs | 3 days | 5 days | 7 days | 10 days | 14 days | >14 days | lead time to aquire |
|---|---|---|---|---|---|---|---|---|---|---|---|---|---|
| Server (specify) | TBD | TBD | TBD | TBD | TBD | TBD | TBD | TBD | TBD | TBD | TBD | TBD | TBD |
| PCs (specify configuration) | TBD | TBD | TBD | TBD | TBD | TBD | TBD | TBD | TBD | TBD | TBD | TBD | TBD |
| Office Systems Server | TBD | TBD | TBD | TBD | TBD | TBD | TBD | TBD | TBD | TBD | TBD | TBD | TBD |
| Printers | TBD | TBD | TBD | TBD | TBD | TBD | TBD | TBD | TBD | TBD | TBD | TBD | TBD |
| Other (specify) | TBD | TBD | TBD | TBD | TBD | TBD | TBD | TBD | TBD | TBD | TBD | TBD | TBD |
| WP software (specify) | TBD | TBD | TBD | TBD | TBD | TBD | TBD | TBD | TBD | TBD | TBD | TBD | TBD |
| Spreadsheet (specify) | TBD | TBD | TBD | TBD | TBD | TBD | TBD | TBD | TBD | TBD | TBD | TBD | TBD |
| Database (specify) | | | | | | | | | | | | | |
| Other software (specify) | TBD | TBD | TBD | TBD | TBD | TBD | TBD | TBD | TBD | TBD | TBD | TBD | TBD |
| Telephones | TBD | TBD | TBD | TBD | TBD | TBD | TBD | TBD | TBD | TBD | TBD | TBD | TBD |
| Telephones (mobile) | TBD | TBD | TBD | TBD | TBD | TBD | TBD | TBD | TBD | TBD | TBD | TBD | TBD |
| Fax | TBD | TBD | TBD | TBD | TBD | TBD | TBD | TBD | TBD | TBD | TBD | TBD | TBD |
| Photocopier | TBD | TBD | TBD | TBD | TBD | TBD | TBD | TBD | TBD | TBD | TBD | TBD | TBD |
| Desks/chairs | TBD | TBD | TBD | TBD | TBD | TBD | TBD | TBD | TBD | TBD | TBD | TBD | TBD |
| Other (specify) | TBD | TBD | TBD | TBD | TBD | TBD | TBD | TBD | TBD | TBD | TBD | TBD | TBD |
| Photocopier—fast | TBD | TBD | TBD | TBD | TBD | TBD | TBD | TBD | TBD | TBD | TBD | TBD | TBD |
| Dictaphone/playback | TBD | TBD | TBD | TBD | TBD | TBD | TBD | TBD | TBD | TBD | TBD | TBD | TBD |
| Specify Stationery: Avery labels | TBD | TBD | TBD | TBD | TBD | TBD | TBD | TBD | TBD | TBD | TBD | TBD | TBD |
| Other | TBD | TBD | TBD | TBD | TBD | TBD | TBD | TBD | TBD | TBD | TBD | TBD | TBD |

Notes:

1. Specify the quantity of each item required and timescale by which that quantity is required under the appropriate timescale column(s)
2. For PC equipment specify memory, hard disk and modem requirements and operating system
3. For software specify make and version
4. Summarize all functions/departmental requirements for use in resupply

### 9.10  Media & PR Business Continuity Activity Log:
_____TEAM

---

**Sheet No:** ..... **Completed by** ........................ **Date:** ......... **Time:** ...................

**Name of Requester:** ................................................ **Tel:** ..........

**Contact Point:** .....................

**Name of Supplier/Service Provider:** ........................... **Tel:** ...........

**Delivery to:** ......................................

**Reason for request:**

**Details of Requirements:**

**Response:**

**Expected Delivery**      **To:** ......................... **Date/Time** .......

**Cost £** .............                          **Account Code** ..........................

**Progress Chasing—Time of calls/result:**

**Delivery Confirmed/Service Completed:** ................. **Date/Time** ..........................

**Delivered/Completed:** ...............

---

*mediaplan.doc*                        *BUSINESS CONTINUITY PLAN*

## Configuration Management

### 1  Document Approval

| Approver | Sections Approved | Signature |
|----------|-------------------|-----------|
| TBD      |                   |           |

### 2  Document Configuration

Title:                              Business Continuity Plan: Appendices
Author:                             W. Shakespear
Reference:                          h:/buscont/mediaplan/doc
Issue and Date:                     Working Draft 2.0 29 June 1999
Location of Electronic Copy:        TBD
Location of Paper Copy:             Project File
Owner:                              TBD
Change Authority:                   TBD

Distribution:
(Each distributee to be specified) Copy No ..... TBD of ........ TBD copies

### 3  Change Log

| Date      | Version | By           | Change detail       |
|-----------|---------|--------------|---------------------|
| 26 Jun 99 | 1.0     | F Bacon      | First Working Draft |
| 29 Jul 99 | 2.0     | W Shakespear | Format changed      |
|           |         |              |                     |
|           |         |              |                     |
|           |         |              |                     |
|           |         |              |                     |
|           |         |              |                     |
|           |         |              |                     |

# Awareness through auditing, training and testing

## 16 Thomas Doemland—USA

Tom is responsible for business continuity management for Farmers Insurance Group in Los Angeles and is a well known figure within the international business continuity community.

## Continuing education and periodic testing are necessary for any plan to be effective

The first section of this chapter will discuss the importance of awareness through auditing a Plan. This includes the purpose of the audits, who is responsible for the auditing, the scope and method of auditing on-site and off-site, frequency of auditing, and evaluation of the audit results. The final stage is to keep senior management awareness level up and involved with the Plan.

The second section will discuss the process of training. This includes the purpose of training, who is responsible for training, scope and method of training frequency, and evaluation of results. The third section will discuss the importance of maintenance testing a Plan. This includes the purpose of testing, and who is responsible for maintaining the Plan. Furthermore, it will explain the scope and method of testing on-site, at a hot site, the frequency of maintenance, and evaluation of results.

## Awarness through auditing

### Purpose

Audits are reports, which continually review Plans, Emergency and Recovery Tests and Exercises. A Plan or Exercise, not continually audited, is less than prepared and effective. The purpose of auditing is to ensure the continuing readiness of the Plan. The continual auditing of the Plan prior, during, and after a test or exercise is

*The Definitive Handbook of Business Continuity Management.* Edited by Andrew Hiles and Peter Barnes. © 1999 John Wiley & Sons Ltd.

invaluable to the overall efficiency and verification of your Recovery plans. While additional time may be needed to do these audits regularly, the value realized is worth the effort.

## Responsibility

The formation of a Contingency Planning Team reporting results to the corporate CEO and his staff is paramount to the success of a Plan. It not only keeps the flow of information and awareness to the highest level of the organization but also allows senior management a method of staying involved by adding their input, support and criticism to the Plan.

The Contingency Planner/Disaster Recovery Coordinator/Business Resumption Planner, as the leading member of the Contingency Planning Team, is responsible for making sure that the Plan is periodically audited. His or her responsibilities include scheduling, conducting, coordinating and evaluating the auditing process, and making sure that senior management is kept aware of the results. Both the internal and external auditing practices will continue being conducted by their appropriate areas. The audits discussed here are conducted along with those established by the Auditing Department, not in place of their audits.

## Scope and method of auditing

On-site and off-site auditing of Critical Applications, Testing of Methodology and Procedures, per the Plan, must be conducted periodically both with and without notification. Calling back critical Datasets from the off-site storage vault, and running the critical application on-site and off-site is a valid way to conduct audits. An audit may also be conducted on a tabletop scenario utilizing random personnel. The Contingency/Disaster Recovery Coordinator/Business Resumption Planner can use all methods of auditing. These audits make senior management aware of the fact that all necessary critical data is being verified and is available should the need occur.

## Frequency

- Off-site storage (Vaults) inventories audits must be conducted a minimum of once every quarter
- Pyramid Call Tree audit must be conducted at least semi-annually or more frequently depending on the amount of personnel movement
- A Hot Site test or exercise conducted no less than semi-annually must also include an audit

- On-site or remote test and exercise audits must be conducted semi-annually
- Critical Application audits must be conducted a minimum of once every quarter

## Evaluation of results

To ensure that auditing is properly conducted, the Contingency/Business Resumption Planner/Disaster Recovery Coordinator will evaluate the results of every audit carried out. Upon conclusion, the Contingency/Business Resumption Planner/Disaster Recovery Coordinator will formulate a written report to senior management, indicating results and recommendations that will help improve the plan. This will keep senior management aware of the progress being made and of the level of involvement generated on the Plan. Remember that all recommendations must be entered in the Plan as quickly as possible. Recommendations are put into practice and tested to familiarize those individuals executing the Plan with any reported and unreported changes. Then repeat the testing and auditing on the findings for strengthened results.

## Types of audits

Examples of the more commonly used On-site and Off-site audits are listed below:

- Telecommunications and work flow verification
- Daily maintenance and debugging of applications
- System problems and resolutions
- Required critical forms
- Off-site and on-site library vaults storage and shipping of critical Datasets
- Outsource Recovery Plans
- Vendor problems and resolutions
- Resource problems and resolutions

These audits must be conducted periodically both with and without notification. Calling back critical Datasets from the vault, and testing/exercising the critical application on-site or off-site, is a viable way to conduct and report on auditing results of the Business Resumption Procedures and Plan. This information is critical to keeping the awareness level up for the senior management and all recovery team participants. The Contingency/Business Resumption Planner/Disaster Recovery Coordinator may also conduct and report audits on a tabletop scenario utilizing recovery team members or random personnel.

Another area to audit is the accuracy of the Pyramid Calling Tree and any information provided by them at testing time. This will periodically audit and verify the accuracy of the telephone numbers and contact personnel as listed in the Contingency/Disaster Recovery/Business Resumption Plan. It will also audit the response and awareness of the Pyramid Calling List, Support Team, and Recovery Team Members. Remember, the audit frequency for the Pyramid Calling List will depend on the frequency of people addition, deletion, or job rotation.

Hot Site procedures enumerated in the Plan must be audited. Being able to bring up the system and reporting on the problems and situations encountered at the Hot Site will accomplish this. Shipping the critical Datasets to a Hot Site and the processing of critical application on the Hot Sites Systems is an excellent method of awareness through auditing. The audit will verify, report on results of the established procedures and keep senior management informed of the Plan readiness.

An exceptional area for awareness through audits is the process of transporting people and media to a Hot Site. The capabilities of these personnel to function at a Hot Site are thoroughly tested. Using only the Hot Sites hardware, software, work area, support personnel and also using only Recovery Media Critical Datasets to process the company's Critical Applications is the purest method of awareness through auditing. Reporting on these results is the best way to exemplify the Plan's readiness to senior management. To audit the endurance of the Disaster Recovery Team Members plus the Support Team Members working under extremely limited conditions, with the added stress and pressures is another excellent way of validating your Plan.

Off-site storage (Vaults) audits is where awareness through auditing will conduct and verify the Off-site storage inventory. This must be conducted periodically. It will ensure that all critical Datasets identified within the Plan are correctly named, saved and accounted for.

The Lessons Learned Reports is the most valuable awareness tool through the Auditing of all Tests/Exercises. The Recovery Planner should not only discuss this audit with all participants of the Test/Exercise but must involve the Internal Auditing departments at the beginning, during and at the end of the test or exercise. The final discussion of the audit is with senior management as the last step to Testing/ Exercising the Plan—this keeps them aware of all achievements in the progress of the Resumption of Business Plan.

# Training

At one time or another we have all been some place, where when the fire alarm went off and, for the lack of effective training, people failed to respond at all or, worse still, panicked. Schoolchildren are usually much better at a fire drill than adults. Adults either take a ho-hum attitude because it is just a drill or they may be totally surprised by it, usually because they are quite unprepared.

No matter how well crafted a Plan may be, it is only as good as the performance of the participants. The purpose of training is to get people to perform instinctively, with the precision that a live disaster requires. To achieve the purpose, the participants must first know the plan. The assumption that people know what to do when the fire bells ring is a dangerous one. Leaving the building by the nearest fire exit, the usual approach from childhood, is not the usual approach in a high-rise office building. Distinguishing the fire bell from other alarms is important, as well.

Throughout this discussion, use of the fire drill represents the most familiar contingency procedure. The Plan includes many more specialized and complex activities. However, everyone has participated in a fire drill. Years of study have proved that the most common of procedures becomes one of the more difficult to coordinate successfully. Knowing the Plan involves everyone in the company at some level. This means everyone in the company requires training of some kind and some may require more than others. This is primarily dependent on the level of their responsibilities. In the most common contingency procedures, the trainees will be the employees. The trainers will be the first line level of management. Can a plan coordinator rely on the first line level of management to accept their role as fire drill trainers? If the first line level of management is not entirely enthusiastic, what happens to the interest of the employees? This concern is a major one. The Plan Coordinator is responsible for securing the support of executive management. He or she is not only responsible for the creation of the Plan, but also for its successful testing and maintenance. The degree to which the Plan succeeds is directly tied to the degree to which management—first line level through executive—supports training, testing, implementation and maintenance of the Plan.

Within the scope of most Contingency Plans, there are many different levels of training activity. The fire drill is an extreme one because it involves everyone. At the other extreme is the training developed through the Plan Coordinator. They must pursue a continuous regimen, which includes reading trade journals, attending seminars, and formal certification, to stay current in Contingency Planning. Between these extremes, the Plan Coordinator must work one-to-one with some participating members to develop the Contingency Planning Team. The Contingency Planning Team groups will vary in size, from one or two people up to the entire first line management.

In training terminology, we call the one-to-one training style mentoring, which is similar to an apprenticeship. Over a considerable length of time and because of frequent contact, the experienced Plan Coordinator, the mentor, must bring his or her replacement into being. At the end of the mentoring relationship, the Plan Coordinator has cloned himself/herself. The apprentice becomes a fully qualified Plan Coordinator who can function independently of the mentor. The apprentice is usually a member of the Contingency Planning Team.

Part of training is evaluation of results, the dreaded test we all faced in our schooldays. Most Contingency Plans prescribe tests and frequency of testing.

Testing is simply the means by which training and the trainers are evaluated. In reality, testing should be nothing more than an information exchange. The connotation of testing usually means senior management will expect and issue some kind of grade for the test. They usually base this on the scope established prior to the test and based upon the results achieved during it. Testing is usually done when it is certain that the Plan will perform as expected. What experienced Plan Coordinators have found out is that it is best to "Exercise" your Plan until it is at a point where a "Test" will produce known results. In this way Senior Management will get results only from those Tests where the results are always positive and the results are always passing. Remember, exercising the Plan will frequently remove most of the problems before presenting a Test for Senior Management's grading. The Plan will address the following training and testing activities.

## Orientation

We conduct Orientation when (i) new procedures are introduced and (ii) when new people enter the workplace. In the first case, the Plan Coordinator is responsible for keeping existing personnel informed of new procedures and their consequences. In the second case, the first line level of management is usually responsible for introducing new personnel to the workplace. Individual employees must be trained on basic emergency procedures, such as:

- Location of fire extinguishers
- Recognition of alarms, emergency exits and evacuation routes
- Basic first aid procedures
- Who to notify in case of an emergency

Although managers and supervisors conduct the training, the Plan Coordinator is responsible for the content of the training and for follow-up to see that training does in fact take place. Training methods include classroom sessions and office tours. Turnover and the rate at which it occurs determine when to conduct orientation of new employees and new hires who enter the workplace. Depending on the circumstance, usually orientation will be conducted on a monthly or quarterly basis.

## On-site emergency preparedness testing (drills)

The chief means by which the Plan Coordinator determines the effectiveness of orientation is by conducting emergency preparedness drills. The objectives of such drills are to validate employee readiness. Employee readiness means the ability of the workers and the ability of essential personnel and their understudies to execute their respective procedures. Other objectives are to verify that equipment is maintained, handled properly and functions as intended. At the same time we also discover any changes in procedures made, but not updated in the Plan.

Drills may be conducted any time, and are usually unannounced ahead of time. Since drills necessarily disrupt the entire workplace, they are expensive exercises. The frequency of conducting drills must be carefully considered in relation to the cost. Simultaneously, drills must occur often enough to keep personnel aware of the procedures and accountable for their execution.

## On-site tabletop/scenario testing

The target audience for tabletop scenarios are those DP and management employees who are responsible for the more detailed and technical tasks in the Plan. This group writes up the circumstances or scopes of an event for consideration. The group response to the event is two-fold. First, the group must brainstorm to develop options. Second, when an option is selected for execution, we write up the option as the correct response. The Plan Coordinator can develop the event through several brainstorming sessions, introducing newly created twists in the plot and more complexity.

The objective is to test the Plan's procedures, and the knowledge of the people enacting the procedures. Another major objective is to test their reaction to a stressful environment where quick but effective reasoning is essential to success. Tabletop/Scenario testing can be conducted any time and should be unannounced.

## On-site functional application testing

As the title suggests, the test is performed to validate application functionality. The purpose is to discover any procedural changes that may affect the Plan. The test is performed "live" on the mainframe or a back-up system that exactly simulates the mainframe environment. Functional Application testing is usually conducted each quarter.

## Off-site functional application testing

This test is performed to test the Hot or Back-up site environment. It is conducted in the same manner as the on-site Functional Application testing except that the environment is off-site. Off-site, testing is usually conducted semi-annually.

These tests are to assess information flow capability and to receive timely statuses on personnel, equipment and procedures. They also assess the ability to establish communication links, and to do damage assessment and restoration activity. They set and direct the restoration priorities, and enable testing of resources, workforce, and supply requirements of both internal and external sources. Finally, testing provides information regarding the status of the Procedures, Plan, Equipment, and personnel. *"There is no such thing as a failed test!"*

Adequate training is obviously necessary to ensure the Plan is properly carried out. Without proper training, personnel's knowledge in responding to a situation may be limited. Proper training will make personnel aware of the many steps detailed in the Plan, which, if used, can result in a timely and satisfactory recovery. The training must be specific in nature to accomplish readiness and maintain employee interest. Remember that through good training the knowledge for responding in a crisis will become second nature to the trainees. The training is not based on all circumstances. It will, however, allow certain actions to be taken specifically every time. The mundane procedures will be covered automatically and allow the Recovery Team more time to focus on the major items.

## Responsibility

In addition, it is the responsibility of the Contingency/Disaster Recovery/Business Resumption Planner to ensure that they train the Disaster Recovery Team Members. They are also responsible for making them aware of their responsibilities. Furthermore, it is the responsibility of the Contingency/Disaster Recovery/ Business Resumption Planner to attend education seminars on disaster recovery, to keep abreast of the latest advances in recovery procedures.

## Scope and method of training

The training should include an introductory classroom session. It must also give tours that show the locations of fire extinguishers, fire alarms, emergency exits, the location of first aid kits and the location of all major utility shut-off.

When available, videotapes will be utilized for training; other materials used are pamphlets, brochures, payroll inserts, and so on. Training will include written tests, to measure levels of understanding and the effectiveness of the training process.

## Frequency

Orientation for new employees must be scheduled once a month, while departmental training must be conducted once every six months. This will ensure all employees are constantly reminded of in-sequence procedure resulting in good effective recovery.

## Evaluation of results

To ensure training has been properly conducted, and to measure the level of employee understanding, the Contingency/Disaster Recovery/Business Resumption Planner will evaluate the results of every test conducted. Upon conclusion, the Contingency/Disaster Recovery/Business Resumption Planner will formulate a written report to management, indicating results and recommendations to improve the training process.

It is also vital to remember that all detrimental or less than accurate results should immediately be corrected in the Plan. This process will not only keep the Plan accurate but will increase the efficiency of the test performance.

Training and repeat testing will allow any corrections made to the Plan to become second nature with those employees responsible for the execution of the Recovery Plan.

# Maintenance testing

## Purpose

Emergency tests are simulations of actual emergency and disaster conditions. *"A Plan formulated, but not tested, is less than useless!" The purpose of testing is to ensure the continuing readiness of the Plan. During the testing period, we can probably determine a realistic timeframe for recovery. But additional time may be needed because of any functional problems such as communications, workflow, transportation, debugging of applications, unique working conditions, system problems, forms and vendor problems.*

## Responsibility

The Contingency Planner/Disaster Recovery Coordinator/Business Resumption Planner is responsible for making sure that the Plan is periodically tested on-site, in both HOT SITES and Back-up storage (Vaults). His or her responsibilities include the scheduling of tests, conducting tests, coordinating departmental tests, and evaluation of the testing process.

## Scope and method of testing

On-site procedures, such as exercising critical applications and testing the Strategies and Procedures stated in the Plan, must be conducted periodically both with and without notification. Planners who call back critical Datasets from the vault, and run them with the critical application on-site, are using a viable way to conduct an exercise. In addition, Testing/Exercising can be conducted in a table-top scenario utilizing random personnel.

Preparation for a test or exercise should include but not be limited to the following items:

- The SCOPE—is the goal you set for the test or exercise. This is what you measure your accomplishments against to deduce how well you have done
- The AGENDA—is a schedule of events and times you plan to follow. This, as you will find out, will not be cast in concrete and should be flexible enough to allow for any changes, which may need on-the-fly corrections
- The LEVEL OF SUPPORT—is the involvement of specific groups, which will aid in the success of the test or exercise. The Pyramid Call Tree members, Hot-Site Operations Support Team or your own Operations Support Team (if you take them along), and your Remote Support Team members are the experts who support the normal day-to-day production operation. Members left at the disaster site who cannot be at the Hot Site, such as Programmers, Operators, Systems Staff, and Technical Support, are also valuable support team members
- The STATISTICS—are taken from the SMF job records. These will give you the exact times used during a recovery test or exercise. This will give you an exact recovery time needed during a real recovery event

Another area of testing is the accuracy of the Pyramid Calling Tree. They should periodically test the Pyramid Calling Tree to verify the accuracy of the telephone numbers and contact personnel as listed in the Contingency/Disaster Recovery/Business Resumption Plan. It will also test the awareness of the Pyramid Calling List Members and Recovery Team Members.

Hot Site procedures as enumerated in the Plan must be tested. Being able to bring up the system at the Hot Site may accomplish this. Shipping critical Datasets to the Hot Site, and processing critical application on their system at the Hot Site is another method of verifying established procedures.

Another area of testing is the process of transporting people and media to the Hot Site. The capability of the personnel at the Hot Site (i.e., hardware, work area, support personnel ECT) is to be able to process the company's critical applications. To test the endurance of the Disaster Recovery Team Members working under limited conditions with the added stress and pressure is an excellent way of validating your Plan.

## Frequency

- On-site/Remote testing must be conducted at least once every quarter
- Hot Site/Off-site testing must be conducted semi-annually
- Pyramid Call Tree testing must be conducted semi-annually

## Evaluation of results

To ensure Testing/Exercising has been properly conducted, the Contingency/Disaster Recovery/Business Resumption Planner will evaluate the results of every test conducted. Upon conclusion, he or she will formulate a written report to management, indicating results and recommendations that will help improve the Plan. Remember that these recommendations must be entered in the Plan as quickly as possible. They must then be put into practice and tested to familiarize those individuals executing the Plan with the changes. Finally, they should again be tested for results.

Over the next few paragraphs there are listed several typical problem areas brought to light by auditing a live recovery test/exercise. A solution for and awareness of these items greatly increases being better prepared for Business Resumption Planning:

## Management issues

1. Lack of awareness of Business Resumption issues and proper practices. Your Business Recovery Plan (BRP) Team can only lead, audit and coordinate its efforts. Senior management must buy into the resources, needs and requirements of Business Resumption Planning. Without their complete support, your efforts will stay less than successful.
2. A lone individual Business Resumption Planner is becoming as outdated as a planner who is only part-time for Resumption Planning. It usually takes a team of from two to three dedicated people having a broad expertise and knowledge base of all the Operations. In addition, they will need supplemental assistance and use of a part-time staff with specific expertise for specific tasks.
3. Business Resumption preparedness requires resources. Not just staffing is needed, but the computer capacity, software automation, and expert consultation (through professional analysts—BIA) and involvement in professional groups (for Networking and information gathering).
4. Broadening the personnel's expertise, in products, applications, auditing and the externals of documentation must be explored.

## Systems issues

1.  System resources must not use the same names at both primary and back-up data centres. Unique names should be considered acceptable. This will ensure maximum production protection and ease of recovery during tests. The top priorities are DASD volumes, Catalogues, Libraries, and Databases. The ultimate protection would come from physically isolating the hardware between your primary and back-up sites, or at least logically isolating the hardware between your primary and back-up sites.
2.  Network Providers (such as ADVANTIS) usually have single connection points to a system. To eliminate this single point of failure multiple gateways must be implemented. This will avoid services disruption in a recovery situation.
3.  Disaster mode NCPs' transitional capacity may not be adequate. They should update Disaster NCPs at least for the final design and confirm the capacities periodically.
4.  Workloads are periodically moved to conserve overall processing capacity. While economically this is beneficial, it may have adverse effects on recovery capabilities. Business Resumption needs must be considered as part of any workload movement decision. Periodic capacity reports should be established to project CPU and DASD needs for disaster situations just as they are done for normal workloads.
5.  Back-up procedures need to be modular, allowing flexibility to recover individual applications at separate times and locations. Redundant back-ups should be eliminated. An analysis tool, such as the Panorama Software product SUNRISE would identify redundant back-up issues.
6.  Maintenance of back-up and recovery activities is too labour intensive. Greater use of automation is needed. In-depth knowledge of disaster recovery methodologies and tools (i.e ABARS, etc.) would be beneficial.
7.  A more effective means of communication with Systems Users in a disaster or extended outage situation needs to be provided. A Network facility for making announcements at the time of an event should be set up as quickly as possible.
8.  A database, which establishes a catalogue of what system products or what facilities need is used by each application, is essential. Temporary software licensing requirements and contact terms should be defined. Procedures for activation must be included in the recovery manual.

## Programming issues

1.  Reduce the complexity of run procedures for applications. Automated balancing controls and procedures may be beneficial for recovery and production. Programmers must understand that personnel performing disaster recovery

activities might have the least expertise available and will be operating under adverse conditions.

2. A standard approach to all back-up and recovery tasks entails adopting some applications which call for modifying a copy of production JCL, others have special job streams, and some do both. Different means of overriding a process are used. Procedures need to be site-independent.

3. Consistent naming conventions for jobs and data need to be enforced I/S wide. All will benefit in many ways, not just the recovery participants.

4. Justification for bypassing normal production files in disaster mode needs to be documented. Operators can only accept the programmers' judgement. The Programmer may not be backing-up some data that would be crucial in a real disaster recovery. Again, automated software similar to a product by Panorama Software called SUNRISE is an excellent tool for verification.

5. Maintenance of disaster recovery procedures is an afterthought and usually handled as a separate project from a production change. Recovery procedures need to be included in Quality Assurance testing and Change Management practices. They should not set up changes without working recovery procedures. At any time, Recovery Problems are identified; they must be handled with the same priority as a production outage

## Operations issues

1. The Hot-site staff needs training to run critical applications without on-site support from the Primary site. They also need the capability to perform initial recovery tasks prior to any Primary site assistance arriving.

2. Highly skilled Recovery participants use their prior knowledge of products and jobs. Documentation suitable for less knowledgeable staff is needed should the experts become incapacitated.

3. Procedures and forms for documenting progress and problems during a recovery operation need standardization. Furthermore, they need formal documentation and inclusion in the Recovery Plan. This process will be essential for effective communications.

4. Currently Disaster Audits are manually performed. They need automated audit software, such as the Panorama Software product SUNRISE, to ensure recovery plans and critical data back-ups are always accurate.

5. Recovery needs an automated method of archiving data. This should be justified and set up prior to data volume growth.

6. Robotics technology should be analysed for disaster situation recovery. There could be a serious contention if both sites are not using similar technology.

7. Critical Forms printing activity should be assessed to consider all recovery possibilities, from in-house reproduction to Outsourcing critical forms reproduction recovery.

REMEMBER, MR MURPHY IS ALWAYS ALIVE AND WELL AT RECOVERY TEST-
ING TIME. BUT, AS THE FATHER OF RECOVERY PLANNING TAUGHT, "*NEVER
IS THERE SUCH A THING AS A FAILED TEST*".

Live Testing is to improve the quality of the written plan and the efficiency of its
execution. Keep this in mind when establishing a maintenance programme and
you can't go wrong.

## Types of testing

There are two primary types of testing methods:

- Component Testing
- Comprehensive Testing

Typically, a disaster programme begins with component testing and, through a
series of successful tests, progresses to comprehensive testing.

### Component testing

This type of test is narrowed in focus and designed to test the recovery capability
of a specific piece of the overall Company Recovery Plan. An example of a component test is the company's first system recovery test conducted at a hot site facility.
This test is usually limited to restoring the operating system, software and
databases if time permits. The component test is considered a "shake down" test
for a new and previously untested recovery strategy or facility. This type of testing
can verify the "readiness" of each of the major "pieces" of the total recovery plan.
Component testing must test the total Company Recovery Plan. This verifies it has
considered all the interdependencies of Plan components. Furthermore, it allows
the restored components to function together.

### Comprehensive testing

This type of test focuses on the entire set of company recovery plans and is
designed to test the recovery capability of the overall Company Recovery Plan. An
example of a comprehensive test includes the restoration of the following:

- Company's mainframe environment (including the operating system, software,
  data, production applications, etc.)
- Its mid-range environment (including the operating system, software products,
  data, production applications, etc.), its various networks (consisting of both
  voice/data)

- Its LAN/WAN environment
- Its Centralized Services (purchasing, legal, forms, mail services, facilities, etc.)
- Finally, the company's Business Operations Areas

Because of its wide scope, comprehensive testing is expensive. The number of staff involved in a large company comprehensive test can range from the twenties and thirties to the hundreds. Testing time at Hot Sites is a rapidly shrinking resource. Therefore, scheduling of a multiday comprehensive Disaster Recovery Test may have to be one or up to two years in advance.

# Maintaining and exercising business continuity plans

**17** Tim Armit and Simon Marvell—UK

This chapter was derived from experience gained across many business continuity assignments by Insight Consulting.

## Introduction

One of the oldest axioms within the field of disaster recovery or business continuity planning is that a plan that is not tested or maintained is of little value, or in some cases worse than no plan at all. The objective of this chapter is to introduce a variety of methods of testing and maintaining your plans, procedures and strategies.

As many organizations have matured in the field of business continuity planning a new concept arises, that of Business Continuity Management. Business continuity is no longer a project but an integral feature of "business as usual" across the organization, and as such it ceases to be planning and becomes management. Maintaining and testing plans is unique within business continuity as all organizations, be they large, small or multinational in whatever field— Finance, Utilities, Manufacturing, Retail or anything else—can adopt a similar approach.

As a part of the business continuity plan development project there is a continual need to prove plans and strategies by testing. Tests will be executed for a variety of technologies and for business areas involved in the planning process to date. The aim will be to raise awareness and give the organization confidence that the approach and strategies adopted could be used in the event of a genuine incident. As planning advances and includes a wider spectrum of business areas and supporting technology, the required tests become more complex and need more detailed planning. To ensure that all parties are aware of tests and appreciate the importance of other ongoing business and technology projects a test schedule needs to be prepared. This chapter will help to identify which areas require testing and what form these tests should take.

*The Definitive Handbook of Business Continuity Management.* Edited by Andrew Hiles and Peter Barnes. © 1999 Tim Armit and Simon Marvell.

Maintaining plans inevitably falls behind established schedules as business units view it as an overhead which is rarely of the highest priority. However, plans must be maintained to hold credibility and to encourage ownership across the organization. Methods of maintaining plans will be discussed within the chapter, especially focusing on how testing improves plans and helps to keep them current. Testing will ensure that projects, change management and operational enhancements address business continuity management as part of their ongoing working method. To assist in this, tests for each year must reflect changes in operation and improvements in recovery planning. The tests selected for each year should build on the organization's past experience and introduce new technological solutions or new business functions to the testing process.

Testing can be used for many reasons and this chapter aims to explain a few of these including:

- Gaining "buy-in" across business areas
- Proving completed plans and strategies
- Proving the adequacy, completeness and accuracy of the current recovery plans
- Component testing of technical elements
- Improving technical or business recovery procedures
- Ensuring that plans incorporate all aspects of the business
- Ensuring that the plans reflect current business priorities
- Building interdepartmental teamwork and relationships
- Working through scenarios

# Testing

Before continuity plans can be signed off as operational, an understanding of their use and value has to be proven. This can only be achieved through structured testing. A business impact analysis will identify critical processes, and the current plans will, in the major part, reflect these. However, over time organizational reviews will be undertaken and current plans are likely to become out of date. To ensure that solutions are implemented across all business areas it is necessary to instigate a series of tests as the first step in enhancing the continuity plans.

## Testing process overview

The testing process should be defined so that all parties involved understand the methodology. Certain organizations have introduced a form of test contract to enable the business and IT areas to define their own test objectives, scope and approach. An example of this is provided later. This means that when a test is being planned all those involved will know what to expect and what is expected of them. The following items are a suggested process for planning a test. These are not all-encompassing but present an overview of a successful operational approach:

- The scope of the test is agreed and all parties to be involved are informed
- The objectives of the test are agreed and published
- A change management request is raised to book time and personnel
- Contracts are raised with external suppliers for any support or equipment that is required
- Agreements are gained from any impacted bodies (internal or external) such as Public Bodies (e.g. Borough Councils), Utilities or Regulatory Bodies
- Briefings of all personnel are held on a number of occasions. These briefings are held with individual recovery teams and with the entire test team. The objective of these is to ensure that all aspects of the test are covered and that all potential risks and failures are identified. They also help the teams to build up their task lists for the tests and to document what they will actually be doing. The combined briefings ensure that all parties understand how they will relate to each other and identify any dependencies between teams. The briefings are key in building the team for the test
- Independent observers are selected to be present at the test and to log events above and beyond the logs kept by each team. These may come either from Internal Audit or an external organization
- Preparation and support for staff is put in place, such as catering, accommodation and transport
- Business areas are briefed about the test and the potential impact on those not involved
- A memo is drafted and distributed informing all areas of the test
- The test is executed to a strict project plan with a clear cut-off time to ensure operations are available post-test
- A post-test review meeting is held to discuss what took place
- A Test Report is written collating all teams' logs and any key findings and observations
- Plans are amended and strategies altered to reflect findings

Figure 17.1 is an example of the internal testing contract described above. It is to be completed by the business area proposing to test its business continuity planning status. Each area containing a note in italics is to be replaced by relevant text.

## Test planning

So when should plans be tested? In almost all instances organizations will follow a structured approach to continuity planning, and having completed a lengthy

| Title: Replace this line with the title of the proposed Test | | | | |
|---|---|---|---|---|
| **Objectives** | | | | |
| People | IT | Vital Records | Facilities | Dependencies |
| Enter the objectives for the test. You are not limited to two, this is displayed for demonstration purposes only. Tick the boxes above which will be proven. 1. 2. | | | | |
| **Exclusions** | | | | |
| Enter specific processes or areas of technology being excluded from the test. | | | | |
| **Method** | | | | |
| Enter the method the test will take. | | | | |
| **Justification** | | | | |
| Enter an explanation as to why this is the best approach to the test and how this will achieve the objectives set. Also explain any exclusions and justify why they have been omitted. | | | | |
| **Requirements** | | | | |
| Enter the requirements for the test at an initial high level. This list should include any dependencies on IT, Facilities or other business areas. It should relate to the method selected and outline what specific requirements are needed to execute the test. | | | | |
| **Sign off** | | | | |

| Business | IT | Facilities | Management |
|---|---|---|---|
| Signed off by the business that the test will satisfy their objectives. | Signed off by IT that the test is feasible and support will be made available. | Signed off by Facilities that support will be made available. | Signed off by management that the test is sufficient to meet periodic testing requirements. |

**Figure 17.1**—Test contract

project will then attempt to prove the deliverables through testing. This is the standard practice and works excellently; however, certain organisations take an alternative approach. Historically plans were initially developed from within the Information Technology departments and later rolled out into the business areas. This has often led to reluctance within the business areas to becoming involved or owning the responsibility for determining strategies. A successful approach to helping the business understand their exposures and responsibilities is to test them before they have been through the structured methodology. This immediately shows the business managers how bad their situation really is and quickly focuses them on their need to plan in detail. This is an unusual approach but is mentioned since it was successfully used in a multinational Investment Bank to encourage the trading floors to take ownership.

There is always a drive towards large-scale multiplatform, multiuser tests but in most cases this is inappropriate in the early stages of the planning cycle. In fact best practice has shown that to improve plans and work towards successful testing a three-year cycle should be adopted. Tests in the early years are probably mis-named and can lead to trepidation; the word test conjures up exams and success or failure criteria, which is not the aim. A better name might be a training exercise or workshop. The aim in the first two years of the programme is to prove the procedures and plans and educate those involved in their roles and responsibilities. To assist in this, exercises should build up in a structured manner. It may be a cliché but don't run before you can walk.

## Stage One—plan audit

The first test to be considered should be to carry out an audit. Whilst it could be argued that an audit is not a test, any process which challenges what is in place and demands proof is testing the credibility of the plans. This approach will ensure that a structured methodology to business continuity has been adopted within plans. The audit should cover the following areas:

- A review of the business continuity management process, including an assessment of the following:

    (i)     the scope of the plans: *This will reveal areas of the business or technology not included in the plans which could lead to services and functions not being recovered;*

    (ii)    whether an appropriate level of business impact analysis has been carried out: *To prove the reasoning behind the strategies selected and to understand if the plans will mitigate the impacts discovered;*

    (iii)   whether an appropriate level of risk analysis has been carried out: *To determine if risk reduction measures have been implemented and potential risks identified and agreed;*

(iv)   whether the recovery strategy has been clearly defined: *If the strategy has not been clearly defined and agreed, the planning will not reflect the actions to be carried out.*

- A document review, including an assessment of whether:

    (i)    the document is logically sequenced: *Plans should be simple to follow and navigate, continual references to other chapters or moving from page to page will cause confusion and lead to errors;*
    (ii)   document version control has been applied: *Change management of plans and the ability to easily correlate many plans through version control is essential to ensure all parties are working from the same copy;*
    (iii)  the document is sufficiently comprehensive and complete;
    (iv)   the document is accurate.

- A review of the plan implementation, including an assessment of whether:

    (i)    the recovery strategies have been successfully implemented;
    (ii)   management involved in the recovery understand and are familiar with their roles and responsibilities;
    (iii)  tests have been undertaken;
    (iv)   there is an ongoing plan maintenance and change management strategy.

## Stage Two—walkthroughs

An integral part of any planning process is to provide an understanding of the plan and its strategies to all key management. A walkthrough of the plan should be undertaken and measured against an agreed scenario. The walkthrough will bring together all key management for a tabletop exercise using the plan as a baseline to measure events against.

The walkthrough will identify whether:

- All managers with roles in the plan understand what is expected of them
- Board-level management understand their roles and responsibilities within the plan
- The disparate business and support areas have equal expectations
- The assumptions made within the plan are accurate
- The plan flows logically to meet the recovery requirements

The walkthrough is a highly visible exercise across all of the business. This will provide a tremendous opportunity to emphasize the importance of planning and ensure "buy-in" from management, and should be used as such. On completion of the walkthrough, any findings should be presented in a report and plans should be amended.

It should always be emphasized that any testing, including the walkthrough type, is not aimed at testing individuals. The main objective of this test is to prove the value and completeness of plans and to validate that the correct infrastructure is in place to facilitate those plans, whilst improving and completing plans and educating the users. Future tests can be created to put individuals under examination.

## Example One—walkthrough

To ensure walkthroughs are successful, management must be able to commit their uninterrupted time to them. As such running them out of working hours, in the evenings or at weekends is sometimes the best approach. Recently a walkthrough was completed which required 7 hours and involved over 20 managers. In terms of commitment, this immediately demonstrates that the organization takes business continuity management seriously. Walkthroughs allow scenarios to be introduced and discussed which allows plans to be tried and proven in alternate ways. This particular walkthrough dealt with a slowly creeping incident which took hours to manifest but resulted in all systems down for three days. As no immediate crisis occurred and no major event happened the organization's plans did not initially cope with the problem. Most plans are based upon incident, crisis, impact, containment and recovery. Where an alternative scenario was presented, it led to confusion and disagreement. Walkthroughs allow this approach to be used and allow the coordinator to have a variety of scenarios into which they can move as the day progresses. In this instance, no information was given out beforehand and only regular update briefings were passed out; this simulated the confusion and lack of information which could be expected. The walkthroughs also brought many disparate parties to the table and in many cases opinions and assumptions held by IT, Facilities and the business areas were very contradictory. These issues were resolved at the tabletop before any physical testing was carried out. The walkthrough completed and led to plans being updated to reflect the findings. This was a very "simple to organize", cost-effective way to raise awareness and involve management from all areas in a planning exercise.

## Stage Three—component testing

The most effective means of identifying that the plans are complete is through a full test. However, this costs time and money which could be wasted if components of the plan fail. Experience shows that there are significant benefits in carrying out tests on individual key components of the plan to avoid this. A series of tests should be identified to assess the effectiveness of the various components of the plan. Once completed, amendments can be made to the plans and a complete plan test can be aimed for with confidence. Examples of component tests are:

- An out-of-hours telephone test to prove the capability of the cascades in place and ensure all key team members can be contacted in a timely manner
- An audit of off-site data with random testing to prove the currency and validity of the data to the business
- Recovery of individual specific technologies to prove in isolation that technological procedures are accurate
- Execution of identified business "workarounds" to prove the business can operate without technology or in a reduced capacity
- An invocation of recovery contracts to ensure the contracts in place are adequate to requirements

On completion of each test a report should be produced in an Audit format to highlight all findings. This will be used to ensure plans are updated and complete.

It is recommended that each of the stages is exercised to ensure that a gradual build up to a future complete test is undertaken. By following this approach organizations will be assured that all personnel and subcomponent areas are aware of their roles and responsibilities before a full test is undertaken.

### Example Two—call-out communication test

In two organizations recent exercising has started with proving the call-out communication cascades. These are simple tests to organize, very cost-effective and are the perfect vehicle for raising awareness of business continuity and how it affects individuals. A key part of any plan is communication, this can be the initial call-out or the ongoing liaison with staff. To ensure this can be done effectively, call-out cascades are a key feature of all plans and generally resemble Figure 17.2.

This test aimed to prove that within three hours of an incident being identified out of hours, key messages could be passed to every member of staff. The primary organization used in this example employed 1500 staff within the scope of the test.

The test specified that every member of staff contacted would complete a log, pass on and record a specific message and answer four questions. The log keeping is essential in any incident for many reasons and encouraging staff to maintain logs in simple exercises ensures that more complex, stressful events will be logged adequately. The message passing was considered important to help to ensure that staff logged key events accurately and could transmit this information to others. The questions were:

- Do you have your plan at home?
- What version is it?
- Do you have a company laptop?
- If yes, is the laptop at home?

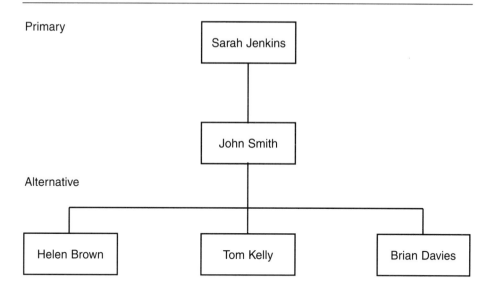

**Figure 17.2**—A call-out cascade

The first two are standard questions which allow the control team to understand how effective their distribution of plans has been and to identify if staff have them to hand. The last two questions were specific to this organization. Many business areas had insisted that they had company laptops and as such planning was not essential as they would have the information on their laptop and would not be impacted.

A single call was made to the initial "out-of-hours" contact. He was then responsible for contacting the initial Crisis Management team and subsequently triggering cascades across the organization. Each member of staff contacted was instructed to call into a central area to allow the flow of the test to be monitored by the BCP management team. This element had been introduced after an earlier exercise which, having been left to run alone, had missed out significant large areas of the business. As at this stage we are still trying to educate not test, there was more value to the organization in triggering these areas independently and logging the event then there was in leaving them to fail. After three hours the exercise finished.

The results showed 672 people, or 45% of the workforce, were contacted directly within three hours, and that over 90% of staff who had company laptops had left them at work. Whilst the contact figure does not look significantly high, no single area of the business had not been contacted and for a first event this was deemed a success. When retested 12 months later over 1000 people were contacted.

The benefits from this exercise were many. As people across the business were contacted in their homes this brought business continuity out of the project phase and into their lives. The next day at work had over 45% of employees talking about business continuity and challenging their management as to what it all meant; there could be no quicker or more efficient way to raise the awareness of business continuity other than a real incident. Business managers now took a real interest in their cascades and ensured that everyone was included. Cascades were revised as people recognized that making over five calls was impractical. Ownership for maintenance was accepted and taken away from the central area into the units affected and plans were amended to show that reliance upon laptops was fatally flawed. The exercise also showed that whilst key management had been issued with pagers many did not know how to use them properly, which led to another minor exercise.

## Example Three—pager exercise for the Crisis Management Team

As mentioned earlier about "not running before walking" the call-out exercise had proved that we should not make assumptions. This exercise was required to prove that all holders of pagers within the critical crisis management team understood how to operate them and how to respond to them.

Both of these tests are incredibly simple, very inexpensive to run and are very high profile. They can be run on a number of occasions per year with no impact on operations. They prove the most important part of planning, that of communication, and quickly give senior management a level of comfort in the business continuity programme.

## Example Four—specific technology tests

An organization had changed its baseline desktop services infrastructure and in upgrading machines had also changed its primary choice of operating system. Plans had been written and proven on a number of occasions for the previous technology. A large-scale test was planned but, before this, an exercise was run to demonstrate that the procedures and understanding were in place to rebuild the new machines. This very small test impacted nobody in the business as it was run off line but did demonstrate a need to alter recovery timescales, as whilst the improved technology simplified the recovery it did take longer. IT had instigated the change in technology and change management had not addressed the impact to the business. A certain level of explanation and rethinking therefore had to be undertaken following the tests.

## Example Five—telephony recovery

Voice recovery is essential to any planning and the rebuilding of a telephone exchange in the shortest possible time will allow for the minimum interruption to operations. Many organizations implement commercial contracts to recover these services but rarely test them, and tests which are conducted often do not test to an appropriate scale. For example, if a telephone exchange handles 20 000 calls a day the value of recovering the system and proving that it can receive a single call should be questioned. A test was undertaken to prove that a mobile telephone exchange could be delivered to the recovery site, be installed and handle all incoming and outgoing services. Included within this were voice, fax, modems for remote access, Internet services and automatic call distribution. Given the number of exchanges available in the market very few service providers will guarantee to match like for like. This in itself caused the first issue—if a different machine was delivered would the installed software work? The answer was no. With the exchange delivered, the problem of how to run services out to extensions arose. Frames running internal services can hold thousands of pairs of wires and can be extremely complicated and time-consuming to rebuild. In fact we learnt that whilst the system could be rebuilt in six hours it was estimated that to reconnect all 800 extensions could take up to a week. A test like this to prove the assumptions meant that once again scale of recovery and timescales had to be revisited.

## Example Six—new technologies

As organizations modernize their technologies, very often this can improve normal operational services to the business, however it does not always simplify the recovery process. The example of the change in desktop technologies was mentioned before. In this case, an organization was moving forward its mainframe-based services towards "state of the art" disk farm technology. The organization had previously relied upon recovery services delivered to its alternative site on the back of lorries. This had meant, with a 24-hour invocation period, that the recovery time for the mainframes was up to 52 hours. The new disk farm technology would bring this down to under 10 hours. Initially this looked ideal and the business areas were obviously relieved. However the new technology implemented in one area (the mainframes), was not being matched in others, in particular the local area network (LAN) servers. During a test to prove the ability to recover the new systems and understand timescales it was observed that the LAN servers and desktop were already in place. As they were beyond the remit of the mainframe team they had not been recovered. However the recovery of the LAN servers, including invocation, needed 32 hours which meant that means to deliver mainframe services were not available until 22 hours after the services themselves were restored. As such, any points of consistency of recovered data were also impacted. Initially this may look like an obvious flaw, but as business continuity is not considered in change management or project planning in many organizations, this is a common finding.

## Stage Four—large-scale testing

As confidence in the business continuity management process grows, and as the strategic infrastructure is proven and known to be in place, the ability to run larger scale tests improves. Tests of both technical support and business areas will prove that plans and strategies in place are accurate, maintained and can operate across the business. This scale of test moves from the rehearsal, practice-type exercise to an actual test of assets in place.

The test itself must be planned in detail; it will be expensive to undertake, bring its own risk to the business and draw on a great deal of operational time and effort. Management must clearly understand why the test is being undertaken and the scope and objectives should be clearly defined. It is important that business areas own these tests and look to IT and Facilities as service providers.

The checklist detailed earlier in this chapter is ideal for the large-scale test. The following example will assist in explaining the set-up and execution of such a test.

## Example Seven—business recovery test

An organization had plans in place for over 40 business functions and the 12 components of the IT department. The organization was divided equally into two buildings and its strategy was for mutual support between the two sites. The test was to prove the ability to recover eight diverse business functions with associated technology services into the alternative site. To do this six mainframe boxes, eight LAN servers and 40 PCs would have to be recovered, in addition to telephony services and an appropriate business environment. In total over 80 personnel from 24 different areas within the business were involved in the test. To bring this number of people together into a test team and to ensure that the dependencies and requirements of all were understood and taken on board by the team involved detailed project planning. The test itself started at 19:00 hrs on a Friday night and had to finish by 13:00 hrs on the Sunday to leave enough time to return the environment to normal operations for the Monday. (A note here, be careful when picking the date, in recent time tests have run on Valentine's Day, Mother's Day and the day of the changeover between British Summer Time and Greenwich Mean Time, all of which caused problems.) The test discovered many issues which had not been considered. For example PCs are delivered in three boxes, as such 40 PCs means 120 boxes. Simply storing and handling this number must be planned for.

Many organizations note that they cannot recreate the stress and anxiety of a real event, which is generally true. This can be an issue when testing on commercial sites, many of which will not allow 24 hour operations for testing—this is unacceptable. In a real event, to ensure the quickest level of recovery personnel will work around the clock, in this particular test some key personnel worked for up to

38 hours, at which stage they were making mistakes and showing signs of tired-ness. However this is what would happen in reality and as such must be addressed through testing. The business areas were closely involved at all stages and this led to a much closer relationship with IT and a much clearer understanding of how services were delivered to them. It also helped them to realize why it took so many hours to restore information and the need for business workarounds for periods without them. These workarounds subsequently were implemented and included procedures for manual operations and agreement with counter-parties for alterna-tive methods of work. In most organizations no matter how often it is explained, the matter of lost data and how you rebuild it is rarely understood by business managers. A test of this scale shows the business what they will get and asks them to function with it. In the post-review meetings it was clear the situation had now been taken on board and solutions would be sought. The test was a success in achieving the aims set and many staff are now involved in the BCM process. However the administration and control of a test of this size should never be underestimated.

# Maintenance

Plans and strategies once implemented reflect the requirements of the business at that time, but these requirements and recovery timescales are not constant and as such both components must be maintained. A business continuity change manage-ment process covering maintenance and review changes is required. Maintenance changes keep plans up to date but do not change the underlying objectives or strategies and can include staff changes, contact detail changes or the correction of errors. Review changes may affect the strategies in place or may alter the plan's objectives and can include business reorganization or the introduction of new business processes or systems.

Testing is an excellent process to maintain plans, but in itself is not enough. A regular testing schedule will ensure that plans are current, proven and maintained by the people needing to use them. However, in addition to this, maintenance schedules need to be produced but experience has shown that implementing these and policing them is time-consuming and rarely successful.

Clear ownership of the change management process is essential to ensure the process is accepted and implemented. The overall strategy, standards and meth-odologies to be implemented and maintained across an organization should be owned by a central business continuity coordinator. A Business Continuity Man-agement Steering Group should be established with responsibility for implement-ing, testing and ensuring that plans are maintained. This group must be empowered to resolve disputes, instruct management of their responsibilities and prioritize projects. The group should meet at least bi-monthly and should be presented with the current status of plans, which will assist in policing plan maintenance.

The ownership of plans must reside with the management teams that require them and they must take responsibility for their maintenance changes. The plan owners will issue new pages to replace those requiring minor changes, and at the same time they will inform the central business continuity coordinator to ensure central copies are consistent. To assist in this, basic document rules should be applied. An agreed schedule for reprints should be determined: for example, a full reprint will occur annually, updates quarterly with key pages replaced on demand. Each page should be version control numbered and show a date of issue. The version numbers should increment by 0.1 for each update or page replacement and by a full integer (1.0) on each annual republication. This number and the date will ensure that plan holders are operating to the most current issue.

Plan owners must also take responsibility for identifying review changes. These should then be actioned centrally by the business continuity coordinator in conjunction with the affected plan owners. These parties should assess any changes required in the recovery strategies and timescales, plans and business impacts and ensure that, if necessary, relevant changes are implemented. These types of changes can negate the entire planning capability and as such may need to be acted on either during the development cycle of the change or very soon after its implementation.

It is always difficult to maintain plans and it is unrealistic to expect plan owners to give business continuity a permanent high priority. As such a proactive approach will often achieve better results and will gain support from the business and IT management involved. This can involve regular questionnaires distributed by the central business continuity coordinator. A proven method to ensure continual ownership and sign off is to distribute a monthly memo to all plan owners requesting sign off that plans are current and accurate. As many organizations use electronic mail this can be set up as an automatic distribution list and thus reduce the effort required. Whilst this does not guarantee that plans are maintained it does put responsibility on the plan owners and the sign off gives a level of confidence.

Testing itself will lead to plans being maintained as the observers will make amendments and the plan holders will see improvements and changes that are required.

Links should be established to personnel systems to ensure that leavers and joiners of an organization are highlighted and that these are reflected in plans. If a specialist software tool has been selected then this can, in some instances, assist in the maintenance process, while conversely it can lead to information being stored and maintained in two places. Some software tools show dates and audit trails against the last time areas were maintained, which can help in policing plans and allowing the central controller to pursue plan owners who are not updating plans. The tools can also assist in identifying links across plans and thus simplify identifying areas requiring updates following a change. Consideration should be given to the method and cost of maintaining plans whilst in the initial planning stage.

Many organizations have established mature change management systems which allow for flags to be incorporated to ask specific questions. Ideally, a flag should be placed on the system asking the change raiser to state "yes" or "no", if the change affects business continuity plans or strategies. This will then ensure that any technical or production alterations consider the impacts on plans and amend them before changes are signed off. This can be taken a step further so that project plans and methodologies recognize business continuity requirements during the development and initiation phase, thus allowing strategies to be developed and tested as an integral part of the project.

## Conclusion

This chapter has outlined an approach to testing which is supported by many examples used in successful implementation of business continuity management programmes. The chapter also outlines an approach to maintaining plans, which although notoriously difficult, is essential if plans are to retain credibility and support.

# Selecting the tools to support the process

**18** Lyndon Bird—UK

Lyndon is Managing Director of UK-based software and consultancy service provider CPA Ltd.

## Introduction

Since the mid-1980s much effort, enthusiasm and originality has gone into developing a wide range of software support tools to assist the Business Continuity planner. Despite some success stories, I think it fair to say that the overall performance of such tools has often been disappointing. This disappointment has been experienced both by the developers (for whom sales have regularly fallen short of predictions) and by end users who have found the tools less valuable than they had expected. Possible causes are discussed later in this chapter but at this stage it is sufficient to suggest that a prime reason has been inconsistency between the Business Continuity Planning (BCP) methodology selected and the BCP software purchased.

This is not, however, a negative observation—it is simply a common problem of any emerging business discipline and supporting technology. Whilst the rules, standards and definitions about what constituted Business Continuity Planning were vague and open to wide interpretation, the software tools available were likely to be equally disparate. Developers either had to produce products which required the end user to conform entirely to their philosophy and approach, or else produce products that were so generic and flexible that they fitted no organization particularly well.

Now the BCP industry is more focused, new software tools are beginning to emerge which are supportive of the process rather than being at odds with it. In addition, there is a much wider appreciation that software tools are purely to assist with developing and maintaining plans—they do not replace the planner, the project methodology or the ongoing management commitment to the process of testing, maintenance and audit.

*The Definitive Handbook of Business Continuity Management.* Edited by Andrew Hiles and Peter Barnes. © 1999 John Wiley & Sons Ltd.

## What are BCP tools?

Within the industry, most professionals tend to think initially of the tools which support the actual development and documentation of corporate or departmental plans. It is in this area that the majority of products are targeted and consequently will be covered in detail later in this chapter.

It is important, however, to recognize that of the 10 certification standards (units of competence) jointly defined by the *Business Continuity Institute (BCI)* and the *Disaster Recovery Institute (DRI)* only two are directly assisted by this type of software. These are:

*Unit Six: Developing and Implementing BCPs*
*Unit Eight: Maintaining and Exercising BCPs*

Other software tools do exist, however, which are valuable additions to the wider BCP armoury. Specifically discussed in this chapter will be tools which support the following certification standards:

*Unit Two: Risk Evaluation and Control*
*Unit Three: Business Impact Analysis*
*Unit Five: Emergency Response and Operations*

The remaining standards will obviously make use of technology and software tools for project management, high-quality presentations and "what-if" modelling. These are not discussed in this chapter because the tools used are likely to be general purpose proprietary products—not specifically designed for BCP use.

Enabling technologies such as the Internet, intranets, multimedia, training, automated call diversion and the like will only be discussed within the context of the BCP tools they may support.

## A brief history

It is difficult to understand why we are where we are today unless the history of BCP tools is fully appreciated. Firstly, it is necessary to reflect back on the early days of Disaster Recovery, even before BCP was conceived.

Disaster Recovery was almost exclusively a data processing function, solely concerned with the technical recovery of mainframe computer systems. The earliest plans concentrated on technical recovery procedures, back-up methods and the logistics of moving tapes and operations staff to a remote back-up facility. They were often documented on the system with printed copies kept off-site. Most were word processed (or even typed) and kept mainly for reference purposes. There was little or no input from the system users and certainly no overall link to the business strategies of the organization.

Once it was realized that Disaster Recovery was a complex and costly business, financial controllers became involved. Naturally they questioned if Disaster Recovery contracts were necessary and whether or not the risk to the business justified the expenditure. Inevitably therefore the earliest tools to emerge (around 1982) were the Risk Assessment products; so called "expert systems" used to justify items of IT expenditure by balancing risks, impacts and vulnerabilities to formulate appropriate counter-measures. An almost universal counter-measure was the need to have a properly written, tested and maintained Computer Disaster Recovery Plan (DRP). The plans to be written were always very similar in structure because they only related to the IT (EDP) department and so the idea of template plans became popular. It was then but a small step before this template concept was automated and software aimed at quickly generating a DRP hit the market. By 1987 there were around 40 such products available in the US, some of which had started to arrive in other English-speaking parts of the world. Today's mainstream BCP planning tools are the descendants of these early DRP products.

As Disaster Recovery Planning gradually evolved towards full Business Continuity Planning in the early 1990s more and more emphasis was placed upon the Business Impact Analysis (BIA) phase. This led to three developments in the support tool arena:

1. The traditional risk assessment tools were extended to identify impacts and incorporate them into overall Risk Profiles.
2. Some of the BCP planning tools started to include a BIA module within their standard packaged software.
3. Specific software tools were introduced to assist with the process of conducting a BIA study and to give a wide range of presentation options for the results.

The most fundamental advance made by developers in this field came with the widespread acceptance of *Windows 3.1* as the *de facto* operating system for corporate PCs. Those developers who realized the implications quickly moved their products from *DOS* to *Windows* and almost overnight generated a wider new base of business user. Those that remained longer with *DOS* products, lost market share and product credibility and often did not survive. Conversely, however, the move towards integrated office suites of programs running under *Windows* made the building of in-house bespoke planning tools (combining elements of word processing, spreadsheets and proprietary databases) more feasible and cost justifiable.

One of the problems faced by potential purchasers of the main proprietary products has been the price—which has always appeared disproportionately high for PC software. The developers have always argued that the price represents a fair return for their investment in a limited and specialist marketplace. Nevertheless the high price did deter all but the largest organizations, whilst simultaneously attracting many small-scale developers into the market with cheaper (and often simpler) products. Whereas in the United States the trend has been market consolidation from around 40 products in 1990 to perhaps 10 in 1998, in the United Kingdom the reverse has happened with all of the newcomers being small UK developers or (more often) BCP consultants launching products at around 20–30% of the price of the main US suppliers. Apart from the US and UK, the only other country which has been very active in tool development for DRP/BCP markets has been the Netherlands—but the products emanating from Holland have not made a major international impact.

Since 1996 there have been further product consolidations in the US and indications that the number of products available in the UK is not sustainable. Consolidation of the UK market is already under way with small developers being acquired by large Business Continuity companies, Salvage companies or Insurance Brokers. Those that do not find a suitor may well not survive long into the next millennium.

In addition the second half of the 1990s has seen a more proactive product range emerging. One example is the use of computerized telephony to automate the whole call-out and emergency response phase of the plan. To some extent these tools are most useful for those organizations which regularly need to activate and notify people quickly. One such example was developed in Sweden, specifically to call out emergency snow-plough crews. Although this application may have only limited value in the UK, much of northern Europe and parts of the US use it exactly for that purpose. In the UK the same product has found a very important market in the nuclear industry sector.

Most tool vendors are exploring ways of making their software available on the Internet and many large corporations are already using internal intranets to maintain and distribute BCPs around their organizations.

In the rest of this chapter the following general groupings will be utilized to designate the types of tool available.

1. **Business Continuity Planning Tools**

    (i)    Templates (WP)
    (ii)   Questionnaire
    (iii)  Relational Databases
    (iv)  Integrated DB/WP
    (v)   Combined products (Project Management, Risk Audits, BIA interface)

2. **Risk Assessment Tools**

    (i)    Methodology products
    (ii)   Audit products

3. **Business Impact Analysis Tools**

    (i)    Analysis and Presentation products

(ii)    Integrated Risk Assessment products
(iii)   Integrated BCP products

4.  **Emergency Response Tools**

(i)     Computerized Telephony
(ii)    Disaster Vendor Databases

## Business Continuity Planning tools

This group of products represents the largest and most significant array of support-ing tools. To an outsider, they may appear perplexing in the sense that there are so many, all claiming to be unique in some way or other. This can be explained by reference to the underlying conflict within the BCP industry about what really constitutes a documented plan. From the beginning, two fundamentally different points of view have existed. These are:

1.  A written plan is simply a document; like a manual, a book or a detailed business report.
2.  A plan is a collection of critical elements of data which may need to be referenced once a disaster has occurred.

The difficulty early developers had to resolve was whether their product should be primarily based upon text processing, or be driven by the need for powerful data management capabilities.
    For those who selected the textual route the reasons put forward were:

1.  People feel comfortable with a well-presented text document which they can easily understand.
2.  Much of the updating can be done by standard WP functions (Find and Replace, etc.) and such concepts are well known by a wide range of business users.
3.  DBMS are more complex to handle than word processing and the volume of really volatile data needed to be included in a place is often exaggerated.
4.  The output quality in terms of presentation is much better from WP than any proprietary database can offer.

The counter-arguments as presented by the developers who favoured the database route were:

1.  Recovery planning is about knowing in precise terms what needs to be done. This can mean generating detailed checklists for teams or individuals, and linking these lists to specific resources.

2.  There are vast amounts of data that can be needed rapidly post-disaster. The only way to ensure this data is accurate, consistent and current is to use proprietary database technology.
3.  Maintenance is even more important than the original plan development. Once you get multilevel plans for multiple locations only a DBMS can hope to handle the maintenance workload.
4.  Although presentation is important—the most crucial aspect is to ensure plans are used in a disaster situation. Large well-written text manuals will simply be ignored in a real disaster.

This argument has not been fully resolved even today although most products now try to interface WP and DB technology in their basic designs.

The simplest form is naturally a word processor-based set of templates. This provides the novice planner with an easy start-set of basic documents, tasks, procedures and resource requirements which he or she can modify to suit a specific organization.

A more sophisticated form of this is the questionnaire-generated template. The user answers questions in an interactive session which automatically triggers appropriate sections of text to form the basis of a documented plan. Further customization is normally possible as for basic templates.

The basic problem with both of these approaches is that the software designer, rather than the BCP planner, specifies the design and framework of the ultimate plan. It tends to lead to a very generic looking format with no (or very limited) buy-in from the organization.

Pure relational database products, on the other hand, give users much more control over the way their plans are formulated and collated. They are, however, more complicated to learn and the final output is often not as attractive as those generated purely from word processors.

Some combined WP/DB products insert selected data variables into predefined text (almost like Mail/Merge does in basic office software programs). These can be difficult to master for infrequent users, and it is almost impossible to incorporate more than a very limited amount of data in this manner.

Other combined DB/WP products try and manage text within a database text editor or provide their own add-on text editor to facilitate the process. This is rarely as satisfactory as using proper word processor software. The emergence of OLE2-compliant products made the linking and embedding to proprietary software like MS Word, Word Perfect and AmiPro a much more attractive route to combine database and text processing needs.

For purposes of competitive edge, rather than real user demand, many vendors have added other functional interfaces to their basic products. Typically these are Project Management, integral BIA modules and sometimes Risk Audit modules.

In many ways the choice of software depends largely upon the methodology you intend to use for plan development and ongoing maintenance. It is recommended that before purchasing any of the available tools, serious thought should be given to how you are actually going to integrate ongoing BCP in your organization. There are numerous examples of clients purchasing extremely sophisticated database products and not using them because their organization decided not to manage the detailed data in its BCP software. Managers felt that a BCP was akin to a procedure manual and did not see any reason why they needed to learn a complex data management tool simply to maintain text. Although their understanding of BCP may be suspect, given their philosophy the selected software may be totally irrelevant to their needs.

The same often applies to the emphasis at the selection stage placed upon the need for compatibility with particular in-house software standards such as multi-user LAN capability. Often clients pay for features they will never need, given the way they intend to manage the BCP process on a regular basis. If you have a centralized approach to plan maintenance, audit and review you may need different software to a company taking a very distributed view. Remember the software is a tool to help you achieve your objectives, not a replacement for management judgement and decision-taking. The criteria list in the following section is useful as a guide but simply because particular software does not support a particular point does not mean it should be excluded from consideration. The bottom line on your decision is not whether the software has every conceivable feature but rather whether it will fit with your method of working and meet your business objectives.

# Criteria for evaluating BCP software

A number of vendors have published criteria lists for comparison of their product with others on the market. I have reviewed a range of their suggested checklists and compiled what I believe to be a definitive list. Many of these criteria are included in all vendor lists but some appear less frequently—obviously when that specific product is possibly weak on that feature.

The following list is unbiased and can be used by anyone evaluating any set of products—without resorting to any vendor supplied listing.

SYSTEM PERFORMANCE

1. Is the product written in a **compiled**, executable programming language?
2. When using the product in a multiuser network environment, with many users accessing the product simultaneously, will the system continue to perform as well as it does when just a few or one user is accessing it?
3. Can the product code and data be separated?

DESIGNING THE PLAN

4.  Does the system provide the capability of defining multiple databases to segregate sets of plans and data for training, change control implementation, planning for separate subsidiaries/divisions, etc.?
5.  Does the system include an advanced Call List module with a graphic hierarchical format (similar to File Manager or Windows Explorer)?
6.  Is a Data File Navigator included to assist new users of the system?
7.  Will the software "roll-up" to create a master, enterprise-wide plan, which includes summarized information by location, building, floor, business unit or department plans?
8.  In the event that a building is inaccessible, can users print the plan at a facility or building level where all the plans in that building are printed automatically, instead of selecting and printing each subplan individually?
9.  In the event that a disruption affects a particular business unit across various locations, can that plan be printed individually, regardless of what building or location it is in?
10. Does the software provide a built-in facility to organize and design all the business continuity planning phases including crisis management, emergency response, business resumption and full restoration?
11. Does the software include a proven step-by-step methodology addressing areas of Prevention, Response, Resumption, Recovery, and Restoration as part of the overall business continuity plan?
12. Using this software, can users develop data centre plans, network plans, telecommunication plans, business unit plans, facilities plans, power system recovery plans and specific scenario plans if needed?

CUSTOMIZING SOFTWARE

13. Does the software include a utility which allows users to change the terminology in all the data entry screens to reflect the vocabulary of a particular industry and company?
14. Does the software include a utility to let users resize data entry fields, to fit unique requirements? Will the system automatically perform the change and display the adjusted screens?
15. Does the software include a utility to eliminate information from the system that does not pertain to a particular industry or company and then automatically display the adjusted screens?
16. When the product is customized, will these changes automatically carry through to the included reports?
17. When the product is customized, will these changes automatically carry forward with all software upgrades?
18. Does the software include a textual "baseline plan" addressing issues such as the purpose of the plans, scope, objectives, assumptions and missions?

19. Does the software let users customize the textual word processing documents using any word processor?
20. Does the software include a tool for creating private picklists on all fields in the entry screens to simplify data entry and ensure data standardization?
21. Can users design and control the output of their plans (what comes out and the order it comes out in) based upon our own unique and specific time-sensitive business requirements?
22. Can users insert pictures, telecom diagrams, floor charts, maps, etc. into the database so that when plans are executed they are automatically printed?
23. Does the software include a utility to customize the standard reports that come with the system?
24. Does the software include a utility to let users create totally new reports?

SECURITY

25. Does the security in the software permit users the right to view specific plan information, even when they cannot build or maintain that information?
26. Does the security in the software restrict users from unauthorized customizing and the use of all administrative functions?
27. Does the security in the software decide which pieces of plan information can be accessed and by whom, by "hiding" that information on any screen?
28. Does the System Administrator have the option of installing the software on a file server as a single or multiuser product?

DEVELOPING THE PLAN

29. Does the system include an **integrated** recovery task scheduling module that is specifically designed for business recovery planning?
30. Are Hint Clouds and Message Panels included to assist new users of the system?
31. Does the software include hypertext Help?
32. Does the software include context-sensitive Help?
33. Does the software include Wizards where users simply answer questions to perform various functions?
34. Does the software provide a direct and seamless interface to the "text" portion of a plan using any word processor?
35. Does the software include an import utility for loading information from other computer systems, such as Purchasing (vendors), and Human Resources (employees)?
36. Does the software include a mapping utility to help specify how our ASCII and database files are laid out (where are the columns and what type of information is in each column)?
37. Does the software include a data gathering tool to send out questionnaires and entry screens to users, via disk, network files, or e-mail?

38. Can users enter data "on the fly" as they build plans instead of having to wait for information to be loaded into Dictionaries before a plan can be built?
39. As users develop multiple plans, can the software display those plans in a graphical hierarchical format, so they can expand and collapse the view, and drag and drop selected plan data?
40. Does the software provide for "drag and drop" functions to move and copy data from plan to plan?
41. As users build plans, can they view and edit data in a "datasheet" format (spreadsheet-like)?
42. Can users view and edit multiple screens simultaneously as in other Windows products?

PRINTING THE PLAN

43. Can enterprise-wide plans be printed as a cohesive document integrating word processor and database information?
44. Can enterprise-wide plans be printed as a two-part document consisting of individual business unit packets and a textual plan overview?
45. Can the standard reports that come with the software be sent to screen, printer or file?
46. Will the software send reports to a specified file (Excel, Lotus 1–2–3, MS Word, etc.) placing it in the correct format?
47. Can plan output include any word processing document and project management schedule whose associated application uses DDE (Dynamic Data Exchange)?
48. Will the software directly send standard and custom reports to users via a compliant e-mail system?
49. Does software come with standard reports which include summarized lists of items that need to be ordered?

MAINTAINING THE PLAN

50. Is the plan data stored in a non-proprietary, relational database which simplifies the maintenance of our plan?
51. Does the software comply with the standard Windows conventions, so our users will feel comfortable using it?
52. Can users view and edit information in a "datasheet" format (spreadsheet-like) for easy plan maintenance?
53. Can users define templates (where data columns begin and what type of data is in each column) to import information from other computer systems on a regular basis?
54. When changes need to be made, such as people moving from one plan to another, does software have a drag and drop function to quickly and easily move information around?

55. Does the software contain a search and replace facility throughout the database portion of the plan?
56. Does the software contain a replacement facility, so that when a person or piece of equipment is replaced, it can be replaced at the click of a button?
57. Can users maintain plans on a LAN file server, where multiple users can maintain their plans simultaneously?
58. Does the software provide an automated data gathering tool, where users can gather and maintain plan information electronically from non-LAN or remote users?
59. Will all plan updates be reflected in the software's audit/history subsystem, from which auditors can print reports on demand?

USING THE PLAN

60. Does the system date and resource stamp each update individually, so auditors can track exactly what part of each plan is updated, when, and by whom?
61. Does the software contain a query utility which allows users to turn data entry screens into query or search forms to quickly and easily find information?
62. Does the software provide an interface to a well respected project management tool, so team tasks checklists, business processes, and their required resources and durations, can be managed in a disaster mode or a test through PERT and Gantt Charts?
63. Does the software include post-exercise or post-disruption assessment forms?

VENDOR

64. Does the vendor provide technical assistance 24 hours a day, 7 days a week?
65. To help with promotions, re-engineering, new hires and corporate-wide planning, does the vendor provide free and unlimited training?
66. Is training **required** to use the software?
67. Is the vendor a recognized leader in advancing the science of business continuity planning, using the latest in technology and industry trends?
68. Does the vendor provide free updates and enhancements as part of the maintenance contract?
69. Does the vendor provide a bulletin board service to quickly get updates, fast answers, and exchange information with other users?
70. Does the vendor publish newsletters to keep abreast of new developments among the user community and industry?
71. Is there an organized open forum for user information exchange and education?
72. Does the vendor provide consulting assistance?
74. Does the vendor have a global network of subsidiaries or distributors to support multinational organizations?

## Risk Assessment tools

Like most software concepts, Risk Assessment tools originated in the United States. Unlike Business Continuity Planning software, however, it has never really become fashionable. In fact in the past decade the Risk Analysis software industry has been largely European driven (particularly from the UK). One reason for this has been a lack of clarity about what Risk Management really is. To many it is synonymous with insurance, which is largely about actuarial data and spreading risk over a range of clients. Consequently, people often assume that Risk Analysis software has something to do with the likelihood of threats being realized based upon statistical data and actuarial calculations. Consequently, a number of quantitative Risk Analysis tools entered the market in the early 1980s. None of them were very successful and few of them remain available today. In the United States, a standard formula was generated to calculate ALE (annualized loss exposure) which became incorporated into all quantitative products. This turned these products into little more than specialized spreadsheets—useful to calculate average annual losses from small exposures (e.g. pilferage), but of no credibility in assessing the risk and consequences of an unlikely but potentially catastrophic large disaster.

It soon became obvious that Risk Management in the Business Continuity sense was different. Since the late 80s the software support tools that have emerged have been what are generally called "Qualitative Risks Analysis" products. All of the main products in this category originated in the UK, but have found a wide acceptance in the southern hemisphere and Pacific Rim. Developers in France and the Netherlands have kept a presence in the market, but have never really challenged the UK domination. The main advantage of the qualitative approach is that no probability database is required and that risk levels are expressed in relative rather than absolute terms.

Unlike BCP planning tools, software in this area is far from generic. Most tools cannot be separated from the conceptual methodology involved. A full and proper understanding of both the terminology being used and the algorithms by which scores are generated is essential.

Benefits claimed for Risk Assessment tools include:

- Better targeting of security
- Cost-justified security
- Increased security awareness
- Consistency between divisions
- Better application of policy and base standards
- Improved business—IT communication
- Greater productivity/Audit savings

Critics of use of automated tools argue that all of the above benefits can be obtained by manual paper-based methods and that software support tools are complicated to learn and provide no real advantages. My personal experience of such products has shown there are significant advantages in using them in the appropriate circumstances. These are:

**SPEED**   Any normal audit inspection or review takes considerable time to plan, undertake, report, discuss and conclude. It becomes a showpiece event. It is not undertaken regularly, it is only a snapshot. With Risk Analysis software a survey can be so easy that perpetual review, improvement and self-audit are the norm.

**CONSISTENCY**   If an organization has hundreds of locations how can you guarantee consistency in standards between branches and different types of site? Imagine having 100 different inspectors visiting 500 locations around the world. Would the results be accepted as fair or consistent, without a common method of measurement?

**PARTICIPATION**   Once the review is non-disruptive and fair, people do buy into it. The best results come from each individual making those small day-to-day decisions (should I clear my desk, back-up my PC, lock my filing cabinet) which cannot be enforced by policy or policing.

Finally, of course, the question comes down to which tool you should select. The following tips will help you decide.

1. Ensure that you understand the benefits you wish to achieve before you start looking.
2. Ensure that you know how your method and software tool will contribute to those benefits. The software should IMPROVE your productivity—NOT tie you to a difficult and inappropriate methodology. Ideally, the software will make your job much easier.
3. The Knowledge Base of the system must be able to be tailored to you. Check that the software allows this.
4. Ensure that you are comfortable with it, it is easy to use, and it makes instinctive sense.
5. Check that the reports are meaningful and that it does not leave you with the task of interpreting difficult computer output.
6. Check that it links RISK and IMPACT. In other words, the reports not only detail the risks, but explain what the implications of these might be. This is critical in selling security to business managers.
7. Make sure that you are not tied to external consultants for support in operating the tool or conducting the risk analysis exercise. The software should give you all the assistance you need.
8. Ensure it is flexible. It must dynamically customize its approach/question-base to suit your environment.
9. Ensure that you can use the software for one-off security reviews or health checks to make your life easier on a day-to-day basis.
10. Ensure that you can experiment on the basis of "what-if . . ." scenarios.

In recent years, the complex methodology-based products have been augmented by a few simpler audit-type products. In particular the BS7799 information security standard in the UK prompted several developers to produce automated tool versions of the standard. With such products, end users can easily audit themselves against BS7799 requirements—to determine the degree of compliance and highlight the areas to be addressed further.

## Business Impact Analysis tools

Conceptually Business Impact Analysis (BIA) products are really only a subset of the functionality which should be provided within a good Risk Assessment product. Unfortunately most Risk Assessment products do not really concentrate upon Business Impact—they tend to be more concerned with threats and the probability of them being realized, rather than the consequences so resulting. Some Risk Assessment tools have attempted to bridge the risk/impact gap and I consider that to be a key factor in evaluating such a product. Nevertheless in recent years the importance of the BIA phase has led developers to produce tools which specialize solely in that element of the process.

Some developers have produced a BIA module as a front end to their full BCP product. This has the advantage of allowing "minimum resource requirements" defined in the BIA to be automatically incorporated into the planning process. The disadvantage of this approach is that a user would be committing to an expensive BCP product, purely to get access to the small BIA module. Separation of the BIA and BCP tools has become the norm, although when developed by the same company they do usually provide some level of integration.

The stand-alone tools have been produced mainly for presentation purposes. They allow a series of results generated by interviews or questionnaires to be analysed and presented in a variety of formats. This is very useful in terms of cost-justifying a particular recovery strategy. Senior executives need to see a professional business presentation which focuses in on the salient points. Products that are modules within a BCP or RA framework often lack sufficiently high-quality output. The main concern I have about stand-alone tools is not in their design, but in their interpretation. The results they provide are only as good as the quality of the data collected. If the user of the software does not validate the answers provided properly, then the analysis produced by the BIA module may be totally erroneous. My rule when shown the output from such tools is to ask "Does it fit with common sense?" If not, then usually the fault lies in a misunderstanding of a question or an incorrect answer given by an inexperienced person.

BIA software does not help an experienced Business Continuity practitioner to get the right answers, but it does help him or her present them more effectively.

Such products, may, however, be useful for an inexperienced planner who is not sure about the questions to ask when conducting a Business Impact Analysis study. Of all the types of software support tools, this is the most dangerous if not correctly implemented because the results from the BIA provide the entire conceptual basis for the remainder of the BCP product.

## Emergency Response tools

The most critical part of a recovery is in the early stages. Failure to properly notify key people and services not only loses time and money—it can cost lives as well. Consequently the use of automated computerized telephony has become increasingly popular in supporting Emergency Response Plans.

In general these consist of pre-programmed instruction sets so that against individual scenarios telephone numbers can be automatically dialled, customized messages given and responses monitored by use of the telephone keypad. Some products link a fairly simple auto-dial facility to a list of disaster recovery vendors—to speed up the acquisition of a locksmith, glazier or the like. Others are much more sophisticated and can be tailored to provide call-out scenarios in a wide range of situations. Usually such products are a combination of hardware, software and telephone network services. Because they are so time critical, users will normally have dedicated equipment to support such products. The cost of ownership of such products is often, therefore, much higher than would appear initially from the vendor software price alone. Technical support for such products is also more complicated than for BCP/RA/BIA tools.

The key things to look for if selecting such a tool are:

- Speed of notification achieved
- Confirmation and feedback of the message delivery service
- Flexibility in type of telecoms utilized
- Ability to modify scenario and call-out lists easily
- Ability to activate the call-out process remotely

These are the five basic criteria. If a product does not successfully achieve good performance in the above categories it will be unlikely to be a valuable aid to your Emergency Response plans.

## Conclusion

Software support tools are now widely used in many major organizations for one or more of the processes described in this chapter. They have not eliminated the need for the experienced BCP practitioner or consultant—and are unlikely ever to do so. When selecting a tool it is important to consider carefully what you need it for and how you intend to utilize it. There is little point in buying a tool because the sales demonstration was slick and it looked functionally advanced. Concentrate more on the benefits it can give you—if there are none do not buy it.

Despite this proviso, there is no doubt that there has been a tremendous advance in the variety and flexibility of such tools—and they can be useful in a wide range of situations. Remember a good plane or chisel will not make you a good carpenter. Neither will a good BCP tool make you a good Business Continuity Manager—but it does help!

# Coping with people in recovery

## 19 Allen Johnson—UK

Allen Johnson is Managing Consultant for Safetynet Plc—a UK-based provider of disaster recovery services.

It is not a disaster that shapes the behaviour of people after the incident, but it is people who shape their own behaviour in their attempt to manage the situation. And it does not have to be an incident of newsworthy proportions for staff to be exposed to a troublesome experience. The Operations Manager in a bank collapsed at work one afternoon with a heart attack. Two female juniors, trained in first aid, applied the appropriate treatment to revive him but their attempts failed and when paramedics arrived he was pronounced dead. The two unfortunate young women became stricken with guilt and remorse, not just at the death of the man, but also at their own frailties which failed to save his life, even though he was probably dead before they began their abortive efforts. This is how they began their journey towards trauma and it was the sensitivity of the Bank's own management team that led to their undergoing treatment to help them to come to terms with the incident. The Bank hired qualified practitioners to help these young women, and within a matter of six elapsed weeks, they were able to discuss the matter cogently and without emotional breakdown. So what do trauma- and stress-related matters have to do with Continuity Planning and Disaster Recovery? Simply this—they must be an integral part of any planning process whose principal aim is to deliver an organization from major difficulties through the unusual efforts of the people it employs.

The people in any organization that has experienced serious and unwanted events, which my colleagues in the industry refer to as *disasters*, have found themselves catapulted down a path of dramatic and rapid change. Maintaining control in what may otherwise be a helter-skelter, swirl of chaotic mystery is the challenge that the management and staff of any such unfortunate organization must face. And because most who face this challenge are meeting it for the first time, it is therefore reasonable to assume that in the challenge between the management of an organization, and the disaster, the smart money is on the disaster. Yet with proper preparation and the right team selection, even major challenges

*The Definitive Handbook of Business Continuity Management.* Edited by Andrew Hiles and Peter Barnes. © 1999 John Wiley & Sons Ltd.

can be overcome; the key is people. Select the wrong man, and you have a disaster within a disaster.

Let us take Tony for example. Tony is a Computer Operations Manager of some standing in his organization. He was responsible for the authorship of all the contingency measures that his employer possesses. The Plan he wrote features mainly IT, as you may appreciate, given his position in the company. One Friday evening after 6 p.m., somebody in the organization entered the male toilets on the fifth floor, plugged all the sinks, stuffed toilet paper in each sink overflow hole and turned every tap fully on. The resulting flood was found on the following Saturday morning and by the early hours of Sunday morning, enough people had gathered at their Disaster Recovery Centre to commence recovery. However, the Plan and all it contained was too orientated to IT and Tony was leading the recovery. In the initial stages, everything appeared to be going as well as could be expected. With computer problems Tony was at ease and had the support of his staff. But business users began to make demands regarding work in progress and other matters regarding their own concerns. Tony was deflected from his main task to answer questions he had not considered and once in unfamiliar territory he became erratic. The realization of the magnitude of the problem and the mounting pressures he was under, served to destabilize him. Simple requests became barked orders, he became aggressive, using abusive language, and this merely compounded his problems. Before long, his user community started to lose confidence in his abilities, as his deteriorating behaviour continued to undermine his performance. Fortunately, his Disaster Recovery Services provider, who provided consultant support under such circumstances, firstly noticed the changes in Tony and secondly noticed that nobody was doing anything to prevent the situation from worsening. The consultant took the initiative by sensitively removing Tony from front line activities and took him to a quiet room to calm him down. Then, carefully shielding Tony from any hostilities, he used him as a guide and eventually ended up successfully leading the recovery. At the end of the recovery process, Tony was publicly thanked and became a hero—as the consultant slipped into the shadows from whence he came. As a point for the reader, at the time of writing, the same staff still work for this organization which means the saboteur is still employed. Nobody knows who it is and the management team is understandably nervous when reminded of this incident from time to time.

Now, it is standard practice that one of the primary tasks for Business Continuity Planners is to identify and analyse those activities which are essential to the organization and to ensure that the resources that underpin those activities are available in the right quantity, in the right way and at the right time. Next is to ensure that the right blend of people is used in the formation of any team which has responsibilities for recovery. To do this the Planner needs to adopt an objective view of the participants, irrespective of status, gender, creed or culture. The Planner must also possess a fundamental understanding that everybody employed by the affected organization, has, potentially, some measure of responsibility for recovery. The parallel to draw here is that everybody employed by the organization is important to the organization—for why else would they be employed? This simple and obvious conclusion is invariably ignored at all planning stages. And, historically, when plans have been written, the employee community is thereby divided into two distinct groups.

The first group comprises the "chosen people"—that is, those deemed senior enough or responsible enough to be accorded one or more recovery roles with definitive responsibilities; either to have to themselves or to share with others, similarly chosen and divided into teams. The Planner may choose these people because he has been told that these are the best people to fulfil this role or that this is the best choice from an internal political viewpoint; ignoring the fundamental, and often more risky, action of picking the best people for the job in hand.

The second group comprises everybody else in the organization, those not mentioned in the Plan as having any recovery role, who for the purpose of this explanation we shall call the "rejects". Thus, even before an incident has occurred, the Planner has introduced unnecessary and unwanted division within the organisation. In certain cases where incidents genuinely occurred, the rejects even arrived on site to help and were turned away by senior management as being surplus to requirement. One such case is *Bank R*, in the aftermath of the Bishopsgate Bomb (London, Saturday 24 April 1993) when staff who, living locally, hearing the explosion, actually went into the City, only to be told by directors of the Bank, who were already on the scene: "Go away. You're not needed. You're in the way." Now that's real, in-your-face rejection. In this instance, and not surprisingly, such treatment of the employee community served more to divide than unite, and supposedly at a time when striving for common goals demands unification. Even five years after the event, the rejected volunteers of *Bank R* still vividly recount their feelings of the rejection experience with some measure of vehemence. And when the disaster has struck and recovery is achieved as the business is put back together again, now what happens? Well, the "rejects" return to a company full of heroes, heroines and champions. The "chosen people" had worked long hours; they had done unusual deeds; they had met severe challenges in testing circumstances; and despite being held in the teeth of adversity, they had come through it all—victorious and euphoric. In reality, the company's employee population has gone through a dramatic cultural change and, to make matters worse, the "rejects" now belong to the previous culture, which has the effect of even further isolating them.

To avoid the negative aspects associated in the creation of these two groups, it will help if one identifies who the "rejects" are and redefines their role and then tells them what is required of them. We do this for such audiences in our client base and the feedback is astonishingly positive. The audiences learn of the investigative processes that have resulted in the plans. They learn that they have a job, even if the building is destroyed, a normal, if selfish, question which frequently arises. They learn that they have not just one role, but probably two and sometimes more and, although any given role may not be within the first 24–48 hours, that the organization cannot make such predictions without knowing what the incident might be, when it will occur and who will be around at the time. So the message is to be somewhere where you can be contacted, do not talk with anybody outside the organization about the incident, and be available at all times because recovering the business is not a 9 a.m.–5 p.m. operation.

However, it is not always thus, as it is the nature of the incident which will be the prime driver in determining how people will react to recovering the business, and, more importantly, to recovering themselves and each other.

According to industry statistics (sources *Survive!* September 1993 and Safetynet Plc July 1998), and ignoring fraud, in excess of 80% of all disasters are still computer-related with hardware, software and NetWare problems. Because these statistics are drawn from incidents that are neither life-threatening nor do they threaten health and safety, they are classified as "soft" disasters. That is to say that they may disturb the operational capacity of an organization without having a detrimental effect upon the staff within, except as nuisance value. But in the case of "hard" disasters, those instances where there has been a violent invasion of one's workspace, such as through criminal act, fire or explosion, then problems visit those personally and directly affected. And those problems tend, in the main, to be emotionally orientated—so why is this the case, and what can be done about it? Let us deal initially with attempting to reduce the emotional impact upon individuals before an incident by first looking at how one's own space at work is both used and treated. In an office environment, the majority of people at work tend to have something at or about their desk or workstation which tells others that this is where they work. There is also a comfort factor in this and it is usually evidenced by such things as favourite cartoons, photographs, a sports trophy, a small soft toy, a child's early attempt at art, and so on. Whatever it may be, it is a "thumbprint" that expresses a message to the world and says, "this area is mine". Although this declaration is made indirectly and implicitly, it is, nonetheless, a very strong statement. But this area can be invaded by unwanted intrusion. For example, you return from lunch one day to find a person, whom you may or may not know, sitting at your desk, using your telephone and writing on your notepad with a pen that was given to you, by a loved one, last Christmas. Now the only thing that is genuinely and legally yours is the pen. The rest—the desk, the chair, and other items—all belong to the company. But that is not the issue. The issue is that you would rather the person be anywhere else other than at this desk, leaving you with the question of *How do you feel about the intrusion?* Mostly the feeling is one of negative reaction because you want that person out of your space. And, depending on how assertive you are, this may happen sooner rather than later. So the relationship between ourselves and the space we are required to operate within is very important. Unless the space is inadequate, the amount we have and are prepared to operate within is largely irrelevant, unless the individual is status conscious and status is important. Take it away, even temporarily, and there is potential for a problem.

If access to the space is denied or removed and it is intact, then an individual has options as to how to manage the situation to regain the territory. If, however, the territory is the subject of an aggressive invasion, then exaggerated and uncharacteristic human reactions may follow, with the nature of such reactions likely to differ from individual to individual because no two people are the same. A flood, or leak, or system outage, or some other temporary reason for denial of access, tends not to carry the same message as that of violence or aggression.

But imagine standing outside your offices, at the proper emergency muster point, only this time it is not a fire drill. This time it is for real; and you can see the building burning and the sounds, the sights and smells of this experience are further magnified by how others around you are reacting. The Emergency Services have not yet arrived and the growing fire spreads to the car park, engulfing vehicles in its path. The Emergency Services eventually arrive and, after asking lots of questions, begin putting out the fire. The intensity of this experience is further swollen by uncertainties such as how you get home, because the jacket containing your railway ticket is in the building; once home, how do you get in, because the front door keys are in the same jacket; and what about the credit cards in the wallet which is in the same jacket; and so on. And then your imagination takes you down the path of twisting reality around "what-if" scenarios, and all the negative reactions that attend such circumstances. There are many other matters which become affected, but if you worked for Digital Equipment Company (DEC) in Basingstoke in the early 1990s, then you will know that this event actually happened.

And where do trauma or stress management sit in all this? Well, it depends whether or not it features as a consideration in the Continuity Plan. But one thing is for certain, and that is, if this matter has not been accorded sufficient attention as an integral part of the recovery process, then for those staff who require such support after a disaster, it may simply leave them stranded with little more than the belief that their self-contained problems are theirs and theirs alone. However, they can show no wound, no bruising, no blood and no scar; no outward evidence that here is a person in trouble. In the absence of proper professional support, each person will have their own way of dealing with this matter.

Take Mary, a slightly built, attractive, highly intelligent businesswoman; a native of New York, working in London. She was, along with all of her colleagues, invited to a presentation in the company's Boardroom, on contingency measures. Whilst still at her desk in her office, Mary asked her new UK boss why the measures were necessary. She was told: "This is London, and in terrorist terms, we are in a war zone." Now, not only did Mary not want to hear this, she was shocked and rapidly became overwhelmed with the desire to stay as far away from the presentation as possible. Her refusal to attend the presentation ended in a very heated discussion between herself and her boss, the latter insisting she attend, which eventually she did. Mary quietly entered the Boardroom and sat down at the back, feeling frightened and anxious in ways she could not fully understand. At the end of the presentation, she approached the presenter and thanked him, "for helping me through one of the most frightening moments of my life". Perplexed by the reply, the presenter gently pressed for more information. He was told that six months earlier, in her New York office, Mary, along with everybody else in her building, was told over the public address system to evacuate immediately because of the threat of an imminent bomb explosion. The elevators were switched off as were the escalators and the only evacuation route available to her was down the emergency stairs at the rear of the building. Mary, incidentally, worked on the 38th floor of a 70-storey block and, on the day in question, she wore shoes that were more of a fashion statement, rather than what she really needed now, which was trainers. Along with over 9 000 others in the same building, she set off on her evacuation route and although she was doing what thousands of others were now doing, she felt very alone with this new trouble. On her descent towards street level, Mary was over-taken, she was shoved, she was buffeted and two or three times she was knocked to the ground. There was a lot of noise, with confusion, people shouting, people crying and a great deal of panic. What also gripped Mary's imagination was that she had absolutely no idea if she was running away from, or towards the bomb. When she got to street level, one of her shoes was broken and she was in shock. But because there was no outwardly obvious indication of her trauma, she understandably con-cluded that it was her own private trouble that nobody else would believe, let alone share. The reality was that she was traumatized and her way of coping with life was to take this experience and "file it away" in the back of her mind where nobody could get to it . . . that is until practically the same subject was raised again. The box in her own mind to which this trouble was consigned was unlocked by the idea of contingency measures and the words "terrorist activity". To satisfy a point of interest, the New York telephoned bomb warning turned out to be a hoax call. And in the fullness of time, Mary sought and got the right treatment.

Now let us look at another incident. At 11:20 hrs on Saturday 15 June 1996, a bomb went off in the Arndale Shopping Centre in the heart of commercial Man-chester. Amongst those businesses affected, was The Boots Company plc. Five months later, there followed an article in *Survive!* Magazine of November 1996 entitled "WHO CARED? THEY DID", which featured support for staff, particularly in the matters of welfare and counselling. Within this, one of the key elements was communication at a time of crisis, addressing both internal and external audiences, which had an interest. In particular, when dealing with the press and media, the spokesperson for the affected organization should have sufficient demonstrable control and authority to convey convincing messages to the outside world. And why is it necessary to tell others that you have an incident under control? Because if this is not done properly, an information vacuum will lead to speculation which could compound known difficulties and create others, but this is a different argu-ment for another time. The principal point is how a company deals with people in crisis. And who does such work? Well, nobody who begins by saying "Now just pull yourself together", whatever that means. What is required is a sympathetic approach by qualified practitioners who have a proven track record, in more than one related field of expertise. Typically it is the role of the Clinical Psychologist that will be particularly appropriate.

According to Michael Stewart, Clinical Psychologist and Partner with the Centre for Crisis Psychology, 50% of those affected by violent incidents will require psychological help from three weeks and up to three months after the incident. Individuals and groups will require information in order to build an understanding so that they may cope. They may already have that information, in part or in whole, but a perfectly normal and unhelpful reaction, such as denial, may prevent the bigger picture being properly understood. The route to that information comprises three elements, namely:

1.  Re-experience of the phenomena. In the case of re-experience, the afflicted parties may endure intrusive recollections: arbitrary and involuntary flashbacks. This may also appear in the form of recurring sleep disturbances and nightmares. It may slip into an imagined re-enaction, leaving the victim in half belief that the incident has been acted out with a feeling that it possibly did not actually happen. Often, with real or symbolic re-exposure, the individual may again experience distress or anxieties.
2.  Avoidance and numbing. In the case of avoidance and numbing, victims deny thoughts and feelings surrounding the situation and may display an inability to recall the incident. Their behaviour may show diminished interest, detachment or estrangement or demonstrate a suggestion that there is a limited or restricted effect through less overt emotive expression; equally, they may display a sense of a foreshortened future or pessimism.
3.  Persistent and increased arousal. In the case of persistent and increased arousal, victims may encounter difficulty in falling asleep, and once asleep, in staying asleep. Victims may display higher levels of irritability through intolerance of others or of observed circumstances, possibly accompanied by angry outbursts; matters that would otherwise draw no comment, become escalated in the individual's sense of what is important. Furthermore, they may have trouble concentrating on matters that demand concentration. Conversely, victims may show increased levels of suspicion or hypervigilance as if guarding against a recurrence of the incident. They may demonstrate exaggerated startle or a physiological reaction against re-exposure.

These three elements describe behavioural traits which may be used to lead to the information that would enable victims to obtain a fuller understanding and managed acceptance of the incident. One display of reaction that is not described is one of complete rejection, not of the incident or the circumstances but of the consequences. This is when one or more employees find matters so unacceptable that they never return to their place of work or if they do, so briefly as makes no difference. This "Can't face it. Won't face it" reaction is an ultimate protective mechanism. An example is Amy, a 24 year-old woman whose offices were severely damaged by one of the London terrorist outrages. Amy was not a front line recovery team member, but nonetheless was a concerned employee who was already on the path of a glittering career, so there was a serious reason not to leave the company, and indeed several very good reasons to stay. Over the weekend Amy rang in and was told to "Come in on Monday morning as usual". The speaker continued: "Everything that can be done is being done and it's really all okay." The latter part of that statement was relative to the experience and judgement of the speaker and not of the caller. When the person turned up for work on Monday morning, such was the shock and dismay of what they saw that their initial feelings were of utter disbelief and overwhelming fear, and turning on their heels, they departed, never to return. Some 18 months or so later, this person was able to relate the story, in this case to the writer, in such detail, that it was as if the event had only just happened. Furthermore, such was the obvious and agitated reaction of the person telling the story, that it was akin to an obsession that the story be told in full; nothing was going to stop the teller. Indeed, psychological trauma is something which most people deal with in their own way, with the majority of us filing it away to the back of our minds and into a mental box wherein it is hidden away until it is unlocked, unleashing all those unwanted memories.

Psychological trauma is not a condition which only affects certain types of people, it also affects people who are normal and healthy. Psychological trauma comes from any life- or injury-threatening incident that causes unusually strong reactions in people and stops them from working normally. It may seriously affect their working life as well as their personal life.

The Board of an organization, through the services of its Contingency Planner, may bathe in the misguided belief that all measures that can be taken, have been taken. Communication with, and advice from, the Emergency Services has been heeded, with recommendations implemented and emergency drills held regularly. First-aid training has been completed and refresher courses scheduled in to the calendar. A Business Continuity Plan has been written and its content has satisfied the scrutiny of auditors, insurers and regulators alike. But despite all these preparations, any major disaster arrives as a complete shock and it is the magnitude and the impact of the incident, combined with the element of surprise, which will begin to shape how people will react. Those directly involved may not display any reactions until some time after the event. People may go back to work, simply because everybody else does, and their manager's impression is that everything, just like everybody, appears to be okay. It is also a common assumption that those who were not directly involved will be unaffected and to ignore these people because of this reason will be an unwise thing to do. Actually, they are often badly affected because their thoughts could lead them to: "There, but for the grace of God, go I." If the management of an organization does not understand, or at least have some sympathy for psychological trauma, then it will be unprepared for the aftermath of a crisis. When confronted by distressing and painful symptoms, management may take completely the wrong steps to remedy the situation or may even seek to avoid the issue altogether in the hope that it disappears as quickly as it arrived. Management reactions that are unsympathetic will discourage staff from declaring their sufferings, which, in turn, may lead to staff resentment and a degradation in job performance. And if left for long enough, such degradation may continue until staff become unmotivated, and a lower morale develops which culminates in staff turnover.

Another contributor to staff post-disaster turnover, is the tolerance of staff to rapid and unwanted change. If recovery from an incident means displacement from the normal place of work, and then temporary relocation is to a similar property with similar facilities within the same neighbourhood, then nobody is unduly disadvantaged. But recovering to a building with less comfortable facilities, or that takes longer to get to, or that is harder to get to, or a combination of these factors, then people may decide that the disaster has acted as the catalyst for leaving the organization. Here is a direct cost to the organization that is not insurable, unless it is a key member of staff and a Key Staff insurance cover is a current policy. Typically, however, with any incident of major proportions, and one where displacement appears to go beyond the average outage (1.85 days— Safetynet Plc data), then once the euphoria surrounding recovery has subsided, staff take a closer look at their new circumstances. And if those circumstances do not suit them, they will take a view and this on average occurs about two weeks after the displacement.

Returning to the Manchester incident, one financial institute that was seriously affected had a Business Continuity Plan that was written and untested. Because the Plan was untested, there was no faith in the document and because nobody, except the author, understood the contents, the Plan largely went unused. However, after a couple of days outage, the Plan was reviewed for a recovery strategy, a strategy which was implemented without a thought of the consequences. The strategy basically had the organization in question spread its Manchester office staff to other regional offices in the north of England. For the sake of confidentiality, the offices are fictionally sited in Leeds, Sheffield, and Birkenhead. The Manchester office was considerably larger than any of the other offices and so each of them got "invaded" by their Mancunian cousins. This had the overall effect of spreading the disaster to those parts of the business that were, up until this point, unaffected. Then suddenly, the discomfort of cramped conditions and demands on resources and space seriously disrupted the business at all of these other offices. On paper, the strategy appeared to work, but in reality, when the people part of the equation was added, the plan failed because the overall reaction was negative. Indeed, the overall reaction leads back to the "invasion of space" issue mentioned earlier, although this invasion was longer and more comprehensive as it embraced the use of PCs, telephones, coffee cups, company documentation, and so on. This experience was not blessed with any "Dunkirk spirit".

When contingency measures are created, they must include the fullest accommodation for all the people who are expected to use them or who will be affected by them, even in a small way. Any Contingency Plan or Continuity Plan will be incomplete without according the fullest consideration to how people feel about the circumstances they encounter, as a result of a serious and unwanted incident. Part of any Plan must seek to address the emotive and psychological needs of people in crisis and this part of the Plan must feature proactive deeds rather than simply waiting to see what happens. As a bare minimum, the Plan should instruct those expected to use it to implement the right approach, which will be to summon the assistance of professional practitioners, usually Clinical Psychologists with a proven track record. These Clinical Psychologists should provide guidance and advice as to what to do and how and when to do it.

It may help to start with the basic understanding that the key resource, and its most volatile resource, for any business, is its staff; without people there is no business. Similarly, no business can fully recover from disastrous circumstances without its staff, and this means *all of them*.

# The missing elements

**20** Andrew Hiles—UK

Andrew is Chairman of *Survive!* The Business Continuity Group and is also Director of the Kingswell Partnership.

## Where next?

What are the trends in business continuity planning and where is it heading? We may get a better glimpse of the future by first looking at the past.

About ten to fifteen years ago, leading edge organizations were coming to grips with their dependency on computers. The Fortune 1000 corporations, led by the finance sector, began to implement disaster recovery plans for computers and vendors responded with standby services. This example slowly filtered to the smaller, dynamic and entrepreneurial companies and through the public sector. As it was doing so, the Fortune 1000 companies began to realize that, while computers were important, so were communications and telephony, production facilities, equipment and offices. Business Continuity Planning was born—again—filtering from the biggest to the smaller.

Blue chip corporations have long held Contingency Plans for specific situations, such as hostage, kidnap, armed robbery. Now, these are being absorbed into full Crisis Management, along with IT disaster recovery planning and wider business continuity planning. And all this is being underpinned by reputation management with an emphasis on managing media.

But, more important, is the underlying reason for this: the message is getting through. More and more Chief Executives are realizing that they simply cannot stick their heads in the sand and pretend a disaster will not happen to their organization. More and more pressure for effective contingency planning and risk reduction is being applied by legislation; by regulation; by auditors; by class actions against negligent directors; by government inspectors and by insurers.

Yet another pressure is the interdependency of corporations through Just-In-Time supply and electronic trading. The big customers have begun to demand that

*The Definitive Handbook of Business Continuity Management.* Edited by Andrew Hiles and Peter Barnes. © 1999 John Wiley & Sons Ltd.

their suppliers have business continuity plans in place: they do not want their supplier's disaster to become their own disaster.

At present the weight of numbers still remains on Information Technology rather than total business recovery planning, but there are unmistakable signs of a swing to comprehensive corporate crisis and continuance management. We really are beginning to see a critical mass on the side in support of aggressive risk prevention and business recovery planning, so that it is rapidly becoming the norm rather than the exception. And as that happens, everybody benefits—the business, the shareholder, staff and the innocent passer-by.

# The business continuity industry

The business continuity market is growing at around 25% a year in most developed countries. Of course, that is good news for suppliers: as long as they provide the services the customer needs at the right quality and the right price, suppliers have a rosy future.

Increasingly customers are looking at a one-stop shop for all their business continuity services. At the same time, customers have an increasingly diverse range of technical platforms to support, taxing the skills and resources of their service vendors. The result has been a series of acquisitions, mergers and partnership arrangements by vendors—a trend that will continue.

This trend has been boosted by the globalization of the industry: global customers want global vendors. Apart from computer manufacturers, there were few truly global players in business continuity say five years ago: now there is a positive stampede to acquire global capability.

Profitability can be high amongst vendors, some of which are showing upwards of 20% profit and 30% annual growth. Once the cost of a standby facility has been covered by subscriptions, every additional sale goes straight to the bottom line. Since the cost of such additional sales is marginal, the astute customer may drive a hard bargain: in one recent case, facilities initially offered at $200 000 were eventually signed up for $60 000. This also means that the earlier subscribers on three- or five-year contracts may not be getting the best deal.

The more subscriptions a facility has, the more profitable it can be. It is incumbent on the customer, therefore, to verify that the vendor does not have so many subscribers that there is a strong possibility of the standby site being occupied by somebody else at the time of invocation. Even a few customers could cause this situation if they are geographically close together.

Service vendors are still primarily focused on providing recovery for the computing and communications technology—albeit with workspace attached. Quick resupply services have developed. Dealing room recovery facilities abound.

General office space is available, with or without office systems. Document protection vaults are also becoming more widely available. However, there remains little in the way of formalized recovery services for manufacturing production, logistics and distribution. In these areas, the business continuity planner remains very much on their own.

## Business continuity professionals

Over the last few years there has been an emphasis within almost every organization on downsizing, right-sizing, outsourcing, "flat pyramids" and various other initiatives for headcount reduction. This has resulted in a number of outcomes impacting the business continuity professional.

1. In Business Continuity Planning, it means that in many corporations skills are just one deep: there are no alternative people to stand in during a disaster. This situation is aggravated by the need to have teams at the damaged site, and at a recovery site, probably working extended hours at each site. Pressure on headcount has become a major challenge for recovery planners.
2. In times of economic stringency, business continuity professionals have sometimes been seen as a soft target for cutbacks. Alert professionals have therefore moved from a technical orientation towards a business orientation. They have been seeking to demonstrate their professionalism by professional qualification and certification. The Business Continuity Institute and the Disaster Recovery Institute International both have a rapidly growing number of certified professionals. The Business Continuity professional has come of age.
3. Reorganization has led to a reappraisal of different roles with responsibilities for various aspects of risk. These include physical security, insurance, health and safety and business continuity. We are increasingly seeing these roles consolidated.

## Corporate resilience

If we have done our risk assessment and business impact analysis effectively, we will already have put in place alternative accommodation, personnel, production capability equipment, logistics and other facilities. These will enable reputation to be protected, operations to continue and customers to be served despite the disaster. You will have rehearsed recovery procedures and you will know they work. So at that stage, has business continuity been effected? Is the business continuity planner still necessary?

Take a few examples.

1.  A bank has its proven and tested in-company, dedicated recovery facility with workspace, equipment and telecommunications capabilities. Its main IT centre suffers major hardware problems causing an immediate and prolonged service outage. Is this a disaster? No—it is an operational decision by IT management to relocate operations to the standby facility.
2.  A Head Office has arranged for standby recovery facilities with a commercial Hot Site vendor. It is planning a major hardware upgrade and agrees with its recovery service vendor that it can conduct equipment operations from the standby site during the upgrade. Is that a disaster? No. And if the cause of the operational relocation was not a planned move but a relocation forced by fire in the Head Office, why should the fire be a disaster?
3.  A gale causes major damage to a manufacturer's production plant: it will take several days to re-establish production. The manufacturer supplies Just In Time components to a major customer. However, its continuity plan involves maintaining one week of buffer stock. Is the gale a disaster? No.

What we have been witnessing over the last few years of business continuity planning is the downgrading of disasters to operational incidents. In many cases, business continuity planning has become simply another (important) element of operational risk reduction. In these cases, we do not necessarily invoke the full business continuity plan, but handle it as an operational incident. Why involve the business continuity planner—it's an operational decision. So are business continuity professionals actually doing themselves out of a job?

There are trends both for and against corporate resilience. Developments supporting resilience include:

*   The growth of expert systems and Artificial Intelligence, reducing reliance on individuals
*   Increasing resilience and fault tolerance in equipment (in part to save field service and maintenance engineering costs)
*   Improved reliability of software
*   Improved resilience of suppliers, including power and telecommunications providers
*   More and more corporations and cities are introducing video surveillance which will reduce business loss through theft, hooliganism and arson
*   Mergers leading to mega-corporations with international multisites—a pain-tolerant situation. An organization worth a trillion dollars can afford to lose a few million!

Trends tending against corporate resilience include:

- Increasing integration of technology across the whole range of operations—for instance, manufacturing control and integrated financial, sales and logistics systems. This complicates recovery and can cause delay. In recovery, modularity rules!
- Time pressures on computer back-ups may prevent interdependent systems from being backed-up in a synchronized fashion, causing integrity and reconciliation problems

We have seen resilience, redundancy and alternative capability increasingly built into equipment and processes to the point where disaster avoidance and mitigation is simply the way we work. But, as always, there is the opposite side of the coin. Again, examples may illustrate this.

1. A retail chain has a central distribution centre and an integrated point-of-sale, logistics, distribution and financial system. The company supplying the software implements a new version without a fallback position in the event the upgrade fails. The upgrade fails. Point of sale tills cannot be polled to feed the logistics chain. The tills' memory fills up: the option is either to stop selling (and preserve system integrity) or to resupply manually (and potentially lose the integrity of the stock control system). Is this a disaster? How many business continuity plans cater for software problems like this?
2. An international courier is prevented from landing its plane through bad weather. Is that an operational incident or a disaster? Is it a disaster if its competitors have been able to land their aircraft?
3. An aerospace company loses its office systems at 10:30 on a Friday morning. There is no indication as to when they will become available. The company is responding to an invitation to tender for a billion dollar contract. Is this a disaster?
4. It is late December. The London offices of a national law firm are handling a high-profile case of sexual harassment. It involves a senior politician and his personal assistant. The law firm is representing the personal assistant, to considerable media interest. News breaks that, in the Manchester office, a Christmas party got a bit out of hand. A senior partner got over-amorous with his young attractive lady clerk. She is claiming that "he kept pouring me drinks and forced himself on me".

Many organizations are fixated on big, physical disasters—the Godzilla scenario. But they have recovery plans to cover these. Companies can die just as easily from being nibbled to death by rats. Does the continuity plan cover this, too?

In summary, probably both corporate resilience and corporate vulnerability are increasing. We cannot afford to be complacent about our resilience: we must be vigilant to a potential disaster situation. Defining "disaster" is fundamental to business continuity planning. Too loose a definition can cause a disaster—either by invoking an unproven and deficient plan unnecessarily, or by failing to recognize that a potential disaster condition exists until irreparable damage has been caused. The lesson is straightforward. Disasters are not always self-evident. There has to be a clear definition of disaster—and escalation procedure from customer complaints, help desks, quality defects, service level failures and production incidents so that decisions can be made about each incident against established disaster criteria.

# Appendix 1
# Case studies

## AN INTRODUCTION TO THE CASE STUDY SECTION

"Disasters" or in the (perhaps) preferred idiom "business-threatening interruptions" are not as uncommon as many managers might wish to believe. Many of the major commercial centres of the world are located in earthquake zones or flood plains; many organizations have hazardous neighbours—railway stations prone to bomb attacks; manufacturers using hazardous materials and so on. Companies located in such conditions need to weigh the threats and prepare for the worst.

Flooding arises not only from natural causes, such as rivers overflowing, dams collapsing, and sea defences being breached, but also from much more mundane occurrences such as faulty plumbing and burst water tanks.

Fire is probably the threat against which most organizations feel best protected. Smoke detectors, alarms, extinguishers and direct communication to fire brigades are widely regarded as almost normal precautions.

The results of bomb attacks can manifest themselves in many different ways. Often the impact is the same as if an earthquake, flood or fire had occurred—in extreme cases all three!

Physical disasters often result in a loss of power. Power blackouts can also be caused by either strikes or sabotage. Just as poor plumbing can cause floods, accidental damage to wiring systems or poor electrical circuitry can lead to power blackouts.

The articles contained in the following pages serve as a reminder that disasters do happen and, yes, they may well happen to you or your organization. There but for the grace of God . . . Disasters range from small fires, to large infernos, floods, explosions, hurricanes, human error. Many lessons can be learnt from the experience of those unfortunate enough to have experienced a disaster and lived to tell the tale.

It is hoped that these lessons, drawn from presentations at Survive! conferences, articles in *Survive!* Magazine, cases from the Survive! database and experiences from authors of the main text of this volume, will provide valuable guidance in enabling disaster recovery and business continuity plans to be drawn up.

*The Definitive Handbook of Business Continuity Management.* Edited by Andrew Hiles and Peter Barnes. © 1999 John Wiley & Sons Ltd.

## 1A STORM, EARTHQUAKE, EXPLOSION—A GENERAL OVERVIEW

We are all familiar with storms, the possibility of explosions has been part of everyday life for some, and even the UK has the occasional earthquake. Each type of occurrence requires a different approach if the damage is to be contained and the status quo restored.

Fire and flood are the most common causes of damage to property, but recent years have seen an increasing incidence of storm and explosion damage. Future weather patterns are unknown, however, and the emergence of new sources of terrorist action is an ever present threat in many parts of the world. Earthquakes are still not predictable, but the continents continue to move and further activity is inevitable. It is therefore important to be able to apply the knowledge and experience gained from past events to those still to come.

## Storm

The Caribbean had major hurricanes in 1988 (Gilbert) and 1989 (Hugo), the United States in 1991 (Andrew), and the United Kingdom experienced severe storms in October 1987 and January 1990.

Hurricane Gilbert focused the damage management industry's attention on storm damage. On arrival in Jamaica it was found that virtually the entire infrastructure had been not destroyed but certainly put out of action. There were no telephones, no power, no piped water, and immediately after the storm the airport runway had been blocked so that access to the island was difficult.

What do you do first in such circumstances? Communication with head office to arrange supplies—of money, men, materials, methods and machines—is impossible, there is nowhere to stay since the hotels are uninhabitable, there is no cooked food for lack of power and gas.

The airport was soon reopened, and major efforts were devoted to loss mitigation by, for example, oiling machinery to arrest corrosion in the warm, moist and salt-laden conditions. Thus damage management contractors were able to reach Jamaica two days after the hurricane, and were soon busy at dozens of damage sites.

Hurricane Hugo and the damage it caused, principally in Puerto Rico, reinforced the lessons learned. The even bigger financial loss caused by Hurricane Andrew was very largely to domestic premises.

Even more unusual was a problem encountered in Indonesia over Christmas 1988. The storm had caused a storage dam to burst, flooding a textile factory 14 kilometres downstream with up to three feet of soft mud. A few days later the panels of a drying machine were opened, revealing two large snakes hissing angrily. Damage management procedure No. 237 was quickly instituted: tap loudly and listen before opening!

## Earthquake

There was an earthquake in remote terrain in the Philippines some years ago. A hydro-electric dam had been constructed and the reservoir contained quantities of silt due to deforestation. The earthquake caused landslides into the reservoir, stirred up the silt, and flooded muddy water through the power-generating equipment.

Minor seismic faults are to be found in the UK, and there are industrial installations downstream from storage dams in the fault zones. The companies concerned would be well advised to include the possibilities of earthquake damage and severe flooding by muddy water in their contingency plans.

# Explosion

The risk of explosion damage has been recognized as being of major concern among business continuity professionals since the IRA bomb-blast in St Mary Axe, London, in April 1992, and even more so since the anniversary blast in Bishopsgate in April 1993 and the New York WTC blast in February the same year. Explosion damage is likely to be restricted to commercial premises, and therefore to include high-rise buildings. One can feel sympathy for those people at the HSB building who, without power and therefore with no lifts, had to climb the stairs as far as the twenty-seventh floor.

Apart from the obvious problems, such as lack of power, rainwater ingress through broken windows, glass falling from windows high up in the building, and the need for structural safety to be established, a few of the problems which may not have been anticipated were:

- Security considerations caused the police to prevent any access to the building for some time after the explosion, even by the structural engineers who would necessarily be first-in to ascertain the building's safety
- Emergency contractors brought in to clear debris caused as much damage as the bomb, including attempts to open safes by force, deliberate deposition of waste material, and deliberate or accidental damage to computers by thrown debris
- There were considerable amounts of money, blank traveller's cheques and other negotiables in the buildings, and their secure removal was difficult and time-consuming, and interrupted access to the buildings by all other parties
- The City did not have sufficient stocks of hard hats, glasses, and safety boots for the number of people requiring to enter the building, and it took time to bring them in
- The site managers took the view that 140 was the absolute maximum number of people which could be allowed into the not-yet-safe building at any one time. This meant that bookings for access had to be made, and everyone experienced further delays

For many affected businesses, it was fortunate that there was a recession at the time, since that made it possible to find alternative premises in the City at short notice. Of course, to organizations with contingency plans in place, this was not a problem.

Electronic equipment in the blast-affected area generally survived extremely well, and many computers continued to operate during and after the explosion. In one case, it would have caused considerable business interruption to switch them off, and the priority was to install plastic sheeting at the windows to protect them from the elements.

Several computers were scrapped unnecessarily, mainly from buildings which lost power, so that direct evidence of continuing function was lacking. One major bank with a developed contingency plan, realizing the complexity of the problems involved in the replacement of several electronic items, decided at once on decontamination. In this case the contamination was from glass fragments as well as ceiling debris and dust, and the contamination from normal use, which includes skin, paperclips, coffee, sugar, staples, and general detritus. The glass fragments came in all shapes and sizes.

There remain two good reasons for thorough removal of the fragments:

1.  Until the device has been dismantled and checked it is not known whether any more damaging large pieces of glass are present.
2.  There is a serious risk of cut fingers of operatives or maintenance personnel, with consequent liability claims.

A car-bomb also set by the IRA exploded at Brent Cross, North London, in April 1992. It released considerable quantities of dust within the warehouse of a company stocking electrical and electronic components, and destroyed all of the perspex rooflight panels. Temporary sheeting was installed over the rooflights, but very strong winds associated with heavy weather in the succeeding weeks blew off the sheeting, and large quantities of rainwater cascaded into the warehouse, to the extent that rainbows were visible within it. To add to dust created by the explosion, there was therefore considerable suspected damage from water. Most of the items remained in a fully functional condition, but they had been new, and the problems of warranties and the unacceptability of damaged items as being new meant that the possibilities of mitigation by reinstatement were reduced.

# Conclusion

Storms, earthquakes and explosions are all forms of damage which need to be considered in contingency planning. Their effects on buildings and equipment are often largely the same as those of fire and flood, with additions such as glass fragments. Electronic equipment is much more robust than is normally credited and reinstatement is probably more successful than it is in the more common cases of fire and flood incidents.

Loss mitigation of over 90% can be achieved by professional reinstatement, and all contingency planning should include damage management procedures. The importance of this step is exemplified by the effects of the bomb at the World Trade Center in New York, where 150 of 350 companies put out on the street subsequently went out of business.

## 1B LIVING NIGHTMARES—SOME APOCRYPHAL TALES

Water in the wrong time and place can be a complete washout for computing and communications equipment, as the management of a bank discovered to their consternation when a chilled water pipe fractured next to its switchboard and ruined it.

The bank's voice capability was restored only after the equivalent of a week's work over a public holiday weekend and at a cost of £175 000. Worse, customers thought the bank had gone out of business because they could not reach it by telephone.

The bank could have used several cellular options to get round the problem, retain customer confidence and plan for recovery of its voice systems at a slower and more economic rate.

## Generators that don't

Many organizations are alive to the problems caused by power failures but can still be caught out if their own contingency plans are not fully thought through. During the power breakdown in Manhattan in 1991 one company was counting on its diesel generator to save the day. They had tested it faithfully for months and were sure they were adequately prepared. Incredibly, the motor to start the generator was connected to mains electricity so when that failed the generator could not be started.

In another instance a consultant called on a customer, asked to see their back-up generators and was introduced to "Bob" who oversaw them. When the consultant asked questions about the start-up procedure Bob had all the answers but, when probed as to whether these were documented the vagueness of his response indicated they were not. One night a few weeks later a 100-mile-an-hour gale tore down the power lines. Alas, the customer could not get its generators started because . . . Bob was on holiday . . . Written procedures now exist, if a little late in the day.

## Litigation and near misses

Whatever the reason, sudden loss of data processing capability can imperil a firm's very existence, as happened to a US company which suffered a loss of no more than four hours processing time. In that relatively short period it was, however, unable to deliver some contracted-for information. In the subsequent court case it was sued for $600m but managed to negotiate an out-of-court settlement of $60m. This problem had not been identified before the computer went down.

All these incidents actually happened. Almost as hair-raising are the near misses—the problems that could have occurred but, mercifully, were spotted or headed-off in time following a business impact analysis.

For example, one particular company factored its receivables. During a business impact analysis it was found that if they could not deliver the receivables to the bank, as contracted for, the bank could assume control of the company.

In another case a firm had halon in a room housing its processing system but the room was found not to be airtight, thus rendering the halon ineffective. Outside the room the building's staff did their welding. The system's batteries emit highly explosive hydrogen— the welding was moved.

## To err is human

The human element is clearly present in all these situations, to a greater or lesser degree. Occasionally the problem is all human in origin. In one company a visiting consultant insisted on visiting the storage location for back-up tapes, which was in a vault in a nearby building. Once inside the vault it was found to contain some rubbish . . . but no tapes! A quick search found the tapes in the company van parked outside the computer centre. These were large old reels each weighing more than two and a half pounds, of which the operators had to take as many as 300 a night up a flight of stairs. They had become rather tired of this so had taken to using the van as the off-site storage location.

## Solid investment

Minimizing the risk of "nightmares" is an investment, that in the event of a disaster will pay for itself in no time. One company has calculated that by using a computer disaster recovery service, all the costs involved with this, including salaries, testing, subscriptions to "hot" sites and consulting costs, would pay for themselves after saving just 42 minutes during the recovery effort.

## 1C  WORLD TRADE CENTER EXPLOSION— 26 FEBRUARY 1993

The World Trade Center in New York City is the second tallest building in the world. Its two familiar twin towers are each 110 storeys tall, 7 floors underground, 7 buildings in the complex which covers 16 acres. There are 2000 parking spaces underground. The complex contains more than 1000 businesses and 8 retail tenants. Some 50 000 workers are employed in the complex and there are 80 000 visitors daily. The WTC is home to 350 firms including commodity exchanges, two major brokerage firms, banks, law firms, a major hotel and a shopping mall. The twin towers alone contain 70 000 phone and data communications lines.

## Problems

Many fire safety systems that are routine in office-building were exempted by New York: no emergency lights in the stairwells; no pressurized fire stairwells to seal them from the rest of the building. New York sets its own standards for high-rise skyscrapers . . . most of the rest of the nation builds skyscrapers to uniform engineering standards. Pipes were broken, causing flooding in the basement and all generators shorted out.

## The explosion

The bomb contained 1200 pounds of explosives and was triggered by nitroglycerin. It had been smuggled in in a van and there appeared to be no difficulty in getting the bomb placed in the WTC. Terrorist involvement was indicated although the target of attack was uncertain. There was immediate concern for "copycat" activities.

The bomb took out all security. The bomb in B-2 in the parking garage created a crater 100 feet wide and down through four floors of concrete. Columns supporting the towers and hotel were damaged. Structural supports had to be reinforced. All emergency lighting and all power were lost. All 250 elevators were inoperative. The underground train station sustained damage. Over 50 000 people had to be evacuated, there were five deaths and more than 1000 injuries.

The explosion was, at the time, the largest single emergency response in United States history:

- 45% of entire New York Fire Department on-duty staff was utilized. Over 700 police officers and federal agents. 170 ambulances responded to the scene
- 2000 personnel were counselled for stress
- Reconstruction cost was estimated at $300m
- Business interruption costs to Port Authority and other business estimated at additional $185m

## Outcome

It was considered that it could take a month just to figure out what needed to be done. At the time 350 businesses were disrupted. Disaster declarations began within one hour of the incident. Many companies were forced to reroute information systems and telecommunications to alternative sites. Most firms did not lose any data and were able to resume operations by Monday morning. Large tenants, such as Dean Witter who employ 5000 personnel, did not have a problem because they had a contingency plan and alternative offices in New York.

Comdisco Disaster Recovery Services, with bases in Illinois, New Jersey, and elsewhere in the USA, accepted three customers totalling 615 employees—the Bank of California and two large Japanese banks. In addition to the Coffee, Sugar and Cocoa Exchange, Sungard Recovery Services had five customers declare disasters. Tower 2 was still closed 31 days after the incident.

## Considerations

Many office workers fled to the stairwells. Some huddled together by windows to await help. Fire fighters arrived two hours after the blast. Some of the workers, after several days, were still coughing black mucous. People believe it could happen anywhere and at anytime. The complex is so huge, it is questionable how a bomb could be prevented. Nevertheless, questions arose:

- Why was it so easy to get the bomb into the car park?
- Why did both WTC power systems fail?
- How well prepared were telecoms organizations in New York City?
- How well prepared were WTC tenants in the event of a disaster?

## Client reactions

"It was hard to believe, during the contingency planning process, that the WTC would ever be brought to its knees!"

"Problem was we didn't acknowledge, in our contingency plan, what was really required to make the problem transparent to our customers."

"I was more worried about having a copy of my resume at home" (as opposed to in my desk) . . . upon returning from lunch and seeing smoke billowing from the WTC.

# Lessons

Harsh lessons were learnt:

- Security in all critical areas of WTC must be increased
- Relocate primary/back-up power systems in WTC
- Install battery-powered lighting in stairwells

Whether you are trapped in an 11-storey office building in New York or a 7-storey hotel in Omaha, there are basic things that can be done to protect oneself:

1. Learn two escape routes, even in the dark. Make sure smoke detectors, sprinklers, emergency lights are there and working.
2. In an emergency, head for fire exits, closing doors behind you to slow the spread of fire and smoke.
3. Before opening a door, feel it with the back of your hand and, if the door is hot, use an alternative exit.
4. Crawl low under smoke, clearer air is near the floor.
5. Never use an elevator.
6. Develop more comprehensive disaster recovery plans which will include what action will be taken by fire, bomb, police and other public safety organizations.

Existing disaster recovery plans must be regularly updated and emergency relocation strategies must be developed and tested.

## 1D   HURRICANE ANDREW, MIAMI—24 AUGUST 1992

Grand Metropolitan Information Services manage three data centres providing IT services and facilities to the Grand Metropolitan Group Companies. [Editor's note: Following continued business developments and mergers, this organization is currently known as Diageo]. One data centre is in the UK and the other two are located in Minneapolis and Miami.

Disaster recovery plans had been developed in the UK over the previous two years and fully tested a number of times. Based on this work, similar projects had been implemented in the USA. The last DRP test for the Miami data centre had been carried out at the hot site in March 1992 so there was a certain level of preparedness when Hurricane Andrew struck Miami in August.

## Background

Because there was some advance warning of the hurricane's arrival a planning meeting was initiated on 23 August, the system was backed-up, gracefully disabled, and the recovery site was put on notice of disaster declaration. Although they were prepared there were many surprises.

The enormity of the disaster had not been comprehended. It was a personal disaster for employees as well as a physical disaster. Many employees lost their homes and this became their priority rather than the company losses. The scale of personal issues therefore impacted the recovery timescales.

Cellular phones proved very inadequate for communication. Ground transportation problems were enormous. The scale of the disaster caused unreal competition for recovery resources. Vendors and suppliers responded beyond expectations and the staff response was outstanding.

Hurricane Andrew arrived in Miami on Monday morning, 24 August 1992. A disaster was formally declared and a control centre set up at an alternative company site in Minneapolis. Attempts were made to move system back-ups to the recovery site in Seattle but ground transportation problems made this impossible. They were eventually dispatched on 25 August.

Even the helicopters being used for transportation purposes encountered problems. They were being given directions using landmarks in and around Miami. Many of the "landmarks" no longer existed in a recognizable form.

BMS-CAT were hired to assess damage and their initial report on 26 August indicated a recovery timescale of "a few weeks". On 26 August the National Guard was moved in and a curfew between 07:00 and 19:00 declared, which caused further logistical problems.

All mainframe processing was eventually transferred back to the restored data centre in Miami by 31 October, two months after the incident.

## Lessons

Grandmet got a lot right—but we also learnt a few things:

- Prior investment in DRP is essential to a recovery capability
- Ability to provide out-of-area resources is essential
- You can't overprepare—discipline is critical
- Expect the unexpected—it will happen
- Good communications are very difficult—but absolutely essential
- Time zones and status updates pose special problems
- Although recovery procedures for mainframe systems were well established those for distributed systems (PCs/LANs) were not so secure
- Be more proactive
- Consider hot site as off-site vault for recovery purposes
- There will be more cooperation and less resistance to DRP now
- The disaster highlighted a critical need for Business Continuity plans
- DRP for data centre-based systems were well established but distributed systems were not so secure

## Hurricane Andrew's toll

The scale of the disaster is hard to imagine:

- 38 deaths in South Florida
- 175 000 homeless in South Florida
- 25 000 homes destroyed; 100 000 homes damaged
- 1.3 million homes and businesses were without power immediately after the storm
- 700 000 people were evacuated from the area
- 80 000 people were housed in temporary shelters
- 7800 businesses were affected
- 22 000 federal troops were deployed; it was the largest US military rescue operation ever
- $20bn in damages
- $10bn in clean-up costs
- $7.3bn in insurance claims
- $1.04bn loss to agriculture

When faced with a disaster of this scale, no plan can handle everything—but a good plan will provide a sound basis for recovery and allow flexibility for some improvisation "on the night"!

## 1E  CHICAGO FLOODS—13 APRIL 1992

One of the features of the Chicago downtown infrastructure is the freight tunnels running beneath the city, constructed in 1904 to enable merchandise, coal and trash to be moved around. They were also designed to reduce the amount of traffic above ground. The tunnels are 60 miles long, 7 feet high by 6 feet wide and 50 feet below ground. They had been unused since 1959, but were later used to house power, phone and TV cables. The tunnels run under the river at several points.

At 5:57 a.m. the first reports of building flooding were received, followed by several additional reports by 09:00. It was originally thought to be a watermain or sewer break. Then a whirlpool was sighted in the river and sonar confirmed a car-sized hole into the tunnel system. The hole was thought to have been created by construction activities nearby.

Water was rising in subbasements at the rate of 2 feet an hour. City, Army Corps and contractors worked to try to slow or stop the leak. Some 250 million gallons of flood water were estimated. The leak was still active on the Saturday with a wide variety of reports on status and repair time estimates being received.

## Impact

At least 200 buildings were without power; 250 000 people were sent home from work; 21 square blocks were affected; $40m per day in lost productivity; the cost impact was estimated at $1.5bn.

The regional headquarters for computer equipment of a large European bank were based in Chicago. US leased line network connects the branches. A disaster recovery plan existed for the IT systems. The plan had been tested three times over the previous six months. No plans existed for business recovery at any site.

## Events

Morning news gave the first reports of the incident. Disaster alert was declared and building evacuation notification given at 10:30. Operations personnel arrived at the alternative back-up processing site by 12:00 and began the system rebuild. Key staff were routed to a nearby restaurant and an initial strategy meeting was held. An operational area was established by 15:30. Customers were notified of the situation and phone notification was used for funds transfer. By the following Wednesday night all work was up-to-date. However the leak in the tunnel system had still not been plugged so it was decided to remain at the recovery site. Systems were eventually reloaded at the home site on 25 April and the disaster situation "stood down" on the 26, 13 days after the incident.

Post-mortems were held and a business recovery project was reprioritized. An initial meeting with the insurance carrier was held.

## What went right

The existing IT recovery plan held up and was reinforced. An off-site operation was successfully established and business losses minimized. Team play by all units provided excellent experience and corporate politics were avoided.

## What went wrong

There was an obvious critical need for a business recovery plan. Communications difficulties with non-key personnel were experienced due to lack of up-to-date information.

# Reflections

Business recovery plans have now become a high priority for all sites. Specific plans are needed for PC system recoveries. A review of the insurance policy was needed. Senior management awareness of potential losses is now acute.

## 1F  THIRTY SECONDS OF TERROR!—THE CALIFORNIA EARTHQUAKE

1993 was a peak year for disasters in Southern California with:

- The Rodney King trial and verdict which ignited into the LA riots
- The firestorms in the Malibu and Pasadena areas
- The mudslides in Malibu and Ventura Canyons caused by fires

1994 began with the earthquake on 17 January.

All catastrophes, natural or man-made, can and will destroy people, property and businesses. Earthquakes, of all natural disasters are the most devastating! We do not know when they will happen, how long they will last or how severe they will be and they impact that which is most dear to us—our home, family and security.

Imagine for a moment an event so enormous in its destruction that its damage will cost £30bn. This is what the majority of LA County survived. Anyone can survive a large magnitude disaster if you know what to do before, during and after.

It has been determined that in some places the ground actually leapt 12 feet. The Santa Monica and Santa Susana mountains are now 15 inches higher and 7–9 inches closer to the ocean because of the quake.

## A personal view

At 04:30 on Monday 17 January I woke to the radio alarm. At 04:31 I thought our world and our lives had ended. The house moved in every direction possible, finally being slammed down with such a force that it drove me so deep into our water bed that I couldn't rise.

After what seemed like an eternity but what was in reality only 10–30 seconds, the violent shaking quit. After dressing we grabbed the portable radio and flashlight which we keep on hand for such emergencies, before we left the house. All this took a couple of minutes during which time the first of many strong aftershocks hit.

Staying outside until dawn, I checked the outside of the house for cracks, gas leaks or any other kind of leak and backed the car out of the garage. After a few minutes in which the initial tremors and immediate aftershocks subsided, I re-entered the house and picked some items of importance like household papers, some jewellery, a video of the house contents, food, water, change of clothes and MONEY! I put all this into the boot of the car where we also keep an Emergency Preparedness Kit for travel. This was in case we had to evacuate the area.

After dawn I again checked the house and found some water leaks which I was able to fix. I tried to call family members to let them know we were all right but all out-of-state phone circuits were shut down. We were one of the fortunate ones having water, gas, intermittent telephone service, shelter and food. The only thing we lacked was power.

About now I figured I had better check with work. After several tries I finally got through to the office and got the recorded message. I was able to find out that the office had some minimal damage and the company was requesting if possible for all employees to report to work in casual clothing for clean-up duty the following day.

The damage in the office consisted of a broken water pipe on the third floor which had soaked some non-essential documents. A few personal computers were thrown to the floor, none of which were severely damaged, and what seemed like tons of paper documents were spilled all over the floor. When the quake hit the back-up generators kicked in and the end users never noticed any problems. Two hours after the quake the system was back on normal power and working as though nothing had ever happened. By Wednesday morning the whole complex was back to business as usual.

The calling tree had been invoked but the Vice-President in charge of the Data Processing operation was unavailable because his home was closer to the epicentre and had received considerable interior damage. The Data Processing manager who lives two blocks from me had little damage but could not get in as our area was cut off because of the freeway damage.

Our power was returned early Tuesday morning and for the first time we could turn on the TV and see the total damage this quake had caused. All the exits from our valley had been damaged and we were physically landlocked.

During work that first week we experienced two severe back-to-back aftershocks. By now the seismology people had calculated over 250 aftershocks, which they were considering normal. They also calculated that we could expect the number of aftershocks to reach in the tens of thousands during the coming year.

Friday of that first week was like a mass exodus from LA. It looked like anybody and everybody who could was packing up all their belongings and leaving the state.

## Situation status

The situation was initially chaotic:

- Large portions of major freeways were closed because of severe damage and several of the secondary roads were opening and closing because of the aftershocks
- Santa Monica freeway at the damaged point was levelled and cleaned up within the first 72 hours. A 64 car freight train derails, spilling toxic chemicals
- Four vehicles travelling along the 5 freeway were caught on an island with a 90 foot drop in front and a 60 foot drop behind
- Utilities were disrupted from day one. Gas and water lines ruptured. Water and gas were temporarily repaired within the first 48 hours but it was estimated to take six months to do the jobs permanently
- Power stations and lines were destroyed

## Summary

People whose homes were destroyed and who were sleeping in open areas were given food and water, and several shelters were open within the first 24 hours.

Insurance companies had plans in place whereby Claims Representatives were out and set up for claims aid and assistance within the first two hours after the quake. It was estimated that over 230 000 victims have filed insurance claims. It is hard to estimate the number of people who had losses and did not have insurance.

Within the first 72 hours loans and aid at 6.6 billion dollars was approved by the government and Federal Management Agency.

Several people needed psychological help following their traumatic experiences.

Only 57 deaths were attributed to the quake, while over 400 were injured. These are small numbers when you look at the devastation caused by the quake.

## Key issues learnt

You can learn a lot from experience! We found out:

- You can survive a large magnitude catastrophic event if you as individuals prepare
- Federal and local government must prepare as they did in California. Government must mobilize quickly and react quickly to the need of the victims. This saves lives and property and aids people in coping
- Business must plan and be prepared for catastrophic events
- Insurance must be on hand to settle claims quickly and equitably
- Government must spend more on per person protection

Our greatest enemy may not be Mother Nature, but rather human nature. Will we soon forget our present earthquake concerns? Or will we take the necessary action to properly plan and prepare? If you stay prepared and learn from these events you can and will survive any catastrophic event.

## 1G  AFTER THE FIRE—FIRST INTERSTATE BANK, LOS ANGELES

On the evening of 4 May 1988 the nightmare began for the tallest building west of the Mississippi river. The 62-storey First Interstate Bank building in Los Angeles, California, had caught fire.

At 10:37 p.m. the Los Angeles Fire Department's Operation Communication Dispatch Section (OCD) received three separate 911 calls from persons reporting a fire on the upper floors of the First Interstate building. At 10:38 the initial fire companies were dispatched. While en route the Battalion Chief observed and reported a large "loom-up" in the general area of the Bank building. On arrival at the scene he requested an additional 15 fire companies and five Chief Officers. The firemen fought the fire successfully and confined it to five floors of the 62-storey building. Even so, the fire had caused multi-millions of dollars damage, the water damage was extensive and the smoke contamination was almost total.

One only has to pause for a moment to realize the catastrophic results that a fire such as this would cause to one of the largest banking corporations in America. In just a matter of hours their corporate headquarters, and one of their main banks, is shut down, totally out of service. All employees, computers, and day-to-day operations conducted in this building are terminated for an undetermined period of time. How would your company handle such a situation?

In this case the costs were minimized because the First Interstate Bank Corporation had a plan. Within minutes after arriving on the scene, the bank management initiated their disaster plan. Their plan took into account catastrophic events such as earthquakes, fires and other types of disasters that could affect the bank's operations. The main objective was to get the bank back into service as soon as possible.

Blackmon-Mooring-Steamatic Catastrophic Incorporated (BMS-CAT, whose headquarters are located in Fort Worth, Texas) were contacted immediately and had supervisors on the scene by 07:00 that morning. BMS-CAT had one specific goal—to put the building in a pre-fire condition—and this would be tough. They had a 62-storey building with five storeys totally destroyed by fire and the entire building had major contamination from the products of combustion.

Cleaning up after a disaster is nothing new to BMS-CAT. The first major job for the Catastrophic Division of BMS was the clean-up of the Las Vegas Hilton after a fire in 1981. Since that time they have cleaned up after floods, fires, earthquakes, and other types of large disasters in the US and Canada.

Initially the parking garage of the bank building was used as a command post where a taskforce was set up with major logistical responsibilities. One of the many obstacles facing BMS-CAT was the restoration of an estimated 7000 electronic data processing equipments. This equipment ranged from small personal computers up to mainframe computers and printers. Priority one equipment was pre-identified in the bank's plans as for immediate restoration. Priority two was equipment that could be restored as they got to it.

A service centre was set up on the 27th floor. Over 200 technicians were hired to clean equipment. Each piece of electronic data processing equipment was taken completely apart and cleaned. After the equipment was reassembled it was given to a representative of the company that serviced that brand for inspection and recertification. There was a less than 5% failure rate for the reassembled equipment. Hundreds of thousands of floppy disks were salvaged by being vacuumed and wiped clean with special materials.

Another obstacle in the cleaning process was the monumental amount of paper materials that had to be sifted through and cleaned. Bank personnel felt sure that the documents in their major vaults would be safe from contamination, but upon opening the vault, they found out differently. It seemed that there was no place safe from the smoke contamination. Thousands and thousands of pieces of paper of all kinds had to be gone through. Each and every shelf, filing cabinet, vault and drawer throughout the building had every paper removed.

After all this was taken care of, the real clean-up effort started. During the reconstruction security consisted of a metal detector and off-duty Los Angeles police officers. All employees were screened daily as they went in and out of the building for the entire 12 weeks that clean-up crews were on site.

On 12 September 1988 the First Interstate Bank was reopened, more than four months after the fire. Due to appropriate planning on the part of the bank the disruption to their operation was kept to a minimum. Why? Because they had a plan.

## 1H   ONE MERIDIAN PLAZA, PHILADELPHIA

## Overview

A major high-rise office building fire occurred on Saturday 23 February 1991 in Philadelphia which resulted in fire extension to nine floors, severe structural damage to the 38-storey building, injuries to 24 and the death of three firefighters. During the 18½-hour effort to control the blaze, the firefighting activities were hampered by the loss of electrical power, including emergency power, and inadequate firehose pressure to suppress the fire. As a result the fire was able to spread from the 22nd floor to the 29th floor with practically no resistance.

The structure at One Meridian Plaza is a 38-storey modern office building rising 491 feet above the streets of downtown Philadelphia. Located directly across from City Hall, at one of the busiest intersections in the city, the building was constructed in 1972 at a cost of $40m.

Generally the floors were arranged with enclosed offices along three perimeter walls. Between these private offices and the building's core there was usually a large, open, unobstructed office work area, subdivided with 5-foot high dividers between workstations. The roof of the building is equipped with two helicopter landing pads that would become vital during the fire.

The building was equipped with a manual and an automatic fire alarm system. Smoke detectors, heat detectors and manual pull stations were installed on every floor. The activation of the alarm system provided an audible alarm signal throughout the building. An audible and visual alarm signal would also sound at both the Security Guard Station and the Annunciator Panel on the ground floor. An automatic transmission of the alarm would also be sent to a Central Monitoring Station in the city.

## The fire

This fire is a prime example of Murphy's Law and would have presented the ultimate challenge to the resources, training, experience and equipment of any major fire department. A total force of over 400 firefighters, 51 engine companies, 11 ladder companies, 21 chief officers, 9 medical units and 14 specialized apparatus were deployed on this incident.

The fire started in a perimeter office near a central window on the 22nd floor. It began by spontaneous combustion from rags that were contaminated by linseed oil, left by contractors who were restoring a large section of wooden panelling. Once ignited, the fire quickly spread into the open ceiling area and continued freely along the top of the unprotected open floor plan.

Very early on in the fire the door to the electrical room on the 22nd floor burned completely away. This immediately destroyed the ducts for both the primary and secondary electrical supply for the building. At 8:23 p.m. the fire alarm system in the building notified personnel of an apparent problem on the 22nd floor. Simultaneously, a telephone call was received from the central alarm monitoring company to inform One Meridian Plaza personnel of an alarm activation.

Neither the building personnel nor the monitoring company bothered to notify the Fire Department. Instead a building maintenance worker determined from the alarm annunciator panel the location of the alarm signal and went to investigate. When the elevator doors opened he was confronted with dense smoke and heat. The security guards were able to override the elevator controls and bring the maintenance worker safely down to the ground floor. Even at this time no one notified the Fire Department but instead, notified the central monitoring company, which finally notified the Fire Department after a considerable delay.

At 8:27 p.m. Dispatch ordered four engine companies, two ladder companies and two battalion chiefs to proceed to One Meridian Plaza. At 8:34 a second alarm was requested, based on initial determinations of the first responding officers. While firefighters were preparing their interior attack the fire had already spread to the 23rd floor.

As the firefighters approached the 22nd floor they were confronted with heavy smoke and heat conditions within the stairwell. Stairwell doors were glowing "cherry red" from the extreme heat. They reported difficulty in forcing the stairwell door open as it had expanded from the heat and was securely locked from the inside. A serious water problem was faced when the "wet" standpipe system did not deliver adequate water. Temperature levels on the fire floor of some 2000 degrees precluded any advancement without adequate water supply.

The early failure of the primary and secondary electrical systems and the total failure of the emergency generator to provide any back-up power were the most significant inhibiting factors faced by the firefighters. Without elevators, all equipment and manpower had to traverse vertically, at least 20 floors. All this in total darkness, depending entirely on limited portable lighting. As a result dozens of firefighters spent as much as eight hours in dark, smoke-filled stairwells, repeatedly shuttling hundreds of pounds of equipment up through the entire length of the darkened building.

As the fire spread both horizontally and vertically, by 2:30 a.m. a total of 12 alarms and numerous special assistance calls were ordered to assist with this incident. The delayed alarm, severe fire conditions, the failure of the electrical and emergency systems and the critical water pressure problems in the standpipe created what was the ultimate challenge of a high-rise fire into the ultimate nightmare of a Fire Department.

While these severe logistical problems were affecting the fire-suppression operations, an emergency arose. Two hours into the fire a Sector Commander ordered that the rooftop doors be opened to "ventilate the stairwells". An officer and two firefighters undertook the task to ventilate stairwell number two. For reasons unknown they never reached their objective. They became disorientated and requested permission to enter the office tower and break out a window for some clean air. The following communication from the team indicated that they were "inside the office tower on the 30th floor".

While the fire was burning out of control many firefighters risked their lives trying to locate their endangered comrades. Firefighters began a room-by-room search of the 30th floor but found no one. They then moved on to the 31st floor and continued upward to the 38th floor. Simultaneously at 10:53 p.m. the Pennstar helicopter was dispatched to pick up a rescue unit of three firefighters and lift them to the roof, to commence another search.

Finally, hours later, a circling helicopter spotted a broken window. The pilot indicated this was on the 28th floor. At 2:30 a.m. rescue teams located the fallen firefighters and removed them to the medical triage area on the 20th floor. The three missing firefighters had run out of air and suffocated.

Despite these severe and formidable conditions, firefighters continued their valiant attempt to contain the blaze. Finally at 1:30 a.m., 5 hours into the inferno, an employee of the contractor that had installed the standpipe system showed up and located the proper tool to adjust the pressure-reducing valves so that the Fire Department could start to produce an effective water supply to the firefighters. By this time the fire had engulfed the 23rd, 24th and 25th floors.

## The ultimate decision

As dawn broke, the fire was still angry and growing. Concern for the structural integrity of the building increased considerably. This was confirmed by an independent Structural

Engineer's examination of the damage inflicted on the building. After completing his assessment he informed the Incident Commanders that there was a very real potential for an internal collapse from the 28th to the 18th floors.

With 280 firefighters inside the building, 3 dead and 24 injured, at 7:30 a.m. Sunday morning, 11 hours into the incident, the Fire Commissioner ordered all personnel to abandon the building in an orderly evacuation. The fire would free burn for 7 hours up through floors 27, 28 and 29 to the 30th where sprinklers would be relied on to stop its spread.

At 3:00 p.m. Sunday afternoon, 18½-hours into the incident, the fire was declared "under control". Smoke was still rising from the building. No one was allowed to approach or enter it for several days.

Some 12 weeks after the fire, restoration work had still not started. Doubt remained on the integrity of the structure. Immediate and direct losses to the building and its contents were estimated at some $150m. Litigation was at a staggering $3.2bn and mounting.

## The conclusions

Investigations revealed that the fire originated on the 22nd floor in a private office. Once the fire had ignited it was able to involve other volatile materials contained within the room of origin and soon engulfed its combustible interior furnishings and finish materials.

Although the building was provided with an emergency electrical generator, designed to operate upon main power supply failure, a post-incident investigation determined that this generator did not produce any output voltage; therefore this was the reason for the complete failure of all elevators, lighting, fire alarm, smoke control systems and fire pumps. One of the toughest decisions a Fire Department Incident Commander has ever had to make is to order all firefighters to abandon all firefighting and immediately leave the building.

The sprinklers on the 30th floor activated because of heat being transferred to that floor from four principal sources:

- Fire lapped at the outside from the 29th floor and entered the floor through broken windows.
- Fire transmitted through spaces between the floor slab and the glass and granite outer curtain wall.
- Conduction and heat transfer through the 5-inch concrete floor plate.
- Fire and heat also impinged on to the floor through cracks in the floor caused by buckling.

Each of these heat-transfer methods resulted in the ignition of combustibles on the 30th floor. Several ignitions were discovered throughout the floor. All were extinguished by sprinklers.

## Significant factors

Some of the key factors influencing the spread of fire and the effect of firefighting efforts were:

1. Lack of automatic fire sprinklers on the 22nd floor.
2. Accelerated growth, development and spread of the fire from the room of origin.
3. The early loss of the main electrical power supply.
4. The complete failure of the emergency back-up power supply system.
5. Lack of early warning smoke or heat detection in the area of fire origin.
6. The effectiveness of Fire Department-supplied, automatic sprinklers to stop the vertical spread of the fire at the 30th floor.
7. Building personnel did not call the Fire Department when the Fire Alarm System first activated. They decided to investigate first.
8. The Central Control Monitoring Company did not call the Fire Department when they received an alarm signal from the building. They instead called the building personnel to verify the alarm.
9. No one from inside the building called the Fire Department. The eventual first call to the Fire Department was placed by someone outside the building.

## The lessons

The facts are outlined above—take a few minutes to study them carefully and identify lessons that can be applied in your organization.

## 1I   THE MERCANTILE FIRE

Churchill Plaza is a 14-storey modern office block in the centre of Basingstoke, Hampshire, UK, housing around 1000 staff with a medium size computer room and large PABX on the ground floor. The basement is used for car parking and a standby generator.

The fire started at 21:40 on Tuesday 16 April 1991 near the 8th floor wiring closet/office equipment area. The fire was detected by smoke sensors, alarms sounded and the Fire Brigade arrived at 21:46 with three pumps. The fire spread rapidly to the 9th floor and part of the 10th floor by failure of external glazing and strong winds. The number of fire appliances and men engaged increased in several stages, peaking at 30 pumps and 200 men. The fire was fully under control by 04:00 on Wednesday 17 April.

What would you do if you were watching the evening TV news and the reports stated that your office was on fire and it was your responsibility to do something about it?

## Major problems

We were faced simultaneously with a number of major problems:

1.  No power, heat or ventilation, hence no computers.
2.  Two floors with around 100 PCs were lost. The paper back-up documentation was also lost, which meant several departments had no information.
3.  A lot of equipment was damaged by water from the firefighting activities.
4.  PC and LAN server back-ups, kept in desks, were burnt, although a number were retrieved and found to be usable.
5.  Much of the cabling was damaged.

Initial assessment indicated that the bottom six floors could be made usable within two to three weeks; however, some key functions needed to be working within a few hours. Senior management fatigue began to set in. How could the 900 displaced staff be best employed?

## Actions

Here are a few questions to ask yourself as "contingency" man in the heat of the moment:

*   Have you confirmed event and scale?—don't overreact and try and get a second opinion
*   Who has been informed? Have the right people been notified?
*   The security guard may have told you, as the nearest convenient person, but has he logged the problem, reported it to management, or is he expecting you to do this?
*   What action has been taken so far? Who will take the decisions?
*   Have the fire, police, ambulance been advised?
*   Do we have a plan we can use? Who has a copy to hand? (It's no good in the vault!)
*   Have all staff been evacuated and sent home if necessary?—do not leave hundreds of people milling around, getting in the way.

Actions often have to be based on inadequate information. We had to decide who needs to be involved (as few as possible). The best way of turning a crisis into a disaster is to assemble the full executive team in the foyer for a committee decision! Among the first actions was to establish a chain of command and a Command Centre.

Selected senior management were able to inspect most of the building at 07:00 on Wednesday morning. The 8th and 9th floors were gutted and the 10th floor partially damaged. On the 7th floor there was serious smoke and water damage and the 6th floor downwards was heavily water damaged (the computer room false floor was floating!), hence there was no power, heat or light, and water was still running down walls. The main structure of the building appeared to have survived in good condition.

## Some advice

As we progressed, we found things out which we can share with you:

1. Having determined who takes what decisions, make sure there is a cross-checking process. Try and communicate simple messages.
2. Beware of Rambos making dynamic decisions, especially if this can risk life and limb. (Some managers feel they must be seen to be dynamic—try to harness this energy by getting them to organize a soup kitchen/mobile canteen!)
3. If you have a plan, great! If not, establish a modus operandi.
4. Ensure accurate feedback from Emergency Services re current status, keep up to date with their chain of command. They may also require information from you.
5. It is essential to appoint a good PR/Press Officer to respond to Press/TV coverage which is inevitably exaggerated and inaccurate. Harness the help of the local radio station to keep staff/local residents briefed on current status.
6. Call staff, using a cascade principle via normal chain of management. To achieve this will need up-to-date home telephone numbers, which must be readily accessible.
7. Establish a help desk, maybe two, one for customers and one for staff. If you don't the switchboard will be swamped!
8. Start to evaluate the likely impact on the business.
9. Do you need to activate third party contingency suppliers (e.g. salvage companies, mobile computer room suppliers)? It may be worth contacting them to put them on notice of potential need.
10. Set up project teams and get the key decision-makers to meet regularly.
11. Discourage other staff from turning up to help (everyone wants to join in the Boys' Own Adventure, especially the guy who forgot to back-up his PC yesterday!).

## Positive factors

It was not all gloom. There were some positive factors in our favour:

1. The main computer centre in North London was unaffected although switching of datacomms was problematic.

2. The branch network and Northern Processing Centre in Manchester was unaffected (all Churchill Plaza voice traffic was switched to Manchester from 08:00 on the Wednesday by BT and their call rate increased from 1000 per day to 3000 per day.
3. A local office two miles away with communication links was used as a command centre and enabled 40–50 key staff to be working by the Wednesday lunchtime.
4. We had plenty of spare office space and computer equipment was available locally in Basingstoke.
5. TV and radio coverage ensured there were plenty of offers of help; however, responding to these offers, sorting out the cowboys, does take a lot of management time.
6. As the fire occurred at night there were no staff injuries.
7. Parts of the ground floor were just about habitable and the PABX worked on standby power.

## Assistance from vendors

The timescales set were very ambitious, asking for items which normally take three months to arrive, to be delivered and installed within four to six days.

1. Acceptable, vacant, local office space (although in three locations) was found and signed up within 24 hours.
2. BT provided 50 mobile phones and several FAXs within hours. They located and installed a PABX extension in the main temporary building and delivered multiple kilostream links within five days.
3. Computer suppliers gave priority with orders for equipment which started arriving in hours rather than days.
4. Local companies installed voice/data mains cabling at breakneck speed (one building for 250 people was completed within 48 hours.

The loss adjustor insisted on a lengthy cleaning process for all the salvaged terminals and PCs. With excellent assistance from the suppliers/maintainers several cleaning "production lines" were set up at their locations. Despite this several hundred vital terminals and PCs were lost for between one to two weeks, whilst the dismantling, cleaning, reassembling and test procedures were followed through.

## Vendor relationships

We received an excellent response from the key vendors. Some of this may have been motivated by the sudden sales opportunity in the middle of a recession, but most did appear to be a genuine desire to help an "old friend". But it is useful to have the home telephone number of your Account Manager to be able to ring him at 2 a.m.!

You need to have a good level of trust to handle major purchases over the phone and agree free loan of equipment if you will be unable to pay for a few weeks. However, with the pressure of the urgent situation there is insufficient time to negotiate discounts. A number of suppliers' staff were extremely helpful over and above the call of duty. Letters of thanks were obviously forwarded to their senior management.

## What went well

The contingency plan was up to date and accessible (probably luck in that they were due to do one of their twice yearly tests the following weekend). Staff enthusiasm, and their willingness to work in difficult conditions, made a huge difference to recovery. We succeeded in reassuring staff that the building was now safe by sending a video to each staff member's home address.

Rapid PR response enabled damage limitation to public image, especially when the competition was mischief making!

## Lessons learnt

These are a few lessons we can pass on:

1. Don't keep PC back-ups in the desk drawers or filing cabinets.
2. Do have an up-to-date directory of home telephone numbers of key staff readily to hand.
3. Avoid day-to-day use of important documents, use photocopies instead.
4. Have easily accessible copies of up-to-date site plans, plans of cable runs, power distribution, etc.
5. A hot standby computer system is not a lot of use if the end users have no terminals or telephones (or desks to put them on!).
6. Don't underestimate the damage water can cause (much of the cabling started failing two to three weeks after it was back in use due to corrosion). It would have been best to replace it from day one.
7. You may need to appoint a Loss Assessor from day one to negotiate on an equal basis with the Loss Adjuster.
8. Maintain a clear desk policy—large amounts of paperwork left lying around can fuel a fire.
9. Beware of overenthusiasm—the same microfilm library duplication was ordered at least twice!
10. Develop a modular contingency plan so that the right components can be quickly assembled for a number of different scenarios as the response will vary depending on the type of incident.

## Summary

We hope you never suffer a similar experience. If you do, recovery will be greatly helped by a few basic principles:

- Do have a plan, if only a simple, general purpose one
- Do determine a simple chain of command
- Keep a copy of the plan and list of home phone numbers at home/in the car.
- When a fire/disaster happens you don't normally have time to plan, and if you don't determine who does what beforehand, abject chaos will occur very quickly!

# 1J   HOW FLOODS CAN RUIN YOUR DAY— LONDON COLLEGE OF PRINTING

The following study tells the story of a disaster and its consequences at the London College of Printing. In addition to the events themselves, several major issues are raised about the role of the manager whose organization is faced with a disaster and how this relates to the role of the disaster management organization.

The London Institute is the largest education organization of its type in Europe, embracing art, design, fashion, distribution and communication. The London Institute was formed in January 1986 when seven colleges, including the London College of Printing, were brought together to form a new major national centre of excellence with the unique feature of providing courses at all levels from apprentice to PhD. The Institute has a major task ahead in improving its range of services to students in the complex inner city environment but work has begun on consolidating and improving upon their building and hostels.

The background to the disaster that occurred at the London College of Printing has to be seen in the transfer of responsibility from the Inner London Education Authority (ILEA) to the London Institute and the College. In spite of the Authority's well-publicized limitations, much of what happened to the College from the early 1980s onwards was out of the Authority's hands. The Authority suffered a severe shortage of funds and this in particular had led to the neglect of the buildings and maintenance under its control, culminating in an enormous backlog of building and maintenance problems for the new college. Even where maintenance was carried out priority was given to schools. Examples of neglect included no window cleaning taking place for five years, long intervals between checks on such things as water, and the building had not been painted for 10 years.

The London Institute began its responsibility for the buildings by taking it on centrally. The management of the College in an education sense was the responsibility of the Head of College but all building matters were handled by the Institute, who in turn handed regular maintenance to a contract company. They also instituted a series of health and safety checks including checking the water system. As a result of such a check in September 1989 the following events unfolded . . .

The London College of Printing had to close down after Legionella bacteria was found in the water system in October 1989. The closure lasted a week, but major flooding followed on the refilling of the water tanks located on the top of the 14-storey building. There were two header tanks and the water supply was not stopped until both were full (determined by a ball valve cutting off the water supply). A faulty ball valve led to both tanks continuing to fill . . . and overflow. The top seven floors were badly damaged. These floors housed courses with very expensive equipment, including film, photography, radio and print journalism. The problem was compounded by the presence of asbestos ceiling tiles which seriously contaminated the top five floors. These had to be removed by specialists and the floors extensively refurbished.

The best advice that can be given to managers faced with disasters is very clear—"don't have them". Unfortunately this is not always possible and it becomes a matter of damage minimization and ensuring the efficient operation of the organization in the meantime. In calling in a Disaster Management Company half of this problem disappeared, leaving the College free to concentrate on reorganizing their internal activities, confident that the other matters were in safe hands.

The initial impact of disasters inevitably provokes the best sort of "blitz" response from all concerned. When things have settled and the extent of damage and disruption becomes clear, management must be alert to morale problems that may surface amongst staff and make sure the response is clear, effective and communicated within their organization.

It is essential that management deals quickly and effectively with questions from, and decisions relating to, those dealing with the crisis, from the Disaster Management Company through to builders, equipment specialists and insurance loss adjustors. The early identification of an individual within the organization able to deal with those companies, and make decisions on major issues, is a further essential step in ensuring disruption is minimized.

# 1K   FLOOD HIGHLIGHTS

In Scandinavia, after a prolonged drought, they had 50 cm of rain in two hours. A hillside stream flooded and 200 cubic metres of water entered a company building, lifting a 20-cm-thick concrete floor 50 cm. The torrent broke down two steel doors and wrecked the communications and tape storage areas. In the computer room, a moisture detector went and a steel door caved in, pushing modem racks across the room towards the operators. Power and UPS were lost. There was 1 cm of mud on the floor. The whole incident took under 15 minutes. A damage management company was called and arrived in half an hour.

The Road Research Laboratory had a retaining wall which had been built to keep rainwater from the computer room. The next time it rained hard a pool of water formed by the retaining wall, which collapsed. The water surged towards the computer room. Unfortunately a delivery was expected and the doors were open! The room was flooded!

In Chicago a datacentre had been located on the 15th floor to avoid flooding from the adjacent Hudson River. Freak weather conditions caused water from the Hudson to be siphoned up through the toilets, flooding the building (including the datacentre) from the top floor downwards.

In the public sector, a sewage pipe ran through the roof void above the false ceiling of the computer room housing a PABX. It blocked! Dynarod was called in to clear it on a Friday and did so, but the pressure had caused an unnoticed fracture to the pipe. Over the weekend sewage seeped into the roof void. Eventually the ceiling collapsed and the sewage fell . . . into the PABX fan!

In Chicago the Household Finance Corporation had fish swimming in the datacentre when 9 inches of rain fell in eight hours, causing water tables to rise and drains to blow back.

A UK insurance company was holding a party to celebrate the opening of their new disaster recovery standby facility. At the same time flash floods took their main datacentre off the air! They fortunately resolved the problem without having to invoke their brand new disaster recovery centre!

In a public utility company, following rain after a dry spell the ceiling of the computer room was found leaking in several places, leaks also went into the engineer's and the plant rooms. Equipment was covered in polythene sheets. A temporary tent roof was built over the existing flat roof of the one-storey block while a new roof was built. It took three months to complete the work. There were no contingency plans and during the three months the computer system had to be powered down each time it rained!

At the *East Anglian Daily Times* in Ipswich a heating engineer was working in the roof on a Sunday afternoon when he damaged a sprinkler pipe which dumped 30 000 gallons of water in 20 minutes, flooding the editorial suite and ruining £250 000 of production systems.

# 1L   A CAUTIONARY TALE

On two separate occasions within two rather grey December weeks in 1991 the Union Bank of Finland (UBF) computer facilities were put out of action.

In their City office they employ some 90 people in the provision of wholesale banking activities, involving Corporate Banking, Trade Finance, Shipping, Property and Syndication and Project Finance, some retail and electronic banking activities, and the full range of Treasury products, as well as Finnish Capital market operations. So, like any other risk management business, they are dependent upon a reliable means of controlling, recording, processing, reporting and monitoring substantial volumes of data, as well as being able to access their database at any moment.

Central to their ability to do this successfully is their AS/400 computer. They had always had back-up procedures of some sort, but on reappraising their recovery plan in late 1991 came to the conclusion that they needed to do things much better, in order to have an acceptable degree of certainty of being able to recover their computing facilities and database within 24 hours and return to normal operations within 36 hours.

In the autumn of 1991 they developed a full-scale disaster recovery programme. As it was to turn out, their timing was immaculate! On Monday 9 December 1991 at 11:23 a.m. the AS/400 system, together with all the peripheral equipment in the computer suite, unexplainedly lost power, and simply closed down. It didn't take long to discover what the problem was: the Water Board had been carrying out maintenance work on the mains in the road outside the building and had accidentally fractured a mains pipe. The escaping water finally worked its way through the foundations of the building, and leaked into the basement directly on top of the uninterruptable power supply (UPS) unit, ruining it in the process.

The Recovery Centre was placed on standby, and the morning save of the data library, together with the most recent systems saves, were retrieved from the off-site security storage centre. At 2:15 p.m. the Fire Brigade began to pump out the basement, and make the area safe. This process was to take two hours, after which UBF were hoping to receive a visit from their UPS maintenance people to inspect the damage.

At 5:10 p.m. the UPS maintenance representative finally confirmed that they would not be able to inspect the equipment and give appropriate advice until the following morning. Since they could see for themselves that the UPS was in any case useless, it was decision time! UBF decided to invoke their recovery plan.

At 5:35 p.m. the operations team left for the recovery site taking with them all the necessary tapes and equipment, and began loading the system. Remote links were established between the bank and recovery site. By 4:00 a.m. on Tuesday morning the system was completely restored. So within 18 hours they were up and running again. Immediately thereafter they began to input Monday's and Tuesday's daily work and this continued throughout the day. All relevant documentation and reports were transferred by taxi between the bank and the recovery site, but then it was realized that courier bikes moved much more rapidly through the traffic; after that they found that one of their messengers travelling on the tube train was even quicker, confirming yet again the old adage that money is not the answer to everything!

Some 25 hours after invoking the disaster recovery plan they were almost back to normal. This continued for the rest of the week, while repairs were being undertaken at the bank. During the following weekend a transformer was installed to smooth the power supply at the bank. By the Monday the system was live again at the bank, the links to the recovery site were cut and disaster recovery status removed.

On the Tuesday the MIS Supervisor left for the recovery site to remove the system from their machines and disconnect. At 10:15 that morning one of the disk drives on the AS/400 at the Bank froze, stopping all input! As a precaution the Supervisor at the recovery site was told not to clear down the system, but to restore the morning save of the data library.

The stoppage had nothing to do with any of the previous difficulties. It turned out to be the result of a broken solenoid, which is just about as unlikely an event as the flood which caught them out in the first place. Later that afternoon the drive was fixed, with no loss of data and all users began to input the current day's work. However, as we all know too well, reassurance, if not actual complacency, is often the mother of big trouble, and only minutes later, disaster struck again!

An unexplained drop in power was followed immediately by a huge electricity surge. It subsequently turned out that despite their best efforts to rectify the previous damage, a loose neutral wire in the fusebox had not been repaired. The effect was to completely destroy the power supplies to all racks, two disk drives and the processor. The popping and crackling noises lasted for a full 10 seconds and they knew they were witnessing the complete destruction of their primary facilities. This hardly seemed a fair reward for all their efforts, and confirmed that lightning does strike twice!

On the Wednesday, with a somewhat weary sense of *deja vu* they again invoked their disaster recovery process. By first thing that morning the system was ready for input, and all remote links re-established to the recovery site. Everybody by now was getting pretty tired and fed up, but they were enormously encouraged by the fact that they were able to provide to the bank a virtually uninterrupted service, to the extent that a lot of people didn't even realize that there had been a second disaster.

On the following Friday the new UPS was delivered and installed, and the system restored at the bank over the weekend. By the Monday morning they were completely restored and up to date again, and finally stood down from the recovery situation, this time without any further mishaps.

You may consider that one disaster is a misfortune, but two in succession is beginning to sound like carelessness! In the comprehensive post-mortem that was carried out to assess how things had gone, one or two conclusions were reached:

1. The time and money spent in devising a well-thought-out plan had justified itself many times over. The recovery process had gone very well, since in spite of the complete collapse of the computer facilities, they had remained in business throughout, and continued to be able to manage the financial risks involved.
2. Although they had not intended that the first disaster should be a practice for the second, the greater speed and efficiency of the recovery on the second occasion demonstrated only too clearly the absolute importance of rehearsal, for the purpose of confirming the logistics of the exercise, and preparing the people involved.
3. Since prevention is better than cure, they reappraised the complete system, looking for the situations that were asking for trouble, such as placing the UPS in a basement liable to flooding. (It's now in the computer room, three floors up!)
4. After any sort of crisis involving electrical power failure they will not again assume that all they need to do is to replace the defective part, and simply plug in and switch on. Every part of the system will be checked first.
5. Where keeping your business operations running is concerned, it's a myth to suggest that lightning doesn't strike twice! It can—and it does (sometimes known as Murphy's Law).

# 1M   IT HAPPENED TO THEM

**How a company with a very small plan survived a major disaster and now has very big plans for the future.**

In the early hours of Thursday, 4 November 1993, thieves broke into the premises of a printing company in Bermondsey, London, and after taking items of office equipment, started a fire on the second floor, "probably to cover their tracks", according to local police, who told reporters: "The firm is virtually wiped out". The fact that the culprits have since been caught and are serving sentences for arson, offers little consolation.

The premises of a working printer will usually contain highly flammable components alongside the expensive and bulky plant and machinery. Although firefighters battled through the night, by 7 a.m. the following morning there was nothing left but an empty shell. Added to the loss of the 150-year-old building was the hefty archive of essential information and reference material that any business accumulates over 30 years, here combined with all the records, client specifications and plant recently bought.

Disaster recovery and business continuity had not been part of the company's day-to-day vocabulary. They had enough problems keeping the business going without worrying about things that might never happen. In short they had no plans to cope with the situation facing them on the morning of Guy Fawkes' day. Nevertheless, by 8 a.m. a temporary office had been set up on the street corner. Production staff were making lists of everything they could remember—clients, work-in-hand, orders, delivery schedules. Sales staff used mobile phones to ring customers to warn them there had been some slight "technical problems". Competitors were contacted to arrange transfer of production to fulfil existing commitments.

By 11 a.m. operations were being directed from an old coach, parked at the side of the road, with a power line running from a nearby sweetshop and, by the following Monday, a temporary office had been established two streets away, with organization of subcontracted production well under way.

In early January the printers were able to commence their own production once more; installation in their own premises was finally completed in May and on 29 June the local MP, Simon Hughes, pressed the button on a new printing press at an Open Day which heralded the return to full commercial operation and a future that had looked impossible on that dark November morning.

"It's true we had no formal disaster recovery plan", said one of the co-directors, "beyond the usual precautions taken by any small business operating reactively. What saved us was the fact that individuals had contingency plans of their own, safeguarding their particular areas of operation. Without them we would certainly have gone under." The Accounts Manager, for example, routinely took home a set of back-up tapes for the accounts package and, by chance, had also taken home the books to prepare wages—due to be paid on the day of the fire.

"We thought we had done enough but our contingencies were woefully inadequate." The fire and burglary alarm systems were in reasonable condition but proved to have a faulty connection to the BT system. This meant that, although the alarm went off, it did not show up at the local police station—a failure which might have been crucial.

Apart from the invaluable safeguards put in place by individuals, the recovery was achieved through the resilience, ingenuity and unflinching support of many of the staff. Employees "mucked in" magnificently. People more used to planning and running departments offered to do all sorts of jobs from shovelling rubbish, to logging refuse and even plastering. One or two wilted under the pressure, and eventually went their separate ways, while others seemed to thrive under the same pressure, determined not to be beaten.

Likewise there were employees who could be relied upon to work uncomplainingly in appalling conditions, while others behaved like spoilt children whining about things that could not be helped.

Initially there was confusion. Staff were used to operating almost robotically, taking few real decisions. Suddenly there was a whole range of new decisions to be taken and there was a period of great frustration with little information available. After the first rush of adrenaline, came a phase of very low morale as staff became aware of the very real difficulties the company was facing. It was mid-winter, managers were clearly preoccupied and employees had no way of knowing what the future might hold.

A sense of direction was restored by an unprecedented meeting of senior staff at which responsibility for the various aspects of redevelopment was allocated, action defined and a programme planned for short, medium and long term. Being forced to rebuild the company, from the ground up, had created opportunities for fresh concepts and methods which might otherwise never have seen the light of day.

New attitudes to marketing ensured that the company now actively seek to promote their services with a computerized database of contacts, direct mailing of a colourful newsletter and regular lobbying of the press. Publicity had not previously been a priority and inviting clients to view the presses in action would have been inconceivable in the old environment. Formalising an existing commitment to adopt a proactive environmental stance is already proving popular, with the company guaranteeing environmentally friendly materials and practices, wherever possible, and a planned environmental audit to reduce waste and improve disposal methods.

Looking back, the company realized that some of the old ingrained habits made the difference between survival and extinction: the attention to detail in negotiating contracts, the most fanatical cost control and the instinct not to spend money on inessentials. There were also decisive moments where a different decision would have wrecked any hopes of continuing. Obviously the insurance company eventually agreeing the claim was a significant milestone, although the waiting was a particularly anxious time.

Deciding on alternative premises, which took six weeks, was the most vital step. Already in train, due to merger negotiations, the move had been in danger of getting bogged down with various options and conflicting dogmatic positions. The urgency created by their situation "concentrated people's minds" and a site was chosen on the basis that, while not ideal, it offered the fastest means to get up and running. In fact they moved in before the previous tenants had moved out.

In the wake of the disaster the very best of the old and the new have been forced to find a harmonious path through the flames and have emerged victorious. They have learned much from the experience, not least the realization that their survival was due to the foresight of those individuals who made their own contingency plans, but it has been a tough education. What they need now is the support of existing and potential customers to ensure their efforts have not been in vain.

# 1N  FIRE HIGHLIGHTS

A 32-year-old man was arrested after he walked into a bank in Hong Kong carrying two canisters of inflammable liquid which he ignited and threw into the bank. The fireball filled the room with black smoke. Six people, including the bank manager, died and many more were injured after being trapped behind bulletproof security doors, unable to escape the flames. A customer using the outside cash machine called the emergency services. The 30-year-old building did not have a fire exit, no sprinkler system or fire-resistant furniture, although it complied with government standards.

An IBM employee was charged with setting fire to his office in San Jose and the home of his supervisor, in March 1993. Witnesses claim he drove his car through the IBM office foyer and then set it alight with camping stove fuel. He had apparently been aggrieved since 1987 when he persistently phoned and wrote to colleagues about the state of work at IBM. He was put on disability leave. He blamed IBM for the break-up of his marriage and accused his supervisor of forcing him to go on disability leave.

A security guard for a large electronics company started two fires to teach another security guard a lesson because he had been abused by him. The first fire was dealt with, but the second, started in a waste bin on another floor, caused fire up to the 15th floor. The ground floor computer centre was untouched, but a message switching centre was destroyed and there was £35 000 worth of damage to terminal equipment. Fire hoses flooded the 8th floor, ruining audit files and security tapes. The culprit was sentenced to four years in jail. He had claimed to be a hero and was expecting the Order of the British Empire for discovering the fire.

At the University of Cambridge, on a Friday evening, a fire started in the Department of Zoology (adjacent to the computer laboratory). To access the fire, the Fire Service had to open fire doors to the lower of two computer rooms, causing entry of smoke, debris and water. Smoke went up a disused lift shaft into the upper computer room and triggered the Halon system. The lower room contained multi-supplier minicomputers and desktop PCs. None avoided damage; the cleaning and replacement took six months.

A £25m new datacentre for a bank at Bracknell was equipped with UPS. It suffered a power cut. The UPS and back-up diesel generator cut in but at 06:00 the duty shift leader smelt burning. The exhaust pipe of the generator was venting near timber, causing the wood to smoulder. Moreover, there was a leak in the diesel fuel pipe leading to the generator. The system was powered down. Mains power was subsequently restored but, as the systems were being rebuilt, the electricity board brought the power down again for 30 minutes: the UPS had not recharged and the system rebuild was lost.

A major supplier of network products set out to develop new security services and took the decision to be underinsured, bearing half the risk themselves. After several months research and development in partnership with another organization who provided market intelligence and a potential customer base, they were poised to launch the new service. A fire destroyed most of their equipment and all of their records. Shortly after, key staff were plundered by a rival; it is rumoured that the rival would market a similar offering within a couple of months.

DEC Customer Services HQ in Basingstoke had a fire which started on the roof, destroying the building which housed 400 staff. Computers were protected by plastic covers after being saved by the Halon. The fire gutted the building in six minutes. Overnight back-ups had protected most orders except any hard copy currently being processed, and that day's orders. Two weeks later, according to press reports, customers were blaming late delivery of spares on the incident. The cost of damage to the building was over £20m and the cost to the business was estimated at between £10m and £38m.

At the Bank of England the rule was to store floppy disks in a metal fire safe. However, some staff persisted in storing their floppies in wooden desk drawers. A fire occurred; the fire safe was not up to standard; the metal safe overheated, ruining the floppies stored in it. Although the wooden desks were charred, the disks stored in them survived, and were readable!

In 1990 a fire at the main Scarborough telephone exchange burned through megastream and kilostream data cables and 23 000 business and residential lines. The cause was believed to be an electrical fault in the computer equipment. It impacted building society and bank ATMs; links between North Sea oil rigs; Scarborough Borough Council; Marks & Spencer.

# 1O  WESSEX REGIONAL HEALTH AUTHORITY

## Picking up the pieces

Few IT professionals have experience of dealing with the press. Yet disasters frequently provoke great public and media interest. Managing press relations should form part of any disaster training. When Wessex Regional Health Authority was forced to write off a £40m systems project it took some explaining.

It started in April 1991 with a phone call from *Computer Weekly.* "Was there any truth in a rumour they had heard concerning two senior staff at Wessex Regional Health Authority (RHA)?" The rumour was true—they had been suspended for gross misconduct and the Fraud Squad were called in to investigate suspected contract fraud on a fairly major scale. Both members of staff were later sacked.

Despite being well briefed, it was one of those inquiries which sets alarm bells ringing somewhere in the darkest recesses of the mind. On the face of it, it was the kind of inquiry which prompts an intensive but short-lived spell of media attention. The issue was relatively straightforward, they had answers to all the likely questions and were prepared to be open and honest about it all.

The difficulty was that the inquiry actually went straight to the heart of a much bigger issue which most people at the RHA thought was dead and buried. The issue was the RHA's abandoned Regional Information Systems Plan (RISP) which had been scrapped in April 1990 and its mismanagement heavily criticized in a National Audit Office report in November 1990. Both milestones had been marked by minor blazes of media attention—after all, they had been dealing with severe criticism of RISP virtually since its inception in 1984, interspersed with occasional media interest surges: such as the story about the mainframe computer that stayed unused in its packaging in a Slough warehouse for 18 months.

The staff suspensions and Fraud Squad involvement came about as a result of an intensive internal investigation into RISP. For the first time ever, the RHA was determined to find out how much had been spent, by whom and on what. They wanted to know what went wrong, who was responsible and to make as much information public as possible.

The scenario was one of serious mismanagement and mishandling of public funds, possible serious fraud, possible exploitation of the RHA by sharp contractors, poor project management and an almost total lack of financial, budgetary and audit controls. There were also some remarkable conflicts of interests. For six weeks a former employee fulfilled the roles of both contractor and client. He was effectively writing the specifications, selecting the company (i.e. his own) to do the work, fixing the price and signing the cheques.

Not surprisingly, journalists with a particular interest in RISP began to put the pieces of the jigsaw together for themselves. In fact, some of them seemed able to eke out details and information very quickly after the RHA had been able to get to the truth themselves! The picture was further complicated by legal battles with various IT suppliers over aspects closely associated with RISP.

They adopted an open stance from the beginning which reflected credit on the organization in the long run but which created painful, time-consuming headaches as more and more details entered the public domain. The District Audit service was brought in to produce a comprehensive, definitive account of the RISP affair. When that report became available to the RHA in July 1993 the true extent of the calamity became clear. The bottom line was that of the £43.6m spent on RISP between 1984 and 1990, about half of it had been effectively wasted. It was time to go public in a very proactive way.

On the basis that it is impossible to keep a £20m public money scandal under wraps, together with a genuine commitment from the authority to openness and accountability, a major news conference seemed the best way to handle the release of information and, to a degree, the way it would be reported. A few frantic weeks of preparation followed before the Regional General Manager was thrown to the mercy of half the nation's press corps. That press conference was an extraordinary event. Many of the assembled media were staggered by the way in which the Authority was prepared to meet the issue head on, to expose and condemn the waste and mismanagement which characterized RISP and to make no excuses. In short they were handed one of the best public cash squandered stories in recent years on a plate—and they were grateful, albeit initially taken aback.

Once the screaming headlines and condemnations which greeted the revelations were past, more considered, analytical pieces began to appear which recognized and highlighted the three issues the RHA hoped the journalists would bear in mind in return for the RHA baring its soul.

Factors which did not receive as much publicity were:

- All those with principal responsibility for RISP were no longer employed by the RHA
- The District Auditor praised the RHA for the remedial action taken since 1990 to ensure that such an inexcusable scenario should never happen again
- It had been the Authority's new administration which had got to the bottom of RISP and made the painful details spectacularly public

There then followed endless hours of explaining the whole story to journalists with no prior knowledge of RISP—an average of 30 minutes per telephone enquiry. Then came follow-up stories, developments in the legal aspects of the saga, sackfuls of critical, probing letters to answer and answers and ministerial briefings to be provided for questions in both Houses of Parliament.

There are a number of lessons that can be passed on in handling the public relations aspects of such an incident:

- It pays to take the initiative
- Openness and honesty are usually the best policies
- There is no substitute for planning and preparation
- Be prepared to believe the unbelievable
- Listen and think carefully before formulating an action plan and/or giving advice
- Remember you are part of a team—others will need to know what you know and vice versa
- There is no substitute for good information, straight from the horse's mouth
- Grow a thick skin and don't take it personally

One other lesson was the importance of being able to relax and switch off. Luckily RISPs don't come along very often, but when they do they can become all-consuming and encroach into one's personal as well as professional life.

Support was forthcoming from the Chairman and RGM, and colleagues and others who became involved in sorting out the nasty mess RISP had left on the corporate carpet. Without that support you would probably crumple under the strain and/or go stark staring mad!

## 1P   THE BISHOPSGATE BOMB—25 APRIL 1993

## Explosions—do they really happen?

Between 1993 and 1995 there were major terrorist explosions in New York, Tokyo, Frankfurt, Bombay, Florence, Madrid, Milan, Rome, Cairo, Paris, London, Oklahoma. Between 1973 and 1993 there were 461 bombings in London alone. Accidental explosion can be as serious: a blast at Sumitomo Chemical, Japan, in April 1993 destroyed 60% of the world's manufacturing capacity for epoxy resin, used to package memory chips and other semiconductor devices, which led to a doubling of the price of computer chips and allegedly delayed computer manufacturers in releasing new models.

## The impact of the Bishopsgate bomb

The home-made fertilizer bomb, exploding at 10:30 p.m., killed one person and forced 91 companies to relocate. In addition:

- 2 buildings were destroyed
- 25 buildings were heavily damaged
- 3 buildings suffered moderate damage
- 100 buildings suffered broken glass—£2m of glass in one building alone
- The estimated damage was £400m (insured loss) and 40 companies were affected

The explosion made many companies face up to reality: lightning can strike twice. Several companies had suffered from the IRA bombings at both St Mary Axe and Bishopsgate in spite of security measures which included additional security guards, increased vigilance and CCTV.

## Some cases from Bishopsgate

SIGITO, a public sector service organization, had held a party during the evening to celebrate moving into their new premises. Catering staff were still on-site when the windows blew out. The heating system flooded computer equipment and important paper records. Papers in steel cabinets survived reasonably well, but water, first from the heating system and later from rain, damaged other documents. Access was denied to the building for three days. It took two days to acquire portable telephones, during which time business was conducted from telephone boxes. A serviced office nearby was rented—initially a short-term measure, but one which lasted in practice for almost a year until the damaged site could be reoccupied; meanwhile, service charges were being levied on a property that was uninhabitable! There were access problems with the temporary offices, cranes were needed to get computer equipment into the building.

Guardian Royal Exchange had four City offices impacted by the explosion: all four nodes on their network were out of action. Fortuitously at that time they were running trials with a software tool that checks network survivability—and so got a flying start in establishing the best way to restore communications!

Commercial Union subsidiary Quilter Goodison was hit by the blast: they decided to continue running the business and clear up later. By 08:00 hours on the Monday morning, fund managers were up and running in another building.

Rea Brothers Group, a City bank, showed £175 000 in their annual accounts for uninsured losses attributable to the bomb. Sir John Hill, Chairman, said: "Although the Bishopsgate Bomb incident in April necessitated our departure from Alderman's House for some months, there was no dislocation of service to clients."

The Hong Kong and Shanghai Bank was severely damaged and they transferred operations to the Sheffield data centre of the Midland bank.

Windows were blown out of the NatWest Tower . . . the day before, the glazier had completed reglazing following the damage from the St Mary Axe explosion and had expressed concern about future business! 200 PCs had to be salvaged.

Other companies seriously impacted included Mocatta, Long Term Credit Bank of Japan, Daewoo Securities, Tokai Bank, Mitsubishi Corporate Finance, Oracle. Many dealers were accommodated on an *ad hoc* basis by other dealers.

## Lessons

The explosion and aftermath showed the need for:

- A broader planning perspective—to cover business, not just IT
- Standby facilities for work areas, dealing rooms, offices, PCs/LANs
- Improved safety measures
- Geographic separation from recovery sites—the police cordon exclusion zone denied access to those who were not affected by the blast
- Bomb-shielded glass; window blinds; entrance canopies to protect people and equipment from flying glass
- Security—9 security guards were charged with theft and cowboy glaziers were breaking windows
- Limiting personal effects left in offices
- A clear-desk policy
- Evacuating the recovery team separately to minimize confusion and speed recovery
- Out-of-hours numbers for contractors
- Staff information—free-phone lines
- Keyholders—information about who they are and contacts (in rented multioccupancy accommodation keyholder bottlenecks can be a real hindrance to gaining access)
- "Disaster packs" to include hard hats
- Patrolling control points for fast access
- Food and drink for the workers!

Planners recovered twice as quickly as those without plans.

## Food for thought

The disaster also provoked thought about things we may take for granted:

- Are suppliers really available 24 hours a day?
- Beware heroes—especially Board Room heroes! They often confuse motion with progress and frequently wreck the best plans.

## 1Q CITY BOMB BLAST: ST MARY AXE— 10 APRIL 1992

## Background

An IRA bomb exploded in St Mary Axe, a sidestreet adjacent to Liverpool Street Station. Three people died; two buildings were destroyed; 40 companies were forced to relocate; damage was out at £1.4bn.

The Baltic Exchange was virtually demolished and the Commercial Union Building took the full brunt of the explosion. All 650 Commercial Union employees had to be relocated. The 5-storey Chamber of Shipping was reduced to rubble. James Capel's computer room ceiling was severely damaged and staff wearing hard hats were bringing the systems back up. By 09:00 hours the following Monday about 30 affected firms had been relocated and were open for business. The account that follows is the personal story of one of them.

## Mocatta's experience

In the 321-year history of gold and silver bullion dealer Mocatta London, the company has seen many disasters hit the capital, but seldom can a disaster have affected it so closely as the massive bomb explosion which caused so much damage in the City during the weekend just before Easter 1992.

Apart from a few shattered windows, the bomb blast caused little damage to the company's substantial nineteenth-century listed building in Crosby Square (only 100 yards or so from the explosion) but police security measures restricted access to the area and threatened the operation of the computer system that is so vital to the success of Mocatta's dealer activities.

Fortunately, Mocatta had for the past eight years been a contracted client with a Disaster Recovery Hotsite Service provider and by the Monday a back-up system was fully operational at their recovery centre in Hertfordshire. It transpired that Mocatta was able to operate the computer system after all, but the recovery centre continued to run the back-up system for a week as a contingency measure.

Manager of the management Information System and Telecommunications at Mocatta was Michael Moore. It was he, a year after joining Mocatta in 1983, who decided that any unforeseen incident could have a catastrophic affect on the running of a precious metals trading company. After looking carefully at the disaster recovery field he signed the contract mentioned above in 1985. Subsequently all the New York processing was transferred to Mocatta House in 1990. It was these systems that Michael was concerned about when he was telephoned at home on the Friday evening of the bomb blast by one of his operators. Later that night he established that the building had not suffered extreme damage and that the computer system was capable of running on generator power.

Very early on the Saturday morning he stepped outside Liverpool Street Station—and was faced with a scene of devastation. There were security cordons around the area, but he managed to convince the police of his need to reach Crosby Square and check on the safety of his computer system. He found Mocatta House standing remarkably unscathed in the midst of the incredible devastation, with the neighbouring insurance company high-rise block across the square reduced to a concrete skeleton. Inside the building, a few window frames had been blown in by the blast and one or two pieces of equipment up-ended. The only human casualty was one of the trading staff who had been knocked bodily out of his chair—but otherwise unhurt—by the shock of the explosion.

A tour of his department showed that the computer system had not been damaged and was capable of normal operation. He was, however, aware that security restrictions imposed on that part of the City, coupled with the continuing danger of falling debris, was likely to prevent the company staff being allowed access on the Monday morning. At this point he decided to give formal warning to the recovery centre that it might be necessary to invoke the disaster recovery contract and he made the necessary telephone calls to key personnel.

Michael stayed in London throughout the weekend and—although other tapes were stored off-site—collected all the current output tapes and documentation for despatch to the recovery centre, confident of the outcome, as he had taken part in a successful disaster recovery test at the site only two weeks beforehand.

The prospects of the Mocatta staff being allowed access to their building after the weekend continued to be uncertain, so early on the Monday morning the Mocatta London management decided on invocation. A member of the Mocatta operations staff travelled to the recovery centre and the backup tapes were delivered. By 10 a.m. the base system had been recovered and by midday the system was fully restored and ready for operation.

Normal computing activities were however resumed at Mocatta House on Tuesday morning. As it turned out the bomb blast, though tragic for some, did not bring total disaster to Mocatta, but it might have done, if they had not been prepared.

## 1R    EXPLOSION ROUNDUP

A one-ton IRA bomb was discovered at Canary Wharf in 1992. Two suspects were challenged by security guards. They drove off in a van, leaving a lorry abandoned with the fertilizer bomb. The other van, later found abandoned, also contained explosives. Access was denied to offices in the area, including the *Daily Telegraph*, which subsequently issued the paper with a blank front page, being unable to complete it in time. The detonator was subsequently found to have been triggered but a wiring fault prevented it from causing the bomb to explode.

In March 1993 ten car bombs exploded in the financial district of Bombay: 255 people were killed, 1100 were injured. The first explosion, in an underground car park beneath the 28-storey Bombay Stock Exchange, killed several dozen people; two traders were blown through windows and fell to their deaths; others died in the stampede to leave the building.

In 1992 two 2-pound bombs exploded in Manchester City Centre. One was in a car parked outside the Inland Revenue and Department of Employment offices and went off at 08:45 (six minutes after a warning was phoned to the Samaritans) and the second at 10:10 at the corner of Cateaton Street near the Arndale Shopping Centre. Some 56 people were injured, one seriously when a two-foot shard of glass went into his back.

In 1994, 600 staff were evacuated from the Croydon HQ of Direct Line after a letter bomb in a jiffy bag, addressed to the Chief Executive, exploded at 11:00. His secretary was treated by ambulance crew at the scene for minor burns and shock. The Chief Executive was away on business at the time. Customer calls were transferred to regional offices as soon as the emergency alarms went off. Business was not "dented".

A 28-pound test bomb was aimed at a target being towed by HMS *Ark Royal*, but hit the aircraft carrier, penetrating the mess deck. Five sailors suffered flash burns, one lost fingers and suffered severe abdominal injuries. The pilot of the plane should aim at the carrier, and a computer program steers the bomb 7 degrees off to hit the target which was 600 yards astern. The software was blamed. The aircraft radar locks on to the ship but the onboard computer automatically aims 600 yards astern. The highly experienced RAF Flight Lieutenant lost radar contact twice with the ship and finally locked on only seconds before firing the bomb, but he was unaware that the computer software was unable to cut in the automatic aim-off so quickly. He will receive a formal warning. The training system has since been suspended.

In another incident London clay shifted under the road, fracturing a cable under the victim's office. Heat build-up caused the pavement to explode, sending molten pitch 15 feet into the air, where it was taken in through the air conditioning intake. The mainframe computer room was filled with smoke so thick it was not possible to see if operators were present. All the equipment had to be checked and cleaned before computing services could be resumed.

Two Kurds walked into the 7th floor branch of the Turkish Bank, and poured a gallon of petrol on the floor on the customer side of the bank: it was set alight, with a customer getting burnt. The customer fled and was arrested by police as a suspect and interrogated for an hour before they realized he did not speak English. About the same time the Turkish Embassy was fire-bombed (it was next to the Turkish Airlines and the terrorists threw the fire-bomb through the wrong window).

# 1S  STOP THIEF!

In 1989 the US National Center for Computer Crime summaries barely mentioned theft of equipment as an issue. Now theft of computer equipment and components in the USA is costing US business around $3.5bn/year. There is hardly a hi-tech manufacturing company that has not suffered a substantial theft of components. One "sting", Operation Grey Chip, resulted in 30 arrests and recovery of $2.1m in cash and $1.5m in equipment.

All these thefts had huge knock-on effects. Memory supplier Datrontech, having suffered a van hijack, now has the permanent overhead of security guards. Intel changed manufacturing processes to include serial numbers on components to aid tracking. The theft of $5m (retail value) of chips from Oki Semiconductor in Oregon caused prices of 1Mb memory to rise by $10 in the USA and £6–£10 in the UK.

When it comes to personal computers, servers, and minicomputers, theft takes on a new dimension. Nearly all the national and regional newspapers, for example, have suffered major equipment raids. It is initially amusing to read of a UK publisher who had their Apple Macintoshes stolen and carried off in a stolen fruit lorry. It is much less amusing when theft of Apples reaches such proportions that publishers are put out of business and at least one insurer is refusing to provide cover for publishers.

In Hampshire, UK equipment theft has risen 70% in one year. Insurers put losses at over £100m/year UK-wide—and that is just replacement equipment value, not the cost to business. Much of the stolen equipment heads for technology-hungry Eastern Europe.

Often the thief steals not just the equipment but any on-site back-ups lying around. Theft to order is commonplace—with thieves waiting for victims to be re-equipped before striking again . . . and again. In some cases the stolen hardware has been recycled and sold back to the original owners ready for a return visit. A Manchester company's office has been robbed 12 times in a year; terrified security guards stood by while armed youths cleared offices during midnight raids.

At the lower level, often a small theft becomes a big, truly personal, disaster. The theft of one PC can destroy a lifetime's work (as several researchers know to their cost). Thefts from doctors' surgeries put health at risk, endanger patient confidentiality and risk sanctions on the victim under data protection legislation. Theft of a computer from the surgery of a doctor in London's Harley Street was said to contain patient details of Princess Diana. The theft of computers from the Institute of Offshore Engineering cost £30 000—but the research they contained, on clearing oil spills, is priceless.

Thieves these days know exactly how long they have to raid premises before police arrive. Alarms don't frighten thieves—but anything that slows them down, or aids identification of equipment will deter theft. Physical security is the poor relation of business protection planning. Maybe it is time it took the limelight.

The burglar has begun to attack the office complex in greater numbers, and premises that are "open" for business. Access in these cases is often gained by walking through the front door unchallenged, or via a rear goods entrance left unguarded. This is the most common method of entry—sometimes assisted by use of a boiler suit, warehouse coat, and invoices sticking out of the pocket. If challenged at all they have a well rehearsed story about collections, repairs, maintenance or some other glib reason for being there, which is rarely checked out. Burglaries still happen after hours but many commercial burglaries occur during the working day and much of the "research" by criminals goes on in the daytime. How many times do you or your security staff pay more than a fleeting attention to the man "repairing" the photocopier, or the person pushing a trolley along the corridor dressed in that overall with papers sticking out of the pocket; and how about the electrical subcontractor or decorators?

---

Burglary, like business, is driven by market forces. A balance between customer and supply is all-important. Market research determines just what and how much the supplier can expect to offload. At one scene of computer theft the police found what was thought to be a "shopping list" of equipment on the office floor.

The right commodity at the right price will ensure a queue of eager customers. At present there is a never ending and fast expanding market place for computer equipment. Following the opening up of Eastern Europe and growth and development in the "Third World", markets are clamouring for hardware and off-the-shelf software packages. In the City of London, the square mile, in 1993 alone the value of property stolen in all reportable crimes from simple theft to burglaries and robberies, totalled £14 961 158. Burglaries in buildings other than houses totalled £1 216 074 worth of property (Police Commissioner's Annual Report 1993).

When one looks at the pressure placed on insurers over the years, payments must be reflected in premiums. These premiums are then offset against profit margins. Inevitably they are passed on to the customer which increases, however insignificantly, the relative cost of products in a very competitive market.

When one looks at the attacks on such premises as colleges, schools, local government buildings and charities, where there is no room to offset loss, the quality of service will suffer. Computer equipment in these premises is often extensive and protection is difficult, with access by the public easy by the nature of their activities.

A computer is not necessarily "logged off" or switched off before it is stolen, it is just pulled from the socket or connection. The disk may well still be in place so, apart from the loss of hardware, damage is caused in several areas. Firstly, valuable information may be lost in the system; processes, customer records, development projects and a lifetime's work could just disappear. The value of information is only just being realized by all concerned. Additionally, if that information does fall into the hands of a skilled or shrewd operator, it could find its way to a competitor. The mere loss of a process in itself can be damaging enough, but for that information to pass into another's hands can double the blow. No insurance can cover that.

# 1T MISCELLANEOUS HIGHLIGHTS

The distribution depot of a PC distributor, was being manned by a security guard, who was called out to help a woman who had apparently crashed into a parked lorry. As he opened the door, an armed gang with sawn-off shotguns entered the warehouse and locked the guard in the van backed against the wall. The gang took the keys from the Transport Manager's office, used them to get a bolt cutter, went to the truck containing 3000 Sinclair Spectrums, cut the locks, loaded up two vans with the Spectrums and drove off. The guard had noted the number plate of the "crashed" car and described the gang: 56 Spectrums were recovered. The retail value of the Spectrums was £390 000.

Following the Iraqi invasion of Kuwait, virtually all datacentres were looted with equipment being ripped out by troops and transported by open lorries to Iraq. Most firms are said to have preserved databases outside Kuwait. One example was the National Bank of Kuwait. They "knocked out" their systems to stop the Iraqis getting into them but had all their records and databases backed-up in the UK, so they could easily fly out and get their computer operations going again.

Mice had nested in the powerhouse of one UK organization. When the back-up rotary generators were switched on, the nest was destroyed and the generators rendered unserviceable.

In the US the Nasdaq electronic share trading system was brought down by a squirrel which had gnawed through the UPS power line.

In a City of London silver dealer, a secretary, Annabel Bird, finds that every time she tries to back up her IBM PC to its internal floppy disk drive an error appears on the screen. She has corrupted boxes of disks. An engineer from the software supplier has reformatted disks and run back-up programs successfully. The secretary has proved she is implementing the back-up procedures correctly. The engineer claims he has discovered the cause. The secretary cannot wear some watches because they break and every time she picks up a disk she scrambles it! He suggests manufacturers who believe their disks are resistant to electrical interference should see if their products pass the "Annabel test".

At London Heathrow Airport, an office block was on the point of collapse in 1994, following subsidence of a tunnel being built for a new rail link. Roads and car parks around the site were closed, causing traffic congestion on the M4 approach to the airport. Tunnelling work was suspended. Torrential rain may then have weakened earth and clay beneath the office block. The building was tilting towards the hole which was 40 yards wide. Millions of tons of concrete were poured into the hole in an attempt to stabilize foundations. The Express Rail Link was due to open in December 1997. The £300m Express Link and the £2bn Jubilee Line Extension are now under question as both use the controversial new Austrian Tunnelling Method!

In 1991 a certain individual sales manager took a back-up tape containing 1700 client details from his company which he later used to target potential customers for his own start-up firm. The Crown Court gave him a conditional discharge for six months. The company discovered the theft after its own records appeared to be scrambled and one of its customers received a mailshot from the new company. The individual claimed he had taken the tape by accident. The company claimed they lost a substantial amount of business.

In another organization over £100 000 was invested in UPS to ensure continuity of computer and network operation. However, when the power failed during the winter, UPS cut in and computer operation continued uninterrupted, but there was no standby power for the central heating, which stopped. It got so cold that staff had to be sent home and computer operation was not able to be supported, so it ceased!

At a disaster recovery seminar in Dublin in 1989 a delegate challenged the speaker about the effectiveness of UPS, saying they had just installed almost 100 for a distributed operation without any problems so far. A lady delegate (from another insurance company) replied that they had installed five—and three had blown up! (Leaking batteries release hydrogen with consequent risk of explosion.) They had discontinued use of UPS on the grounds that they felt it represented a greater potential threat than power failure.

At a food processing plant in Northern England a computer system was installed without anyone realizing the impact of frequent electrical storms which were common in the area. Although there were standby generators for the food store, there were none for the computer. Each storm took out power for 1–2 seconds, causing computer failure. After every power failure back-up copies of data had to be used to restore processing. Often power failure recurred during this process. As a result back-ups were taken four times daily and computer operations suspended when a storm looked likely! UPS was eventually installed.

## 1U    LESSONS IN RISK MANAGEMENT FROM THE AUCKLAND POWER CRISIS

### Introduction

PricewaterhouseCoopers performed a survey of companies located in the Auckland Central Business District affected by the February 1998 power crisis. The purpose of the survey was to gather and share information about how the crisis affected organizations, the lessons learnt, recovery strategies that worked well, and those that did not. The survey also aimed to identify how risk management and business continuity planning disciplines helped organizations during the crisis.

The power crisis affected all organizations surveyed. Some had only minor disruption, while for others the crisis was in fact a disaster. As disasters go, this should have been, operationally, easier to cope with than most. There was not the destruction of equipment and records that would have been experienced in a fire. Neither was there any limitation of access to normal premises, such as in disasters which affect building safety. The comment was made, by more than one participant in the survey, that the crisis had the benefit of showing what they are able to achieve in a recovery situation, whilst allowing them to change strategies which were not working.

By sharing this information more organizations may be better prepared for the next crisis, whatever that may be.

### How long did it take to get started?

As each of the four power cables supplying Auckland's Central Business District (CBD) failed it became increasingly likely that a crisis would develop. Events came to a head late on Friday 20 February 1998, when Mercury Energy stated publicly that there would be little or no power in the Auckland CBD during the following week. It would have been feasible to prepare for this over the weekend, to minimize disruption by Monday morning, but many people did not hear about the crisis, or did not understand its significance for a couple of days, which resulted in recovery times being eroded—time lost.

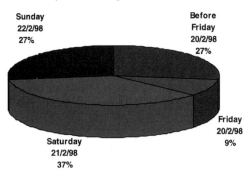

**Figure A1U.1**—(A) When did you become aware of a crisis?

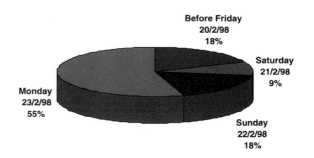

**Figure A1U.1**—(B) When did you start to take action?

Although more than 90% of the organizations surveyed had heard about the crisis before Monday 23 February, fewer than half took any action. The reasons for this time being lost included:

- Did not hear news of the crisis until late in the weekend
- Where power was on over the weekend it was not clear who would be affected and how badly
- Difficulty contacting colleagues over the weekend to agree on actions
- Plans were made over the weekend, to be put in effect on Monday morning

## Lesson One

> **Businesses which had identified their critical business processes and analysed the impact of risks to business continuance appeared to be able to assess the significance of the disaster early and take timely action.**

# What strategies were used to continue business?

The main strategies for a power crisis fall naturally into two alternatives:

- use generator power, or
- relocate to facilities with power

A mixture of these strategies was used, with some organizations relocating part of their staff while the remainder struggled on with or without power. In many cases the strategy used was determined by the nature of the business. Hotels, for example, could not relocate. Other organizations found that their alternatives were limited, usually by a shortage of generators. Generators were arriving in the city, from various parts of the world, for more than a week after the crisis started.

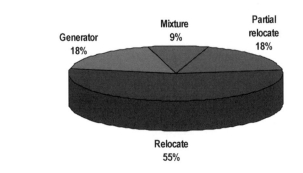

**Figure A1U.2**—Strategies used

## Difficulties encountered

### Information

Not surprisingly the most difficult aspect of the crisis was obtaining reliable information about when power would be available. The uncertainty this caused delayed action being taken by some organizations at the start of the crisis.

### Staff

Most organizations were impressed with the way their staff coped with the crisis, particularly where they were working in unfamiliar and far from ideal surroundings. As the crisis dragged on morale became more difficult to sustain. Staff safety was an issue in some cases.

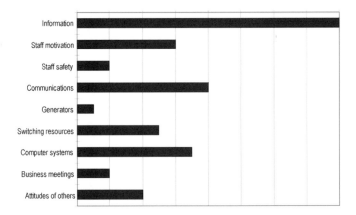

**Figure A1U.3**—Difficulties encountered

## Communications

Communications were frequently difficult, particularly where staff were in different locations. While cell phones were useful, there were periods when the analogue network was overloaded. They should not be relied upon totally. Many organizations found it useful to have a communications centre, which kept track of where staff were and forwarded messages. In some cases e-mail servers were also moved to somebody's home, so that staff could dial-in for their mail.

## Generators

Organizations who had or were able to find generators appeared to cope more easily with the crisis, although generator use was not without pitfalls.

## Resource relocation

Switching resources to a new location was surprisingly easy, with the Telcos being proactive in setting up call diversion where required. Installation of new data circuits was also speeded up, but still took up to three days. Couriers and other services were diverted with only a small amount of confusion and delay.

## Computer systems

Computer systems were difficult to move in a few cases, particularly where new data circuits had to be installed and some reconfiguration was required.

## Recovery times

The time taken to return to a satisfactory level of operations, given the circumstances, varied greatly.

## External attitude

Generally organizations outside the CBD were understanding about the crisis, although a couple of parent companies became impatient about reporting delays. Offshore attitude was of concern to some.

## Lesson Two

> **Businesses which chose appropriate back-up and recovery options based on a business impact analysis appeared to cope well with the disaster.**

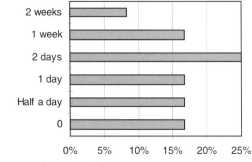

**Figure A1U.4**—Time to achieve satisfactory recovery

# How bad was the crisis?

Impacts from a disruption generally fall into the following classifications:

- **Financial**—loss of revenue and additional costs
- **Operational**—the effect of not working at normal efficiency, which may result in backlogs, missed deadlines, and delayed projects
- **Intangible**—such as poor customer service, leading to loss of goodwill, reduced staff motivation and loyalty, etc.

## Financial impacts

The main feature of the financial impacts was the number of organizations who do not know what the crisis has cost them. Nearly 30% of organizations surveyed, however, believed the crisis had cost them over $100 000. The biggest and most difficult to measure impacts were in lost revenue, and it is likely that at least some organizations will suffer for some months after the crisis. Loss of profits insurance, where held, will be difficult to assess in many cases.

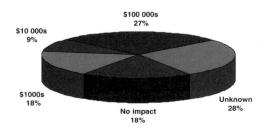

**Figure A1U.5**—Financial impact of crisis

## Operational impacts

Most companies, in the first one to three days of the crisis, were operating well below normal efficiency. However most improved to about 85–95% over the remainder of the crisis. As a result of this reduction in efficiency a number of projects have been delayed, including due diligence exercises, and the backlogs will take some time to clear.

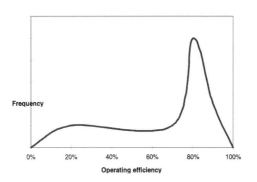

**Figure A1U.6**—Operational impacts

## Intangible impacts

The intangible impacts considered did not appear to have been greatly felt. Respondents were asked to estimate the intangible impact of the crisis on a scale of 1–9, one being of very little impact. The impact on staff morale and welfare was greatest, followed by customer service and the ability to communicate with business partners. The impact of poor publicity overseas was raised as an additional concern by a number of respondents.

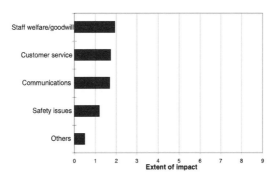

**Figure A1U.7**—Intangible impacts

# Status of business continuity plans

No organisation surveyed had a full business continuity plan. Some had risk management plans, some had IT recovery plans, and others were in the process of writing plans.

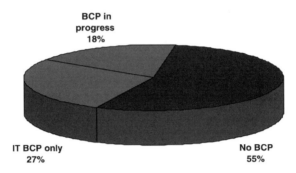

**Figure A1U.8**—Status of business continuity plans

Relating the impact suffered to the state of planning cannot be conclusive in a small sample, where there were a mixture of industries and head office/operational locations. However, the indication is that prior planning helped the recovery by reducing the impacts. In fact, just thinking about the plan, and going through the first phases of a continuity planning process, seems to have helped, largely because the alternatives had already been identified and considered.

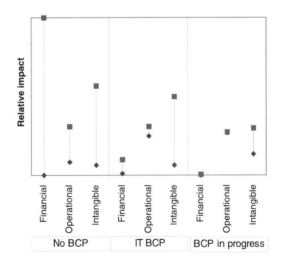

**Figure A1U.9**—Impact vs BCP status

## Lesson Three

> **Businesses which progressed business continuity to a formal planning stage appeared to cope with financial, operational and intangible aspects of the disaster.**

# The pitfalls of generators

A lot of lessons have been learnt about running generators, including the fact that they need fuel and regular maintenance.

Many of the lessons are less obvious, such as the issues relating to the tower blocks around the city. Some have emergency generators, many do not. Emergency generators enable limited lift access, security systems to operate, and keep emergency lighting on after the batteries run down. However, on their own these emergency facilities are not sufficient to make offices habitable for the longer term.

Some buildings have more powerful generators, which are capable of running 70–80% of the building's needs. However, care needs to be taken running computer equipment on these facilities, as it may be difficult to control the load, and hence the supply to equipment. Some uninterruptible power supplies, which provide protection against fluctuations in mains power, were unable to cope with fluctuations in generator power.

The cabling of buildings also influences how generators may be used. Some buildings have individual circuits for each floor or group of floors. This enables a generator to supply a localized area for which it may be easier to control the load.

## Lesson Four

> **Operational issues need to be considered in the plan, for example:**
>
> - **Build the logistical support for your generator, such as fuel and servicing, into your plan**
> - **Know your building and the structure of its cabling**
> - **If generator supply is a strategy, check that the uninterruptable power supply will cope.**

# Risk management and business continuity planning

**Risk Management** is the process of identifying the organization's risks, their impact and probability, and establishing a plan to manage the risks to an acceptable level. There are many sources of risk to an organization, some representing hazards while others are opportunities.

A high level review (see Figure A1U.10) of key business risks can reveal much about the organization's risk exposures and profile, and provides senior management with comfort that they are aware of, and understand, the material exposures.

**Figure A1U.10**—Key business risks

The key to effective risk management is to understand that to be **reactive** is **not enough** in today's business environment. A demonstrable and proactive approach is needed if stakeholders are to have faith in the competence of the senior management team.

**Business Continuity Planning** is a response to manage identified risks which involve a disruption to business operations. It is performed in four phases:

**Figure A1U.11**—Business Continuity Planning process

1. **Business impact analysis**, to identify the critical functions performed by the organization, the impact of disruptions and the maximum acceptable time to recover.
2. **Strategy selection**, to compare and select the most appropriate, cost-effective strategies for risk reduction, continuity of critical functions, and recovery.

3. **Plan preparation**, involving documentation of the plan, including measures to reduce the risk and impact of disruption.
4. **Testing and Maintenance**, to ensure that the documented plan works, and that any changes to the business are properly reflected in the continuity plan.

The benefits of this approach are that it:

- protects the business not just computer systems
- focuses on critical business processes not disaster scenarios
- balances the cost of strategies against the impact of disruption
- reduces the risk and impact of disruption as well as enabling effective recovery

*The aim is to prevent an unfortunate event from becoming a disaster.*

# Appendix 2
# General guideline notes

## 2A  RISK: A PROCESS APPROACH

Many countries run national lotteries—the biggest payout I have heard of was the recent US$185m prize. In the UK, payouts can be over £12m. The Irish National Lottery is popular throughout Europe. And if you win El Grande in Spain you will need a wheelbarrow to cart your cash away. Do you buy lottery tickets? I admit I do. Strange, isn't it? We are prepared to accept odds of tens of millions to one against winning, on the basis that someone has to win and it could just be us. It is even stranger, then, we dismiss the odds of hundreds to one that a disaster will actually happen to us!

A comprehensive approach to risk starts with an examination of business processes—ideally at the inception of a new process, project or product.

We were impressed recently by the process approach developed by a parastatal organization responsible for a country's entire infrastructure. They examine risk in planning, development, implementation, operational use and after-use. Geographically, they examine risk associated with the place of use—the area, the line (end to end topography of the infrastructure) and point. This covers process and technology and process and infrastructure. Management risks are reviewed in terms of strategy, of the production process and operations. In terms of the production activities, risk data are gathered concerning preprocess activity, the core process itself, and post-process activities. These risks are related to operational strategy, management and operations. They examine interaction with associated (dependent) processes and parallel processes (e.g. using the same facilities) and any consequential processes.

They are currently developing a geographic warehouse, which literally maps all identified risks and includes navigational information, topographical information, infrastructure information and process information. It is possible to zoom in on a large-scale map; identify their infrastructure; zoom in on specific sites to site plans and photographs and thence on to buildings for building photographs and building plans.

Critical Component Failure Analysis will examine the statistical possibility of the failure of components and the lead time to recover. A mathematical model (Monte Carlo Analysis) can be run to identify the likelihood of multiple component failures. When the impact of the loss

*The Definitive Handbook of Business Continuity Management.* Edited by Andrew Hiles and Peter Barnes. © 1999 John Wiley & Sons Ltd.

of the component is identified, a cost/benefit case may be made to introduce redundancy, resilience or alternative paths and processes.

Some risk assessment methods seek to identify the cash and non-cash cost of the risk happening against the likelihood of the risk occurring (e.g. a fire costing $10m once every ten years). The cost of loss can then be averaged out on an annual basis. The spend on preventive measures can then be justified against the annual cost of loss. But we should remember that real life does not usually happen like that: nothing may happen for 20 years, then it all happens at once.

The most common form of risk assessment is to identify risks and the impact if they occur (at its simplest, catastrophic, high, medium, moderate or sustainable—cash values can be used for cash loss, "points" can be used to weight non-cash loss). Each risk may be identified by a letter or number. An assessment is then made of the likelihood of the risks occurring (inevitable, probable, possible, unlikely—or timescales could be used if they can be estimated). A matrix can then be developed (Figure A2A.1) with the implication that the highest impact, probable risks should have highest priority in the risk reduction programme. Traffic-light colours can be used to identify priorities.

| Impact | Sustainable | Medium | High | Catastrophic |
|---|---|---|---|---|
| **Probability** | | | | |
| Inevitable | 1,3 | | | 1,8 |
| Probable | | 2,6 | 17 | |
| Possible | 15 | | 4,7 | |
| Unlikely | 14,16 | 13 | 10 | 9,11,12 |

**Figure A2A.1**—A simple risk assessment matrix

Software tools may help to take some of the grind out of risk assessment. There are many risk assessment software tools available and some provide a good structure for risk assessment and a sound checklist of risks. Some are too generic and do not adequately relate these risks to the specific situation. Some simply massage subjective risk data and lend it a (perhaps specious) authenticity.

Combining a top-down process approach and a bottom-up assessment of risk will provide not just a powerful tool-set for risk management, but a risk-aware culture which benefits the whole operation. We often find that a risk and impact assessment provides the stimulus for improved control, procedures, resilience or processes—and this benefits the organization every day, not just in disaster!

## 2B    BACK-UP OR BE BACKED INTO A CORNER

The importance of backing-up vital records and materials cannot be overstated. But all too often, the mindset stops at backing-up computer data and programs. Vital materials can be almost anything—not just disks and tapes. If you have conducted a critical component failure analysis, you may have found areas within your organization where there is a single point of failure. Applying redundancy or keeping a spare off-site may be the answer.

A few examples will illustrate the point:

1.  A £35m installation needed four air conditioner compressors to cool it in summer. There was no redundancy. The manufacturer of the air conditioning had long since gone out of business. There was a 16-week manufacturing lead time to produce a one-off compressor in balance with the others. The compressor cost £15 000. Worthwhile to have one made and keep it in reserve?
2.  A retail fashion chain depends on its top selling lines. Some of these are classics and may be regularly reordered from manufacturers. The only way you know if you are getting the same colour, cut, quality is by checking the new batch against a sample—photographs and colour swabs are inadequate. Therefore among vital materials backed up off-site could be, for instance, samples of the top 20 lines.
3.  A manufacturer depends for its unique market position on patented designs produced by special dies and moulds: the dies and moulds are vital materials and should be backed-up off site.
4.  A sauce, spice and condiment supplier operation depends on its unique recipes—the recipes are vital materials.
5.  A market research operation receives input via audio tapes of interviews around the world. Until the tapes are captured on to a computer system, are these vital materials?
6.  Many companies receive vast amounts of paper—orders, Invitations to Tender, contracts, work in progress. Some of it may be irreplaceable. When thinking about back-up, don't forget the paper or the mission critical work in progress. In many cases the need to recover vital paper documents has been the justification for microfilm, microfiche or document management systems.

In a £100m outsourcing contract, Scottish National Health Service complained of loss of patient records, both digital and paper. Records had been misdirected to other hospitals and some cases had pages lost. A British Medical Association spokesman said: "This is a serious breach of security." In another sensitive case, thieves stole a PC and back-up disks from the National Association for the Care and Resettlement of Prisoners: it held data on prisoners. Voters were disenfranchised in a UK election when they were deleted from the electoral role by a data processing firm.

Back-ups are not always what you think they are. A colleague was inspecting a client's IT operations when he noticed an operator load a tape and key in a few instructions. Almost instantly the tape drive leapt into life—and stopped just as quickly. "What was that?" my colleague asked. "Oh", the operator replied. "That was the back-up. It used to take hours, but it's ever so quick now we've got the new program." Yes, you have guessed: when checked, the program merely wrote a header to tape. Effective back-ups had not been taken for weeks. A similar case arose when one organization tried to restore from its back-ups: it found it had been writing zeros to tape for months.

Another issue can arise when trying to restore: some devices have such sensitive head alignment that only the device which wrote the cartridge can read it. It pays to check read capability *before* it's really needed!

Yet another problem can arise where the device reads a block from memory, transfers it to tape, verifies the data on tape is the same as was read, then moves along a track repeating the process. A stepping motor then drops down to the next track and the process is repeated. On some devices, if the stepping motor is jammed, the device may simply go back over the same track, overwriting what was previously saved.

One survey by SecuricIT found that over half of respondents had recently suffered data loss and 75% of them blamed faulty or non-existent back-ups. Theft accounted for 8% of the loss. The survey also noted a steady increase in the amount of mission critical data held on networks—up from 34% to 80% in two years. The occurrence of a serious network problem at least once a month was reported in 28% of networks. Data loss is costing UK business over £1bn a year, according to a Prodata survey. In Germany, a survey of national computer centres a few years ago resulted in a call for risk analysis and back-up plans.

Theft of PCs, with their data, is an increasing concern. The UK company, Cosmetics to Go, went bankrupt after the theft of a PC containing its full customer database.

Disgruntled employees are often the cause of loss of data—and frequently they destroy or remove back-ups, too. Digital Technologies of Hartford, Connecticut, discovered this to their cost when an employee deleted their web pages. The non-presence of the web site cost lost business for a week while the web site was recreated. In another case, a tyre distributor lost nearly $2m when a Credit Controller was fired: he kept a spare set of keys, re-entered the building, destroyed all invoice records and planted logic bombs in systems and programs—including the payroll.

Sometimes data may be erased that protect fraud. In the infamous case of the Bank of Credit and Commerce International (BCCI) investigations were ongoing in the UK, Luxembourg and the USA. An attorney admitted that he had erased parts of a diary kept by Zafar Iqbal, former Chief Executive of the Ubu Fhabi based bank. The entries were thought to show when the Abu Dhabi authorities first became aware of fraud at the bank. The attorney's defence was that he had erased the entries because they were held in an insecure location.

A UK company, BAC Computer, discovered its client records were scrambled—later finding that an ex-employee had set up a similar business and was targeting their clients. The cost of damage was put at some £300 000 a month.

Data terrorism and extortion is also a cause for concern. Guylain Olivera de France de Terfant and Michel Bruchon (both French) gained entry to Barclays International Bank at Trafalgar Square, London, and stole computer disks. They were sentenced to four years in prison.

Motivation may be political as well as commercial: Members of Parliament in the UK have complained that computer disks have been stolen from the House of Commons, and party leader Paddy Ashdown discovered his constituency computer had been tampered with, and access was gained to constituency member information. At about the same time private documents were stolen from his London solicitors' offices.

A brief review of Comdisco's list of invocations shows a number of cases where invocation occurred as a result of data loss or corruption. In one typical case a computer failure when archiving a database journal rendered the log file useless and the Carlstadt, New Jersey, recovery site was invoked.

Are back-ups accessible in a disaster? Charles Schwab & Co suffered when trying to recover their back-ups following the California earthquake: tapes were stuck in gridlock on the highway in transit to the airport and onward flight to the back-up site. By the time the highway had cleared, the airport was closed down.

Data loss may sometimes be comic if it were not so serious. One organization kept all its back-ups in a fireproof safe on site: when thieves broke in, all they took was the fireproof safe. And data loss can happen to comedians: entertainer Ruby Wax threatened to "murder" an operator who accidentally wiped her script.

The lessons? Back up *all* vital materials. Unless recovery has been tested, do not assume back-ups will work. And when testing recovery, do not restore so as to overwrite the live system!

## 2C  THE ROLE OF INSURANCE

Myths, misconceptions and delusion abound in the customer's perception of insurance. It is comforting to take out a policy and believe the insurer will pay out when the worst happens. But will they? Many insurance companies have been going through lean times and wish to avoid unnecessary payments: and insurers have a duty to shareholders to return decent dividends. So insurers generally are getting more picky about accepting claims as valid and, when accepting valid claims, about how much will be paid out. Increasingly, negligence on the part of the insured may lead to a reduced payout . . . and the interpretation of negligence is open to debate. For instance, is failure to have a business continuity plan (to limit loss) negligence? Indeed, recent conferences in London are designed to help insurers interpret clauses and legitimately to avoid paying out on claims.

All too often, the business continuity manager or the line manager does not know what insurance is in force—they just assume the corporate insurance manager or risk manager has it taped.

So, what is covered? Often, insurers do not understand the detail of the business they are insuring (especially high-tech businesses) and the insurance is negotiated with the insurer by, say, a finance person who again may not fully understand the technology. The result may be an ambiguous insurance policy which misses the point and leaves much inadequately covered. Please, check your policy—and, if in doubt, ask the insurer for an unambiguous definition or clarification. Here are just a few examples of ambiguous words found in insurance policies:

- "Data carrying materials"—so disk arrays, floppies and tapes should be covered—shouldn't they? But does this include copper or fibre-optic cable? Filing cabinets? Safes? PCs? Laptops? Just the hard or floppy disk in PCs and laptops?
- "Computer"—with chips in virtually all equipment, do we know what a computer is any more?
- "Maintenance must be in force"—to what level and by whom? If we have not advised the insurer of a third party maintenance contract, does this mean we have withheld "relevant information"?

Self-insurance is not necessarily a help. If you are self-insured, does that mean "corporate" have reinsured loss or are they carrying the risk themselves? All of the risk . . . or do they have an insurance reserve? As a business continuity planner, do you know how to get your hands on the insurance reserve? If not, you need to find out—or you could get bogged down in multinational conglomerate style financial politics where "corporate" expects individual business units to cover themselves and individual business units think "corporate" has it covered. Do you know how big the insurance reserve is? Is it enough? In any event, one way or the other the insurance reserve has to be funded and eventually it comes back to the bottom line.

What value do we place on the asset? Depreciated cost? Depreciated how . . . tax depreciation or book value? Do our corporate depreciation policies really reflect the true cost of acquiring similar equipment? And what if the asset is worth more to the business than its book value? Are we insured for exact replacement of an asset (like for like) or for the nearest equivalent—and if for the nearest equivalent, what if it is not fully compatible (say with existing software applications or with other parts of a production process)? Who pays for redesign? Is just the equipment cost covered, or the full project cost of reinstatement to the pre-disaster status?

What risks are insured? The one thing we can be certain of, is that an "all risks" policy does not cover all risks! In some policies (notably cases concerning malicious damage or fraud) for an effective claim we may have to prove the identity of the perpetrator. Could we?

We can insure for loss of profits, cost of cashflow disruption, interest, extra cost of working and many other things. But to be sure of getting paid, we have to prove the loss beyond reasonable doubt. So do we have pre-agreed formulae with the insurers . . . do we have inventories . . . videos, photographs?

Often we see in the headlines following a disaster huge figures for loss and, reading the level of claims or the actual payout in the insurance press, we note a large discrepancy. Sometimes the first figure reflects journalistic sensationalism: but sometimes it also reflects a high element of uninsured loss.

Insurance is full of pitfalls, and my view may seem jaundiced: it is not intended to be. Insurance companies have a perfect right to protect themselves and their stakeholders from frivolous, ambitious or fraudulent claims. It isn't all doom and gloom—a client recently had a claim of almost £1m agreed for a flood which, in the strict interpretation of the policy, our consultant believed could have been excluded from cover! It is in the interests of both the insurer and the insured to make sure the risks are clearly understood—and covered.

## 2D WHAT THE YEAR 2000 MEANS FOR BUSINESS CONTINUITY PROFESSIONALS

We are all familiar with the doomsday scenario: cars, aircraft, ships, lifts, safe vaults, cookers, building monitoring systems, computers and telecommunications all plagued by the Year 2000 glitch. Government, defence, utilities and power, banking, trading, manufacturing, transport, commerce—especially electronic commerce—and security are all imperilled. Throw in monetary union, the ECU and the ghosts of the problems laid at decimalization rise from their graves. We cannot avoid the birth of the millennium—but Europe does have a choice about EMU. Where was the risk assessment in wilfully coinciding two such challenges?

It could all cause disaster in under three years—but what is the angle for the business continuity professional now? We should be conducting risk assessment and business impact analysis to establish the downside of failure to comply. We should be looking at risk reduction, avoidance or transfer methods.

The extent to which it is a problem will depend entirely on the extent of changes to firmware or programs that are required—not just to our own computer systems but also to those of our suppliers. Therefore all businesses should itemize their reliance on external vendors who may be prone to the Year 2000 glitch and to their own computer systems or chip-controlled equipment—not only those working in the IT system but also telephone exchanges, automated production equipment and anything else that uses automation to perform the business function.

This list should then be divided into two categories:

- Software/hardware/firmware or other mission-critical supply which is provided by external vendors
- Software maintained by the business

## External vendors

We can think about our exposure to our vendors—if they are not already compliant, can we be sure they will be? We can consider dual or multiple sources of supply and start placing contracts—it may be more expensive and the business has to decide whether resilience is worth it. For software/hardware/firmware maintained by external suppliers, the business should obtain assurances that any incidence of this problem will be dealt with by the supplier.

Treat with serious cynicism any vendor who has recently set up a new company for current trading, while leaving its existing operation with the "old" company. Does this mean they want to ring-fence their exposure to their pre-2000 legacy? It they are not confident enough of their robustness to Year 2000, why should you be?

Get an assurance of compliance from the standby facilities vendor that they themselves can handle Year 2000 and find out what their contingency plans are in case they cannot— and for overload if they have multiple invocations from customers who cannot.

We can ensure Year 2000 compliance (and EMU compliance) is written into new contracts with other vendors—especially for software, telecommunications and hardware supply and especially if we use JIT resupply. We can raise the issues with every supplier and at every user group until we see our suppliers proving their capability to withstand 2000 and EMU.

## Internal supply

For those items supplied or maintained by the business, establish the complexity of changes and resources required to effect them—and decide whether changes can be implemented in time. Steps could include:

- setting up a project to make the changes
- deciding to replace old systems with packages
- deciding that the system will be redundant by 1999 because of other proposed changes in the business or the supporting systems

Accounting, and possibly other, records need to be retained for various legally defined periods in addition to any business requirements. One key aspect will be to decide how best to store the retained records; whether to convert them to the new format or transfer them to other media such as microfilm.

## General precautions

One thing we can do is to test any equipment that it is safe to test. Turn the clock on and see what happens—but ensure there is a fallback position from which to recover! Use your business continuity standby services vendor's testing time to check out your systems, procedures and applications against Year 2000 and EMU. If you use software for safety critical systems, production control or project management, check it out. We may not be able easily to identify all applications and equipment which embed clocks, but some are pretty obvious: human resource, financial, trading, building monitoring. And wouldn't it be ironic if your disaster recovery plan was not compliant!

We can bring forward capital spend to replace suspect equipment or we can use preemptive maintenance to replace suspect components.

And finally, it you have to travel on 1 Jan 00—walk. Even better, go to bed early on New Year's Eve, listen to the speaking clock at midnight, saying "Oh ****!"—and stay in bed.

# 2E  CONSULTANCY WITHOUT TEARS

A consultant is a person who borrows your watch to tell you the time, charges you for doing so, and then sells you back your watch. Consultants have had a bad press—sometimes they have themselves to blame. Once they get into an organization they can infest it like wood-worm, creeping through every part of the company—and business consultants have a vested interest in reorganization, since it makes work for them—hence a cycle of centraliza-tion and distributed operations, consolidation and diversification. I know one consultancy responsible for a corporate culture change programme who told the client "you are going to go through three years of chaos, and we will not know the outcome until it's all over"—and charged a £350 000 fee for doing so. From the consultant's viewpoint, this was neat: it you set off for an unspecified destination with out a map, you cannot blaim the consultant if you never arrive—alternatively at any convenient point the consultant can say "hey, we're here". To my simple mind, one ought to have a good idea of the destination before setting out.

Is business continuity consultancy any different? As a director of a consultancy company, I admit to being embarrassed at times at the quality of work we see from other consultants—large companies as well as small. But, on the whole, business continuity consultancy is different.

Companies serious about Business Continuity frequently use consultants for some or all of the business continuity project life cycle: risk analysis, business impact analysis, business continuity strategy, plan design, implementation, testing, plan audit. Where software is used, the consultant may help the client to exploit its full potential and train the client in its use. In some cases, the business continuity planning activity is outsourced to consultants.

Effective use of consultants depends on the client having a good idea of what they are looking for in the consultant. Does the client want a partner in solving problems, a guru, a silent influencer, a technical assistant, skilled resource, or a skills transferrer? In each case, the role of the consultant—and that of the client—may be different.

The problem solver consultant:

- Acts as a facilitator whenever it is appropriate
- Avoids "quick-fixes" and produces solid lasting solutions
- Understands and acts to further the client's mission
- Does not confuse the client by talking in a different language
- Only makes promises when they can be kept
- Keeps a good relationship with others in the company
- Minimizes dependency of the client on the consultant
- Encourages the client's competence, confidence and commitment
- Works with the client on the problem solution
- Focuses on the relationship with the client and technical problems
- Doesn't take on any of the client's responsibilities

The consultant will concentrate on two-way communication, developing an attack plan, accumulating and analysing data, solution finding and managing his or her side of the project. The client usually defines the problem and subsequently implements the solution, often in concert with the problem solver.

The guru generates the plan, develops the solution, makes technical judgements and organizes data collection while the client's role is typically to define the problem and effect the solution.

The silent influencer is viewed as a leader with potential to change the pattern of events, acts as an objective, detached sounding board and returns feedback to the client. Often their contribution is enormous but, at the end of the contract, those not immediately involved may say "what did he do?" because the resultant actions have been owned and delivered by client managers. It's a little like the effective manager who goes into his slightly bemused but flattered boss and says "I've been thinking about what you said the other day—it's a great idea, I've just developed it a little for you."

The technical support consultant or skilled resource pursues the implementation while the client defines the project plan, constructs requirement specifications, describes the required solution and advises on implementation.

The skills to be transferred are defined by the client, while the skills transferrer consultant passes on expertise in the most appropriate and effective way. In many ways, this is the most effective use of consultants: suck their brains out and throw them away as quickly as possible!

Of course, sometimes the edges between these approaches may be blurred, some assignments involve the consultant acting in more than one of these roles—and one can debate the detail of the roles endlessly. The real point, however, is that the client must know what they want from the consultant and both client and consultant must define and deliver against their roles. Expectations of each have to be set out clearly from the outset, or they will not be met.

How do you pick a good consultant? Asking for references may help, but many consultancy contracts contain confidentiality agreements and the consultant may not be able to divulge appropriate clients' names. Also, with the extent of reorganization and downsizing that has been going on in recent years, it may be difficult to track down the individuals with whom the consultant worked on relevant contracts. So the best way is to make sure the consultant has an appropriate qualification and profile in business continuity—and it would be surprising if I did not put in a plug for the Business Continuity Institute. Why risk your whole business at its most critical time by employing someone whose effectiveness cannot be determined until it is too late? One thing to avoid is accepting a proposal without knowing specifically who the consultant will be: the world is full of disappointed clients thinking they were getting a superman and ending up with an acne-covered newly qualified MBA literally practising on the client and learning at the client's expense. When a consultant has been identified, examine their c.v. carefully. If it is a reasonable sized project, they will be pleased to discuss client requirements on site, which gives the client the opportunity to assess the consultant's interpersonal skills and how relevant their knowledge and experience is to the client's industry, culture and approach.

Please, don't ask every consultant in the book to put in a proposal—it simply wastes everybody's time. It also sets the whole project off on the wrong foot, because it usually means price is the key determining factor rather than the quality of the finished project at a fair price. By making consultancy a commodity, you are likely to get a commodity product and the consultant may be looking for ways to cut corners. If you have identified a suitable consultant, there may not be a need to do more than have them provide a detailed breakdown of time and costs: often the best assignments—for both parties—are those which were not competitive. If you intend to get competitive proposals, a shortlist of say three or four consultants should be enough to ensure you are getting a good deal.

Business Continuity Planning is a project like any other project, and a reasonable sized assignment should be accompanied by a project plan identifying timescales, deliverables and milestones. However, unlike many other projects, business continuity planning often gets downgraded in priority as a result of higher business priorities arising. The consultant depends on interviews being arranged and kept, information being received, reports being read and decisions being made by the client to agreed timetables. If this does not happen, the cost may go up, the timescale may go out or the result will be less effective—sometimes all three.

So, do we consultants deserve a poor image? Well, check your wrist. You're still wearing your watch, the time here is 11.00 a.m.—and there's no invoice overleaf.

## 2F FINANCING BUSINESS CONTINUITY: WHY IS IT A PROBLEM?

Why are we so hung up about money? Why is the financial and business case always such a pain?

The creation of a Business Continuity Plan can typically be justified on one or more of the following grounds:

- Marketing
- Financial
- Statutory requirement
- Quality

## Marketing

It is crucial to retain customer confidence in the event of a disaster. Seamless integration with the customer is often crucial to retention of market share. Competition is intense and market share, once lost, would be hard to regain.

Often the most powerful corporate advertising can work just as powerfully against an organization in the event of a disaster. Just imagine the effect on the Commercial Union if, when hit by the IRA bombers, it had not lived up to its slogan: "We don't make a drama out of a crisis." The marketing image of competence and capability so carefully built up over many years could be destroyed in two cartoons.

How much is your annual advertising budget? What increased market share does it buy you? Typically an organization may spend three or more times its normal annual marketing budget in the aftermath of a disaster to retain customer confidence and to retain and regain market share.

## Financial

Many contracts contain liquidated damages or penalty clauses. Increasingly penalty clauses are being expressed as a percentage of contract value per week or month of delay, or provable liquidated damage clauses may be invoked.

Although contracts may include Force Majeure clauses, increasingly Force Majeure defence is being contested in the courts on the basis that events should have been foreseen and safeguards should be in place to eliminate them or to limit the damage caused by them.

Other sources of loss could include:

- Loss of interest on overnight balances; cost of interest on lost cashflow
- Delays in customer accounting, accounts receivable and billing/invoicing

- Loss of control over debtors
- Loss of credit control and increased bad debt
- Delayed achievement of benefits of profits from new projects or products
- Loss of revenue for service contracts from failure to provide service or meet service levels
- Lost ability to respond to contract opportunities
- Penalties from failure to produce annual accounts or produce timely tax payments
- Where company share value underpins loan facilities, share prices could drop and loans be called in or be rerated at higher interest levels

## Statutory requirement

Many organizations may have to meet legal requirements to maintain records or audit trail, or regulatory requirements of industry regulators, Health & Safety, government agencies, tax authorities, customs requirements and import and export regulations. Loss of capability to comply could lead to severe penalties.

## Quality

A BS5750 organization is subject to QMS and BSI audits and surveillance visits. There is a strong move to include disaster recovery capability as part of the BS5750/ISO 9000 series requirements. In addition, there are the requirements of British Standard 7799, (code of practice for information security management). These are being offered as ISO standards with which a BS5750/ISO 9000 organization should comply.

These guidelines require, inter alia, that: "Business continuity plans should be available to protect critical business processes from major failures or disasters" and go on to outline a planning process consistent with the approach recommended in this report. Loss of service, aggravated by lack of disaster recovery plans, could result in non-compliance action and possibly withdrawal of accreditation. This could have a serious impact since customers may require contractors to be BSI/ISO certified.

A quality accreditation—ISO or national—leaves the organization open to audit. A disaster may destroy the capability to document consistency or process, batch tracking or other requirement of the standard. Loss of quality accreditation could have a severe impact on production costs or market share (or else why did you go through the quality accreditation in the first place?).

## Summary

So—we have just written your business case for you—all you have to do is fill in the blanks. Easy, isn't it? So now all you have to do is to manage the politics and a few million other minor details. Good luck!

Table A2F.1 is indicative of the nature of costs which could be incurred.

**Table A2F.1**  Cost of disaster: causes

| Cause of Loss |
| --- |
| Cost of replacement of buildings and plant |
| Cost of replacing equipment and software |
| Salaries paid to staff unable to undertake billable work |
| Salaries paid to staff to recover work backlog and maintain deadlines |
| Cost of re-creation and recovery of lost data |
| Loss of cashflow |
| Interest value on deferred billings |
| Penalty clauses invoked for late delivery and failure to meet Service Levels |
| Loss of customers and market share |
| Additional cost of advertising to reassure customers and prospects to retain market share |
| Additional cost of working; administrative costs; travel and subsistence, etc. |

Some of these costs may be insured but:

1. The risk would fall back on the organization for aspects which are self-insured and thus would still be a real corporate cost.
2. In the event of payout of self-insurance, the insurance reserve fund would need topping up, leaving less capital available for productive investment.
3. Commercial insurers and reinsurers are increasingly limiting their liability, reducing or denying claims if there is any suggestion of negligence (questioning Force Majeure defence on the basis that the events should have been foreseen and guarded against) and charging punitive subsequent premiums.

## 2G   PROTECTING DATA: WHERE DID IT GO?

It sounds self-evident that if data is worth collecting and keeping, it—and access to it—is worth protecting. But all too often it is vulnerable to loss or denied access.

In the UK, a recent survey showed that half the respondents had recently suffered data loss and 75% of these companies blamed faulty or non-existent back-ups. It really is amazing how many organizations fail adequately to check that back-ups really are working—the only real way to prove it is to do a restore (but not to a live system, you might find out back-up deficiencies the hard way!). Theft accounted for 17% of data loss. One of the trends is the steady increase in the amount of mission-critical data held on networks, up from 34% to 80% over two years; 28% of networks suffer severe problems at least once a month. Another survey claims data loss is costing UK business £1bn a year.

There are many reasons for loss of data, amongst them lack of systems integrity or systems inadequacy. A few real examples will prove the point. The British Army computerized supply system "lost" millions of pounds worth of stores. At one point £6.7m of ammunition could not be accounted for—500 separate consignments went walkabout and 452 Milan anti-tank missiles were "lost".

Operator or user error is another common cause of lost data. In the USA, Comdisco has reported a number of invocations over the last few years because of data loss. Their Carlstadt New Jersey facility came to the rescue of several of these. In one case a user mistakenly deleted a user journal; in another case a production IDMS database was rendered useless.

Malicious damage by unauthorized access or virus can also destroy data. There are around 12 000 viruses, growing at a rate of 200 new viruses each month—many capable of destroying a database. In Italy for example, there are some 2000 new virus cases reported a year. In the UK 90% of companies see a virus attack each month. The US Army and the USAF were hit by virus in Bosnia.

Theft of PCs and no back-up are a lethal combination: a UK cosmetics firm lost its customer database this way—the £1m company subsequently went bankrupt! When burglars emptied a fire extinguisher into a server at Clifton Securities, causing severe data loss, the Securities authorities closed the firm down.

Hardware failure—a diskhead crash during a routine back-up—hit 17 north London hospitals causing cancellation of appointments and failure to find patient records. And when a power supply unit failure in a Scottish bank's IBM mainframe failed, the result was a lock of all IMS database files.

Software failure can be equally damaging: in 1994, American Express UK cardmember services division systems, serving all of Europe, were down for two and a half hours because a software application bug prevented access to customer history database, stopping files from being updated and causing telephone queries to be unanswered. It took another five hours to bring systems back on line.

Data loss can have its lighter side: for two weeks, British Rail "lost" a £1m 17-metre long inter-city 125 engine weighing 75 tons. Cases like this may seem like a joke—but not if they happen to you! The lessons are self-evident: back-up frequently and ensure you can restore from back-up; keep back-up off-site; ensure you are fire-walled against hacking and virus.

# Appendix 3: Certification standards for Business Continuity Practitioners

These certification standards form the basis of the professional certification programme offered by the Business Continuity Institute and have been agreed in collaboration with the Disaster Recovery Institute International. Contact details for both organizations can be found in Appendix 4.

## Units of competence

1. PROJECT INITIATION AND MANAGEMENT—To establish the need for a Business Continuity Plan (BCP), including obtaining management support and organizing and managing the project to completion within agreed upon time and budget limits.
   The professional's role is to:

   (i)     Lead Sponsors in Defining Objectives, Policies, and Critical Success Factors.
   (ii)    Coordinate and Organize/Manage the BCP Project.
   (iii)   Oversee the BCP Project Through Effective Control Methods and Change Management.
   (iv)    Present (Sell) the Project to Management and Staff.
   (v)     Develop Project Plan and Budget.
   (vi)    Define and Recommend Project Structure and Management.
   (vii)   Manage the Process.

2. RISK EVALUATION AND CONTROL—To determine the events and environmental surroundings that can adversely affect the organization and its facilities with disruption as well as disaster, the damage such events can cause, and the controls needed to prevent or minimize the effects of potential loss. Provide cost-benefit analysis to justify investment in controls to mitigate risks.
   The professional's role is to:

*The Definitive Handbook of Business Continuity Management.* Edited by Andrew Hiles and Peter Barnes. © 1999 John Wiley & Sons Ltd.

(i)     Understand the Function of Probabilities and Risk Reduction/Mitigation Within the Organization.
(ii)    Identify Potential Risks to the Organization.
(iii)   Identify Outside Expertise Required.
(iv)    Identify Vulnerabilities/Threats/Exposures.
(v)     Identify Risk Reduction/Mitigation Alternatives.
(vi)    Identify Credible Information Sources.
(vii    Interface with Management to Determine Acceptable Risk Levels.
(viii   Document and Present Findings.

3.  BUSINESS IMPACT ANALYSIS—To identify the impacts resulting from disruptions and disaster scenarios that can affect the organization and techniques that can be used to quantify and qualify such impacts. Establish critical functions, their recovery priorities, and interdependencies so that recovery time objective can be set.
    The professional's role is to:

(i)     Identify Knowledgeable and Credible Functional Area Representatives.
(ii)    Identify Organization Functions.
(iii)   Identify and Define Criticality Criteria.
(iv)    Present Criteria to Management for Approval.
(v)     Co-ordinate Analysis.
(vi)    Identify Interdependencies.
(vii)   Define Recovery Objectives and Timeframes, including recovery times, expected losses, and priorities.
(viii)  Identify Information Requirements.
(ix)    Identify Resource Requirements.
(x)     Define Report Format.
(xi)    Prepare and Present Business.

4.  DEVELOPING BUSINESS CONTINUITY STRATEGIES—To determine and guide the selection of alternative business recovery operating strategies for recovery of business and information technologies within the recovery time objective, while maintaining the organization's critical functions.
    The professional's role is to:

(i)     Understand Available Alternatives, their Advantages, Disadvantages, and Cost Ranges, including mitigation as a recovery strategy
(ii)    Identify Viable Recovery Strategies with Business Functional Areas
(iii)   Consolidate Strategies.
(iv)    Identify Off-Site Storage Requirements and Alternative Facilities.
(v)     Develop Business Unit Consensus.
(vi)    Present Strategies to Management to Obtain Commitment.

5.  EMERGENCY RESPONSE AND OPERATIONS—Develop and implement procedures for responding to and stabilizing the situation following an incident or event, including establishing and managing an Emergency Operations Centre to be used as a command centre during the emergency.
    The professional's role is to:

(i)     Identify Potential Types of Emergencies and the Responses Needed (e.g., fire, hazardous materials leak, medical).
(ii)    Identify the Existence of Appropriate Emergency Response Procedures.
(iii)   Recommend the Development of Emergency Procedures Where None Exist.
(iv)    Integrate Disaster Recovery/Business Continuity Procedures with Emergency Response Procedures.

(v)     Identify the Command and Control Requirements of Managing an Emergency.
(vi)    Recommend the Development of Command and Control Procedures to Define Roles, Authority, and Communications Processes for Managing an Emergency.
(vii)   Ensure Emergency Response Procedures are Integrated with Requirements of Public Authorities *(Refer also to Subject Area 10, Coordination With Public Authorities)*.

6.  DEVELOPING and IMPLEMENTING BUSINESS CONTINUITY PLANS—to design, develop, and implement the Business Continuity Plan that provides recovery within the recovery time objective.
    The professional's role is to:

    (i)     Identify the Components of the Planning Process.
    (ii)    Control the Planning Process and Produce the Plan.
    (iii)   Implement the Plan.
    (iv)    Test the Plan.
    (v)     Maintain the Plan.

7.  AWARENESS and TRAINING PROGRAMMES—to prepare a programme to create corporate awareness and enhance the skills required to develop, implement, maintain, and execute the Business Continuity Plan.
    The professional's role is to:

    (i)     Establish Objectives and Components of Training Programme.
    (ii)    Identify Functional Training Requirements.
    (iii)   Develop Training Methodology.
    (iv)    Develop Awareness Programme.
    (v)     Acquire or Develop Training Aids.
    (vi)    Identify External Training Opportunities.
    (vii    Identify Vehicles for Corporate Awareness.

8.  MAINTAINING and EXERCISING BUSINESS CONTINUITY PLANS—to pre-plan and coordinate plan exercises, and evaluate and document plan exercise results. Develop processes to maintain the currency of continuity capabilities and the Plan document in accordance with the organization's strategic direction. Verify that the Plan will prove effective by comparison with a suitable standard, and report results in a clear and concise manner.
    The professional's role is to:

    (i)     Pre-plan the Exercises.
    (ii)    Coordinate the Exercises.
    (iii)   Evaluate the Exercise Plans
    (iv)    Exercise the Plans.
    (v)     Document the Results.
    (vi)    Evaluate the Results.
    (vii)   Update the Plan.
    (viii)  Report Results/Evaluation to Management.
    (ix)    Understand Strategic Directions of the Business.
    (x)     Attend Strategic Planning Meetings.
    (xi)    Coordinate Plan Maintenance.
    (xii)   Assist in Establishing Audit Programme for the Business Continuity Plan.

9.  PUBLIC RELATIONS and CRISIS COORDINATION—To develop, coordinate, evaluate, and exercise plans to handle the media during crisis situations. To develop, coordinate, evaluate, and exercise plans to communicate with and, as appropriate, provide trauma counselling for employees and their families, key customers, critical suppliers,

owners/stockholders, and corporate management during crisis. Ensure all stakeholders are kept informed on an as-needed basis.

**Note: Details of this subject area vary from country to country, and from industry to industry. The following basic components should be considered in addition to those specific to your country and/or industry.**

The professional's role is to:

(i) Establish Public Relations Programmes for Proactive Crisis Management.
(ii) Establish Necessary Crisis Coordination with External Agencies.
(iii) Establish Essential Crisis Communications with Relevant Stakeholder Groups.
(iv) Establish and Test Media Handling Plans for the Organization and its Business Units.

10. COORDINATION WITH PUBLIC AUTHORITIES—To establish applicable procedures and policies for coordinating continuity and restoration activities with local authorities while ensuring compliance with applicable statutes or regulations.

**Note: Details of this subject area vary from country to country, and from industry to industry. The following basic components should be considered in addition to those specific to your country and/or industry.**

The professional's role is to:

(i) Coordinate Emergency Preparations, Response, Recovery, Resumption, and Restoration Procedures with Public Authorities.
(ii) Establish Liaison Procedures for Emergency/Disaster Scenarios.
(iii) Maintain Current Knowledge of Laws and Regulations Concerning Emergency Procedures.

# Appendix 4:
# Useful international contacts

## Part One—*Survive!* international contacts

The following provides details of the main contacts for each of our regional and international offices.

*Survive! United Kingdom and Survive! International*
(For general enquiries or information about *Survive!* activities in countries for whom no local contact is listed.)

General Manager—Peter Barnes MBCI
*Survive!* Ltd
The Chapel
Royal Victoria Patriotic Building
Fitzhugh Grove, London, SW18 3SX
United Kingdom
Tel: +44 181 874 6266
Fax: +44 181 874 6446
Email: pbarnes@survive.com

Chairman—Andrew Hiles FBCI
c/o The Kingswell Partnership
The Forge, Faringdon Road
Kingston Bagpuize
Oxon, OX13 5AG, United Kingdom
Tel: 01865 822010
Fax: 01865 822011
Email: admin@kingswell.net

*The Definitive Handbook of Business Continuity Management.* Edited by Andrew Hiles and Peter Barnes. © 1999 John Wiley & Sons Ltd.

*South East Asia*
For information about *Survive!* in Thailand, Malaysia, Laos, Cambodia, Vietnam, Myanmar, Indonesia, Bangladesh, Brunei, Singapore, Hong Kong, Macau, Philippines.

Director—Alan Craig MBCI
Survive! in Asia Ltd
119 Soi 2
Sukhumvit 22
Klong Tooey
Bangkok
10110
Thailand
Tel: +662 258 2012
Fax: +662 261 0874
Mobile: +661 841 2631
Email: acraig@comnet3.ksc.net.th

*Australia*
For information about Survive! throughout Australia.

Manager—Michelle Smith
Survive! Australia
PO Box 350
Black Rock, VIC 3193
Australia
Tel: +613 9533 5161
Fax: +613 9533 4822
Email: surviveaustralia@pobox.com

*Germany*
For Germany and German-speaking areas of Switzerland and Austria.

Director—Lutz Dorn
Survive! Germany
c/o Professional Infotech
Bert-Brecht Strasse 2
63069 Offenbach
Germany
Tel: +49 69 831061
Fax: +49 69 844292
Email: professionalinfotech@compuserve.com

*Ireland*
For membership in the Irish Republic and Ulster.

Peter Comerford
Survive! Ireland
c/o Forum Connect
Maro House
Belgard Road
Dublin 24
Republic of Ireland
Tel: +353 1 494 1460
Fax: +353 1 494 1473
Email: survive@survive.com

*Netherlands*
For Dutch-speaking members in the Netherlands and Belgium.

Chairman: Survive! Europe—Ron Ginn FBCI
Survive! Europe
Ruys De Beerenbroucklaan 20
1181 XS Amstelveen
The Netherlands
Tel/Fax: +31 20 643 3219
Email: 100711,2152@compuserve.com

*New Zealand*
For information about Survive! throughout New Zealand.

Manager—Alec Carlisle FBCI
Survive! New Zealand
10 Alexandra Road
Roseneath
Wellington
New Zealand
Tel/Fax: +644 386 1075
Email: carlisle@actrix.gen.nz

*North America*
For information about Survive! in the USA and Canada.

General Manager—Peter Barnes MBCI
Survive! Ltd
The Chapel
Royal Victoria Patriotic Building
Fitzhugh Grove, London, SW18 3SX
United Kingdom
Tel: +44 181 870 0048
Toll Free (Int Access Code—usually 011) 800SURVIVE 5
Fax: +44 181 874 6446
Email: survive@survive.com

*Philippines*
For information about Survive! throughout the Philippines.

See South East Asia

*Southern Africa*
For information about Survive! throughout South Africa and neighbouring states within the Southern African region.

Membership Secretary—Louanne Bruton
Survive! Southern Africa
PO Box 1618
Cramerview 2060
South Africa
Tel: +27 11 465 3663
Fax: +27 11 465 6335
Email: survive@shadow.co.za

# Part Two—Other useful contacts

This section includes details of a selection of organizations which will be of interest to business continuity management professionals.

- **Suppliers of products and services to the business continuity/disaster recovery community.**

A comprehensive directory can be located on the Internet at http://www.survive.com.

- **Professional certification and accreditation bodies**

The Business Continuity Institute (BCI)
PO Box 4474
Worcester
WR6 5YA
United Kingdom

The Disaster Recovery Institute International
1810 Craig Road Suite 213
St Louis
MO 63146
USA

- **Emergency Preparedness, Business Continuity & Disaster Recovery Information Exchange Associations**

There are large numbers of regional "DRIE" (Disaster Recovery Information Exchange) groups throughout the world. As the contacts for these groups frequently change—many on an annual basis—we recommend that you contact Survive! International in the UK (Tel: +44 181 874 6266) who will provide the most current information available for your region of interest.

Listed below are a selection of national and international organizations

American Society for Industrial Security (ASIS)
1655 North Ft Myers Drive, Suite 1200
Arlington
VA 22209
USA

Association of Contingency Planners
USA National HQ
POB 341
Brigham City
UT 84302–0341
USA

EPIX (Emergency Preparedness Information Exchange)
Center for Policy Research on Science and Technology
Simon Fraser University—Harbor Centre Campus
515 W. Hastings St
Vancouver
V6B 5K3
BC
Canada

(USA) International Association of Fire Chiefs
4025 Fair Ridge Drive
Fairfax
VA 22033–2868
USA

(USA) National Coordinating Council on Emergency Management
7297 Lee Highway Suite N
Falls Church
VA 22042–1707
USA

(USA) National Fire Protection Association
Batterymarch Park
Quincy
MA 02269
USA

The American Civil Defense Association
POB 1057
Starke
FL 32091
USA

(USA) National Association of Flood and Storm Water Management Agencies
1225 Eye Street N.W. Suite 300
Washington
DC 20005
USA

United Nations International Decade for Natural Disaster Reduction
IDNDR Secretariat
United Nations
Palais des Nations
CH-1211
Geneva 10
Switzerland

The Federal Emergency Management Agency (FEMA)
500 C Street, SW
Washington DC
20472
USA

Emergency Management Australia
Department of Defence
PO Box 1020
Dickson
ACT 2602
Australia

Joint Assistance Centre
G-17/3
Qutab Enclave—1
Gurgaon
122002 (Haryana)
India

Minsiterio del Interior
Officina Nacional Emergencia
Beaucheff 1637
Clasificador 1-C
Correo 25
Santiago
Chile

# Appendix 5:
# About *Survive!* The Business Continuity Group

*Survive!* is the international, industry-wide group for business continuity practitioners. With membership of almost 3000 professionals around the globe, *Survive!* is recognized as the world leader in providing information and expertise for all with an interest or responsibility for business continuity and disaster recovery planning. Through a wide schedule of member meetings, conferences, training, a quarterly magazine and a variety of information services presented via the world-wide-web, *Survive!*'s mission is to facilitate the spread of best practice throughout industry so that organizations are better prepared to maintain critical business functions in the face of any interruption to normal processes.

## *Survive!* membership benefits

### Free services

- Free Guide to Disaster Recovery and Contingency Planning
- Free Quarterly Magazine, *Survive!*
- Free Quarterly, Members-only Newsletter
- Free Membership Directory
- Free Video Loan Library
- Free Attendance to Regular Special Interest Group (SIGs) Meetings
- Free Members-only, Quarterly Working Meetings
- Free Access to Databases of Disaster Cases/Surveys/Suppliers' Products and Services

### Other services

- Regularly updated documents and reports, exclusive to *Survive!*
- Discount on attendance at *Survive!* training courses and conferences in UK and overseas
- Discount on exhibiting at *Survive!* exhibitions in UK and overseas

*The Definitive Handbook of Business Continuity Management.* Edited by Andrew Hiles and Peter Barnes. © 1999 John Wiley & Sons Ltd.

## We can help you by:

- Searching through our comprehensive list of features, surveys and articles from back issues of our quarterly magazine *Survive!*
- Putting you in touch with our members who share similar interests, technical environments or planning issues
- Searching for relevant data about disaster case studies and statistics from our comprehensive databases.
- Accessing relevant speakers' notes and slides from past *Survive!* events.

For full details and for a registration form please call any of the *Survive!* offices listed in Appendix 4 of this publication or call *Survive!* International on +44 181 874 6266. Alternatively you may register via the Internet at www.survive.com.

# Glossary of general Business Continuity terms

**Activation**  The implementation of recovery procedures, activities and plans in response to an emergency or disaster declaration

**Alert**  A formal notification that an incident has occurred which may develop into a disaster

**Alternative Site**  An alternative operating location for the usual business functions (i.e. support departments, information systems and manufacturing operations) when the primary facilities are inaccessible. (*Associated term: Back-up site*)

**BS 7799**  A UK BSI Standard for information security management. Section 9 deals with Business Continuity Management

**Backlog Trap**  The effect on the business of a backlog of work that develops when a system or process is unavailable for a long period, and which may take a considerable length of time to reduce

**Building Denial**  Any damage, failure or other condition which causes denial of access to the building or the working area within the building, e.g. fire, flood, contamination, loss of services, air conditioning failure, forensics

**Business Continuity**  *A proactive* process which identifies the key functions of an organization and the likely threats to those functions; from this information plans and procedures which ensure key functions can continue whatever the circumstances can be developed

**Business Continuity Coordinator**  A member of the Recovery Management Team who is assigned the overall responsibility for coordinating the Recovery Planning Programme, ensuring team member training, testing and maintenance of recovery plans. (*Associated terms: Business Recovery Planner, Disaster Recovery Planner, Business Recovery Coordinator, Disaster Recovery Administrator*)

**Business Continuity Management**  Those management disciplines, processes and techniques which seek to provide the means for continuous operation of the essential business functions under all circumstances

**Business Continuity Plan**  A collection of procedures and information which is developed, compiled and maintained in readiness for use in the event of an emergency or disaster. (*Associated terms: Business Recovery Plan, Disaster Recovery Plan, Recovery Plan*)

**Business Continuity Planning** The advance planning and preparations which are necessary to identify the impact of potential losses; to formulate and implement viable recovery strategies; to develop recovery plan(s) which ensure continuity of organizational services in the event of an emergency or disaster; and to administer a comprehensive training, testing and maintenance programme. (*Associated terms: Contingency Planning, Disaster Recovery Planning, Business Recovery Planning*)

**Business Continuity Programme** An ongoing process supported by senior management and funded to ensure that the necessary steps are taken to identify the impact of potential losses, maintain viable recovery strategies and recovery plans, and ensure continuity services through personnel training, plan testing and maintenance. (*Associated terms: Disaster Recovery Programme, Business Recovery Programme, Contingency Planning Programme*)

**Business Critical Point** The latest moment at which the business can afford to be without a critical function or process

**Business Impact Analysis (BIA)** A management level analysis which identifies the impacts of losing company resources. The BIA measures the effect of resource loss and escalating losses over time in order to provide senior management with reliable data upon which to base decisions on risk mitigation and continuity planning. (*Associated terms: Business Impact Assessment, Business Impact Analysis Assessment*)

**Cold Site** One or more data centres or office space facilities equipped with sufficient prequalified environmental conditioning, electrical connectivity, communications access, configurable space and access to accommodate the installation and operation of equipment by critical staff required to resume business operations

**Contingency Fund** An operating expense that exists as a result of an interruption or disaster which seriously affects the financial position of the organisation. (*Associated term: Extraordinary Expense*)

**Contingency Plan (***a general non-specific point***)** A plan of action to be followed in the event of a disaster or emergency occurring which threatens to disrupt or destroy the continuity of normal business activities and which seeks to restore operational capabilities

**Crisis** An abnormal situation, or perception, which threatens the operations, staff, customers or reputation of an enterprise

**Crisis Management Team (CMT)** A group of executives who direct the recovery operations whilst taking responsibility for the survival and the image of the enterprise

**Crisis Plan** or **Crisis Management Plan** A plan of action designed to support the Crisis Management Team when dealing with a specific emergency situation which might threaten the operations, staff, customers or reputation of an enterprise

**Critical Data Point** The point to which data must be restored in order to achieve recovery objectives

**Critical Service** Any service which is essential to support the survival of the enterprise

**Decision Point** The latest moment at which the decision to invoke emergency procedures has to be taken in order to ensure the continued viability of the enterprise

**Declaration (of disaster)** A formal statement that a state of disaster exists

**Disaster**  Any accidental, natural or malicious event which threatens or disrupts normal operations, or services, for sufficient time to affect significantly, or to cause failure of, the enterprise

**Disaster Recovery (DR)**  The process of returning a business function to a state of normal operations either at an interim minimal survival level and/or re-establishing full scale operations

**Disaster Recovery Plan (DRF)** or **Recovery Plan**  A plan to resume, or recover, a specific essential operation, function or process of an enterprise

**Emergency**  An actual or impending situation that may cause injury, loss of life, destruction of property, or interfere with normal business operations to such an extent as to pose a threat of disaster

**Emergency Control Centre**  The location from which disaster recovery is directed and tracked; it may also serve as a reporting point for deliveries, services, press and all external contacts

**Emergency Data Services**  Remote capture and storage of electronic data, such as journalling, electronic vaulting and database shadowing

**Emergency Management Plan**  A plan which supports the Emergency Management Team by providing them with information and guidelines

**Emergency Management Team**  The group of staff who command the resources needed to recover the enterprise's operations

**Enterprise**  An organization, a corporate entity; a firm, an establishment, a public or government body, department or agency; a business or a charity

**Enterprise (Large-Scale or Super)**  An enterprise that is large and complex, in the sense that it could absorb the impact of losing a complete location or business unit. The normal terminology, and perspective, needs to be scaled down by regarding individual locations or business units as self-sustaining entities

**Financial Impact**  An operating expense that continues following an interruption or disaster, which as a result of the event cannot be offset by income and directly affects the financial position of the organization

**Hot Site**  A data centre facility or office facility with sufficient hardware, communications interfaces and environmentally controlled space capable of providing relatively immediate back-up data processing support. (*Associated terms: Warm Site, Cold Site*)

**Immediate Recovery Team**  The team with responsibility for implementing the business continuity plan and formulating the organization's initial recovery strategy

**Impact**  Impact is the cost to the enterprise, which may or may not be measured in purely financial terms

**Incident**  Any event which may be, or may lead to, a disaster

**Information Security**  The securing or safeguarding of all sensitive information, electronic or otherwise, which is owned by an organization

**Invocation**  A formal notification to a service provider that its services will be required

**Logistics/Transportation Team**  A team comprised of various members of departments associated with supply acquisition and material transportation, responsible for ensuring the most effective acquisition and mobilization of hardware, supplies and support materials

**Mobile Standby**   A transportable operating environment, usually complete with accommodation and equipment, which can be transported and set up at a suitable site at short notice

**Mobilization**   The activation of the recovery organization in response to an emergency or disaster declaration

**Off-Site Location**   A storage facility at a safe distance from the primary facility which is used for housing recovery supplies, equipment, vital records, etc.

**Operational Impact**   An impact which is not quantifiable in financial terms but its effects may be among the most severe in determining the survival of an organization following a disaster

**Outage**   The interruption of automated processing systems, support services or essential business operations which may result in the organization's inability to provide service for some period of time

**Period of Tolerance**   The period of time in which an incident can escalate to a potential disaster

**Pre-positional Resource**   Material (i.e. equipment, forms and supplies) stored at an off-site location to be used in business resumption and recovery operations. (*Associated terms: Pre-positioned Inventory*)

**Reciprocal Agreement**   An agreement in which two parties agree to allow each other to use their site, resources or facilities during a disaster

**Recovery**   *See* System Recovery

**Recovery Exercise**   An announced or unannounced execution of business continuity plans intended to implement existing plans and/or highlight the need for additional plan development. (*Associated terms: Disaster Recovery Test, Disaster Recovery Exercise, Recovery Test, Recovery Exercise*)

**Recovery Management Team**   A team of people, assembled in an emergency, who are charged with recovering an aspect of the enterprise, or obtaining the resources required for the recovery

**Recovery Plan**   A plan to resume a specific essential operation, function or process of an enterprise. Traditionally referred to as a Disaster Recovery Plan (DRP)

**Recovery Site**   A designated site for the recovery of computer or other operations, which are critical to the enterprise. (*Associated terms: Recovery Time Scale*)

**Recovery Strategy**   A pre-defined, pre-tested, management-approved course of action to be employed in response to a business disruption, interruption or disaster

**Recovery Team**   A group of individuals given responsibility for the coordination and response to an emergency or recovering a process or function in the event of a disaster

**Recovery Window**   The timescale within which a function or business unit must be restored, usually determined by means of a Business Impact Analysis

**Resilience**   The ability of a system or process to absorb the impact of component failure and continue to provide an acceptable level of service

**Response**   The reaction to an incident or emergency in order to assess the level of containment and control activity required

**Restart**   The procedure or procedures that return applications and data to a known start point. Application Restart is dependent upon having an operable system

**Restoration**   The process of planning for and implementing full-scale business operations which allow the organization to return to a normal service level

**Resumption**   The process of planning for and/or implementing the recovery of critical business operations immediately following an interruption or disaster

**Risk Assessment and Management**   The identification and evaluation of operational risks that particularly affect the enterprise's ability to function and addressing the consequences

**Risk Reduction** or **Mitigation**   The implementation of the preventive measures which Risk Assessment has identified

**Scenario**   A pre-defined set of events and conditions which describe an interruption, disruption or disaster related to some aspect(s) of an organization's business for purposes of exercising a recovery plan(s)

**Security Review**   A periodic review of the security of tangible and intangible assets which should cover security policy, effectiveness of policy implementation, restriction of access to the assets, accountability for access and basic safety

**Service Level Agreement (SLA)**   An agreement between a service provider and service user as to the nature, quality, availability and scope of the service to be provided

**Site Access Denial**   Any disturbance or activity within the area surrounding the site which renders the site unavailable, e.g. fire, flood, riot, strike, loss of services, forensics. The site itself may be undamaged

**Social Impact**   Any incident or happening that affects the well-being of a population and which is often not financially quantifiable

**Standby Service**   The provision of the relevant recovery facilities, such as cold site, warm site, hot site and mobile standby

**Stand Down**   Formal notification that the alert may be called off or that the state of disaster is over

**Structured Walkthrough**   An exercise in which team members verbally review each step of a plan to assess its effectiveness, identify enhancements, constraints and deficiencies. (*Associated terms: Bench Test*)

**System Denial**   A failure of the computer system for a protracted period, which may impact an enterprise's ability to sustain its normal business activities

**System Recovery**   The procedures for rebuilding a computer system to the condition where it is ready to accept data and applications. System Recovery depends on having access to suitable hardware

**System Restore**   The procedures that are necessary to get a system into an operable condition where it is possible to run the application software against the available data. System Restore depends upon having a live system available

**Tabletop Exercise**   The exercising and testing of a BCP, using a range of scenarios whilst not effecting the enterprise's normal operation

**Tolerance Threshold**   The maximum period of time which the business can afford to be without a critical function or process

**Vendor**  An individual or *company* who provides a service *to a department* or the organization as a whole. (*Associated terms: Supplier, Third Party Vendor*)

**Vital Record**  A record that it is essential for preserving, continuing or reconstructing the operations of the organization and protecting the rights of the organization, its employees, its customers and its stockholders

**Warm Site**  A data centre or office facility which is partially equipped with hardware, communications interfaces, electricity and environmental conditioning capable of providing back-up operating support. (*Associated terms: Hot Site, Cold Site*)

**Work Area Standby**  A permanent or transportable office environment, complete with appropriate office infrastructure

This Glossary of Terms originally appeared in *"Continuity"—The Journal of the Business Continuity Institute—***2**:3 (October 1998) and is reproduced with permission of the BCI. The data from which it has been collated was originally drawn from information supplied by Jim Burtles FBCI and Steve Yates of Corporate Integrity Ltd, and from the Glossary contained in *Business Continuity Demystified*, an EPS publication.

# Index

*Index compiled by Geoffrey Jones*